AN
INTRODUCTION
TO THEORIES
OF
LEARNING

B. R. HERGENHAHN

Hamline University

PRENTICE-HALL, INC., *Englewood Cliffs, New Jersey*

Library of Congress Cataloging in Publication Data

HERGENHAHN, B R   (date)
   An introduction to theories of learning.

   Bibliography: p.
   Includes indexes.
   1. Learning, Psychology of.   I. Title.
LB1051.H42   370.15'2   75–41353
ISBN 0–13–498733–0

Printed in the United States of America

10   9   8   7   6

Prentice-Hall International, Inc., *London*
Prentice-Hall of Australia Pty. Limited, *Sydney*
Prentice-Hall of Canada, Ltd., *Toronto*
Prentice-Hall of India Private Limited, *New Delhi*
Prentice-Hall of Japan, Inc., *Tokyo*
Prentice-Hall of South-East Asia Pte. Ltd., *Singapore*

Contents

part 5   Some Final Thoughts

Preface

The development of widely divergent theories of learning has been one of the most exciting aspects of psychology's history. In the period between about 1900 and 1950, a great debate raged between those who sought to explain learning as a cognitive phenomenon and those who sought to explain learning as a behavioral phenomenon. There was also debate within the behavioral camp over the importance of reinforcement in the learning process. The controversy over these issues continues to this day but it does not have nearly the religious fervor that it once had. From this era of debate came most of the great learning theories covered in this book.

An unusually large amount of information contained in earlier theories of learning has withstood the test of time and is still very useful both in explaining various learning phenomena and as a guide for solving practical problems. In addition, the major traditional theories of learning are an important starting point for a great deal of advanced work in psychology. For example, much of the current research on the learning process can be best understood within the framework of one of the theories of learning that was developed during the first half of this century. Likewise, it is quite common today for the student to encounter either a traditional theory of learning, or an extension of that theory in such areas as counseling, clinical psychology, personality theory, child psychology, and educational psychology.

This book has four main purposes. First, it attempts to define learning and to show how the learning process is studied (Chapters 1 and

2). Second, it attempts to place learning theory in historical perspective. Early philosophers sought the answers to such questions as How do ideas originate?; How are ideas related to one another?; and How are complex ideas related to simpler ones? Attempts to answer these questions go back at least as far as Plato and Aristotle. Chapter 3 shows how answers to these ancient questions gradually evolved into what we now refer to as modern learning theory.

The third and most important purpose of this book is to introduce students of psychology and education to the essential features of the major theories of learning. Chapters 4 through 12 describe the nine major theories of learning. Although some research is discussed in relationship to each of the theories, it is mentioned mainly to clarify and/or exemplify some aspect of the theory.

Chapter 13 is included mainly to give the student an idea of some of the current developments in learning theory. It samples some research designed to discover the neurophysiological basis of learning. A search for the biological correlates of learning represents one of the most active areas of research in psychology today.

The fourth purpose of the text is to point out some of the relationships that exist between learning theory and educational practices. Chapter 14 is devoted exclusively to that topic, but examples of how a particular principle of learning might be related to teaching or childrearing are interwoven throughout the text.

This text is arranged so that it can easily be used in an individualized course. Each chapter can be considered as a self-contained segment of such a course. The Glossary, along with the Discussion Questions following each chapter, can be thought of as the objectives for that chapter. If the student can answer the Discussion Questions and knows the concepts, terms, and names contained in each Glossary, he should feel ready to be tested on the contents of that chapter. In such a course, the student typically moves from segment (chapter) to segment at his or her own pace, and is tested on a particular segment only when he or she feels ready to be tested. A more detailed description of individualized courses is given in Chapter 14.

Finally, it should be noted that this text attempts to do, at an introductory level, what Hilgard and Bower's *Theories of Learning* (1975) does on an advanced level. Both books attempt to provide the student with an overview of a wide variety of learning theories, but the Hilgard and Bower text assumes that the reader has a considerable background in both learning theory and in experimental psychology. The two books, therefore, should not be seen as competing with each other. In fact, if the student's interest in learning theory is aroused by this text, there is probably no better place to seek additional information than the Hilgard and Bower text.

Acknowledgments

If there is anyone who believes writing a book is an individual effort they are in for a shock if they ever attempt to write one. Clearly, writing a book is a highly cooperative effort. First, it takes time, a great deal of time. I am indebted to Hamline University for making a sabbatical leave available to me during which I was able to work exclusively on this book. Also, Hamline's Faculty Enrichment Fund helped make it possible for me to work on the book for the better part of three summers.

Second, in order to publish a book one needs a publisher. Few realize the enormous influence a publisher has on a book, and few authors would deny that that influence is a positive one. I would like to thank Neale E. Sweet, Psychology Editor for Prentice-Hall for his faith and support in this project. I would like also to thank Natalie Krivanek of Prentice-Hall for her tolerance while working with me on many loose ends just prior to and during the time the manuscript entered production. I would also like to express my appreciation to an anonymous copyeditor who made the entire manuscript more legible and who must have been amazed that anyone with as little understanding of the English language as I demonstrated would have attempted to write a book.

Third, an author needs criticism to shake him loose from the tunnel vision he develops from existing for years without adequate criticism. The reviewing process is vital in the production of any worthwhile manuscript. I would like to thank Dr. Howard R. Pollio from the University of Tennessee, Dr. John W. Donahoe from the University of Massachusetts and Dr. Alfred Karlson also from the University of Massachusetts for their many reactions to the manuscript. Their suggestions, which sometimes bordered on actual hostility, vastly improved the final manuscript. Most of all I would like to thank James J. Jenkins from the University of Minnesota. Dr. Jenkins read and digested the manuscript and made suggestions that resulted in its complete reorganization. Others who have worked with Dr. Jenkins have been impressed both by his knowledge of psychology and by his compassion and, after working with him myself, it is easy to see why. This is not to suggest that Dr. Jenkins would agree with everything in this book; clearly he would not. The final product is my own responsibility but the Jenkins influence is everywhere and for that I am grateful.

Fourth, most books evolve through several stages before they finally enter production and this one was no exception. This evolutionary process involves thousands of pages of typing and, therefore, a number of typists. The first two drafts of this text were typed by Joy Kromschroeder at Hamline University. After the second draft was typed, both Joy and I began to develop some idea of what the book was going to be about. The third draft was typed by Ann Drake at Western Washington College while I was on sabbatical leave there in 1973. Typing manuscripts was nothing new to Ann, and I benefited greatly from her experience. The last two drafts were typed by Madelon Cassavant at Hamline University. Madelon combines patience, understanding, tolerance and professional competence. Since Madelon typed the final drafts of the manuscript she probably has a distorted view of my intelligence, only Joy knows the truth.

Fifth, writing a book requires a certain amount of knowledge. In this regard, I have been extremely fortunate to have had some truly excellent teachers. To attempt to list them would be unfair to those I would inadvertently omit, but Dr. Halldor Karason at Western Washington State College and Dr. Clyde Noble at the University of Georgia stand out most vividly at this moment. Dr. Karason instilled an interest in philosophy in me while I was an undergraduate that has lasted to this day. Dr. Noble, who taught me learning theory while I was a graduate student, was such a good teacher that I'm sure if I had taken a course in religion from him, this book would be about theology.

Lastly, one does not write a book without encouragement and emotional support. For this I am grateful to the Hamline students who experienced various editions of my learning theory course over the last nine years. Their initial reactions to the subject matter and subsequent feedback from them nurtured my belief that there is something very special about learning theory. In the book's final stages one student, Dawn Kloster, was especially helpful in tracking down elusive information and references and with the proofreading of the galleys. Dartmouth is fortunate to be getting Ms. Kloster; we will certainly miss her. Jane E. Bowers, Jill Fischer, Margaret Cassavant, Laura Ann Hergenhahn and Mary Ann Hergenhahn also helped with proofreading at various stages of the manuscript's development.

Dr. Donald E. Swanson, who was chairman of the Psychology Department at Hamline University before his recent retirement, was completely supportive to the idea of writing this book, as he was with all my projects through the years. Don and his wife Mary have been truly good friends.

B. R. HERGENHAHN

Photo Credits

P.249   Wolfgang Köhler (Garrett, H. E. *Great Experiments in Psychology,* New York: The Century Co., 1930).

P.259   Kurt Koffka (Murchison, C. [Ed.], *Psychologies of 1925: Powell Lectures in Psychological Theory,* Worcester, Mass.: Clark University, 1926).

P.267   Jean Piaget (Courtesy of the Universite de Geneve).

P.286   Edward Chace Tolman (Carl A. Murchison, [Ed.], *A History of Psychology in Autobiography,* Vol. IV, Worcester, Mass.: Clark University Press, 1952).

P.319   Karl Lashley (Garrett, H. E. *Great Experiments in Psychology,* 3rd ed. New York: Appleton-Century-Crofts, 1951).

P.326   Donald Olding Hebb (Photograph by Chris Payne).

P.333   James Olds (Courtesy of James Olds).

P.336   Roger W. Sperry (photo by Ronald Meyer).

P.342   Neal E. Miller (Courtesy of Neal Miller).

P.362   Robert F. Mager (Courtesy of R. F. Mager).

P.366   Fred S. Keller (Courtesy of F. S. Keller).

Introduction to Learning

1

What Is Learning?

Learning is one of the most important areas in present day psychology and yet it is an extremely difficult concept to define. The *American Heritage Dictionary* defines learning as follows: "To gain knowledge, comprehension, or mastery through experience or study." Most psychologists, however, would find this definition unacceptable because of the nebulous terms it contains, such as knowledge, comprehension, and mastery. Instead, the trend in recent years is to accept a definition of learning that refers to changes in observable behavior. The most popular of these definitions is the one suggested by Kimble (1961, p. 6), which defines learning *as a relatively permanent change in behavioral potentiality that occurs as a result of reinforced practice.* Although popular, this definition is far from universally accepted. Before reviewing sources of disagreement over Kimble's definition, let us look at it a bit more carefully.

First, learning is indexed by a change in *behavior;* in other words, the results of learning must always be translated into observable behavior. After learning, the learner is capable of doing something that he could not do before learning took place. Second, this behavioral change is *relatively permanent;* that is, it is neither transitory nor fixed. Third, the change in behavior need not occur immediately following the learning experience. Although there may be a *potential* to act differently, this potential to act may not be translated into behavior immediately. Fourth, the change in behavior (or behavior potentiality) results from *experience*

3

or practice, according to the definition. Fifth, the experience, or practice, must be reinforced; that is, only those responses that lead to reward will be learned. In this text, the terms *reinforcer* and *reward* will be used synonymously. Both refer to something that an organism wants.

Kimble's definition of learning provides a convenient frame of reference for discussing a number of important issues that must be confronted when attempting to define learning. We will review these issues below.

MUST LEARNING RESULT IN A BEHAVIORAL CHANGE?

As we shall see in Chapter 3, psychology has tended to become a *behavioral* science for good reason. A science requires an observable, measurable subject matter, and within the science of psychology, that subject matter is behavior. Thus, whatever we study in psychology must be expressed through behavior, but this does not mean that the behavior we are studying *is* learning. We study behavior so that we can make inferences concerning the process believed to be the cause of the behavioral changes we are observing. In this case, that process is learning. Most learning theorists covered in this text agree that the learning process cannot be studied directly; instead, its nature can only be inferred from changes in behavior. B. F. Skinner is the only theorist who takes exception to this contention. For Skinner, behavioral changes are learning and no further process needs to be inferred. Other theorists say that behavioral changes *result from* learning. We will have more to say about Skinner's antitheoretical point of view in Chapter 5.

Except for Skinner, then, most learning theorists look upon learning as a process that mediates behavior. For them, learning is something that occurs as the result of certain experiences and precedes changes in behavior. In such a definition, learning is given the status of an intervening variable. An intervening variable is a theoretical process that is assumed to take place between the observed stimuli and responses. The independent variables cause a change in the intervening variable (learning), which, in turn, causes a change in the dependent variable (behavior). The situation can be diagrammed as follows:

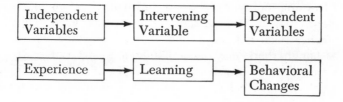

How Permanent is Relatively Permanent?

Here we run into at least two problems. First, how long must a be-havior change last before we say learning has been demonstrated? This was originally inserted into the definition to differentiate between learn-ing and other events that may modify behavior, such as fatigue, illness, and drugs. Clearly, these events and their effects come and go quite rapidly, whereas learning lingers until forgetting takes place over time or until new learning displaces old learning. Thus temporary states as well as learning modify behavior, but with learning the modification is relatively more permanent. However, the duration of the modification that results from either learning or temporary body states cannot be given exactly.

A related problem is more serious. Recently, a number of psychologists have turned their attention to a phenomenon called short-term memory (see Chapter 13). Psychologists have found that if unfamiliar information, such as a nonsense syllable, is presented to human subjects who are pre-vented from rehearsing the information, they will retain the material almost perfectly for about three seconds. In the following fifteen seconds, however, their retention drops to almost zero (Peterson and Peterson, 1959; Murdock, 1961). Despite the fact that the information is lost over such a short period of time, we would hesitate to say that no learning had occurred.

Accepting the qualification of "relatively permanent" in a definition of learning will also determine whether the processes of *sensitization* and *habituation* are accepted as crude examples of learning. Both sensitization and habituation are examples of behavior modification that results from experience, but both are short-lived. Sensitization is the process whereby an organism is made more responsive to certain aspects of his environ-ment. For example, an organism that may not ordinarily respond to a certain light or sound may do so after receiving a shock. The shock, therefore, sensitized the organism, making him more responsive to his environment. Feeling "touchy" or hypersensitive following an upsetting experience is a form of sensitization that we are all familiar with.

Habituation is the process whereby an organism becomes *less* respon-sive to his environment. For example, there is a tendency for an organism to attend to novel stimuli as they occur in his environment. This tendency is referred to as the orienting reflex, and is exemplified when a dog turns in the direction of a sound that suddenly occurs. After attending to the sound, however, the dog will eventually ignore it (assuming that it poses no threat to him), and go about his business. We say, in this case, that the dog's response to the sound has habituated. Similarly, Sharpless and

Jasper (1956) found that a tone, when first presented, will arouse a sleeping cat. With repeated presentations, however, the tone loses its ability to arouse the cat. Again, we say that habituation has occurred.

Learning and Performance.

As mentioned above, what is learned may not be utilized immediately. A football player, for example, may learn how to play his position by watching films and listening to lectures during the week, but may not translate that learning into behavior until Sunday's game. In fact, he may be prevented from actually performing for a prolonged period of time because of an injury or an illness. We say, therefore, that the *potential* to act differently resulted from learning, even though behavior was not immediately affected.

This type of observation has led to the very important distinction between learning and performance, which will be considered in detail in Chapters 6 and 12. Learning refers to a change in behavior potentiality; and performance refers to the translation of this potentiality into behavior.

Why do We Refer to Practice or Experience?

Obviously not all behavior is learned. Much simple behavior is reflexive. A *reflex* can be defined as an unlearned response in reaction to a specific stimulus. Sneezing in response to a tickling in your nose, or producing a sudden knee-jerk when your knee is tapped sharply, or instantly withdrawing your hand when it touches a hot stove are examples of reflexive behavior. Clearly, reflexive behavior is unlearned; it is a genetically determined characteristic of the organism rather than a result of experience.

Complex behavior can also be unlearned. When complex behavior patterns seem to be genetically determined, they are generally referred to as *instinctive*. Instinctive behavior includes such activities as nest building, migration, hibernation, and mating behavior.

For a while psychologists explained complex behavior patterns by referring to them as instincts. Thus, we said, birds and fish migrate because they possess a migration instinct; birds build nests because of a nest-building instinct. Because the term instinctive was offered as an *explanation* of behavior, we now use the term *species-specific behavior* (Hinde and Tinbergen, 1958) because it is more descriptive. Species-specific behavior refers to complex unlearned, and relatively unmodifiable, behavior patterns engaged in by a certain species of animal under certain circumstances.

Controversy continues, however, over whether species-specific behavior is completely determined by the makeup of the organism or whether some learning is involved. Do birds fly instinctively, or do they learn to fly? Some say that the young bird learns to fly through trial and error while falling to the ground from a tree. Others say that the bird responds reflexively to falling by flapping his wings and therefore flies without learning to do so.

A few examples, however, seem to demonstrate complex behavior that is clearly not influenced by learning. For example, many species of the cuckoo bird lay their eggs in other birds' nests and the young cuckoo is raised by its foster parents. Since each adult cuckoo behaves this way regardless of the foster parents' species, it is very difficult to imagine how such behavior could be learned.

Another example of what appears to be unlearned behavior is given by Beach (1942), who studied the copulatory behavior of 55 male rats. The rats were divided into three groups, following weaning. In Group I, each animal was maintained in isolation. Group II was segregated from females but lived together in one big cage. Group III animals were raised with females and were permitted to copulate. After about 100 days, each rat was given the opportunity to copulate with a receptive female, and the frequency and pattern of sexual behavior was observed. Results indicated that 69 percent of the isolation rats (Group I), 53 percent of the cohabitation group (Group III), and 25 percent of the segregation group (Group II) engaged in copulatory behavior when given the opportunity to do so. Note that the isolation group, which had no opportunity to learn this kind of activity, had the largest proportion of copulators. In addition, 12 of the 15 copulators in this group had normal sexual relations with a female upon their first contact with her.

Other research supports the contention that species-specific behavior is both learned and unlearned (Lorenz, 1952, 1965, 1970; Hess, 1958; Thorpe, 1963). Lorenz found, for example, that a newly hatched duckling would form an attachment to any kind of moving object and follow it as its mother, provided the object was presented at just the right moment in the duckling's life. Lorenz demonstrated attachments between ducklings and a wooden box on wheels, a human being, and a bird of a different species. The formation of an attachment between an organism and an environmental object is called *imprinting*. Imprinting was found to occur only during a *critical period*, after which it was difficult, if not impossible, to imprint the duckling on anything. With imprinting, we have a combination of learned and instinctive behavior. It appears that the animal's genetic endowment causes it to be maximally sensitive to a moving object

Konrad Lorenz and a group of ducklings that have imprinted on him. (Thomas McAvoy/Time-Life Picture Agency, © 1973.)

for a short period of time, during which it can learn the strong habit of following a specific object. If the learning does not occur during that interval, however, it may never occur. Furthermore, the strong habit of following an object does not seem to be built up over time with practice. Rather, the habit seems to be learned at full strength in a single trial. We will have more to say about one-trial learning in Chapters 8 and 9.

Studies about imprinting raise a number of questions. The kind of learning, if any, involved in species-specific behavior, and to what extent it is involved must be determined by future research. The main point to emphasize, however, is that to attribute a behavioral change to learning, the change must be relatively permanent and must result from *experience*. If an organism engages in a complex behavior pattern independent of experience, that behavior cannot be referred to as learned behavior.

Does Learning Result From a Specific Kind of Experience?

According to Kimble's definition, learning results from *reinforced practice*. In other words, only rewarded behavior will be learned. On this

Gregory A. Kimble

point, there is widespread disagreement among learning theorists. Theorists not only disagree over what constitutes reinforcement (reward), but also over whether it is a necessary prerequisite for learning to take place. In a sense, this book is an attempt to review various interpretations of the nature and importance of reinforcement. This is a question, therefore, to which we will return often.

A Modified Definition of Learning.

It is now possible to revise Kimble's definition of learning so that it would be neutral on the matter of reinforcement, thereby making it more widely accepted: *learning is a relatively permanent change in behavior or in behavioral potentiality that results from experience and cannot be attributed to temporary body states induced by illness, fatigue, or drugs.* Such a definition still stresses the importance of experience, but leaves it to the theorist to specify the kind of experience he feels is necessary for learning to take place, e.g., reinforced practice, or contiguity between a stimulus and a response. It also reminds us that experience can cause events other than learning that modify behavior. Fatigue is one such event.

modified definition of learning

Are There Differert Kinds of Learning?

Learning, as we have seen, is a general term that is used to describe changes in behavior potentiality resulting from experience. Conditioning, however, is a more specific term used to describe actual procedures that can modify behavior. Since there are two kinds of conditioning, instrumental and classical, many theorists conclude that there are at least two kinds of learning, or that learning ultimately can be understood in terms of classical and/or instrumental conditioning. Although both conditioning procedures will be discussed in detail later on in this book, we will summarize both procedures briefly.

Classical Conditioning.

We will look at classical conditioning in detail when we discuss Pavlov's views on learning in Chapter 7, but for now we can summarize classical conditioning as follows:

1. A stimulus, such as food, is presented to an organism which will cause him to have a natural and automatic reaction, such as salivating. The stimulus causing this natural reaction is called the unconditioned stimulus (UCS). In this case, the food was the UCS. The natural, automatic reaction to the UCS is called the unconditioned response (UCR). In this case, salivation was the UCR.
2. A neutral stimulus (one that does not cause a UCR), such as a tone or a light, is presented to the organism **just prior** to the presentation of the UCS. This neutral stimulus is called the conditioned stimulus (CS).
3. After the CS and UCS are paired a number of times, with the CS always preceding the UCS, the CS alone can be presented, and the organism will salivate. This salivating response, similar to the organism's response to the UCS, is now given in response to the CS, the tone or the light. We now say that a conditioned response (CR) has been demonstrated.

In classical conditioning, the UCS is called reinforcement, since the entire conditioning procedure depends on it. Note, however, that in classical conditioning, the organism has no control over reinforcement: it occurs when the experimenter wants it to occur. In other words, in classical conditioning, reinforcement is not contingent on any overt response made by the organism.

Instrumental Conditioning.

The relationship between reinforcement and the organism's behavior is distinctively different in instrumental conditioning. With instrumental conditioning, the organism must act in a certain way *before* he is rein-forced; that is, reinforcement is contingent on the organism's behavior. If the animal does not emit the desired behavior he is not rewarded. Thus in instrumental conditioning, the animal's behavior is "instrumental" in getting him something he wants, i.e., a reward.

A small experimental test chamber called the Skinner Box is often used to demonstrate instrumental conditioning (or a closely allied form of conditioning called operant conditioning). Such a box is a plexiglas cage with a grid floor that can be electrified, and a lever that, when pressed, activates a feeder mechanism that delivers food pellets to the animal inside. The experimenter introduces a hungry rat (for example) into the Skinner Box. As the rat explores the enclosure, it will eventually activate the lever and receive a pellet of food. Soon the rat will associate lever-pressing with the appearance of food, and his rate of lever-pressing will increase. In this case, the rat must engage in lever-pressing in order to get food. The lever-pressing is the conditioned behavior; the food is the reinforcement. If the Skinner Box is programmed so that when a hungry animal presses the lever he is given a pellet of food, the rate at which he presses the lever will increase.

Escape and avoidance conditioning are special kinds of instrumental conditioning. For example, the rat is placed in the Skinner Box and the electrified grid is activated, with the lever connected to an off-switch. As the rat leaps around from the shock, he accidentally will hit the lever and terminate the shock. The rat will associate the lever-pressing with the termination of the shock. In this case the lever-pressing is the conditioned behavior, and the termination of shock is the reinforcement. This is an example of *escape conditioning*.

To demonstrate avoidance conditioning, let the Skinner Box grid be activated at intervals, with a signal, such as a light, set up to precede the onset of shock by, say, five seconds. The rat will soon learn to associate the light with the onset of shock, and he will press the lever in order to avoid the shock whenever he sees the light go on. The arrangement where an organism can avoid an aversive stimulus by performing some appro-priate response is referred to as *avoidance conditioning*.

Recently, learning theorists have become increasingly aware that con-fining themselves to research involved with just classical and instrumental conditioning leaves out vast areas of human experience. For example, Gagné (1970) feels it is more realistic to assume that there are eight kinds of learning. Gagné believes that the eight kinds of learning are arranged in a hierarchy, with one sort being a prerequisite for the next. Thus, for Gagné, simple conditioning simply provides the basis for the more ad-vanced kinds of learning. As we shall see in Chapters 10 and 12, Tolman and the Gestalt theorists took a similar position much earlier. Although many theorists believed that complex behavior ultimately could be understood in terms of classical or instrumental conditioning, other influential theorists opposed that contention.

WHY STUDY LEARNING?

Since most human behavior is learned, investigating the principles of learning will help us understand why we behave as we do. An awareness of the learning process will not only allow greater understanding of normal and adaptive behavior, but will also allow greater understanding of the circumstances that produce maladaptive and abnormal behavior. More effective psychotherapy might result from such an understanding.

Child rearing practices can also utilize the principles of learning. Obviously, individuals differ from one another and these individual differences may be explained in terms of differing learning experiences. One of the most important human attributes is language and there is little doubt that specific language development results mainly from learning. No doubt, many other human attributes are molded in a similar way by the interaction of the environment with the learning process. When parents know more about the learning experiences that create what they would call desirable traits, they may wish to organize the environment of their child so that it encourages these traits. Likewise, learning experiences that tend to produce socially maladaptive behavior can be avoided.

Moreover, there is a close relationship between the principles of learning and educational practices. In many cases, principles that have been uncovered while studying the learning process in the laboratory have eventually been utilized in the classroom. The widespread utilization of programmed learning and teaching machines offer two examples of how research on learning influences teaching practices. The current trend in American education toward personalized systems of instruction or individualized instruction can also be considered a spinoff from research on the learning process. We may reasonably conclude that as our knowledge of the learning process increases, educational practices should become more efficient and effective.

DISCUSSION QUESTIONS

1. List the requirements that must be met before a change in behavior can be attributed to learning.

2. Describe the processes of sensitization and habituation as they have occurred in your life.
3. Differentiate between learning and performance.
4. Give a few examples of complex unlearned behavior. Do you feel that complex unlearned behavior exists on the human level? Explain.
5. Why was the term *instinct* replaced with the term *species-specific* behavior?
6. Differentiate between the terms learning and conditioning.
7. How many kinds of learning are there? Explain how you arrived at your answer.
8. What is meant by the statement, "Imprinting seems to result from both learning and instinct"?
9. Give a few reasons why it is important to study the learning process.

GLOSSARY

Avoidance conditioning. The experimental arrangement where an organism can avoid experiencing an aversive stimulus by engaging in appropriate behavior.

Behavioral potentiality. The ability to perform some act although the act is not being performed at the present time. Learning may result in a change in behavioral potentiality although the learning may not be translated into behavior until some time after the learning has taken place.

Classical conditioning. An experimental arrangement whereby a stimulus is made to elicit a response that was not previously associated with that stimulus, i.e., the conditioned stimulus (CS) comes to elicit a response similar to the one elicited by the UCS.

Conditioning. An experimental procedure used to modify behavior. Most learning theorists believe that there are two kinds of conditioning–classical and instrumental–and that all learning involves conditioning. To those holding such a belief, learning is a term used to summarize a large number of conditioned responses.

Critical period. A period in an organism's life during which time an important development occurs. If the development does not occur during that time, it may never occur. For example, if imprinting does not occur shortly after a duckling is hatched, it is difficult, if not impossible, to establish it. The period of time immediately following hatching, therefore, is the critical period for imprinting.

Escape conditioning. The experimental arrangement where an organism can terminate an aversive stimulus by engaging in appropriate behavior.

Habituation. The decreased tendency to respond to a stimulus that results from prolonged exposure to that stimulus.

Imprinting. The rapid formation, during a critical period, of a close attachment between an organism and an environmental object.

Instinct. The inborn capacity to perform a complex behavioral task. In recent years, the term has been replaced by *species-specific behavior.*

Instrumental conditioning. An experimental procedure whereby the rate or probability of a response is changed from a relatively low value before conditioning to a relatively high value following conditioning. With instrumental conditioning, the organism must perform an appropriate response in order to be rewarded.

Learning. A relatively permanent change in behavior or behavioral potentiality that comes from experience and cannot be attributed to temporary body states such as illness, fatigue, or drugs.

Overt behavior. Behavior that is observable and is, therefore, measurable. This is contrasted with covert behavior, such as thinking or reasoning, which is not directly observable and, therefore, cannot be measured directly.

Performance. The translation of learning into behavior.

Reflex. An unlearned response to a specific stimulus.

Reinforced practice. Repeated performance under the conditions where a correct response is followed by reinforcement. Reinforced practice is thought by many learning theorists to be a necessary condition for learning to take place; other theorists do not agree.

Sensitization. The tendency to be more responsive to the environment following an arousing experience.

Short-term memory. The memory of an experience that lasts for only several seconds after the termination of the experience. This is opposed to long-term memory that lasts considerably longer.

Temporary body state. A temporary condition of the body such as fatigue, illness, emotion, the presence of drugs, and sleep loss, that cause a modification in behavior. Such modifications in behavior are differentiated from those caused by learning.

2

Approaches to
the Study of Learning

We noted in Chapter 1 that most learning theorists contend that learning can be observed only indirectly through changes in behavior. Therefore when we study learning, we observe behavior and based on these observables, we infer that learning has taken place or that a particular type of learning has or has not occurred. The inaccessibility of learning is one reason why there are so many approaches to its study. Some feel, for example, that the best place to study learning is in the field rather than in the laboratory. This method of studying a phenomenon as it occurs naturally is called *naturalistic observation*. Using this technique, one would make detailed observations and recordings of what is being studied. Such research often results in a grouping or classification of the various elements of the phenomenon being investigated. For example, while using naturalistic observation to study learning in the classroom one might classify learning to read or spell as verbal learning, the learning of athletic prowess as perceptual-motor skill learning, and the learning that requires complex mental processes as problem solving or concept formation.

Two major drawbacks of naturalistic observation become apparent. First, because the classroom situation is extremely complex it is very difficult to observe and record accurately. Second, there is a tendency to classify events into chunks that may be too comprehensive; for example, what is classified as concept formation may in reality consist of many different phenomena whose distinctions get lost in the classifying process. Classifications that seem rather straightforward at first may become extraordinarily complex under closer scrutiny.

Naturalistic observation can be an important first step for a study of learning but eventually the psychologist must break up the recorded chunks of behavior for closer and more detailed analysis. He must become more *reductionistic* in order to discover the various laws operating in the learning situation, and discovering laws usually involves experimentation. That is, naturalistic observation may be important in isolating groups of events for further study, but these must then be reduced into smaller components for further analysis. Such an approach is called reductionistic.

THE SYSTEMATIC STUDY OF LEARNING

In recent times, that portion of psychology concerned with the learning process has become more scientific. We will see in the next chapter that using the scientific method in the psychology of learning has been very productive. It is important, therefore, that we look at such a productive method in more detail.

What is Science?

According to Stevens (1951): ". . . science seeks to generate confirmable propositions by fitting a formal system of symbols (language, mathematics, logic) to empirical observations [p. 22]." Stevens's statement points to a number of important characteristics of science. For example, science deals with *confirmable propositions*. The propositions of science must be capable of having their truth or falsity demonstrated publicly, so that any other interested researcher can replicate the experiment and obtain the same results. This insistence on publicly verifiable propositions is what characterizes a science. Science is not concerned with private or unique events, but only with statements that are empirically verifiable. The statement, "I ate pickles last night and subsequently dreamt of elephants," is scientifically useless because it refers to a personal experience that is unique and undemonstrable. However, the statement, "People who eat pickles tend to dream of elephants," can be thought of as scientific because it is in principle verifiable. If we feed pickles to a large number of people and they subsequently report dreaming of elephants, and if we repeat the procedure a number of times with the same outcome, we have discovered a *scientific law*. A scientific law can be defined as a consistently observed relationship between two or more events. *All sciences seek to discover laws.* The lawful relationship we have discovered in the example above is between the eating of pickles and the *verbal report* of having dreamt of elephants. Again, if there is no way of publicly demonstrating whether a statement is true or false, it is scientifically useless.

Aspects of Theory.

Scientific theories have two important aspects. First, a theory has a *formal aspect*, which includes the words and symbols the theory contains. Second, a theory has an *empirical aspect*, which consists of the physical events that the theory is attempting to explain. Although the relationship between the formal and empirical aspects of a theory is very complex, it should be noted briefly that the formal part of a theory can make sense by itself even though it may make erroneous predictions about the physical world. The statement, "All learning depends upon drive reduction," makes sense formally, but may not accurately explain learning. The point here is that a theory can sound good, but it is devoid of scientific meaning unless it withstands the rigors of experimental test. There is always the danger of being overly impressed by the wording of a theory and forgetting to check how accurately it predicts and describes empirical events.

It is important to remember that no matter how abstract and complex a theory becomes, it must ultimately relate to *physical thing language,* that is, it must at some point make contact with observable physical events. All scientific theories, no matter how abstract their formal aspects become, begin and end with statements about observable events.

From Research to Theory.

As a general example of the use of theory in psychology, we can refer to research examining the relationship between food deprivation and rate of learning, with food as the reinforcer. In this case, learning rate will be indexed by the number of trials it takes for an animal to learn to turn left on every trial in a T-maze. After many separate experiments, a researcher finds that as hours of food deprivation goes up, learning occurs more rapidly. That is, animals deprived of food the longest, learn to turn left in a T-maze most rapidly.

These results can be looked upon as the demonstration of a law. Here the observed relationship is between degree of food deprivation and performance on a learning task. The researcher turns next to study water deprivation. Again, he finds that as hours of water deprivation goes up, learning time goes down. Now we have a second law: as hours of water deprivation go up the faster an animal learns to turn left in a T-maze when water is used as a reward.

Next, with a sense of urgency, the researcher turns to the study of sexual behavior. This time the opportunity to copulate is used as a reward for the rat to turn left in the T-maze. Again, it is found that increased hours of sexual deprivation results in faster learning.

Although the goal of science is to discover laws (observed relationships between events), it is seldom enough to simply observe and record hundreds or perhaps thousands of empirical relationships. Scientists usually attempt to make sense out of the laws they discover, i.e., they attempt to group them in some coherent fashion. This grouping has at least two functions: (1) to synthesize a large number of observations and (2) to point the way to further research. The latter aspect of grouping or attempting to make sense out of data is called its *heuristic function*.

At this point, therefore, the researcher may wish to go beyond his data. He may make statements such as "Hungry animals tend to learn faster than food-satiated ones," or "Thirsty animals tend to learn faster than water-satiated ones." Both statements plunge the researcher into the realm of theory. Although his experiments involved specific situations (e.g., 2, 4, 6, and 8 hours of deprivation) the concept of hunger, which is an abstraction, covers all states of deprivation, even those not involved in his research (e.g., 26, 30, 37, 37½, and 50 hours of deprivation). Thus, by postulating the unobservable inner state of hunger, the researcher is at the same time attempting to tie together some of his observations and predicting the outcome of future research. The same is true when he uses the concepts of thirst and sexual arousal.

The researcher can take an additional step and attempt to synthesize his three theoretical terms into still another theoretical term. He can conclude, for example, that deprivation increases drive, and animals with high drive learn faster. Note, in doing this, he is using the two functions of a theory: synthesizing, and predicting avenues of future research. By stating that "animals with high drive learn faster than animals with low drive," he is suggesting research on oxygen deprivation, heat deprivation, or pain reduction. The relationship between the concepts of drive, hunger, thirst, sexual arousal and the empirical events from which they stem is shown in Figure 2–1.

The researcher could take still an additional step and postulate the

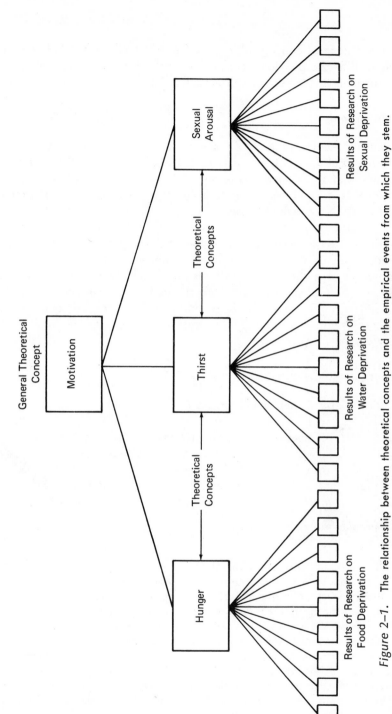

Figure 2-1. The relationship between theoretical concepts and the empirical events from which they stem.

19

even more general concept of motivation and include psychological factors as well as the physiological ones we have been considering, e.g., the need for achievement or for self-actualization.

Theories as Tools.

Because a theory is merely a research tool it cannot be right or wrong; it is either useful or it is not useful. If a theory clarifies the various observations that have been made, and if it generates additional research, the theory is a good one. If it fails in either respect, the researcher is likely to search for a new theory.

If a hypothesis generated by a theory is confirmed, the theory gains strength. If a hypothesis generated by a theory is rejected, the theory is weakened and must either be revised or abandoned. Again we see how confirmation of a theory depends on empirical observation. Whether a theory is maintained, revised, or abandoned is determined by the outcome of the empirical research generated by the theory. Thus, we see that *theories must continually generate the very hypotheses that may prove they are ineffective.*

The Principle of Parsimony.

We noted above that one characteristic of science is that science deals only with statements that are in principle empirically verifiable. Another characteristic of science is that it follows the principle of parsimony (sometimes called the principle of economy, Occam's Razor, or Morgan's Canon). This principle states that when two equally effective theories can explain the same phenomenon, but one explanation is simple and the other is complex, we must use the simpler explanation.

Summary of Characteristics of a Scientific Theory.

1. A theory synthesizes a number of observations.
2. A good theory is heuristic, that is, it generates new research.
3. A theory must generate hypotheses that can be empirically verified. If such hypotheses are confirmed, the theory gains strength; if not, the theory is weakened and must be revised or abandoned.
4. A theory is a tool and as such cannot be right or wrong; it is either useful or it is not useful.
5. Theories are chosen in accordance with the law of parsimony: of two equally effective theories, the simpler of the two must be chosen.
6. Theories contain abstractions, such as numbers or words, which constitute the formal aspect of a theory.

7. The formal aspect of a theory must be correlated with observable events, which constitute the empirical aspect of a theory.
8. All theories are attempts to explain empirical events and they must, therefore, start and end with empirical observations.

THE LEARNING EXPERIMENT

In the previous section we considered the course from research to theory; here we will look briefly at the course from theory to research. First, we must delineate a subject matter. This usually takes the form of a general definition of learning or a general description of the phenomenon to be studied. Next, we attempt to specify the conditions necessary for the phenomenon to occur. Lastly, we must convert our theoretical statements about the learning process in terms of identifiable and repeatable activities or experimental performances. This way of measurably defining a theoretical term is called an *operational definition.* In other words, an operational definition relates what is being defined (in this case learning), to the operations used to measure it. For example, a common operational definition of difficulty of learning is *trials to criterion,* which is the number of times an experimental subject needs to experience the material to be learned before being able to perform at some specified level; for instance, how many times he had to see a list of nonsense syllables before he could recite the entire list accurately. Once the researcher has operationally defined his theoretical terms, he is ready to experiment.

Every experiment involves something whose changes are measured, *the dependent variable,* and something the experimenter manipulates to see its effect on the dependent variable, the *independent variable.* In the previously mentioned experiment concerning the relationship between the number of hours of food deprivation and rate of learning, rate of learning was measured and was, therefore, the dependent variable. Rate of learning was operationally defined as how many trials it took for the animal to learn to make a left turn in a T-maze. Thus, trials to criterion was used as the dependent variable. In learning experiments, the operational definition indicates the kind of behavior that will be used to index learning. Hours of food deprivation was systematically manipulated by the researcher and it, therefore, was the independent variable.

Arbitrary Decisions in Setting Up a Learning Experiment.

Science is often thought of as a cold, highly objective means for arriving at the "truth." Scientists, however, are often highly emotional, very subjective, and the "truth" they disclose is dynamic and probabilistic. This can be seen in the number of arbitrary decisions that go into the setting up of any learning experiment. A number of these arbitrary decisions are summarized below.

1. What Aspects of Learning Should be Investigated?   This, of course, will be partially dictated by one's theory concerning learning. One can study learning in the laboratory, or one can observe learning as it occurs in a schoolroom setting via naturalistic observation. In addition, one can study instrumental conditioning, classical conditioning, concept formation, problem solving, or verbal or perceptual-motor learning. Although a theory of learning attempts to specify the conditions under which learning takes place, it is up to the experimenter to choose which conditions should be investigated.

2. Idiographic versus Nomothetic Techniques.   Should the researcher intensely study the learning process of a single experimental subject under a wide variety of circumstances (idiographic technique), or should he use groups of experimental subjects and study their average performance (nomothetic technique)? Although quite different, both techniques are respectable and both yield useful information about the learning process. As we shall see later, Skinner uses the idiographic technique, and Hull used the nomothetic technique. As we shall see in Chapter 9, the two techniques can result in entirely different conclusions about the nature of learning.

3. Humans versus "Lower" Animals as Subjects.   If the researcher chooses to use humans as his experimental subjects, he is concerned about how his results generalize from the laboratory situation to the real world outside the laboratory. If, however, he uses subhuman subjects, such as rats, pigeons, or monkeys, he is concerned about how the learning process generalizes from one species to another in addition to the above concern.

Why, then, use anything but human subjects? There are many reasons why researchers use subhuman subjects instead of humans despite the difficulties involved.

1. Humans are often too sophisticated for certain learning experiments, that is, their previous experience interferes with a clear study of the learning process. The learning history of subhuman subjects can be controlled with relative ease.
2. Often learning experiments are long and boring, and it would be difficult to find humans willing to run in them. Subhuman subjects don't complain.
3. Some experiments are designed to test the effects of genetics on learning ability. By using subhuman subjects, the genetic background of subjects can be systematically manipulated.
4. The relationship between certain drugs and learning can be investigated

using subhuman subjects, whereas using human subjects for such research would be difficult, if not impossible.

5. Various surgical techniques can be used on subhuman subjects, not on humans. The surgical removal of certain brain areas and direct brain stimulation via electrodes implanted in the brain are but two examples. Likewise, human subjects can't be sacrificed after the experiment to check on such things as neuronal effects of the treatment condition.

6. Last, but not least, human subjects sometimes miss appointments to run in experiments, whereas subhuman subjects almost always show up.

4. Correlation versus Experimental Techniques. Some researchers may want to correlate learning (as defined by a score on an achievement test) with intelligence (as measured by an IQ test). Since this involves correlating one response (performance on the achievement test) with another response (performance on the IQ test), the resulting relationship is called an R-R law (response-response law). R-R laws are said to be correlational in that they describe how two classes of behavioral events vary together.

Other researchers may want to systematically vary one or more environmental events and note their effect on the dependent variables. Since the relationship examined here is between environmental events (stimuli) and responses (changes on the dependent variable), it is said to be an S-R, or stimulus-response, law.

While one may argue about the relative merits of correlational or experimental techniques, the point here is that there are at least these two general approaches available for doing research. Both approaches yield distinctly different information about learning. Which approach is taken depends on the preference of the individual researcher.

5. Which Independent Variables Should be Studied? Once learning has been operationally defined, the dependent variable in an experiment has been automatically set. If, for example, learning is operationally defined as "trials to criterion," then this is what is measured in the experiment. Next, the researcher must ask "What variable or variables are likely to have an effect on the behavior being measured?" The answer to that question could involve a long list of possible independent variables for him to choose from. A sample list follows.

Sex difference	Intelligence
Age differences	Drugs
Size of the stimulus materials used	Intertrial Interval
Rate of presentation	Interaction with
Meaningfulness of the material used	other tasks
Instructions	

An additional function of a theory, by the way, is to give the researcher some guidance in choosing his independent variable or variables.

6. What Levels of the Independent Variables Should Be Studied? Once one or more independent variables have been chosen, the researcher must consider how many levels of it should be represented in the experiment. For example, if age is chosen as an experimental variable, how many ages and which ones should be studied. There are some guidelines that could be used here to assure that the levels chosen will have the greatest effect on the dependent variable (see Anderson, 1971), but this choice is basically arbitrary.

7. Choice of Dependent Variables. Common dependent variables in learning experiments include the following:

scores on tests	trials to criterion
trials to extinction	latency
running speed	probability of response
rate of responding	number of errors
time to solution	response amplitude

Because each results from an operational definition of learning, it should be clear that there are many acceptable operational definitions of learning available to the researcher. Although which he chooses is arbitrary, his choice may have a profound effect on the conclusions he draws about the outcome of his experiment. In experiments having two dependent variables, it is common for one variable to show an effect due to the independent variable, and for the other to show no effect. For example, when investigating the transfer of training from one hand to the other in our laboratory, we consistently find that practice with one hand increases the speed with which a task can be performed with the other hand (speed of responding being one dependent variable). Using speed as our dependent variable, we would find evidence for positive transfer of training from one hand to the other. If, however, we used number of errors as our dependent variable we would discover that practice with one hand did not facilitate performance with the other hand. Thus we would conclude that no transfer of training took place–two altogether dissimilar conclusions resulting from our choice of the dependent variable.

8. Data Analysis and Interpretation. Once the data (scores on the dependent variable) has been gathered in an experiment, how does one analyze it? Although it is beyond the scope of this book to discuss them, the reader should be aware of the fact that there are many statistical techniques available to the researcher for data analysis. Here again, his choice of a statistical test is somewhat arbitrary and may have a significant effect on his conclusions.

Once the experiment has been designed, run, and analyzed, it must be interpreted. There are usually many interpretations of the data provided by an experiment, and there is really no way of knowing if the one finally decided upon is the most adequate. It is possible that even after following the most rigorous scientific procedures in the gathering of experimental data, the interpretation of those data could be totally inadequate. For example, there is the story of the researcher who trained a flea to jump every time he said "jump." After this preliminary training, the researcher began pulling legs off the flea, and after the removal of each leg, he said "jump" and the flea jumped. The experiment continued in this manner until the flea's last leg had been pulled off. Now when the experimenter said "jump," the flea did not move. The researcher jotted his conclusion in his notebook: "Fleas without legs are deaf." We exaggerate only to stress the point that there are any number of possible conclusions that could be drawn about the same experimental data.

It should be noted that although we refer to the decisions in this section as arbitrary, they are arbitrary only in the sense that there are a number of ways of arranging an experiment in a given area and any one of the ways might be scientifically correct. In a more practical sense, however, the choice of what to study, the kind of subject to use, independent and dependent variables, and approach to data analysis and interpretation will be at least partially determined by such factors as cost, practicality, theoretical orientation, social and educational concerns, and availability of apparatus.

THE USE OF MODELS

In *The Random House Dictionary of the English Language* (1968) simile is defined as "A figure of speech in which two unlike things are explicitly compared, as in 'she is like a rose.'" Other examples of similes would be, "clumsy as a bull in a china shop," "gentle as a lamb," "he dropped like a rock," or "the engine purred like a kitten." In each case, something we know quite well is being used to describe something we do not know as well. We say that the well-known condition is acting as a *model* to describe the less known condition. Even though the two things involved may be dissimilar in most respects, they have enough in common so that they are comparable in at least one respect. Similes and scientific models are used in much the same way, in that something known is used to describe something that is relatively less known.

Unlike a theory, however, a model is not used to explain a complicated process; rather it is used to simplify the process and make it more understandable. When Freud used the concepts of id, ego, and superego, he was using them as a model to describe the interaction of various processes of human behavior. Lewin (see Chapter 10) used the concept of "life space" in much the same way. Life space, to Lewin, was really a diagram showing the many influences acting on a person at any given time. Used in this way, life space was a model simplifying a situation that was otherwise very complicated.

A theory, as opposed to a model, attempts to describe the processes underlying a complex phenomenon. Reinforcement theory, for example, is an attempt to explain why learning occurs. It is not an attempt to show what learning is *like*, as would be the case with a model. In the area of motivation, one might say that an organism acts like a mule with a carrot dangling before him, or one might say that the physiological state of hunger is interacting with previously learned habits, causing the organism to run. In the former case, a model is being used to *describe* behavior; in the latter case, a theory is being used in an attempt to *explain* behavior. Estes (see Chapter 9) is an example of a theorist who uses a model to clarify his views about the learning process.

Learning in the Laboratory Versus Naturalistic Observation

Remember that science deals in statements that are verified through experimentation. Contrasted with naturalistic observation, where the researcher has no control over what is being observed, an experiment can be defined as controlled observation. Information is both gained and lost in laboratory experimentation. On the plus side, the experimenter controls the situation, and therefore is able to systematically examine a number of different conditions and their effect on learning. On the negative side, the laboratory creates an artificial situation that is much different from the circumstances under which learning would ordinarily occur. This always brings into question how information gained in the laboratory is related to learning situations outside the laboratory.

Kuhn's Views of How Sciences Change

To picture science as an activity that gradually evolves toward an increasingly accurate understanding of nature, as we have done above, may be somewhat misleading. In his book *The Structure of Scientific Revolutions* (1973), Thomas Kuhn portrays a much different view of science. According to Kuhn, scientists working in a given area usually accept a certain point of view about what they are studying. For example, at one time most physicists accepted the Newtonian point of view in their study of physics. Kuhn calls a point of view shared by a substantial number of scientists a *paradigm*. A paradigm provides a general framework for empirical research and, as such, is usually more than just a limited theory. A paradigm corresponds more closely to what is called a school of thought or an "ism" such as behaviorism, introspectionism, or functionalism (these terms will be explained in the next chapter).

The activities of scientists who accept a particular paradigm consist mainly of elaborating and verifying the implications of the framework it superimposes over the subject being studied. In other words, a paradigm is a way of looking at a subject matter which illuminates certain problems and suggests ways of solving those problems. Kuhn calls the problem solving activities of scientists following a paradigm *normal science*. Normal science is what most of this chapter has been about.

The positive result of a community of scientists following a certain paradigm is that a certain range of phenomena, those upon which the paradigm focuses, are explored thoroughly. The negative result is that following a particular paradigm blinds the scientists to other, perhaps more fruitful, ways of dealing with their subject matter. Thus, while research generated by a certain paradigm results in depth, it may inhibit breadth.

According to Kuhn (1973), scientists following a particular paradigm, that is, those engaged in normal science, are providing little more than a "mop-up operation." Kuhn puts the matter as follows:

> Mopping-up operations are what engage most scientists throughout their careers. They constitute what I am here calling normal science. Closely examined, whether historically or in the contemporary laboratory, that enterprise seems an attempt to force nature into the preformed and relatively inflexible box that the paradigm supplies. No part of the aim of normal science is to call forth new sorts of phenomena; .indeed, those that will not fit the box are often not seen at all. Nor do scientists normally aim to invent new theories, and they are often intolerant of those invented by others. Instead, normal-scientific research is directed to the articulation of those phenomena and theories that the paradigm already supplies [p. 24].

How then do new paradigms emerge? According to Kuhn, innovations in science come when scientists following a particular paradigm are consistently confronted with events that are inconsistent with the point of view they are holding. Eventually, as the anomalies persist, an alternative paradigm will emerge that will be able to explain the anomalies as well as the events supporting the previous paradigm. The new paradigm will usually be associated with one individual or a small group of individuals who attempt to convince their colleagues that their paradigm is more effective than its predecessor. Typically, the new paradigm meets with great resistance and converts are won very slowly. Kuhn says this resistance comes from the fact that a particular paradigm has implications for every aspect of one's scientific life and, therefore, changing from one paradigm to another involves an enormous change in how one does science; for this reason, there is emotional involvement in the decision. Kuhn says:

> Like the choice between competing political institutions, that between competing paradigms proves to be a choice between incompatible modes of community life [p. 94].

Because of this emotional involvement, a scientist will usually do everything possible to make his accepted paradigm work before pondering a change. At some point, however, the older paradigm will be "overthrown" and the new one will replace it. The displacement of Newton's theory by Einstein's theory would be one example and the displacement of religious notions concerning the creation of man by Darwin's theory of evolution would be another.

It appears, then, that a science changes (although it does not necessarily advance) through a series of revolutions, which are similar to political revolutions, rather than through a continuous evolutionary process within a single theoretical framework. To Kuhn, the evolution of a science is at least as much a sociological phenomenon as it is a scientific phenomenon. We might add that it also appears to be a psychological phenomenon.

As valid as Kuhn's argument appears to be, it seems most forceful when applied to the physical sciences rather than the behavioral sciences. Within the more mature physical sciences, it is the rule that most scientists accept some prevailing paradigm and, therefore, a change in paradigm tends to be revolutionary. In the younger behavioral sciences, however, a variety of paradigms exist simultaneously. The book you are now reading provides a good example since it offers various ways of looking at the learning process. Every theory in this book is accepted to some extent by a substantial number of researchers of the learning process. Although followers of one theory tend to form a camp, they still communicate and influence members of other camps. It would be difficult to find an area in physics for which this would be true. For example, one could not find a book on theories of gravity, since there are not as many paradigms that exist simultaneously in that area.

Thus, it seems that under the conditions that exist in the behavioral sciences, the revolutionary change of paradigms is less possible and/or necessary. One possible exception to this contention would be the widespread acceptance of associationism, one of psychology's oldest and most widely accepted doctrines. In fact, most theories in this book assume some aspect of associationism. At the present time, there is growing dissatisfaction with the assumptions underlying associationism; thus we have the necessary condition for the kind of scientific revolution that Kuhn so eloquently elaborates in his book. When we discuss the ideas of Jean Piaget in Chapter 11, we will review a theory that radically departs from an associationistic viewpoint.

DISCUSSION QUESTIONS

1. In what way(s) do you feel science differs from other fields of inquiry, such as philosophy and theology?
2. What is a scientific law? How does the scientific concept of law differ from how the term is used in a legal or a religious sense?
3. Discuss the strengths and weaknesses of naturalistic observation.
4. Briefly discuss the characteristics of a scientific theory.
5. Discuss the steps involved in going from experimentation to theory.
6. Discuss the steps involved in going from a theory to experimentation.
7. Differentiate between a theory and a model.
8. List and briefly describe the arbitrary decisions that are involved in setting up, running, and analyzing a learning experiment.
9. What does Kuhn mean when he says normal science is a "mop-up" operation?
10. Describe the process of scientific revolution as it is viewed by Kuhn.

GLOSSARY

Confirmable proposition.   A proposition whose truth or falsity can be publicly demonstrated. Such a proposition is also called verifiable.

Correlational techniques. Research where two response measures are related. Such research is usually interested in detecting how two kinds of behavior vary together. For example, how is performance on an IQ test related to performance on a creativity test? Correlational techniques generate R-R laws, since two response measures are being related.

Dependent variable. The variable that is measured in an experiment, usually some kind of behavior, e.g., trials to criterion.

Empirical aspect of a theory. The empirical events that the theory purports to explain.

Experimental techniques. Research where one or more independent variables are systematically manipulated in order to detect their effects on one or more dependent variables. Since an experiment attempts to relate stimuli (independent variables) to responses (dependent variables), it is said to generate S-R laws. This is contrasted with correlational techniques which demonstrate R-R laws.

Formal aspect of a theory. The signs, symbols, or words that a theory contains.

Heuristic function of a theory. A theory's ability to generate research.

Idiographic technique. The intense study of a single experimental subject.

Independent variable. The variable that is systematically manipulated in an experiment. Typical independent variables would include hours of deprivation, sex of subject, age, rate of presentation, or degree of meaningfulness.

Model. When a fairly well known situation is used to describe a relatively less known situation. Models are used to show that the two situations are alike in some respects.

Naturalistic observation. A technique to study a phenomenon as it occurs naturally in the environment.

Nomothetic techniques. .The study of a group of experimental subjects, the interest being in the *average* performance of the group.

Normal science. Those activities of scientists as they are guided by a particular paradigm.

Operational definition of learning. A definition that states the procedures to be followed in determining whether, and to what extent, learning has taken place. Operational definitions of learning can range from grades on achievement tests to some behavioral measure in a learning experiment, such as trials to criterion or the number of errors in maze-running.

Paradigm. A point of view shared by a substantial number of scientists, that provides a general framework for empirical research. A paradigm is usually more than just one theory and corresponds more closely to what is called a "school of thought" or an "ism."

Physical thing language. Language that refers directly to physical objects that can be pointed at or touched.

Principle of parsimony. When a researcher has a choice between two equally effective theories, he is obliged to choose the simpler of the two.

Reductionism. The belief that a meaningful way to study a complex phenomenon is to divide it up into smaller components.

Science. A method of inquiry that involves the use of experimentation to test theories about various aspects of nature.

Scientific law. A consistently observed relationship between two or more empirical events.

Scientific revolution. The displacement of one paradigm with another. Such a displacement usually occurs over a fairly long period of time and after great resistance. A paradigm is associated with the scientist's total view of his science—what counts as a good problem, what counts as a good answer, what a good experiment is like, and so on. Thus, a change in paradigm is a widespread change for the scientist which invalidates almost every aspect of his previous scientific life. There is, therefore, emotional involvement in such a change.

Theory. An attempted explanation that makes sense out of a large number of observations, and indicates to the researcher where to look for additional information.

Trials to criterion. The number of trials an experimental subject requires to reach the criterion that the experimenter sets as a definition of learning. For example, if perfect recall of a list of nonsense syllables is defined as learning the list, then trials to criterion is the number of times the subject had to go through the list before he could recall the items without error.

3

Early Notions About Learning

EPISTEMOLOGY AND LEARNING THEORY

Epistemology is a branch of philosophy that is concerned with the nature of knowledge. The epistemologist asks questions such as, What is knowledge? What can we know? What are the limits of knowledge? What does it mean to know? What are the origins of knowledge? Questions of this kind go back at least as far as the early Greeks. In fact, the views of Plato and Aristotle concerning the nature of knowledge have set philosophical trends that have persisted until this day. Plato believed that knowledge was inherited and was, therefore, a natural component of the human mind. According to Plato, one gained knowledge by reflecting on the contents of one's mind. Aristotle, on the other hand, believed that knowledge was the result of sensory experience and was not inherited.

The position taken by Plato is an example of *rationalism*, since it stresses the activities of the mind in explaining the nature of knowledge. The rationalist believes that the mind must somehow become involved before knowledge is obtainable. Plato's particular brand of rationalism is also called *nativism*, since he stressed the fact that knowledge was innate.

The position taken by Aristotle has come to be called *empiricism*, since it stresses the importance of sensory experience as the basis of all knowledge. The rationalist and empiricist explanations of knowledge that started with Plato and Aristotle over 2000 years ago are still very much alive in the area of learning theory, as we shall see throughout this book.

Since the views of Plato and Aristotle concerning the nature of knowledge have played such an important role in the history of learning theory, we will look at them in greater detail below.

PLATO

Plato (427–347 B.C.) was Socrates' most famous student. In fact, Socrates never wrote a word about his philosophy—it was all written by Plato. This is a most significant fact, since the early dialogues were designed primarily to show the Socratic approach to knowledge and were memories of the great teacher at work. The later dialogues, however, seem to represent Plato's own philosophy and have little to do with Socrates. Plato was so upset by the execution of Socrates for impiety that he went on a self-imposed exile to southern Italy, where he came under the influence of the Pythagoreans. This fact has profound implications for western man and is directly related to all approaches to epistemology, including learning theory, that have occurred since.

The Pythagoreans believed that the universe was governed by numerical relationships that influenced the physical world. In fact, numbers and their various combinations *caused* events in the physical world. And both events, the number and the empirical event that it caused, were real. Thus, to the Pythagoreans, the abstract had an independent existence and was capable of influencing physical objects. Furthermore, physical events are but manifestations of the abstract. Although number and matter interact it is matter that we experience with our senses, not number. This results in a dualistic view of the universe, where one aspect can be experienced through the senses and the other cannot. Following this notion, the Pythagoreans made great strides in mathematics, medicine, and music. Through time, however, they developed into a mystical cult, allowing only a few individuals to become members and share their wisdom. Plato was one such individual.

Plato's later dialogues reflect complete acceptance of the dualistic universe that the Pythagoreans believed in. He developed a theory of knowledge based on the Pythagorean notion that the abstract has an independent and influential existence. This theory has profoundly influenced epistemology in general, and psychology in particular. Because all approaches to explaining human knowledge or learning refer back to Plato's ideas it is important for us to look at his theory of knowledge in some detail.

Plato's Theory of Knowledge.

Every object in the physical world has a corresponding abstract "idea" or "form" that causes it. For example, the abstract idea of *chair* interacts with matter to produce what we call a chair. The idea of *tree* interacts with matter to form what we see as a tree. All physical objects have such an origin. Thus, what we experience through our senses is a chair, a tree, or a house, but not chairness, treeness, or houseness. The pure idea of these things exists independent of matter, and something is lost when the idea is translated into matter. Therefore, if we attempt to gain knowledge by examining things that we experience through the senses, we will be misled. Sensory information provides only opinion; the abstract ideas themselves are the only bases of true knowledge.

But how do we obtain information about the ideas if we cannot experience them through the senses? Plato says we experience through the "mind's eye." We turn our thoughts inward and ponder what is innately available to us. Every human being has in his mind complete knowledge of all the ideas that make up the world; thus true knowledge comes from introspection or self-analysis. One must learn to divorce himself from sensory information that can only deceive or, at best, remind him of what he already knows.

How does one come to have knowledge of the ideas? Here Plato becomes extremely mystical. All humans possess a soul. Before being placed in the body at birth, the soul dwells in pure and complete knowledge. Thus, all human souls know everything before entering the body. Upon entering the body, the knowledge of the soul begins to be "contaminated" by sensory information. According to Plato if one accepts what he experiences through the senses as truth, he is doomed to live a life of opinion and ignorance. Only by turning away from the physical impure world to the world of ideas, pondered by the mind's eye, can we hope to gain true knowledge. Thus, all knowledge is reminiscence or recollection of the experience our soul had in the "heaven which is beyond the heavens." Plato advises the astronomer to "let the heavens alone" and use "the natural gift of reason" (*Republic* VII, p. 296).

As we have already seen, Plato was a nativist because he felt knowledge was inborn. He was also a rationalist, because he felt this knowledge could only be made available through reasoning. As we shall see later, other rationalists were not as extreme as Plato in their negative attitude toward sensory information. However, it was Plato's philosophy that dominated Europe for the first twelve centuries of the Christian Era. It is through this early influence on Christianity that we still have remnants of Platonism in western culture today. Time and time again, Plato's nativism has appeared in psychology. We will see one example of it when we discuss Gestalt psychology in Chapter 10.

ARISTOTLE

Aristotle (384–322 B.C.) was one of Plato's students who first followed Plato's teachings quite closely and later broke away from them almost completely. A basic difference between the two thinkers was in their attitude toward empirical information. To Plato, it was a hindrance and something to be distrusted, but to Aristotle, sensory information was the basis of all knowledge. With his favorable attitude toward empirical observation, Aristotle compiled an extraordinarily large number of facts about physical and biological phenomena.

Reason, however, was in no way abandoned by Aristotle. He felt sense impressions were only the beginning of knowledge—the mind must then ponder these impressions to discover the lawfulness that runs through them. The laws that govern the empirical world are not knowable through sensory information alone, but must be discovered by active reason. Thus, Aristotle believed that knowledge was gained from sense experience *and* thinking.

There are two major differences here between Aristotle's and Plato's theory of knowledge. First, the laws, or forms, or universals that Aristotle was looking for did not have an existence independent of their empirical manifestation, as they did for Plato. They were simply observed relationships in nature. Second, for Aristotle, all knowledge is based on sensory experience. This, of course, was not the case with Plato. Because Aristotle contended that the source of all knowledge was sensory experience he is labelled an empiricist.

In elaborating his empiricistic view of knowledge, Aristotle formulated his *Laws of Association*. He said the experience or recall of one object will elicit the recall of things similar to that object (Law of Similarity), or recall of opposite things (Law of Contrast), or recall of things that were originally experienced along with that object (Law of Contiguity). Aristotle also noted that the more frequently two things are experienced together, the more likely it will be that the experience or recall of one will stimulate the recall of the second. Later in history, this came to be known as the Law of Frequency. Thus, according to Aristotle, sensory experience gives rise to ideas. The ideas stimulated by sensory experience will stimulate other ideas in accordance with the laws of Similarity, Contrast, Contiguity, and Frequency. Within philosophy, the attempt to explain the relationship between ideas using these or other laws has come to be called *associationism*. An example of how ideas become associated through contiguity is shown in Figure 3-1.

Besides making empirical investigation respectable, Aristotle made several other contributions to psychology. He wrote the first history of psychology, which was entitled *De Anima*. He wrote extensively on man's sensory apparatus, which he listed as consisting of sight, hearing, smell, taste, and touch. He contributed greatly to later conceptions of memory, thinking, and learning. As we saw above, his associative principles of similarity, contrast, contiguity, and frequency later became the bases for the Doctrine of Associationism, which is still very much part of modern psychology. In view of his immense contributions, we can forgive him for locating the mind in the heart and treating the brain as a system for cooling the blood. About Aristotle's great influence on learning theory, Weimer has recently said the following (1973):

> A moment's recollection . . . shows that Aristotle's doctrines are at the heart of contemporary thought in epistemology and the psychology of learning. The centrality of associationism as the mechanism of the mind is so well known as to require only the observation that *not one single learning theory* propounded in this century *has failed to base its account on associative principles* [p. 18].

With Aristotle's death died the hope for the development of empirical science. In the centuries following Aristotle there was no follow-up to the scientific study that Aristotelian thinking had promoted. The collapse of the Greek city-states, barbarian invasions throughout Europe, and the rapid spread of Christianity stunted the growth of scientific inquiry. Early medieval thinkers depended on the teachings of past authorities instead of seeking new information.

Plato was by far the most important influence on early Christianity. The conception of man that prevailed during these times is described by Marx and Hillix as follows (1963):

> He [man] was regarded as a creature with a soul, possessed of a free will which set him apart from ordinary natural laws, subject only to his own willfulness and perhaps to the rule of God. Such a creature, being free-willed, could not be an object of scientific investigation. Even the body of man was regarded as sacrosanct, and dissection was dangerous for the dissector. These strictures against observation hindered the development of anatomy and

The child associates seeing and feeling a chair
with hearing the word "chair."

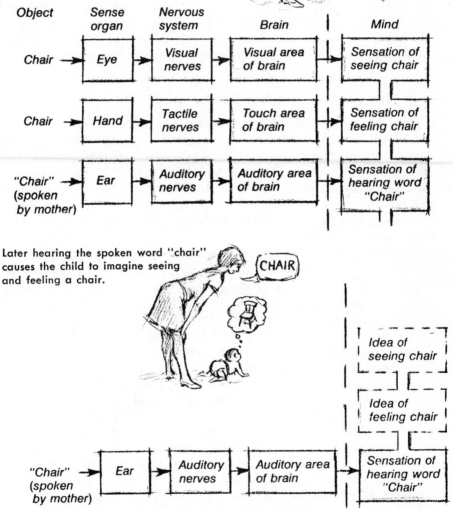

Figure 3–1. An example of how seeing and touching a chair and hearing
the word "chair" become associated through contiguity. (From Introduction
to Modern Behaviorism by Howard Rachlin. W. H. Freeman and Co. Copyright © 1970.)

medicine for centuries, and misconceptions that are today considered incredible persisted for over a thousand years. A science of man could not flourish in such an atmosphere [p. 24].

Religion has been defined as philosophy in the absence of dialogue; when Plato's views concerning the nature of knowledge were incorporated into Christian dogma, they could not be challenged. Some 1500 years elapsed before the rediscovery of Aristotle's writings challenged the antiempiricism of the Church. When inquiry into the nature of man did begin, it spread like wildfire. For psychology, the writings of René Descartes is one of the most important examples of this renaissance.

THE BEGINNING OF MODERN PSYCHOLOGY

René Descartes (1596–1650) tried to approach all philosophical inquiry with an attitude of complete doubt. "I can doubt everything," he argued, "except one thing, and that is the very fact that I doubt. But when I doubt I think; and when I think I must exist." He thus arrived at his celebrated conclusion, "I think, therefore I am." He went on from that point to prove the existence of God and from there he inferred that our sensory experiences must be a reflection of an objective reality, since God would not deceive us.

Descartes went on to postulate a separation between the mind and the body. He viewed the human body as a machine that moves in predictable ways; in this respect we were the same as any other animal. The mind, however, is a uniquely human attribute. The mind was free and could decide the actions of the body. Descartes believed the pineal gland to be the point of contact between the mind and body. The mind could move the gland from side to side and could thus open or close the pores of the brain. Through these pores, the "animal spirits" flowed down tiny tubes to the muscles, filling and swelling them and making them become short and thick, thus moving the parts of the body to which they were connected. Although that is what happens when the mind causes behavior, sensory experience can also cause behavior. Motion outside the body exerts a pull on the "taut strings" that lead to the brain; the pull opens the pores of the brain, releasing the "animal spirits" which flow into the muscles and cause behavior. Therefore, the mind or the physical environment can initiate behavior. This description of *reflex action* was to have a long-lasting influence on psychology. Descartes can be considered a predecessor of the stimulus-response psychologists.

By comparing the human body to a machine, Descartes helped to make it accessible to scientific study. He urged physiologists to use the method of dissection in order to better understand the machinery of the body. Because Descartes believed that humans and animals were physiologically similar, the study of animals to learn about man was given greater respectability. Descartes, therefore, did much to pave the way for physiological and comparative psychology.

The mind, however, was free and possessed by man alone. In explaining the working of the mind, Descartes relied heavily on *innate ideas*, thus showing Plato's influence on his philosophy. Innate ideas were not derivable from experience but were integral to the mind. Examples of innate ideas would include the concepts of God and the self; the axioms of geometry; and the ideas of space, time, and motion. The question of innate ideas caused much philosophical discussion following Descartes, and it is still very much an issue in psychology today.

Thomas Hobbes (1588–1679) opposed the notion that innate ideas are a source of knowledge. He maintained that sense impressions are the source of all knowledge. With this belief, Hobbes reopened the philosophical school of empiricism and its related school of associationism. As we have seen, rationalism looks upon the mind as the source of knowledge. Empiricism, on the other hand, maintains that sensation is the source of knowledge and explains memory, thinking, and imagination as combinations of persistent sense impressions held together by association.

Hobbes also believed that stimuli either help or hinder the vital functions of the body. A stimulus that aids in the vital functioning of the body causes a feeling of pleasure; therefore, the person seeks to experience this pleasure again. Stimuli that hinder the vital functioning of the body cause an aversive feeling, and the person seeks to retreat from it. According to Hobbes, human behavior is controlled by these "appetites" and "aversions." Those events approached by a person are called "good," and those avoided are called "evil." Thus, the values of good and evil are individually determined; they are not absolute. Later, Jeremy Bentham (1748–1832) said man's behavior was governed by the "pleasure principle," an idea that was picked up by Freud, and later by the reinforcement theorists.

John Locke (1632–1704) also strongly opposed the notion of innate ideas. For him, the mind is made up of ideas, and ideas come from experience. He indicated that children have no awareness of most universally accepted truths and that racial groups differ markedly in what they believe. Thus, the infant mind at birth is a *tabula rasa,* a blank tablet, and experience writes upon it. The mind becomes what it experiences; *there is nothing in the mind that is not first in the senses.* Simple ideas come directly from sense experience, complex ideas come from combining simple ideas.

Locke also distinguished between "primary" and "secondary" qualities. Primary qualities are characteristics of physical objects, such as size, weight, solidity, shape, and mobility. The secondary qualities are in the mind of the perceiver and include such things as colors, odors, and tastes.

For Locke, ideas are elements that constitute the mind, and therefore, the mind could be understood by analyzing its elements. The laws of association explain how the ideas come to be combined. To postulate a separate faculty of willing or understanding, Locke said, is as ridiculous as postulating a faculty of singing or dancing.

George Berkeley (1685–1753) claimed Locke did not go far enough. There was still a kind of dualism in Locke's view that physical objects cause ideas about them. While Locke contended that there is an empirical world about which we have ideas, Berkeley claimed there are no primary qualities, only secondary qualities. *The only reality is the mind.* What we call physical characteristics, such as shape and size, are constructs that we project upon the environment. The ideas themselves are the only things we can be sure of. Despite such beliefs, however, Berkeley is still considered an empiricist because he believed the contents of the mind were derived from experience.

David Hume (1711–1776) carried the argument one step further. Although he agreed with Berkeley that we could know nothing for sure about the physical environment, he added that we could know nothing for sure about ideas. *We can be sure of nothing.* Mind, for Hume, was no more than a stream of ideas, memories, imaginings, and feelings.

This is not to deny Hume's empiricist and associationist leanings. He believed strongly that human knowledge consists of ideas which somehow come from experience and which come to be associated through the principles of similarity and contiguity. Hume was saying, however, that we only experience the empirical world indirectly through our ideas. Even the laws of nature are constructs of the imagination; the "lawfulness" of nature is in man's head, not in nature. General concepts such as causation, for example, come from what Hume referred to as the "habitual order of ideas."

Needless to say, Hume upset everyone. To accept Hume was to question the foundation of rational thought, science, psychology, and religion. All dogma, whether religious or scientific, now became suspect.

Immanuel Kant (1724–1804) attempted to correct the impractical features of both rationalism and empiricism. Rationalism can only involve the manipulation of concepts, and empiricism confines knowledge to sensory experience and its derivatives. Kant attempted to reconcile both points of view.

Kant felt that careful analysis of our experience revealed certain categories of thought. These categories of thought, or "faculties," are neither part of our sensory experience, nor derived from it. If these thoughts are not the result of sensory experience, Kant reasoned, they must be innate. These innate mental faculties are superimposed over our sensory experiences, thereby providing them with structure and meaning. Kant believed that there were twelve of these innate faculties that give meaning to our experiences of the physical world; examples included unity, totality, reality, existence, necessity, reciprocity, and causality.

What we experience, according to Kant, is a combination of sensory experience, caused by the empirical world, and the components of the mind, which are innate. The faculties of the mind modify sensory experience, giving it greater organization and meaning. Any attempt to determine the nature of knowledge must, according to Kant, also take into consideration the active contribution of the mind. We will see a current example of this point of view when we review Jean Piaget's theory in Chapter 11.

Thus, Kant kept alive rationalism by showing that the mind is the source of knowledge. In other words, he kept alive an approach to explaining knowledge in terms other than its reduction to sensory experience. By taking a nativistic point of view—that knowledge is inborn—Kant revived the Platonist point of view that had been losing ground since the time of Descartes.

John Stuart Mill (1806–1873) was disturbed by the contention of the early associationists, such as Hobbes and Locke, that complex ideas are nothing more than combinations of simple ideas. Although he remained an empiricist and an associationist, he made a very important revision in the position taken by other associationists. Accepting the notion that complex ideas are made up of simpler ideas, Mill added the notion that simple ideas combine into a new totality that may bear little resemblance to its parts. For example, if we combine blue, red, and green lights, we get white. In other words, Mill believed that *the whole is more than the sum of its parts*. We will encounter this idea again when we discuss Gestalt psychology in Chapter 10.

OTHER HISTORICAL INFLUENCES ON LEARNING THEORY

Thomas Reid (1717–1796) also opposed the extreme reductionism of the empiricists, but his opposition took a different form than that of John Stuart Mill. Like Kant, Reid believed that the mind had powers of its own which strongly influence how we perceive the world. Unlike Kant, however, Reid believed these powers or faculties corresponded to specific areas of the brain. He hypothesized twenty-seven discrete areas of the brain, each corresponding to a specific faculty. These faculties were believed to be innate and not the product of experience. The belief in the existence of such faculties in the mind later was called *faculty psychology.* The faculty psychologist is a strange mixture of nativism, rationalism, and empiricism. Kant, for example, explored sensory experience (empiricism) in order to discover categories of thought (rationalism) that were innate (nativism).

Franz Joseph Gall (1758–1828) carried faculty psychology one step further. He believed that the faculties of the mind did not exist to the same extent in every individual. Furthermore, he believed that if a faculty was well developed, there would be a bump or protrusion on the part of the skull corresponding to the place in the brain that houses that faculty. Likewise, if a faculty was poorly developed, a hollow or depression would be found on the skull. Armed with these assumptions, Gall set out to examine the shape of people's skulls. He developed an elaborate chart showing what faculties the various parts of the skull correspond to. Using this chart and analyzing the bumps and hollows of a person's skull, Gall and his followers believed they could tell which of the person's faculties were the most highly developed, and which were underdeveloped. This analysis of mental attributes by examining the characteristics of the skull is called *phrenology.* A typical phrenology chart is shown in Figure 3–2.

Phrenology had two lasting effects on psychology, one good and one questionable. First, it lead to research designed to discover the function

Figure 3–2. **A typical phrenology chart.**

of various parts of the brain. It was this very research, however, that disproved the assumptions upon which phrenology was based. Second, many faculty psychologists believed that the faculties became stronger with practice just like the biceps become stronger with practice. For this reason the faculty psychologists were said to have taken a "mental muscle" approach to learning. Learning, to them, meant strengthening faculties by practicing those traits associated with them. One could improve his reasoning abilities, for example, by formally studying such topics as mathematics or Latin. The belief that a particular course of training would strengthen certain faculties was called *formal discipline*, a concept that provides one answer to the question of how learning transfers from one situation to another. We will have more to say about the transfer of training when we discuss E. L. Thorndike in Chapter 4. It should be noted here, however, that the idea of formal discipline, based on faculty psychology, dominated school curricula for many years and was used to justify requiring students to intensely study the most difficult topics available, such as mathematics and Latin, regardless of their vocational aspirations. One suspects that many present day educators still believe in the benefits of formal discipline.

Charles Darwin (1809–1882) supported the notion of biological evolution with so much evidence that it had to finally be taken seriously. The Church bitterly opposed Darwin's notions. In fact, Darwin himself was so worried about the impact his findings would have upon religious thought that he wished to have his research published only after his death.

The final acceptance of evolutionary theory by the scientific community marked a blow to man's collective ego equal only to the one dealt by Copernicus and the future one dealt by Freud. Evolution restored the continuity between humans and other animals that had been denied for centuries. No longer was there the clear-cut distinction between man and other animals that had been the cornerstone of so many systems of thought, such as those of Plato, Aristotle, Descartes, and Kant. If we are biologically related to the "lower" animals, do they also have minds, souls, and innate categories of thought, and if so, to what extent? Obviously, animal research was now to take on a much greater respectability. Descartes' thinking tolerated animal research as a way of finding out how the human body works, but from his point of view, it could not disclose anything concerning the human mind. Until Darwin, man's behavior was thought to be rational and animal behavior thought to be instinctive. With Darwin, that handy dichotomy was lost. Many questions arose such as "can animal's behavior also be rational, at least in part?" "Can man's behavior be instinctive, at least in part?" A mind resulting from a long evolutionary process is looked at differently than a mind which is divinely implanted into the body by God.

Darwin changed all thoughts about human nature. A human being was now looked upon as a combination of his biological heritage and his life's experiences. The pure associationism of the empiricists was now coupled with physiology in a search of the underlying mechanisms of thought, and the function of behavior as a way of adjusting to the environment was studied intensely. Individuality was appreciated as never before and its study became popular. This new attitude was exemplified by Darwin's cousin, *Francis Galton* (1822–1911), who devised a number of methods, such as the questionnaire, psychological scales, and the method of correlation, specifically designed to measure individual differences. Probably the most famous person directly influenced by Darwin was *Sigmund Freud* (1856–1939), who explored the problems of the human animal living in a civilized world.

Such philosophic questions as "How does man think?" and "What can man know?" changed to "How does man adjust to his environment?" and "Given certain circumstances, what does man *do*?" Thus, the mood was set for a science of behavior. If human behavior was now to be studied like any other aspect of the environment, then the experimental approach that had been so successful in the physical sciences should be applied to the study of the human being.

Hermann Ebbinghaus (1850–1909) is said to have emancipated psychology from philosophy by demonstrating that the "higher mental processes" of learning and memory could be studied experimentally. Rather than assuming that associations had already been formed, and studying them through reflection, as had been the case for many centuries, Ebbinghaus studied the associative process as it was taking place. This way, he could systematically study the conditions that influenced the development of associations. He was an extremely careful researcher and repeated his experiments over a period of many years before he finally published his results in 1885. Many of his findings concerning the nature of learning and memory are still valid.

An important principle of association was the law of frequency, on which Ebbinghaus focused in his research. The law of frequency stated that the more frequently an experience occurred, the more easily the experience was recalled. In other words, memory gains strength through repetition. In order to test this notion, Ebbinghaus needed material that was not contaminated by the subject's previous experience. In order to control for the effects of previous experience, he invented his now famous *nonsense syllable*, which consisted of a vowel between two con-

Hermann Ebbinghaus

sonants (e.g., *qaw, jiq, xuw, cew,* or *tib*). The nonsense syllables were usually arranged in groups of twelve, although he varied group size to measure rate of learning as a function of the amount of material to be learned. He found that as the number of nonsense syllables to be learned became larger, it took a greater amount of time to learn them. Ebbinghaus was the first to demonstrate this fact that sounds so obvious to us today.

Using himself as a subject, Ebbinghaus would look at each syllable in the group for a fraction of a second, and he would pause fifteen seconds before starting through the group again. He continued in this manner until "complete mastery" had occurred, which meant he could recite each syllable in the group without making a mistake. At that point, he noted how many exposures to the group of syllables it took before mastery was reached. Also, he plotted the number of errors made as a function of successive exposures to the group of syllables, thus creating psychology's first learning curve.

At various intervals following original "mastery," Ebbinghaus went back and relearned a group of nonsense syllables. He noted the number of trials it took to relearn a group of syllables and subtracted that number from the number of exposures it took to originally learn the list. The difference was called *savings*. He plotted savings as a function of time elapsed since original learning, thus creating psychology's first retention curve. His graph indicated that the rate of forgetting is very fast for the first few hours following a learning experience, and very slow thereafter. He also found that *overlearning* reduces the rate of forgetting considerably. That is, if he continued to expose himself attentively to a group of nonsense syllables even after they had been mastered, they would be retained much better than if his learning stopped with only one perfect recitation of the syllables.

Ebbinghaus also studied the effects of what is now called meaningfulness on learning and retention. He found, for example, that it took nine readings to memorize eighty syllables of material from Byron's *Don Juan*, but about nine times as many exposures to learn eighty nonsense syllables. Not only was learning rate much faster for the more meaningful material, but retention was far superior also.

Ebbinghaus's research revolutionized the study of the associative process. Instead of hypothesizing about the law of frequency, he demonstrated how it functioned. Ebbinghaus brought the "higher mental processes" into the laboratory, where they have been ever since.

PSYCHOLOGY'S EARLY SCHOOLS

Structuralism.

As far as learning theory is concerned, associationism has been one of the most important developments in psychology's long philosophical history. As we have seen, philosophers over the centuries studied the problems of how ideas were associated with other ideas and how simple ideas combined to form complex ones. As the scientific technique was being successfully applied to investigate physics and chemistry, it was to be only a matter of time before it would be applied to study psychology as well. Thus the first school of psychology, called structuralism, developed out of the philosophical school of associationism combined with the scientific method. Although the structuralists had good intentions, their subject matter was unreliable, thus making their scientific effort a dubious one.

Within the structuralist school, which was headed by *Wilhelm Wundt* (1832–1920), and later by his student, *Edward Titchener* (1867–1927), psychology was the systematic study of human consciousness. The structuralists believed that human consciousness could be studied the same way as chemical substances, that is, complex entities could be broken down into simpler elements. Thus, the structuralist, like all associationists, believed that the mind is made up of various combinations of ideas, and that the smallest element of consciousness was the idea.

The structuralists set out to discover the structure of the mind. In analyzing the elements of thought, the major tool of the structuralist was *introspection,* or self-analysis. Experimental subjects had to be carefully trained not to misuse the introspective technique. They were trained to report their *immediate experience* as they perceived an object, and not to report their interpretations of that object. In other words, Wundt and Titchener were interested in the subject's "raw" experiences, but not in what they had learned about those experiences. In that sense, learning was looked upon as more of a hindrance than a topic worthy of study for itself. When shown an apple, for example, the subject was supposed to report hues, brightnesses, and spatial characteristics, rather than labelling the object as an apple. Naming the object of experience during an introspective report was called a *stimulus error.* An example of a stimulus error would be calling an apple an apple. In other words, the subject is reporting a compound idea rather than simple ones, and therefore the building blocks of the mind remain obscure. Clearly, the structuralists were more interested in the contents of the mind than with the origins of those contents.

As a school of psychology, structuralism was short-lived and died within Titchener's own lifetime. There were many reasons for the death of structuralism, but the most important one was probably the rising popularity of functionalism, which we will consider below. The structuralists made a rather sterile attempt to use the methods of science to substantiate an ancient philosophical belief. It failed to take into consideration one of the most important developments in man's history— the doctrine of evolution. As the importance of the evolutionary process became more apparent, there was increased attention given to the organism's adaptation to his environment. Also, the doctrine of evolution made the study of "lower" animals a legitimate way of learning about people. Structuralism ignored both of these trends. It also ignored the growing evidence for the existence of unconscious processes that was being provided by researchers such as Sigmund Freud. For these and other reasons, structuralism came and went. It has been said that perhaps the most important thing about structuralism was that it appeared, it was tried, and it failed. Psychology was able, therefore, to get such an approach out of its system.

Functionalism.

Structuralism, scientific psychology's first school of thought, originated in Germany when Wundt founded his laboratory in 1879 in Leipzig. Functionalism, however, originated in this country and was America's first school of psychology. Although functionalist beliefs diverged, their emphasis was always the same—*the utility of consciousness and behavior in adjusting to the environment.* Clearly, the functionalists were strongly influenced by Darwin's doctrine of evolution.

The founder of the functionalist movement is usually thought to be *William James* (1842–1910). In his highly influential book, *The Principles of Psychology* (1890), James took the structuralists to task. Consciousness, he said, cannot be reduced into elements. Rather, consciousness functions as a unity whose purpose is to allow the organism to adjust to his environment. The "stream of consciousness" changes as total experience changes. Such a process should not be studied reductionistically because a person's conscious processes as a whole are involved with adaptation to his environment. The most important thing about consciousness, as far as James was concerned, was that it had a purpose. James also wrote about the importance of studying psychology scientifically. He emphasized that man is both rational and irrational (emotional). He pointed out the importance of understanding the biological foundations of mental events, and urged the study of lower animals to learn more about humans. Many of James's ideas are still current. It should be noted that James had a profound influence on psychology, both through his writings and through his ability to inspire as a teacher. Many consider James as one of the greatest psychologists of all times.

In addition to James, two of the most influential members of the functionalist movement were John Dewey (1867–1949) and James R. Angell (1869–1949). In Dewey's famous article, "The Reflex Arc Concept in Psychology" (1896), he attacked the growing tendency in psychology to isolate a stimulus-response relationship for study. He argued that isolating such a unit for study was a total waste of time since the purpose of behavior is overlooked. The goal for psychology should be to study the significance of behavior in adapting to the environment. The main contribution of Angell was that he built up a department of psychology at the University of Chicago around the functionalistic point of view. Under his leadership, the department trained many functionalistic psychologists.

The main contribution the functionalists made to learning theory, is that they studied the relationship of consciousness to the environment, rather than studying it as an isolated phenomenon. They opposed the introspective technique of the structuralists because it was reductionistic, not because it studied consciousness. The functionalists were not opposed to studying mental processes, but they insisted that they always be studied in relationship to survival.

Behaviorism.

The founder of behaviorism was *John B. Watson,* whom we will discuss further in Chapter 7. Watson noted that consciousness could only be studied through the process of introspection, a notoriously unreliable research tool. Because consciousness could not be reliably studied, he said, it should not be studied at all. To be scientific, psychology needed a subject matter that was stable enough to be reliably measured, and that subject matter was behavior. Watson felt that the main concern for the psychologist should be with behavior and how it varies with experience. Leave the study of consciousness to the philosophers, he said. Thus, what was the focal point of epistemological inquiry for thousands of years was looked upon by the behaviorist as only a hindrance in the study of human behavior.

Of course, the behaviorist's main point was that behavior should be studied because it could be dealt with directly. Mental events should be ignored because they could not be dealt with directly. Behaviorism had a profound effect on American learning theory. In fact, most of the theories of learning in this book can be thought of as behavioristic. It is possible, however, to make subdivisions within the behavioristic camp. Some theories concentrate on behavior related to an organism's survival. Such behavioristic theories can be called functional theories. Other behavioristic theories are less concerned with adaptive behavior, and explain all learned behavior in terms of the laws of Association. Such theories tend to treat functional and nonfunctional behavior in the same way. Thus, under the general heading of behaviorism we can list both functionalistic and associationistic theories. Whether a behavioristic theory is labelled as functionalistic or associationistic depends on the kind of behavior the theory concentrates on and how the theory explains the origins of that behavior.

Summary and an Overview.

From the brief history presented in this chapter, it can be seen that learning theory has a rich and diverse heritage. As a result of this heritage, numerous viewpoints concerning the learning process exist today. In Chapter 2, we referred to a point of view shared by a substantial number of scientists as a paradigm. At least three such points of view can be identified among modern theories of learning.

One paradigm we will refer to as *functionalistic*. This paradigm reflects the influence of Darwinism in that it stresses the relationship between learning and adjustment to the environment. A second paradigm we will refer to as *associationistic,* since it studies the learning process in terms of the laws of association. This paradigm originated with Aristotle and was perpetuated and elaborated on by Locke, Berkeley, and Hume. As mentioned before, both the functionalistic and associationistic paradigms are considered behavioristic. The third paradigm we shall label *cognitive,* since it stresses the cognitive nature of learning. This paradigm originated with Plato and came to us through Descartes, Kant, and the faculty psychologists.

These paradigms should be viewed as only very crude categories, since it is difficult to find any theory of learning that fits unambiguously into any one of them. We will place a theory in a particular paradigm because of its major emphasis. However, within almost every theory, certain aspects of other paradigms can be identified. For example, even though Hull's theory is listed under the functionalistic paradigm below, it relies heavily on associationistic ideas. Similarly, Piaget's theory is listed under the cognitive paradigm only because of its major emphasis. Piaget's theory, as much influenced by Darwinism as any other, has a great deal in common with the theories listed under the functionalistic paradigm. Tolman's theory is also difficult to categorize since it has both functionalistic and cognitive elements. We list it as a cognitive theory only because the main emphasis of the theory is cognitive.

With these reservations in mind, the major theories of learning covered in this book are organized as follows:

Functionalistic Paradigm
    Thorndike
    Skinner
    Hull

Associationistic Paradigm
    Pavlov
    Guthrie
    Estes

Cognitive Paradigm
    Gestalt Theory
    Piaget
    Tolman

Which paradigm is correct? Probably all of them. No doubt, they all emphasize certain truths about the learning process and ignore others. At this point in history, it appears that in order to obtain the most accurate picture of the learning process, one must be willing to view it from a number of different angles. It is hoped that this book will allow the student to do just that.

DISCUSSION QUESTIONS

1. Compare Plato's theory of knowledge with that of Aristotle. Include a definition of the terms *rationalism, nativism,* and *empiricism* in your answer.
2. Summarize Descartes' influence on psychology.
3. Briefly describe what Kant meant by an "innate category" of thought.
4. What important departure from traditional associationistic thinking did John Stuart Mill suggest?
5. Discuss phrenology and the theory of the mind upon which it is based.
6. Discuss Darwin's influence on learning theory.
7. What was the significance of the work of Ebbinghaus as far as the history of learning theory is concerned?
8. Summarize the important features of the schools of structuralism, functionalism, and behaviorism.
9. What caused the downfall of structuralism?
10. List each individual discussed in this chapter and indicate which of them can be labelled a rationalist, a nativist, and/or an empiricist.

GLOSSARY

Aristotle (384–322 B.C.).   Because he believed sensory experience to be the basis of all knowledge, he was the first major empiricist. He also proposed the laws of similarity, contrast, contiguity, and frequency to explain how ideas became associated with other ideas. Therefore, he was the first associationist.

Associationism. The philosophical belief that the relationship between ideas can be explained by the laws of association.

Behaviorism. A school of psychology, founded by J. B. Watson, that completely rejected the study of consciousness. In order to be scientific, psychology needed a subject matter that could be reliably measured, and according to the behaviorist, that subject matter was behavior.

Berkeley, George (1685–1753). He said we have no direct knowledge concerning the empirical world; we only have ideas caused by the empirical world. He disagreed with Locke's distinction between primary and secondary qualities and said there are only secondary qualities. The only reality we can ever know is the ideas contained in the mind.

Darwin, Charles (1809–1882). He demonstrated the utility of behavior in adjusting to the environment, and that human development is biologically continuous with that of lower animals. Both observations had a profound and lasting effect on psychology, especially on learning theory.

Descartes, René (1596–1650). He postulated that the mind and the body were governed by different laws. The mind was free and possessed only by humans, whereas the body was mechanical and its functions were the same for both humans and other animals. He is responsible for creating the duality of mind and body, stimulating interest in physiological and comparative psychology, and for updating Plato's belief in innate ideas.

Ebbinghaus, Hermann (1850–1909). He was the first to study learning and memory experimentally. Demonstrating how the law of frequency worked in the forming of new associations, he invented the nonsense syllable to control for previous experience in a learning situation.

Empiricism. The philosophical belief that sensory experience is the basis of all knowledge.

Epistemology. The study of the nature of knowledge.

Faculty psychology. The belief that the mind contains certain powers or faculties.

Formal discipline. The belief held by many faculty psychologists that specific training can strengthen a specific faculty. For example, practicing being friendly would strengthen the friendliness faculty, thereby making the person more friendly.

Functionalism. America's first school of psychology. The primary goal of the functionalist was to discover how mental and behavioral processes are related to an organism's adaptation to his environment. Members of this school were strongly influenced by Darwin's writings.

Gall, Joseph Franz (1758–1828). He believed that a person's strong and weak faculties could be detected by analyzing the bumps and depressions on the person's skull. This system of analysis is called phrenology.

Hobbes, Thomas (1588–1679). He reasserted Aristotle's doctrine of associationism and also suggested that experiences of pleasure and pain influence how associations are formed.

Hume, David (1711–1776). He said we can know nothing with certainty. All ideas are products of the mind and do not necessarily relate to a reality outside of the mind. Therefore, the so-called natural laws are more the result of "habits of thought" than of any lawfulness in nature.

Immediate experience. The raw psychological experience that was the object of introspective analysis; experience that was not contaminated by interpretation of any kind.

Innate category of thought. A genetically determined faculty of the mind that molds our cognitive experiences by giving them greater structure and meaning than they otherwise would have.

Introspection. The reporting of one's own mental events while experiencing a certain object or situation; the technique employed by the structuralists to study the structure of the mind.

James, William (1842–1910). The founder of the functionalist movement. He attacked the way that the structuralists used the introspective method to search for the elements of thought. Consciousness, he felt, could not be subdivided since it acted as a functional unit that was constantly changing. The most important thing about consciousness is that it aids human survival. He also encouraged psychology to embrace the scientific method, to search for the physiological correlates of mental processes, and to investigate human emotions nature as well as the intellect.

Kant, Immanuel (1724–1804). He believed that the mind was active and not passive, as the empiricist-associationists had assumed. The mind has innate powers or faculties which act upon sense impressions and give them meaning. The concept of causality, for example, cannot be derived from sensory experience; therefore it must be innate.

Laws of association. Principles such as similarity, contrast, contiguity, and frequency that are supposed to explain how one idea is related to another or how one experience elicits ideas related to it.

Locke, John (1632–1704). He strongly opposed the notion of innate ideas and suggested that at birth, the mind was a *tabula rasa,* or a blank tablet. He said "there is nothing in the mind that is not first in the senses." He distinguished between primary qualities, the physical characteristics of an object, and secondary qualities, the psychological experience caused by a physical object, such as the experience of color or taste.

Mill, John Stuart (1806–1873). An associationist who disagreed with his fellow associationists' contention that complex ideas are nothing more than a compound of simpler ones. He felt that ideas could fuse together and the fusion could create an idea distinctly different from the simple ideas that made it up.

Nativism. The philosophical belief that a mental attribute is inherited and therefore is independent of experience.

Nonsense syllable. A meaningless consonant-vowel-consonant combination invented by Ebbinghaus to control for previous experience in a learning situation.

Phrenology. The study of the location of bumps and depressions on a person's skull in order to determine his strong and weak faculties.

Plato (427–347 B.C.). He proposed a reminiscence theory of knowledge where knowing was explained as remembering the pure knowledge that the soul had experienced before entering the body. Plato was the first rationalist and the first nativist.

Pythagoreans. Followers of Pythagoras who believed abstractions, such as numbers, were just as real as physical objects and that these abstractions could influence the physical world. Such beliefs had a strong influence on the development of Plato's theory of knowledge.

Rationalism. The philosophical belief that the mind must become actively involved before knowledge can be obtained.

Reid, Thomas (1717–1796). Believed that the faculties of the mind corresponded to certain areas of the brain. Later individuals, such as Kant and Reid who attributed certain powers or faculties to the mind, were called faculty psychologists.

Reminiscence theory of knowledge. The belief held by Plato that all knowledge is present in the human soul at birth; thus to know was to remember the contents of the soul.

Savings. The difference in the time it takes to relearn something as compared to the amount of time it took to learn it originally; a measure of retention used by Ebbinghaus.

Stimulus error. The error of naming an object while introspecting about it instead of reporting one's immediate experience.

Structuralism. The first school of thought in psychology. The goal of structuralism was to discover the basic elements of thought by using the technique of introspection.

Wundt, Wilhelm (1832–1920). Founder of the structuralist school; also founded psychology's first psychological laboratory in Leipzig, Germany, in 1879.

part 2

Predominantly Functionalistic Theories

4

Edward Lee Thorndike

It is fitting that we begin our discussion of the major learning theorists with Edward L. Thorndike (1874–1949), perhaps the greatest learning theorist of all time. He did pioneer work not only in learning theory but also in the areas of educational practices, verbal behavior, comparative psychology, intelligence testing, the nature-nurture problem, transfer of training, and the application of quantitative measures to socio-psychological problems (for example, he developed scales with which to compare the quality of life in different cities). It may be of interest to note that Thorndike began this latter project, as well as many others, when he was more than sixty years old.

His research started with the study of mental telepathy in young children (which he explained as the unconscious detection on the part of the child of minute movements made by the experimenter). His later experiments involved chicks, cats, rats, dogs, fish, monkeys, and finally adult humans. He wanted to use apes also but could not afford to buy and maintain them.

Thorndike's scientific productivity was almost unbelievable. At his death in 1949 his bibliography comprised 507 books, monographs, and journal articles. Always attempting to measure everything, Thorndike reports in his autobiography that up to the age of sixty he had spent well over 20,000 hours reading and studying scientific books and journals—this in spite of the fact that he was primarily a researcher rather than a scholar.

Thorndike was born in Williamsburg, Massachusetts, in 1874, and was the second son of a Methodist minister. He claims never to have seen or heard the word psychology until he was a junior at Wesleyan University. At that time he read William James's *Principles of Psychology* (1890) and was deeply impressed. Later, when he went to Harvard and took a course from James they became good friends. When Thorndike's landlady forbade him to go on hatching chicks in his bedroom, James tried to get him laboratory space on the Harvard campus. When this failed, James allowed Thorndike to continue his studies in the basement of his home— much to the dismay of James's wife and to the delight of his children.

After two years at Harvard, where he earned a living by tutoring students, he accepted a fellowship at Columbia working under James McKeen Cattell. Although Thorndike carried two of his "most educated" chicks with him to New York, he soon switched from chicks to cats upon arrival at Columbia. His years of animal research were summarized in his doctoral dissertation entitled, *Animal Intelligence: An Experimental Study of the Associative Processes in Animals* which was published in

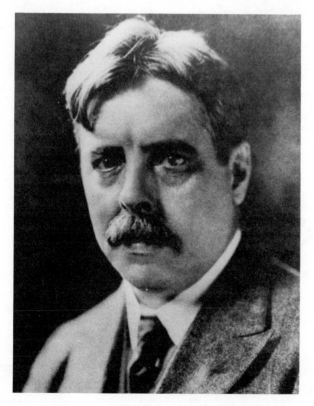

Edward L. Thorndike

1898 and expanded and republished in 1911 as *Animal Intelligence*. The fundamental ideas put forth in these documents permeate all of Thorndike's writings and, in fact, all of learning theory. The extent of Thorndike's influence is indicated by the following quote from Tolman (1938):

> The psychology of animal learning—not to mention that of child learning—has been and still is primarily a matter of agreeing or disagreeing with Thorndike, or trying in minor ways to improve upon him. Gestalt psychologists, conditioned-reflex psychologists, sign-Gestalt psychologists—all of us here in America seem to have taken Thorndike, overtly or covertly, as our starting point. And we have felt very smart and pleased with ourselves if we could show that we have, even in some very minor way, developed new little wrinkles of our own [p. 11].

MAJOR THEORETICAL NOTIONS

Connectionism.

Thorndike called the association between sense impressions and impulses to action a bond or a connection. This marked the first formal attempt to link sensory events to behavior. Earlier brands of associationism attempted to show how *ideas* became linked together; thus Thorndike's approach is quite different and can be regarded as the first modern theory of learning. Thorndike's emphasis on the functional aspects of behavior is due mainly to the influence of Darwin. In fact, Thorndike can be understood as a combination of associationism, Darwinism, and the methods of science.

Thorndike's concern was not only for stimulus conditions and tendencies to action, but for what held the stimulus and response together. He believed they were connected by a neural bond. His theory is called connectionism, with the connection referred to being the neural connection between stimuli (S) and responses (R).

Selecting and Connecting.

To Thorndike the most basic form of learning is trial and error learning, or what he originally called selecting and connecting. He reached this basic notion of trial and error learning through his early experimentation, which involved putting an animal in an apparatus that was arranged so that when the animal made a certain kind of response he escaped. The

Figure 4–1. One kind of puzzle box that Thorndike used in his research on learning.

apparatus shown in Figure 4–1 was a small confining box with a pole sticking up in the middle of it, or a chain hanging from its top. Pushing against the pole or pulling on the chain enabled the animal to escape. Some arrangements, however, required the animal to engage in a complex series of responses before he could escape. Different responses were called for at different times in Thorndike's experiments but the idea was always the same—the animal had to perform in a certain way before it was allowed to leave the box. The following quote from *Animal Intelligence* (1911) summarizes his work with the puzzle box.

> The behavior of all but 11 and 13 was practically the same. When put into the box the cat would show evident signs of discomfort and of an impulse to escape from confinement. It tries to squeeze through any opening; it claws and bites at the bars or wire; it thrusts its paws out through any opening and claws at everything it reaches; it continues its efforts when it strikes anything loose and shaky; it may claw at things within the box. It does not pay very much attention to the food outside, but seems simply to strive instinctively to escape from confinement. The vigor with which it struggles is extraordinary. For eight or ten

minutes it will claw and bite and squeeze incessantly. With 13, an old cat, and 11, an uncommonly sluggish cat, the behavior was different. They did not struggle vigorously or continually. On some occasions they did not even struggle at all. It was therefore necessary to let them out of the box a few times, feeding them each time. After they thus associate climbing out of the box with getting food, they will try to get out whenever put in. They do not, even then, struggle so vigorously or get so excited as the rest. In either case, whether the impulse to struggle be due to instinctive reaction to confinement or to an association, it is likely to succeed in letting the cat out of the box. The cat that is clawing all over the box in her impulsive struggle will probably claw the string or loop or button so as to open the door. And gradually all the other non-successful impulses will be stamped out and the particular impulse leading to the successful act will be stamped in by the resulting pleasure, until after many trials, the cat will, when put in the box, immediately claw the button or loop in a definite way [pp. 35–40].

Thus, whether working for a piece of fish or for release from confinement, all his animals learned to do whatever was necessary to escape from the box.

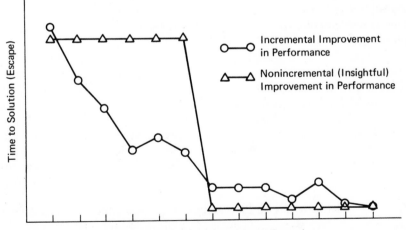

Successive Trials (Opportunities to Escape)

Figure 4–2. The figure exemplifies both the incremental improvement in performance observed by Thorndike and the non-incremental (insightful) improvement which Thorndike did not observe.

Thorndike plotted the time it took the animal to solve the problem as a function of the number of opportunities the animal had to solve the problem. Every opportunity was a trial and the trial terminated when the animal hit upon the correct solution. A typical graph generated under these circumstances is shown in Figure 4–2. In this basic experimental arrangement Thorndike consistently noted that the time it took to solve the problem (his dependent variable) systematically decreased as the number of trials increased, that is, the more opportunities the animal had, the faster it solved the problem.

Learning Is Incremental, Not Insightful.

Noting the slow decrease in time to solution as a function of successive trials, Thorndike concluded that learning was incremental rather than insightful. In other words, learning occurs in very small systematic steps rather than in huge jumps. He noted that if learning was insightful the graph would show that the time to solution would remain relatively stable and high while the animal was in the unlearned state. At the point where the animal would gain insight into the solution, the graph would drop very rapidly and would remain at that point for the duration of the experiment. Figure 4–2 also shows how the graph would look if the learning that took place was insightful.

Learning Is Not Mediated by Ideas.

Based on his research, Thorndike also concluded emphatically that learning was direct and was not mediated by thinking or reasoning. He said in 1895:

> The cat does not look over the situation, much less *think* it over, and then decide what to do. It bursts out at once into the activities which instinct and experience have settled on as suitable reactions to the situation *"confinement when hungry with food outside."* It does not ever in the course of its success realize that such an act brings food and therefore decide to do it and thenceforth do it immediately from decision instead of from impulse [p. 45].

Elsewhere (1911) Thorndike makes the same point with regard to monkeys:

> In discussing these facts we may first of all clear our way of one popular explanation, that this learning was due to "reasoning." If

we use the word reasoning in its technical psychological meaning as the function of reaching conclusions by the perception of relations, comparison and inference, if we think of the mental content involved as feelings of relation, perceptions of similarity, general and abstract notions and judgments, we find no evidence of reasoning in the behavior of the monkeys toward the mechanisms used. And this fact nullifies the arguments for reasoning in their case as it did in the case of the dogs and cats. The argument that successful dealings with mechanical contrivances imply that the animal reasoned out the properties of the mechanisms, is destroyed when we find mere selection from their general instinctive activities sufficient to cause success with bars, hooks, loops, etc. There is also positive evidence of the absence of any general function of reasoning [pp. 184–86].

Thus, following the law of parsimony, Thorndike rejected reason in favor of direct selection and connection in learning. The demotion of reasoning and of the importance of ideas in learning was the beginning of what was to become the behavioristic movement in America.

All Mammals Learn in the Same Manner.

Many were disturbed by Thorndike's insistence that all learning is direct and not mediated by ideas especially because he also insisted that the learning of all mammals including humans followed the same laws. According to Thorndike, no special processes need to be postulated when one is attempting to explain human learning. The following quote (1913a) serves both to point out Thorndike's belief that the laws of learning were the same for all animals, and to introduce other aspects of Thorndike's theory to which we will turn next:

> These simple, semi-mechanical phenomena . . . which animal learning discloses, are the fundamentals of human learning also. They are, of course, much complicated in the more advanced states of human learning, such as the acquisition of skill with the violin, or of knowledge of the calculus, or of inventiveness in engineering. But it is impossible to understand the subtler and more planful learning of cultural men without clear ideas of the forces which make learning possible in its first form of directly connecting some gross bodily response with a situation immediately present to the senses. Moreover, no matter how subtle, complicated and advanced a form of learning one has to explain, these simple facts— the selection of connections by use and satisfaction and their elimination by disuse and annoyance, multiple reaction, the mind's

set as a condition, piecemeal activity of a situation, with prepotency of certain elements in determining the response, response
by analogy, and shifting of bonds—will as a matter of fact, still
be the main, and perhaps the only, facts needed to explain
it [p. 16].

THORNDIKE BEFORE 1930

Thorndike's thinking about the learning process can be conveniently
divided into two parts: one part consisting of his thoughts prior to 1930,
and the second part consisting of his views after 1930 when some of his
earlier views changed considerably.

The Law of Readiness.

The law of readiness, proposed in his book *The Original Nature of Man*
(1913b), had three parts, abbreviated as follows:

1. When a conduction unit is ready to conduct, conduction by it is satisfying.
2. For a conduction unit ready to conduct, not to conduct is annoying.
3. When a conduction unit is not ready for conduction and is forced to
   conduct, conduction by it is annoying.

We notice some terms here whose subjectivity might worry the modern
learning theorist. We must remember, however, that Thorndike was
writing before the behavioristic movement and that many of the things
that he discussed had never been systematically analyzed before. It is
also important to note that what appear to be subjective terms in Thorndike's writing, may not be. For example, what he meant here by a conduction unit ready to conduct is merely a preparedness for action or goal
directedness. Using current terminology we can restate Thorndike's law
of readiness as follows:

1. When someone is ready to perform some act, to do so is satisfying.
2. When someone is ready to perform some act, not to do so is annoying.
3. When someone is not ready to perform some act and is forced to do so,
   it is annoying.

Generally, we can say that interfering with goal-directed behavior
causes frustration and causing someone to do something they do not
want to do is also frustrating.

Even terms such as "satisfying" and "annoying" were defined in such
a way as to be acceptable to most modern behaviorists (1911):

By a satisfying state of affairs is meant one which the animal does nothing to avoid, often doing such things as attain and preserve it. By a discomforting or annoying state of affairs is meant one which the animal commonly avoids and abandons [p. 245].

These definitions of satisfiers and annoyers should be kept in mind throughout our discussion of Thorndike.

The Law of Exercise.

Before 1930, Thorndike's theory included the law of exercise, which had two parts.

1. Connections between a stimulus and a response are strengthened as they are used. In other words, merely exercising the connection between a stimulating situation and a response strengthens the connection between the two. This is the part of the law of exercise called the **law of use.**
2. Connections between situations and responses are weakened when practice is discontinued or if the neural bond is not used. This is the portion of the law of exercise called the **law of disuse.**

What did Thorndike mean by the strengthening or weakening of a connection? Here again he was ahead of his time and on this issue he could be speaking today. He defined strengthening as an increase in the probability that a response will be made when the stimulus recurs. If the bond between a stimulus and a response is strengthened, the next time the stimulus occurs, there is an increased probability that the response will occur. If the bond is weakened, there is a decreased probability that the next time the stimulus occurs, the response will occur. In brief, the law of exercise says we learn by doing and forget by not doing.

The Law of Effect.

The law of effect, before 1930, refers to the strengthening or weakening of a connection between a stimulus and a response as a result of the consequences of the response. For example, if a response is followed by a satisfying state of affairs, the strength of the connection is increased. If a response is followed by an annoying state of affairs, the strength of the connection is decreased. In modern terminology, if a stimulus leads to a response, which in turn leads to reward, the S-R connection is strengthened. If, on the other hand, a stimulus leads to a response which leads to punishment, the S-R connection is weakened.

The law of effect was a historical break from traditional associationistic theory that claimed frequency of occurrence or mere contiguity to be the determiners of the strength of an association. Although Thorndike accepted both the law of frequency and the law of contiguity, he went further by saying that the consequences of a response are important in determining the strength of association between the situation and the response to it. The importance of the consequences of an act in forming associations was only hinted at previously by philosophers such as Hobbes and Bentham. Here we see Thorndike's concern with the utility of behavior in helping the organism adjust to its environment, a concern which he shared with the functionalists who were, of course, strongly influenced by Darwin.

Thorndike's law of effect was attacked on several grounds. Critics said his argument was circular: If the response probability went up, it was said to be due to the presence of a satisfying state of affairs; if it did not go up, it was claimed none was present. It was believed that such a situation did not allow for a test of the theory, since the same event (increased or decreased probability of a response) was used to detect both learning and a satisfying state of affairs. Later defenders of Thorndike have shown this criticism to be invalid since once something has been shown to be a satisfier, it can be used to modify behavior in other situations (Meehl, 1950). In other words, it is the "transituational" nature of satisfiers that save the law of effect from circularity.

A second criticism has been concerned with the fact that the effect of a response appears to work back in time on the neural bond that caused it. First, there is a stimulus which causes a certain response to occur, since there is a neural connection between that stimulus and that response. The response results in a satisfying state of affairs that is supposed to strengthen the S-R connection. How can this happen, since the conduction unit has already fired before the satisfying state of affairs had occurred? This criticism has been answered by postulating the existence of a neural trace that is still active when the satisfaction occurs; therefore, in a sense, the conduction unit is still firing at the time the organism experiences the satisfying state of affairs. Although the neural trace idea became a popular answer to this question, the problem of how reward strengthens a response is still essentially unsolved. Learning theorists have usually adjusted to this problem by ignoring it.

A third criticism concerned the automatic way that the connections were strengthened or weakened. Even with the law of effect, Thorndike believed learning to be direct and not the result of any conscious mechanism such as thinking or reasoning. This criticism began a theoretical debate that we shall encounter again in subsequent chapters.

SECONDARY CONCEPTS BEFORE 1930

Before 1930, Thorndike's thinking included a number of ideas that were less important than the laws of readiness, effect, and exercise. These secondary concepts included multiple response, set or attitude, prepotency of elements, response by analogy, and associative shifting.

Multiple Response.

Multiple response, or varied reaction, was, for Thorndike, the first step in all learning. It refers to the fact that if our first response does not solve the problem we try other responses. Trial and error learning, of course, depends upon the animal trying first one response and then another until a response that works is hit upon. When this happens the probability of that response being made again goes up.

Set or Attitude.

What Thorndike called "attitudes," "dispositions," "preadjustments," or "sets" was his recognition of the importance of what the learner brings to the learning situation. He says (1913a):

> It is a general law of behavior that the response to any external situation is dependent upon the condition of the man, as well as upon the nature of the situation; and that, if certain conditions in the man are rated as part of the situation, the response to it depends upon the remaining conditions in the man. Consequently, it is a general law of learning that the change made in a man by the action of any agent depends upon the condition of the man when the agent is acting. The condition of the man may be considered under the two heads of the more permanent or fixed and the more temporary or shifting, attitudes, or "sets" [p. 24].

Thus, individual differences in learning can be explained by the basic differences among people: their cultural and genetic heritage or by temporary states such as deprivation, fatigue, or various emotional conditions. What can act as a satisfier or an annoyer depends on both the learner's background and his temporary bodily state at the time of learning.

Prepotency of Elements.

This is what Thorndike called "the partial or piecemeal activity of a situation." It refers to the fact that only some elements of any situation will govern behavior. He says (1913a):

> One of the commonest ways in which conditions within the man determine variations in his responses to one same external situation is by letting one or another element of the situation be prepotent in effect. Such partial or piecemeal activity on the part of a situation is, in human learning, the rule. Only rarely does man form connections, as the lower animals so often do, with a situation as a gross total—unanalyzed, undefined, and, as it were, without relief. He does so occasionally, as when a baby, to show off his little trick, requires the same room, the same persons present, the same tone of voice and the like. Save in early infancy and amongst the feeble-minded, however, any situation will most probably act unevenly. Some of its elements will produce only the response of neglect; others will be bound to only a mild awareness of them; others will connect with some energetic response of thought, feeling or action, and become positive determiners of the man's future [pp. 26–27].

With the notion of prepotency of elements, Thorndike recognized the complexity of the environment and concludes that we respond selectively to aspects of it. In other words, we could respond to some of the elements in a situation and not respond to others. Therefore, how we respond to a situation depends on both what we attend to and what responses are attached to what we attend to.

Response by Analogy.

What determines how we respond to a situation we have never encountered before? Thorndike's answer was that we respond to it as we would to a related situation that we had encountered before. The amount of transfer between the familiar situation and the unfamiliar one is determined by the number of elements that the two situations have in common. This is Thorndike's famous *identical elements* theory of the transfer of training.

With his theory of transfer, Thorndike opposed the long-held view of transfer based on the doctrine of *formal discipline*. As we saw in Chapter 3, formal discipline was based on faculty psychology which contended that the human mind was made up of several powers or faculties such as reasoning, attention, judgment, and memory. It was believed that these faculties could be strengthened with practice, e.g., practicing reasoning made one a better reasoner. Thus, the study of mathematics and Latin were justified because they strengthened the reasoning and memory faculties. It should be obvious why this position was referred to as the "mental muscle" approach, since it claims that faculties of the mind are strengthened with practice just as one would strengthen his biceps. This position also maintained that if one was forced to solve a number of difficult problems in school he would be an able problem solver outside of school. Thorndike felt that there was little evidence that education generalized so readily. In fact, he believed that education resulted in highly specific skills rather than general ones. He says (1906):

> A man may be a tip-top musician but in other respects an imbecile; he may be a gifted poet, but an ignoramus in music; he may have a wonderful memory for figures and only a mediocre memory for localities, poetry or human faces: school children may reason admirably in science and be below the average in grammar: those very good in drawing may be very poor in dancing [p. 238].

Thorndike and Woodworth (1901) critically examined the formal discipline theory of transfer and found no support for it. Instead they found transfer from one situation to the next only occurred to the extent that both situations had elements in common. These elements, according to Thorndike, may be actual stimulus conditions or they may be procedures. For example, looking up words in a dictionary in school may transfer to a variety of situations outside of school that have nothing to do with the exact words you were looking up in the classroom, but the ability to look things up may transfer. This would be the transfer of procedure rather than of substance. Learning to pay attention for long periods and learning to be punctual would be further examples of the transfer of procedures rather than stimulus elements.

Why is it, then, that the more difficult courses seem to produce brighter students? Because, says Thorndike, the brighter students went into these courses to begin with. Thorndike summarizes his elaborate study with Woodworth on the transfer of training involving 8,564 high school students as follows (1924):

> By any reasonable interpretation of the results, the intellectual values of studies should be determined largely by the special information, habits, interests, attitudes, and ideals which they demonstrably produce. The expectation of any large differences in general improvement of the mind from one study rather than an-

other seems doomed to disappointment. The chief reason why good thinkers seem superficially to have been made such by having taken certain school studies, is that good thinkers have taken such studies, becoming better by the inherent tendency of the good to gain more than the poor from any study. When the good thinkers studied Greek and Latin, these studies *seemed* to make good thinking. Now that the good thinkers study Physics and Trigonometry, these seem to make good thinkers. If the abler pupils should all study Physical Education and Dramatic Art, these subjects would seem to make good thinkers. . . . After positive correlation of gain with initial ability is allowed for, the balance in favor of any study is certainly not large. Disciplinary values may be real and deserve weight in the curriculum, but the weights should be reasonable [p. 98].

Concerning the question of how many elements two situations must have in common before the same behavior occurs in both, Thorndike says (1905):

The case may be likened roughly to that of the direction taken by a four horse team at a fork in the roads, when the team has never travelled either road *as a team* but some one horse or a pair *has*. Their previous habit of taking, say, the left turn, will cause the whole team to go that way [pp. 212–13].

Since all schools are attempting to influence the way students behave outside of school, the problem of the transfer of training is a central one for educators. Thorndike urged that the school curriculum be designed to include tasks that would be similar to those the student will be asked to perform when he leaves school. Thus, the study of mathematics should not be included because it strengthens the mind, but because the student will be actually using mathematics when he leaves school. For Thorndike, schools should emphasize the direct training of those skills thought to be important beyond the school.

The transfer of identical elements theory was Thorndike's solution to the problem of how we respond to a novel situation and to the problem of the transfer of training in general. Thorndike offered what some thought was a weakness in his theory, namely, the fact that we respond smoothly to new situations, as supportive evidence for his theory (1913a):

There is no arbitrary *hocus pocus* whereby man's nature acts in an unpredictable spasm when he is confronted with a new situation. His habits do not then retire to some convenient distance while some new and mysterious entities direct his behavior. On the contrary, nowhere are the bonds acquired with old situations more surely revealed in action than when a new situation appears [pp. 28–29].

Associative Shifting.

Associative shifting is closely related to Thorndike's identical elements theory of the transfer of training. The procedure for demonstrating associative shifting is to begin with a connection between a certain situation and a certain response. Then one gradually drops out stimulus elements that were part of the original situation, and adds stimulus elements that were not part of the original situation. According to Thorndike's identical elements theory, as long as there are enough elements from the original situation in the new situation, the same response will be given. In this way the same response can be carried through a number of stimulus changes and finally be made to stimulating conditions totally dissimilar to those associated with the original response. Thorndike says (1913a):

> Starting with response X made to $abcde$, we may successively drop certain elements and add others, until the response is bound to $fghij$, to which perhaps it could never otherwise have become connected. Theoretically the formula of progress, from $abcde$ to $abcfg$ to $abfgh$ to $afghi$ to $fghij$, might result in attaching any response whatever to any situation whatever, provided only that we arrange affairs so that at every step the response X was more satisfying in its consequences than balking or doing anything else that the person could do [pp. 30–31].

With his notion of associative shifting, Thorndike answers the question "What are the limits of learning?" According to Thorndike (1913a), "it is theoretically possible to associate any response that an organism is capable of making with any stimulus he is capable of responding to" [p. 15].

An example of associative shifting is found in the work of Terrace (1963) on discrimination learning. Terrace first taught pigeons to make a red-green discrimination by rewarding them with grain when they pecked at a red key but not when they pecked at a green key. Next Terrace superimposed a vertical bar over the red key and a horizontal bar over the green key. Gradually the red and green colors were faded out leaving only the vertical and horizontal bars on the keys. It was found that the discrimination previously associated with red and green was transferred without the pigeons making any errors to the vertical and horizontal bar discrimination. Now the pigeons pecked at the vertical bar and ignored the horizontal bar. The shifting process is shown in Figure 4–3.

The association shifts from one stimulus (red) to another (vertical bar) because the procedure allows enough elements from the preceding situation to guarantee that the same response is made to the new stimulus. This, of course, demonstrates transfer of training according to Thorndike's identical elements theory.

In a more general way much advertising is based on the principle of associative shifting. The advertiser need only find a stimulus object that elicits positive feelings, such as a picture of a beautiful female or handsome male, a respected personality, a medical doctor, a mother, or a romantic outdoor scene. Then the advertiser pairs this stimulus object with his product—a brand of cigarettes, an automobile, or a deodorant—as often as possible so that his product will elicit the same positive feelings elicited by the original stimulus object.

In reading Thorndike, we should note that associative shifting is really quite different from trial and error learning, which is governed by the law of effect. Unlike learning that depends on the law of effect, associative shifting depends only on contiguity. Associative shifting represents, therefore, a second kind of learning that is similar to the theories of Pavlov and Guthrie which we consider in chapters 7 and 8.

THORNDIKE AFTER 1930

In September 1929, Thorndike stood before the International Congress of Psychology in New Haven and started his address by saying "I was wrong." This points out an important aspect of good scientific practice: a good scientist is obliged to change his conclusions if the data require it.

Revised Law of Exercise.

Thorndike practically renounced the law of exercise. The law of use that stated that mere repetition strengthened a connection was found to be inaccurate. By the same token, simple disuse did not weaken a connection to any large extent. Although Thorndike still maintained that practice led to minor improvement and that lack of practice led to slight forgetting, for all practical purposes he discarded the entire law of exercise after 1930.

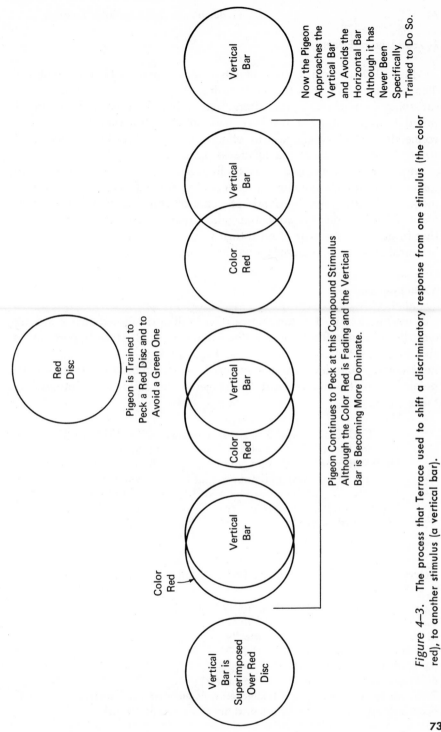

Figure 4-3. The process that Terrace used to shift a discriminatory response from one stimulus (the color red), to another stimulus (a vertical bar).

Revised Law of Effect.

After 1930, the earlier law of effect was found to be only half true. The salvaged half was the half stating that a response followed by a satisfying state of affairs was strengthened. For the other half, Thorndike found that punishing a response had no effect on the strength of the connection. His revised law of effect stated that *reward increases the strength of a connection, whereas punishment does nothing to the strength of a connection.* This finding still has profound implications today. Thorndike's conclusion concerning the effectiveness of punishment ran contrary to thousands of years of common sense and has numerous implications for education, child rearing, and behavior modification in general. We will often return to the question of the effectiveness of punishment as a means of modifying behavior in the following chapters.

Belongingness.

With his notion of belongingness Thorndike disagreed that contiguity was the sole basis for an association's being formed. More important than the mere fact that two things occur together is the fact that they somehow belong together. In one experiment designed to investigate this phenomenon Thorndike read his subjects the following sentences ten times (1932):

> Alfred Dukes and his sister worked sadly. Edward Davis and his brother argued rarely. Francis Bragg and his cousin played hard. Barney Croft and his father watched earnestly. Lincoln Blake and his uncle listened gladly. Jackson Craig and his son struggle often. Charlotte Dean and her friend studied easily. Mary Borah and her companion complained dully. Norman Foster and his mother bought much. Alice Hanson and her teacher came yesterday [p. 66].

Afterwards his subjects were asked the following questions:

1. What word came next after **rarely?**
2. What word came next after **Lincoln?**
3. What word came next after **gladly?**
4. What word came next after **dully?**
5. What word came next after **Mary?**
6. What word came next after **earnestly?**
7. What word came next after **Norman Foster and his mother?**
8. What word came next after **and his son struggle often?**

If mere contiguity was important in forming connections, all sequences of words should be remembered equally well. This, however, was not the case. The average number of correct associations from the end of one sentence to the beginning of the next was 2.75, whereas the average number of correct associations between the first and second word combinations was 21.50. Clearly, something is operating here beyond mere contiguity or proximity and that something is what Thorndike called *belongingness*, that is, subjects and verbs belong together more than the last word in one sentence and the first in another. Thus, the structure of the learning situation will influence what is attended to and therefore what is learned and retained.

Spread of Effect.

After 1930, Thorndike added another major theoretical concept, which he called the *spread of effect*. During one of his experiments Thorndike accidentally found that a satisfying state of affairs not only increased the probability of recurrence of the response that led to the satisfying state of affairs, but also increased the probability of recurrence of the responses surrounding the rewarded one.

One typical experiment demonstrating this effect involved the experimenter calling out a word to which the subject was instructed to respond with a number. The number that was called out was entirely arbitrary; the subject was simply instructed to say a number when the experimenter said a word. At some preconceived place the experimenter said "correct" or "that's right" when the subject responded with a certain number to a certain word, and sometimes he said "incorrect" or "wrong." Using this procedure Thorndike found that reward increased the probability of a number being repeated. More importantly, he found that the numbers that preceded and followed the rewarded number also increased in probability of recurring, even though they were not rewarded or the experimenter may have even said "wrong." Thus, what Thorndike called a satisfying state of affairs apparently "spread" from the rewarded response to neighboring responses. He called this phenomenon the spread of effect. Thorndike also found that the effect diminishes with distance. In other words, the rewarded response has the greatest probability of recurring, then the responses next to the rewarded one, then the responses next to those, and so on.

In discovering the spread of effect, Thorndike felt that he had found additional confirmation for his revised law of effect, since reward not only increased the probability of a rewarded response, but also increased the probability of neighboring responses even though these may have been punished. He also felt that the spread of effect demonstrated the automatic, direct nature of learning.

Thorndike on Education.

Thorndike believed strongly that educational practices should be studied scientifically. It was obvious to him that there should be a close relationship between the knowledge of the learning process and teaching practices. Thus, he expected that as more was discovered about the nature of learning, more could be applied to improve teaching practices. Thorndike says (1906):

> Of course present knowledge of psychology is nearer to zero than to complete perfection, and its applications to teaching must therefore be often incomplete, indefinite and insecure. The application of psychology to teaching is more like that of botany and chemistry to farming than like that of physiology and pathology to medicine. Anyone of good sense can farm fairly well without science, and anyone of good sense can teach fairly well without knowing and applying psychology. Still, as the farmer with the knowledge of the applications of botany and chemistry to farming is, other things being equal, more successful than the farmer without it, so the teacher will, other things being equal, be the more successful who can apply psychology, the science of human nature, to the problems of the school [pp. 9–10].

At many points Thorndike's thinking ran contrary to traditional thinking about education; we saw one clear example of this with his identical elements theory of transfer. He also had a low opinion of the lecture technique of teaching that was so popular then (and now). He says (1912):

> The lecture and demonstration methods represent an approach to a limiting extreme in which the teacher lets the pupil find out nothing which he could possibly be told or shown. They frankly present the student with conclusions, trusting that he will use them to learn more. They ask of him only that he attend to, and do his best to understand, questions which he did not himself frame and answers which he did not himself work out. They try to give him an educational fortune as one bequeaths property by will [p. 188].

Elsewhere he says (1912):

> The commonest error of the gifted scholar, inexperienced in teaching, is to expect pupils to know what they have been told.

But telling is not teaching. The expression of the facts that are in one's mind is a natural impulse when one wishes others to know these facts, just as to cuddle and pat a sick child is a natural impulse. But telling a fact to a child may not cure his ignorance of it any more than patting him will cure his scarlet fever [p. 61].

What then is good teaching? Good teaching involves first of all knowing what you want to teach. If you do not know exactly what it is you want to teach you will not know what material to present, what responses to look for, and when to apply satisfiers. This principle is not as obvious as it sounds. Only recently have we realized the importance of behaviorally defining educational objectives. Although Thorndike's seven rules that follow were formulated for the teaching of arithmetic, they represent his advice for teaching in general (1922):

1. Consider the situation the pupil faces.
2. Consider the response you wish to connect with it.
3. Form the bond; do not expect it to come by a miracle.
4. Other things being equal, form no bond that will have to be broken.
5. Other things being equal, do not form two or three bonds when one will serve.
6. Other things being equal, form bonds in the way that they are required later to act.
7. Favor, therefore, the situations which life itself will offer, and the responses which life itself will demand [p. 101].

One can see here the seeds of B. F. Skinner's attitude toward educational practices which we will consider in Chapter 5.

Science and Human Values.

Thorndike was also criticized for assuming determinism in the study of human behavior. Reducing human behavior to automatic reactions to the environment destroys human values, the critics said. On the contrary, Thorndike answered, the science of man offered mankind his greatest hope for the future (1940):

The welfare of mankind now depends upon the sciences of man. The sciences of things will, unless civilization collapses, progress, extend man's control over nature, and guide technology, agriculture, medicine, and other arts effectively. They will protect man against dangers and disasters except such as he himself causes. He is now his own worst enemy. Knowledge of psychology and of its applications to welfare should prevent, or at least diminish, some of the errors and calamities for which the well-intentioned have been and are responsible. It should reduce greatly the harm done by the stupid and vicious [p. v].

Elsewhere Thorndike states (1949):

> Thus, at last, man may become ruler of himself as well as of the rest of nature. For strange as it may sound man is free only in a world whose every event he can understand and foresee. Only so can he guide it. We are captains of our own souls only in so far as they act in perfect law so that we can understand and foresee every response which we will make to every situation. Only so can we control our own selves. It is only because our intellects and morals—the mind and spirit of man—are a part of nature, that we can be in any significant sense responsible for them, proud of their progress, or trustful of their future [p. 362].

Obviously, Thorndike was a very colorful person who expressed opinions on a wide variety of topics. In this chapter we have concentrated on outlining his thoughts on the learning process, and his views concerning the relationship between the learning process and educational practices. The student who is interested in knowing more about Thorndike is urged to read *The Sane Positivist: A Biography of Edward L. Thorndike*, by Geraldine Joncich (1968).

DISCUSSION QUESTIONS

1. Do you agree with Thorndike's contention that the same laws of learning apply to both human and subhuman animals? Explain.
2. Assuming Thorndike's revised law of effect to be valid, do you feel classroom practice in this country is in accordance with it? Child rearing practices? Explain.
3. How would you arrange schoolroom practices so that they take into consideration Thorndike's theory concerning the transfer of training?
4. How would Thorndike answer the question, "What are the limits of learning?"
5. Design an academic curriculum taking into consideration as many of Thorndike's ideas as you can.

6. Describe how you could reduce the probability of a child being fearful of a new situation, such as a new babysitter, using the procedure of associative shifting.
7. Which laws of association did Thorndike accept? Did he create any new laws of association? Defend your answer.
8. Respond to the statement "Practice makes perfect," as you think Thorndike would have responded to it.

GLOSSARY

Annoying State of Affairs.   A condition that an organism actively avoids. If such a condition occurs the organism attempts to abandon it as soon as possible.

Associative Shifting.   The process whereby a response is "carried" from one set of stimulating conditions to another by gradually adding new stimulus elements and subtracting old ones. The result is that a response that was originally given to one set of circumstances is now given to an entirely new set of circumstances. Associative shifting is based on the principle of contiguity.

Belongingness.   Material is learned more readily when it is structured in certain ways. Contiguity alone does not determine how well something will be learned. How the material "fits together" must also be taken into consideration.

Connectionism.   A term often used to describe Thorndike's explanation of learning since he assumed learning involved the strengthening of neural bonds (connections) between stimulating conditions and the responses to them.

Formal Discipline.   See Glossary for Chapter 3.

Identical Elements Theory of Transfer.   The theory which states that the likelihood of something which was learned in one situation being applied in a different situation is determined by the number of common elements in the two situations. As the number of common elements goes up the amount of transfer between the two situations goes up. The elements can be either stimuli or procedures.

Incremental Learning.   Learning that occurs a little bit at a time rather than all at once.

Insightful Learning.   Learning that occurs all at once rather than a little bit at a time. (See also the Glossary for Chapter 10).

Law of Disuse. That portion of the law of exercise which states that the strength of a connection diminishes when the connection is not used. The law of disuse was discarded by Thorndike after 1930.

Law of Effect. The law which states that the strength of a connection is influenced by the consequences of a response. Before 1930, Thorndike believed that pleasurable consequences strengthened a connection and annoying consequences weakened a connection. After 1930, however, he believed that only pleasurable consequences had an effect on the strength of a connection.

Law of Exercise. The law which states that the strength of a connection is determined by how often the connection is used. The law of exercise has two components—the law of use and the law of disuse.

Law of Readiness. The law which states that when an organism is ready to act it is rewarding for it to do so, and annoying for it not to do so. Also, when an organism is not ready to act, forcing it to act will be annoying to it.

Law of Use. That portion of the law of exercise which states that the strength of a connection increases with its use. The law of use was discarded by Thorndike after 1930.

Multiple Response. Refers to the fact that if one response does not solve the problem the organism continues to try other responses until it hits upon one that is effective in solving the problem; a prerequisite to trial and error learning.

Prepotency of Elements. Refers to the fact that different aspects of the environment have different responses connected to them; similar to what we now refer to as selective perception.

Response by Analogy. Refers to the fact that our response to an unfamiliar situation is determined by its degree of similarity to a familiar situation. Insofar as two situations are similar they will tend to be similarly responded to. Thorndike describes similarity in terms of the number of elements that the two situations have in common. This is related to his identical elements theory of transfer of training.

Satisfying State of Affairs. A condition that an organism seeks out and attempts to preserve. Once such a condition exists, the organism does nothing to avoid it.

Selecting and Connecting. See *Trial and Error Learning.*

Set (Attitude). Temporary conditions, such as food deprivation, fatigue, or emotion, that determine what will be annoying or pleasurable to a given organism.

Spread of Effect. The observation that reward not only strengthens the response that produced it, but that it strengthens neighboring responses as well.

Strength of a Connection.   Determined by how likely a certain response is in a given set of circumstances. In other words, the strength of a connection is equated with response probability.

Transfer of Training.   When something learned in one situation is applied in another situation.

Trial and Error Learning.   The trying of different responses in a problem solving situation until a response which is effective in solving the problem is hit upon. Thorndike originally called this phenomenon selecting and connecting.

5

Burrhus Frederic Skinner

Skinner was born in Susquehanna, Pennsylvania, in 1904 and is considered by many to be the most famous, influential psychologist alive today. He received his Masters degree in 1930 and his Ph.D. in 1931 from Harvard University. His B.A. degree was obtained from Hamilton College in New York where he majored in English.

While at Hamilton, Skinner had lunch with Robert Frost, the great American poet, who encouraged Skinner to send him a sample of his writing. Frost reviewed favorably the three short stories that Skinner sent and Skinner decided definitely to become a writer. This decision was a great disappointment to his father who was a lawyer and who wanted his son to become a lawyer.

Skinner's early efforts to write were so frustrating that he thought of seeing a psychiatrist. He eventually went to work for the coal industry summarizing legal documents. In fact, his first book, coauthored by his father, concerned those legal documents and was entitled *A Digest of Decisions of the Anthracite Board of Conciliation*. After finishing this book, Skinner moved to Greenwich Village in New York City where he lived like a Bohemian for six months before going to Harvard to study psychology. By that time he had developed a distaste for most literary pursuits. In his autobiography, he says (1967):

> I had failed as a writer because I had had nothing important to
> say, but I could not accept that explanation. It was literature which
> must be at fault [p. 395].

When he failed in describing human behavior through literature,
Skinner attempted to describe human behavior through science. Clearly
he was much more successful at the latter pursuit.

Skinner taught psychology at the University of Minnesota between
1936 and 1945, during which time he wrote his highly influential text,
The Behavior of Organisms (1938). One of Skinner's students at the
University of Minnesota was W. K. Estes, whose work has had a considerable impact on psychology (see Chapter 9). In 1945 Skinner went
to the University of Indiana as chairman of the psychology department,
and in 1948 he returned to Harvard where he has been ever since.

As we shall see, Skinner's position is similar to Thorndike's position
after 1930 in that it emphasizes the effects of a response on the response
itself. Moreover, like Thorndike, Skinner concludes that the effects of
reward and punishment are not symmetrical, that is, reward changes the
probability of a response's recurring, but punishment does not.

Through the years, Skinner has been a highly prolific writer. One of
his main concerns has been to relate his laboratory findings to the solution of human problems. His work has led to the development of programmed learning and teaching machines. Two representative articles in
this area are "The Science of Learning and the Art of Teaching" (1954),
and "Teaching Machines" (1958). Following his own ideas on this topic,
he and his co-author, Holland, produced a programmed text on his theoretical notions entitled *The Analysis of Behavior* (1961). In 1948 he
wrote a Utopian novel called *Walden Two*. The title paid tribute to
Thoreau's *Walden*. In *Walden Two*, which Skinner wrote in only seven
weeks, he attempts to utilize his principles of learning in the building of
a model society. Skinner has recently written *Beyond Freedom and
Dignity* (1971) where he shows how a technology of behavior can be
used in designing a culture. In *Beyond Freedom and Dignity* he discusses
many reasons why the idea of cultural engineering is met with so much
opposition. Skinner's writings have been extended into the area of child
development through the efforts of Bijou and Baer (1961, 1965). His
thoughts have been related to the area of personality through the writings
of Lundin, who wrote *Personality: A Behavioral Analysis* (1974), and to
child rearing by Hergenhahn, who wrote *Shaping Your Child's Personality*
(1972).

Most students of psychology are well aware of the widespread utilization of Skinnerian notions in the area of psychotherapy. For example,

Lovaas's early work with autistic children relied heavily on Skinner's ideas. Today the behavior modification approach, based on Skinner's ideas, has become the most widely used and most effective way of working with autistic or retarded children. Behavioral engineering, however, is by no means limited to children. The technique has been successfully applied to the alleviation of a number of adult problems such as stuttering, phobias, homosexuality, and psychotic behavior.

During the Second World War, while at the University of Minnesota, Skinner attempted to apply his theory to the problem of national defense. He trained pigeons to peck at discs upon which moving pictures of enemy targets were being shown. The discs and the motion pictures were ultimately to be contained in a glider loaded with high explosives. The glider was called the *Pelican,* thus, the name of the article describing these events, "Pigeons in a Pelican" (1960). The pecking of the pigeons closed various electronic circuits and thereby kept the vehicle on target. This American version of kamikaze fighter planes would involve no losses of human lives. Although Skinner demonstrated to a group of America's top scientists that he and his co-workers had perfected a homing device that was practically immune to electronic jamming, was capable of reacting to a wide variety of enemy targets, and was simple to build, their proposed project was turned down. Skinner speculates that the whole idea was simply too fantastic for the committee to cope with.

MAJOR THEORETICAL NOTIONS

Respondent and Operant Behavior.

Skinner distinguishes two kinds of behavior: *respondent* behavior, which is elicited by a known stimulus, and *operant* behavior, which is not elicited by a known stimulus but is simply emitted by the organism. Unconditioned responses would be examples of respondent behavior since they are elicited by unconditioned stimuli. Examples of respondent behavior would include all reflexes, such as jerking one's hand when jabbed with a pin, the constriction of the pupil of the eye when it is exposed to bright light, and salivation in the presence of food. Because operant behavior is *not* initially correlated with known stimuli it seems to appear spontaneously. Examples include beginning to whistle, standing up and walking about, a child abandoning one toy in favor of another, and moving one's hands, arms, or legs arbitrarily. Most of our everyday activities would be operant behaviors. Note that Skinner does not say that operant behavior occurs independently of stimulation; rather, he says that the stimulus causing such behavior is unknown and that it is not important to know its cause. Unlike respondent behavior which is dependent on the stimulus that preceded it, operant behavior is controlled by its consequences. We will say more about how consequences influence operant behavior.

Type S and Type R Conditioning.

Along with the two kinds of behavior described above, there are two kinds of conditioning. Type S conditioning is also called *respondent conditioning* and it is identical to classical conditioning. It is called Type S conditioning to emphasize the importance of the stimulus in eliciting the desired response. The type of conditioning that involves operant behavior is called Type R because of the emphasis on the response. Type R conditioning is also called *operant conditioning*.

It is important to note that in Type R conditioning the strength of conditioning is shown by *response rate*, whereas in Type S conditioning,

Burrhus Frederic Skinner

strength of conditioning is usually determined by the *magnitude* of the conditioned response. We see, then, that Skinner's Type R conditioning very closely resembles Thorndike's instrumental conditioning, and Skinner's Type S conditioning is very close to Pavlov's classical conditioning. After making the distinction between Type S and Type R conditioning, Skinner's research has been concerned almost entirely with Type R, or operant conditioning.

Although Skinner and Thorndike are in close agreement on a number of important issues, there are still important differences between them. For example, the dependent variable in Thorndike's learning experiments, (his measure of the extent to which learning took place) was *time to solution.* Thorndike was interested in measuring how long it took an animal to perform whatever task was necessary to release him from confinement. Skinner, on the other hand, uses *rate of responding* as his dependent variable. Although Skinner sometimes talks about how reward affects the probability of a response's recurring, his main concern is with how reward affects the rate with which an operant response occurs. In other words, Thorndike was mainly interested in noting how long it took an animal to make a certain response, whereas Skinner is interested mainly in what variables affect rate or pattern of responding.

Operant Conditioning Principles.

Two general principles are associated with Type R conditioning: (1) any response that is followed by a reinforcing stimulus (reward) tends to be repeated; and (2) a reinforcing stimulus (reward) is anything that increases the rate with which an operant response occurs. Or, as we saw above, we can say that a reward is anything that increases the probability of a response's recurring.

Skinner does not provide a rule that one would follow in discovering what would be an effective reinforcer. Rather, he says that whether or not something is reinforcing can only be ascertained by its effect on behavior. He says (1953):

> In dealing with our fellow men in everyday life and in the clinic and laboratory, we may need to know just how reinforcing a specific event is. We often begin by noting the extent to which our own behavior is reinforced by the same event. This practice frequently miscarries; yet it is still commonly believed that reinforcers can be identified apart from their effects upon a particular organism. As the term is used here, however, the only defining characteristic of a reinforcing stimulus is that it reinforces [p. 72].

In operant conditioning, the emphasis is on behavior and its conse-quences; with operant conditioning, the organism must respond in such a way as to produce the reinforcing stimulus. This process also exemplifies contingent reinforcement, because getting the reward is contingent (de-pendent) upon the organism's emitting a certain response. We will have more to say about contingent reinforcement in our subsequent discussion of superstitious behavior.

The principles of operant conditioning can apply to a variety of situa-tions. To modify behavior, someone merely has to find something that is rewarding for the organism whose behavior he wishes to modify, wait until the desired behavior occurs, and immediately reward the organism when it does. When this is done, the rate with which the desired response occurs goes up. When the behavior next occurs, it is again rewarded, and the rate of responding goes up even more. Any behavior that the orga-nism is capable of performing can be manipulated in this manner.

The same principles are thought to apply to the development of human personality. According to Skinner, we are what we have been rewarded for being. What we call personality is nothing more than consistent be-havior patterns that summarize our reinforcement history. We learn to speak English, for example, because we have been rewarded for approxi-mating the sounds of the English language in our early home environ-ment. If we happened to be brought up in a Japanese or Russian home, we would learn to speak Japanese or Russian because when we approx-imated sounds in that language, we would have been attended to or rewarded in some other way. Skinner (1971) says:

> The evidence for a crude environmentalism is clear enough. People are extraordinarily different in different places, and possibly just because of the places. The Nomad on horseback in Outer Mon-golia and the astronaut in outer space are different people, but, as far as we know, if they had been exchanged at birth, they would have taken each other's place. (The expression "change places" shows how closely we identify a person's behavior with the en-vironment in which it occurs.) But we need to know a great deal more before that fact becomes useful. What is it about the en-vironment that produces a Hottentot? And what would need to be changed to produce an English conservative instead [p. 185]?

Skinner defines culture as a set of reinforcement contingencies. His answers to the above questions would be that a particular set of rein-forcement contingencies produce a Hottentot and another set produces the English conservative. Different cultures reward different behavior patterns. This fact must be clearly understood before an adequate technology of behavior can be developed. Skinner (1971), says:

> The environment is obviously important, but its role has remained obscure. It does not push or pull, it *selects,* and this function is difficult to discover and analyze. The role of natural selection in evolution was formulated only a little more than a hundred years ago, and the selective role of the environment in shaping and maintaining the behavior of the individual is only beginning to be recognized and studied. As the interaction between organism and environment has come to be understood, however, effects once assigned to states of mind, feelings, and traits are beginning to be traced to accessible conditions, and a technology of behavior may therefore become available. It will not solve our problems, however, until it replaces traditional prescientific views, and these are strongly entrenched [p. 25].

If one controls reward, one can also control behavior. However, this need not be looked upon as a negative statement, since behavior is constantly being influenced by reward whether we are aware of that fact or not. It is never a question of *whether* behavior is going to be controlled, but who or what is going to control it. Parents, for example, can decide to give direction to their child's emerging personality by rewarding certain behavior, or they can let society rear their child by letting the TV, his peers, his school, his books, and his babysitter reward him. Giving direction to a child's life is difficult, however, and any parents wishing to do so must take at least the following steps (Hergenhahn, 1972):

• 1. Decide the major personality characteristics you want your child to possess as an adult. Let's say, for example, you want the child to grow up to be a creative adult.
• 2. Define these goals in behavioral terms. In this case, you ask, "What is the child doing when he is being creative?"
• 3. Reward behavior that is in accordance with these goals. With this example, you would reward instances of creativity as they occurred.
• 4. Provide consistency by arranging the major aspects of the child's environment so that they too reward the behavior you have deemed important [p. 152].

Without a knowledge of these principles, a parent could easily misapply them without knowing it. Skinner says (1951):

The mother may unwillingly promote the very behavior she does not want. For example, when she is busy she is likely not to respond to a call or request made in a quiet tone of voice. She may answer the child only when it raises its voice. The average intensity of the child's vocal behavior therefore moves up to another level. . . . Eventually the mother gets used to this level and again reinforces only louder instances. This vicious circle brings about louder and louder behavior. . . . The mother behaves, in fact, as if she has been given the assignment of teaching the child to be annoying [p. 29].

According to Skinner, living organisms are constantly being conditioned by their environment. We can either allow the principles of learning to operate capriciously on our children, or by systematically applying those principles, we can give some direction to their development.

The Skinner Box.

Most of Skinner's early animal work was done in a small test chamber which has come to be called the Skinner box. It is a direct descendant of the puzzle box used by Thorndike. The Skinner box usually has a grid floor, a light, a lever, and a food cup. It is arranged so that when the animal depresses the lever, the feeder mechanism is activated and a small

Figure 5–1. A typical Skinner box (courtesy of the Gerbrands Company, Inc.).

pellet of food is released into the food cup. A typical Skinner box is shown in Figure 5–1.

The Cumulative Recording.

Skinner uses a cumulative recording to keep track of an animal's behavior in the Skinner box. A cumulative recording is quite different from other ways of graphing data in learning experiments. Time is recorded on the X-axis and total number of responses is recorded on the Y-axis. The cumulative recording never goes down— the line either climbs or remains parallel to the X-axis. Let's say we are interested in how often the animal presses the lever. When the cumulative recording shows a line parallel to the X-axis, it indicates no responding, that is, the animal is not pressing the lever. When the animal makes a lever-pressing response, the pen goes up a notch and remains at that level until the animal makes another response. If, for example, the animal presses the lever when he is first placed in the Skinner box, the pen will go up a notch and remain

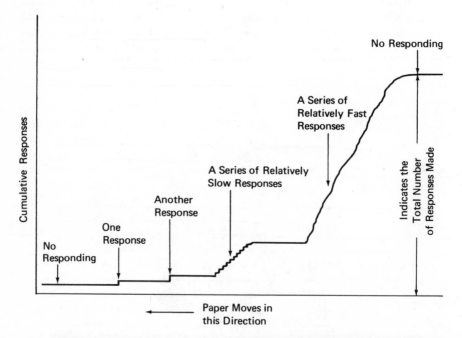

Figure 5–2. A cumulative recording. Note that the steeper the line, the faster is the rate of responding. A line parallel to the baseline indicates no responding.

there until the animal responds again, at which time the pen will go up another notch, and so on. If he responds very rapidly, the line will rise very rapidly. The rate with which the line ascends indicates rate of responding; a very steep line indicates very rapid responding, and a line parallel to the X-axis indicates no responding. If at any time you want to know the total number of responses made by the animal, you just measure the distance between the line of the graph and the X-axis, and this can easily be transformed into total number of responses. Sample cumulative recordings are shown in Figure 5–2.

Conditioning the Lever Press Response.

Typically, conditioning the lever press response involves the following steps:

• 1) **Deprivation.** The experimental animal is put on a deprivation schedule. If food is to be used as the reinforcer, then the animal is deprived of food for a 23-hour period for a number of days prior to the experiment, or he is maintained at 80 percent of his free-feeding body weight. If water is to be used as the reinforcer, the animal is deprived of water for a 23-hour period for a number of days prior to the experiment. (Some Skinner boxes are designed to deliver small pellets of food and others small drops of water.) Skinner does not say that these procedures "motivate" the animal; he even hesitates to say that they produce a drive state. Deprivation is simply a set of procedures that is related to how an organism performs on a certain task; nothing more needs to be said.

• 2) **Magazine training.** After being on a deprivation schedule for a number of days, the animal is placed into the Skinner box. Using an external hand switch, the experimenter periodically triggers the feeder mechanism (also called the magazine), making sure the animal is not in the vicinity of the food cup when he does so (otherwise the animal would learn to remain near the food cup). When the feeder mechanism is activated by the hand switch, it produces a fairly loud clicking sound prior to delivering a pellet of food into the food cup. Gradually the animal associates the click of the magazine with the presence of a food pellet. At that point, the click has become a secondary reward through its association with a primary reward (food). (We will discuss secondary reinforcement in a later section.) The click also acts as a cue or signal indicating to the animal that if he responds by going to the food cup, he will be rewarded.

• 3) Now the animal can be left in the Skinner box on his own. Eventually, he will press the lever, which will fire the food magazine, producing a click that reinforces the bar press, and also signals the animal to go to the food cup where he is reinforced by food. According to operant conditioning principles, the lever press response, having been rewarded, will tend to be

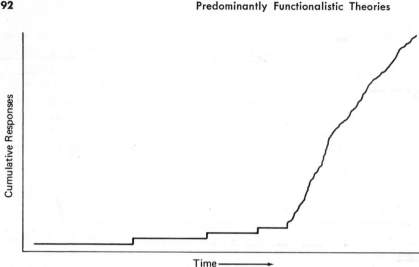

Figure 5–3. A typical cumulative recording which reflects the acquisition of a lever press response.

repeated and when it is, it is again rewarded, which further increases the probability that the lever press response will be repeated, and so on. A typical cumulative recording generated by an animal placed in a Skinner box after magazine training is shown in Figure 5–3.

Shaping.

The process of operant conditioning we have described so far takes considerable time. As we saw above, one way to train the lever press response is to place the deprived animal in the Skinner box and simply leave it there. The experimenter merely checks the cumulative recording periodically to see if the lever press response has been learned. Under these conditions the animal either learns or he dies.

There is another approach to operant conditioning that does not take as long as the procedure described above. Again, the animal is placed on a deprivation schedule and is magazine trained, and again, the experimenter uses the hand switch to trigger the feeder mechanism externally. This time, however, the experimenter decides to fire the feeder mechanism only when the animal is in the half of the Skinner box containing the lever. When the animal gets rewarded for being near the lever, he will tend to remain in that part of the test chamber. Now that the animal remains in the vicinity of the lever, the experimenter begins to reward him only when he is still closer to the lever. Next he is rewarded only when he touches the lever, then only when he is putting pressure on it, and finally, only when he is pressing it by himself.

The process is similar to a childhood game called "You're Hot, You're Cold," where a child hides something and his playmates try to find it. As they get closer to the hidden object, the child who hid the object says, "You're getting warm, you're warmer, you're boiling hot, you're on fire." As they get farther from the object the child says, "You're getting cold, colder, very cold, you're freezing." When this game is played in the laboratory, it is called shaping. In the shaping procedure described above, the lever press response was shaped rather than waiting for it to happen.

Shaping has two components: *differential reinforcement,* which simply means some responses are reinforced and others are not; and *successive approximation,* which refers to the fact that only those responses are reinforced that become increasingly similar to the one the experimenter wants. In our example, only those responses which successively approximated the lever press response were differentially reinforced.

Extinction.

As with classical conditioning, when we remove the reward from the operant conditioning situation, we produce extinction. During acquisition, the animal gets a pellet of food whenever he presses the lever. Under these circumstances, he learns to press the lever and persists in doing so until he is satiated with food. If the feeder mechanism was suddenly disconnected, thus preventing a lever press from producing a pellet of food, we would note that the cumulative recording would gradually become shallower and would eventually become parallel to the X-axis, indicating that no lever press responses are being made. At that point, we say that extinction has occurred.

We are being somewhat inaccurate when we say that after extinction a response is no longer made; it is more accurate to say that after extinction, the response rate goes back to where it was before reward was introduced. This baseline rate is the frequency with which the response occurs naturally in the life of the animal without the introduction of reward. This is called the *operant level* for that response. When we remove reward from the experimental arrangement, as in extinction, the response tends to go back to its operant level.

Spontaneous Recovery.

After extinction, if the animal is returned to his home cage for a period of time and then brought back into the experimental situation,

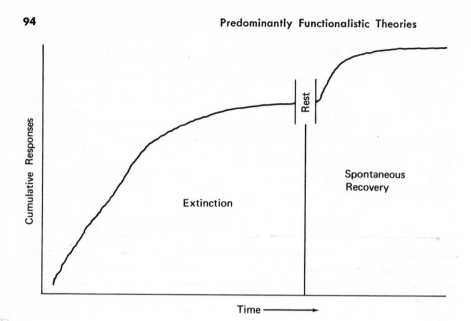

Figure 5–4. A cumulative recording which depicts the extinction and spontaneous recovery of a lever press response.

he will again begin to press the lever for a short period of time without any additional training. This is referred to as spontaneous recovery. A cumulative recording showing both extinction and spontaneous recovery is shown in Figure 5–4.

Superstitious Behavior.

In our earlier discussion of operant conditioning, we briefly mentioned *contingent reinforcement*. Reward following the lever press response is an example of contingent reinforcement since the reward is dependent on the response. What would happen, however, if the situation was arranged so that the feeder mechanism would fire every now and then, independently of the animal's behavior? In other words, we are now going to arrange the situation so that the feeder mechanism delivers a pellet of food periodically *regardless of what the animal is doing.*

According to the principles of operant conditioning, we can predict that whatever the animal is doing when the feeder mechanism is activated will be rewarded, and the animal will tend to repeat the rewarded behavior. At some time the rewarded behavior will be repeated when the feeder mechanism randomly fires again, and the response will be strengthened. Thus the animal is apt to develop strange, ritualistic responses; he may bob his head, turn in a circle, stand up on his back legs, or perform a series of actions according to what he was doing when the feeder mechanism fired. This ritualistic behavior is referred to as superstitious because the animal looks as if he believes that what he is doing is causing a pellet of food to appear. Because the reward in this situation is independent of the animal's behavior, it is referred to as *noncontingent reinforcement.*

One can think of numerous examples of superstitious behavior on the part of humans. Organized sports, for example, are filled with many examples. Imagine what happens to the baseball player who, after stepping to the plate, adjusts his hat in a certain way, and hits the very next pitch out of the ball park. There will be a strong tendency on his part to adjust his hat in a similar way the next time he is at bat.

It is interesting to speculate as to the effects of Christmas or birthday presents on children. It is clear that rewards influence behavior and no doubt presents are rewards. It is not clear, however, what behavior is being rewarded. Are we rewarding a child for becoming a year older, for example, or for what he did just prior to receiving the reward? In the former case, it seems impossible for "getting a year older" to increase in frequency. In the latter case, if the behavior prior to the reward is strengthened, we have an example of noncontingent reinforcement, since the response preceding the reward did not produce the reward. Obviously it is not what the child receives that is important in shaping his personality, but when he receives it.

Discriminative Operant.

Now we return to the Skinner box and discuss the light that we referred to earlier. After we have conditioned the animal to press the lever, we can make the situation more complex. We can arrange the situation so that the animal receives a pellet of food only when the light in the Skinner box is on, but not when the light is off. Under these conditions, we refer to the light as an S^D or a *discriminative stimulus*. The light being on defines the S^D conditions and the light being off defines the S^Δ conditions (Δ = delta). With this arrangement, the animal learns to press the lever when the light is on and not to press when the light is off. The light, therefore, has become a signal (cue) for the lever press response. We have developed a *discriminative operant,* which is an operant response given to one set of circumstances but not to another. The arrangement can be symbolized as follows: $S^D \rightarrow R \rightarrow S^R$ where R is the operant response and S^R is the reinforcing stimulus or the reward.

The concept of the discriminative stimulus allows for a more detailed statement about which association is of interest in operant conditioning. For Thorndike, the association of interest was between a general environmental situation and a response effective in solving a problem. For Skinner, the association of interest can be diagrammed as follows:

discriminative stimulus $\rightarrow$ operant response $\rightarrow$ reinforcing stimulus
$\quad\quad$ (S^D) $\qquad\qquad\qquad$ (R) $\qquad\qquad\qquad$ (S^R)

association of interest

Except for slight differences in terminology, Skinner's views of learning are quite similar to those of Thorndike after 1930. In fact, except for the way each researcher measured the dependent variable, which was difference pointed out earlier in this chapter, instrumental conditioning and operant conditioning can be considered the same procedures.

There is some slight similarity between the discriminative operant and respondent conditioning. You will recall that respondent behavior is elicited by a known stimulus. The behavior occurs because of its association with the stimulus. Such behavior, as we have seen, is not under the control of its consequences. In the case of the discriminative operant, the light becomes a signal associated with a certain response that the organism has learned will be followed by reward.

Operant behavior is emitted behavior, but Skinner (1953) says:

Most operant behavior, however, acquires important connections with the surrounding world. We may show how it does so in our pigeon experiment by reinforcing neck-stretching when a signal light is on and allowing it to be extinguished when the light is off. Eventually stretching occurs only when the light is on. We can then demonstrate a stimulus-response connection which is roughly comparable to a conditioned or unconditioned reflex: the appearance of the light will be quickly followed by an upward movement of the head. But the relation is fundamentally quite different. It has a different history and different current properties. We describe the contingency by saying that a *stimulus* (the light) is the occasion upon which a *response* (stretching the neck) is followed by reinforcement (with food). We must specify all three terms. The effect upon the pigeon is that eventually the response is more likely to occur when the light is on. The process through which this comes about is called *discrimination*. Its importance in a theoretical analysis, as well as in the practical control of behavior, is obvious: when a discrimination has been established, we may alter the probability of a response instantly by presenting or removing the discriminative stimulus [pp. 107–8].

Thus, the discriminative operant involves a signal which leads to a response which, in turn, leads to reward. With the conditioned reflex (a kind of respondent behavior), a signal leads to a response, but reward (the UCS) precedes the conditioned response rather than following it. In other words, the CS elicits a response, but the S^D becomes the occasion for a certain response to be emitted and subsequently rewarded.

There are numerous examples of discriminative operants in everyday life. A certain time of the day (S^D) indicates that you must be in a certain place (R) in order to transact some business (S^R). As you're driving down the street, you encounter a red light (S^D), which causes you to stop (R), thereby avoiding a ticket or an accident (S^R). You see someone you don't care for (S^D), causing you to change the direction you are walking in (R), thereby avoiding him (S^R).

Secondary Reinforcement.

Any neutral stimulus paired with a primary reward (e.g., food or water) takes on reinforcing properties of its own; this is the principle of secondary reinforcement. It follows then that every S^D must be a secondary reinforcer since it consistently precedes primary reinforcement.

One way to demonstrate the reinforcing properties of a previously neutral stimulus is to wire the Skinner box so that a lever press switches on the light and also produces a pellet of food. Thus, a lever press results in both the light coming on and in primary reward (food). According to the principle of secondary reinforcement, the pairing of the light with food should cause the light to take on reinforcing properties of its own. One way to test this notion is to extinguish the lever press response so that the animal presses the lever and neither light nor food is produced. When the response rate decreases, we arrange for the lever press to turn on the light but not deliver a pellet of food. We note that the response rate goes way up. Since the light alone has increased the response rate and thereby prolonged extinction, we say it has developed secondary reinforcing characteristics through its association with food during acquisition (training). A light not associated with a primary reward will not produce a similar effect during extinction.

In addition to maintaining the lever press response, we can now use the light to condition other responses. Once a previously neutral stimulus

takes on rewarding properties through its association with primary reinforcement, it can be used to reward any number of responses.

Keller and Schoenfield (1950) provide an excellent summary of secondary reinforcement:

1. A stimulus that occasions or accompanies a reinforcement acquires
   thereby reinforcing value of its own, and may be called a conditioned,
   secondary, or derived reinforcement. A secondary reinforcement may be
   extinguished when repeatedly applied to a response for which there
   is no ultimate primary reinforcement.
2. A secondary reinforcement is positive when the reinforcement with which
   it is correlated is positive, and negative when the latter is negative.
3. Once established, a secondary reinforcement is independent and nonspecific; it will not only strengthen the same response which produced the
   original reinforcement, but it will also condition a new and unrelated
   response. Moreover, it will do so even in the presence of a different
   motive.
4. Through generalization, many stimuli besides the one correlated with
   reinforcement acquire reinforcing value—positive or negative [p. 260].

Generalized Reinforcers.

A generalized reinforcer is a secondary reinforcer that has been paired
with more than one primary reinforcer. Money is a secondary reinforcer
because it is ultimately associated with any number of primary rewards.
The main advantage of the generalized reinforcer is that it does not
depend upon a certain condition of deprivation to be effective. Food, for
example, is only reinforcing for an organism deprived of food, but money
can be used as a reward whether or not someone is deprived of food.
Grades, trophies, medals, and awards would also classify as generalized
reinforcers.

Moreover, the very activities that once led to reward may themselves
become reinforcing. Skinner (1953) says:

> Eventually generalized reinforcers are effective even though
> the primary reinforcers upon which they are based no longer
> accompany them. We play games of skill for their own sake. We
> get attention or approval for its own sake. Affection is not always
> followed by a more explicit sexual reinforcement. The submissive-
> ness of others is reinforcing even though we make no use of it. A
> miser may be so reinforced by money that he will starve rather
> than give it up [p. 81].

With these comments, Skinner comes very close to Gordon Allport's
concept of *functional autonomy*. Allport (1961) maintains that although

an activity may once have been engaged in because it led to reward, after awhile the activity itself may become rewarding. In other words, the activity may become independent of the reward upon which it was originally dependent. For example, a man might originally join the merchant marines in order to make a living, but later in life go sailing because it is enjoyable for him to do so even though sailing no longer provides an income. In the latter case, we say that sailing has become functionally autonomous, that is, it continues in the absence of the original motive. Skinner would say that such an activity must ultimately result in primary reinforcement or it would extinguish. Allport, on the other hand, would say that the activity no longer depends on primary reinforcement.

Chaining.

One response can bring the organism into contact with stimuli that act as an S^D for another response, which in turn causes him to experience stimuli that cause a third response, and so on. This process is referred to as *chaining*. In fact, most behavior can be shown to involve some form of chaining. For example, even the lever press in the Skinner box is not an isolated response. The stimuli in the Skinner box act as S^Ds, causing the animal to turn toward the lever. The sight of the lever causes him to approach it and press it. The firing of the feeder mechanism acts as an additional S^D which elicits the response of going to the food cup. Consuming the food pellet acts as an S^D causing the animal to return to the lever and again press it. This sequence of events (chain) is held together by the food pellet, which, of course, is a primary positive reinforcer. It can be said that various elements of a behavioral chain are held together by secondary reinforcers, but that the entire chain depends upon a primary reinforcer.

In order to explain how chaining comes about from Skinner's point of view, one must utilize the concepts of secondary reinforcement and associative shifting. Because of their association with the primary reinforcer, the events prior to the delivery of the food pellet take on secondary reinforcing properties. Thus, the sight of the lever itself becomes a secondary reinforcer, and the response of looking at the lever is reinforced by the sight of the lever. Now, through a process similar to associative shifting (or higher order conditioning which we will discuss in Chapter 7), other stimuli more remote from the lever develop reinforcing properties. Thus, after considerable training, when the animal is placed in the Skinner box, the initial stimuli he encounters will act as an S^D, causing him to orient toward the lever. The sight of the lever at this point acts both as a reinforcer and an S^D eliciting the next response in the chain. The situation is diagrammed in Figure 5–5.

Figure 5–5. An example of chained behavior.

It is important to note that the development of a chained response always acts from the primary reward backwards. As more and more related stimuli take on reinforcing properties, the chain is extended. It is possible, for example, for the chain to gradually extend all the way back to the animal's home cage.

Occasionally rats have been trained to perform complex chained responses such as climbing a staircase, riding in a cart, crossing a bridge, playing a note on a toy piano, entering a small elevator, pulling a chain, riding the elevator down, and receiving a small pellet of food. This chain, too, is developed backwards so that the events that precede the primary reward gradually become secondary reinforcers. When they do, they reward the responses prior to them, and so on along the chain of behaviors.

Chained responses can also occur between two people. For example, seeing someone you know acts as an S^D to say "hello." Your hello acts as an S^D for your friend to say "hi." His "hi" acts not only as a reward for your "hello" but also acts as an S^D for you to say "How are you?" This two-person chain can be diagrammed as follows:

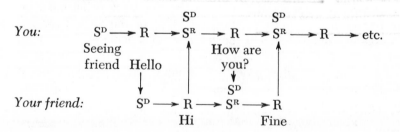

Not only do the consequences of certain responses act as cues for other responses, but certain thoughts can act as S^Ds for other thoughts. Skinner (1953) says,

A response may produce or alter some of the variables which control another response. The result is a "chain." It may have little or no organization. When we go for a walk, roaming the countryside or wandering idly through a museum or store, one episode in our behavior generates conditions responsible for another. We look to one side and are stimulated by an object which causes us to move in its direction. In the course of this movement, we receive aversive stimulation from which we beat a hasty retreat. This generates a condition of satiation or fatigue in which, once free of aversive stimulation, we sit down to rest. And so on. Chaining need not be the result of movement in space. We wander or roam verbally, for example, in a casual conversation or when we "speak our thoughts" in free association [p. 224].

Positive and Negative Reinforcers.

To summarize Skinner's position on reward, we have first of all *primary positive reinforcement*. This is something that is naturally rewarding to the organism and is related to survival, such as food, or water. Any neutral stimulus associated with primary positive reinforcement takes on positive secondary reinforcing characteristics. A *positive reinforcer, either primary or secondary, is something which, when added to the situation by a certain response, increases the probability of that response's recurring*. A *primary negative reinforcer* is something naturally harmful to the organism, such as an aversive high pitched tone or an electric shock. Any neutral stimulus associated with a primary negative reinforcer takes on negative secondary reinforcing characteristics. A *negative reinforcer, either primary or secondary, is something which, when removed from the situation by a certain response, increases the probability of that response's recurring*. For example, if a Skinner box is arranged so that an aversive tone is discontinued when the lever is pressed, the lever press response will soon be learned. In this case, by pressing the lever, the animal avoids experiencing an aversive stimulus.

Thus, reinforcement consists of either giving an organism something it wants, or taking away something it does not want. Each one increases the probability of a response's recurring. Negative reinforcement, however, should not be confused with punishment. Skinner (1953) says:

> Events which are found to be reinforcing are of two sorts. Some reinforcements consist of *presenting* stimuli, of adding something—for example, food, water, or sexual contact—to the situation. These we call *positive* reinforcers. Others consist of *removing* something—for example, a loud noise, a very bright light, extreme cold or heat, or electric shock—from the situation.

These we call *negative* reinforcers. In both cases the effect of reinforcement is the same—the probability of response is increased. We cannot avoid this distinction by arguing that what is reinforcing in the negative case is the *absence* of the bright light, loud noise, and so on; for it is absence after presence which is effective, and this is only another way of saying that the stimulus is removed. The difference between the two cases will be clearer when we consider the *presentation* of a *negative* reinforcer or the *removal* of a *positive*. These are the consequences which we call punishment [p. 73].

Punishment.

Punishment involves either taking away what is positively reinforcing to an organism or applying a negative reinforcer. Thus, punishment is either taking away something someone wants, or giving him something he does not want. Skinner and Thorndike agree on the effectiveness of punishment: it does not decrease the probability of a response. Although punishment suppresses a response as long as it is applied, it does not weaken the habit. Skinner (1971), says:

> Punishment is designed to remove awkward, dangerous, or otherwise unwanted behavior from a repertoire on the assumption that a person who has been punished is less likely to behave in the same way again. Unfortunately, the matter is not that simple. Reward and punishment do not differ merely in the direction of the changes they induce. A child who has been severely punished for sex play is not necessarily less inclined to continue; and a man who has been imprisoned for violent assault is not necessarily less inclined toward violence. Punished behavior is likely to reappear after the punitive contingencies are withdrawn [pp. 61–62].

A typical experiment which led Skinner to this conclusion was done by one of his students, Estes (1944). Two groups of eight rats each were trained to press the lever in a Skinner box. After training, both groups were placed on extinction. One group was extinguished in the regular way, that is, food was withheld following a lever press. Rats in the second group, in addition to not receiving food, received a shock when they pressed the lever. Rats in this group were shocked an average of nine times. There were three extinction sessions and the rats were only shocked during the first of the three sessions. The second and third sessions were the same for both groups. The results indicated that the punished group made fewer responses during the first extinction session than did the nonpunished group. The number of responses made during the second extinction session was about the same for both groups, with the nonpunished group making slightly more responses. From the data of the first two sessions, one can conclude that punishment was effective since the number of responses to extinction was much lower for the punished group. During the third extinction session, however, the previously punished group made many more responses than did the nonpunished group. Thus, in the long run, the originally punished group caught up in the total number of responses to extinction to the nonpunished group. The conclusion was that simple non-reward (extinction) is as effective in extinguishing a habit as non-reward plus punishment. The results of the Estes' study are summarized in Figure 5–6.

Skinner's main argument against the use of punishment is that it is ineffective in the long run. It appears that punishment simply suppresses behavior and when the threat of punishment is removed, the rate with which the behavior occurs returns to its original level. Thus, punishment often appears to be very successful when, in fact, it has produced only a temporary effect. Other arguments against the use of punishment follow.

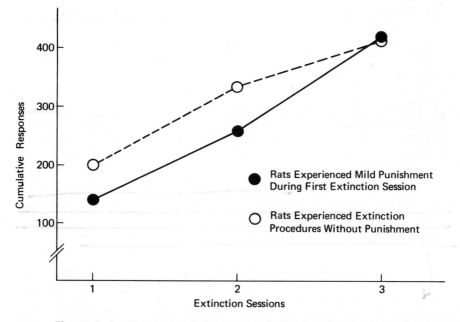

Figure 5–6. The results of Estes' research showing that the effect of punishment is to only temporarily suppress rate of responding (from Estes, 1944, p. 5).

ot her side
effects. [suppresses behavior around one being punished
[tolerance

104   Predominantly Functionalistic Theories

effects of
punishment

1.) It causes unfortunate emotional by-products. The punished organism becomes fearful and this fear generalizes to a number of stimuli related to those present as the punishment was occurring.

2. It indicates what the organism should not do, not what it should do. Compared to reward, punishment conveys practically no information to the organism. Reward indicates that what was done is effective in the situation; therefore, no additional learning is required. Very often punishment informs the organism only that the punished response is one that will not work to bring reward in a given situation, and additional learning is required to hit upon a response that will work.

3.) It justifies inflicting pain on others. This, of course, applies to the use of punishment in child rearing. When a child is spanked, the only thing he may be learning is that under some circumstances it is justifiable to inflict pain on others.

4.) Being in a situation where previously punished behavior could be engaged in without being punished may excuse a child to do so. Thus, in the absence of a punishing agent, children may swear, break windows, be disrespectful to elderly people, push smaller children around, etc. These children have learned to suppress these behaviors when they could lead to punishment, but in the absence of a punishing agent, there is no reason to avoid engaging in these activities.

5.) Punishment elicits aggression toward the punishing agent and others. Punishment causes the punished organism to become aggressive and this aggression may cause additional problems. For example, our penal institutions which use punishment as their major means of control, are filled with highly aggressive individuals who will continue to be aggressive as long as punishment or the threat of punishment is used to control their behavior.

6.) Punishment often replaces one undesirable response with another undesirable response. For example, a child who is spanked for making a mess may now cry instead, just as a man punished for stealing may now become aggressive and commit even more crimes when he has the opportunity.

In their study of how 379 New England suburban mothers brought up their children from birth to kindergarten age, Sears, Maccoby, and Levin (1957) concluded the following concerning the relative effects of emphasizing reward as opposed to punishment in child rearing:

> In our discussion of the training process, we have contrasted punishment with reward. Both are techniques used for changing the child's habitual ways of acting. Do they work equally well? The answer is unequivocally "no"; but to be truly unequivocal, the answer must be understood as referring to the kind of punishment we were able to measure by our interview method. We could not,

as one can with laboratory experiments on white rats or pigeons, examine the effects of punishment on isolated bits of behavior. Our measures of punishment whether of the object-oriented or love-oriented variety, referred to *Levels of Punitiveness* in the mothers. Punitiveness, in contrast with rewardingness, was a quite ineffectual quality for a mother to inject into her child training.

The evidence for this conclusion is overwhelming. The unhappy effects of punishment have run like a dismal thread through our findings. Mothers who punished toilet accidents severely ended up with bedwetting children. Mothers who punished dependency to get rid of it had more dependent children than mothers who did not punish. Mothers who punished aggressive behavior severely had more aggressive children than mothers who punished lightly. They also had more dependent children. Harsh physical punishment was associated with high childhood aggressiveness and with the development of feeding problems.

Our evaluation of punishment is that *it is ineffectual over the long term as a technique for eliminating the kind of behavior toward which it is directed* [p. 484].

Why, then, is punishment so widely used? Because, says Skinner, it is rewarding to the punisher (1953).

Severe punishment unquestionably has an immediate effect in reducing a tendency to act in a given way. This result is no doubt responsible for its widespread use. We "instinctively" attack anyone whose behavior displeases us—perhaps not in physical assault, but with criticism, disapproval, blame, or ridicule. Whether or not there is an inherited tendency to do this, the immediate effect of the practice is reinforcing enough to explain its currency. In the long run, however, punishment does not actually eliminate behavior from a repertoire, and its temporary achievement is obtained at tremendous cost in reducing the over-all efficiency and happiness of the group [p. 190].

It is interesting to note that Skinner himself was never physically punished by his father and only once by his mother, who washed his mouth out with soap for swearing (Skinner, 1967, p. 390).

Alternatives to Punishment.

Skinner lists a number of alternatives to the use of punishment. The circumstances causing the undesirable behavior can be changed, thereby changing the behavior. For example, removing fine china from the living room will eliminate the problem of a child's breaking fine china. The undesirable response can be satiated by letting the organism perform the undesired response until he is sick of it, such as letting a child continue to light matches or eat candy (advice similar to that given by Guthrie as we shall see in Chapter 8). If the undesirable behavior is a function of the child's developmental stage, it can be eliminated by simply waiting for him to outgrow it. Skinner says about the latter approach (1953):

> It is not always easy to put up with the behavior until this happens, especially under the conditions of the average households, but there is some consolation if we know that by carrying the child through a socially unacceptable stage we spare him the later complications arising from punishment [p. 192].

Another method is simply to let time pass, but this approach may take too long. Habits are not soon forgotten. For example, in his "Pigeons in a Pelican" project, mentioned earlier, Skinner found that his trained animals "immediately and correctly" performed their task after six years of inactivity.

Still another alternative to punishment is to reinforce behavior incompatible with the undesirable behavior, e.g., a child is rewarded for reading in the presence of matches rather than striking them.

The best way to discourage an undesirable habit, however, is to ignore it. Skinner says (1953):

> The most effective alternative process (to punishment) is probably *extinction*. This takes time but is much more rapid than allowing the response to be forgotten. The technique seems to be relatively free of objectionable by-products. We recommend it, for example, when we suggest that a parent "pay no attention" to objectionable behavior on the part of his child. If the child's behavior is strong only because it has been reinforced by "getting a rise out of" the parent, it will disappear when this consequence is no longer forthcoming [p. 192].

Generally speaking, behavior persists because it is being rewarded; this is true of undesirable as well as desirable behavior. To eliminate objectionable behavior one needs to find the source of reward and remove it. Behavior that does not lead to reward extinguishes.

Schedules of Reinforcement.

Although Pavlov had done some work with partial reinforcement, using classical conditioning (1927, pp. 384–86), it was Skinner who has thoroughly investigated the topic. Skinner had already published data on the effects of partial reinforcement when Humphreys (1939a, 1939b) startled the psychological world by showing that the extinction process was more rapid following 100 percent reinforcement than after partial reinforcement. That is, if an organism receives a reward every time he makes an appropriate response during learning, and then is placed on extinction, he will extinguish faster than an organism who had only a certain percent of his correct responses rewarded during acquisition. In other words, partial reinforcement leads to greater resistance to extinction than continuous, or 100 percent reinforcement, and this fact is called the *partial reinforcement effect* (PRE).

Skinner studied the partial reinforcement effect extensively and eventually wrote a book with Ferster called *Schedules of Reinforcement* (1957). This book summarized years of research on various types of partial reinforcement. Five schedules of reinforcement have become the most common and they are described below.

1. *Continuous Reinforcement Schedule* (CRF). Using a continuous reinforcement schedule, every correct response during acquisition is rewarded. Usually in a partial reinforcement study, the animal is first trained on a 100 percent reinforcement schedule and then switched to a partial reinforcement schedule. It is difficult to bring about the acquisition of any response when partial reinforcement is used during the initial training period.

2. *Fixed Interval Reinforcement Schedule* (FI). Using a fixed interval reinforcement schedule, the animal is reinforced for a response made only after a set interval of time. For example, only a response following a 3-minute interval is reinforced. At the beginning of the fixed time interval the animal responds slowly, or not at all. As the end of the time interval approaches the animal gradually increases his speed of responding, apparently anticipating the moment of reward. This kind of responding produces a pattern on the cumulative recording referred to as the *fixed-interval scallop*. Such a pattern is shown in Figure 5–7.

The behavior of an animal under this schedule is somewhat similar to the way a person behaves as a deadline approaches. After putting off a certain task as long as possible, the due date is rapidly approaching and activity increases accordingly. Often a student preparing a term paper will act in this manner.

3. *Fixed Ratio Reinforcement Schedule* (FR). An FR schedule of rein-

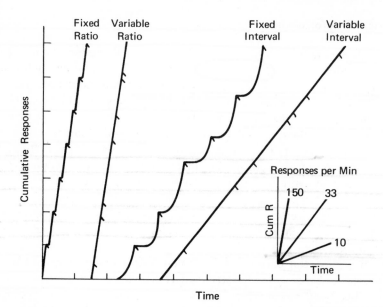

Figure 5–7. Typical cumulative recordings generated by fixed ratio, variable ratio, fixed interval and variable interval reinforcement schedules. The slash marks in the recordings indicate a reinforced response.

forcement occurs when every *n*th response that the animal makes is rewarded. FR5, for example, means that the animal will get rewarded at every fifth response. Here the important factor in determining when a response is rewarded is the number of responses made. Theoretically, an animal on a fixed interval schedule could make just one response at the end of the interval and be rewarded each time he responds. With a fixed ratio schedule, this is not possible; the animal *must* respond a fixed number of times before he is rewarded.

For both the FI and FR reinforcement schedules, a rewarded response is followed by a depression in the rate of responding. This is called the *post-reinforcement pause*. There is considerable speculation as to why such a pause exists. Perhaps the animal learns that the responses immediately following a rewarded response are never rewarded. However, the scallop on the cumulative recording of an FI schedule is usually not found on that of an FR schedule. The FR schedule usually generates a steplike cumulative recording, indicating that the animal temporarily stops responding after a rewarded response and then, at some point, resumes responding at a rapid rate. Such behavior has been characterized as "break and run." In fact, recent evidence suggests that with overtraining on an FI schedule, the scalloping effect gradually disappears and is replaced by the break and run behavior characteristic of FR schedules of reinforcement. A cumulative recording generated by an animal under an FR schedule is shown in Figure 5–7.

4. *Variable Interval Reinforcement Schedule* (VI). With the VI schedule, the animal is rewarded for responses made at the end of time intervals of variable durations. That is, rather than having a fixed time interval, as with FI schedules, the animal is rewarded on the *average* of say, every three minutes, but he may be rewarded immediately after a prior reinforcement, or he may be rewarded after thirty seconds or after seven minutes. This schedule eliminates the scalloping effect found in FI schedules and produces a steady, moderately high response rate. A typical cumulative recording generated by an animal on a VI schedule is shown in Figure 5–7.

5. *Variable Ratio Reinforcement Schedule* (VR). With the FR schedule, an animal is rewarded after making a specific number of responses, say five. With the VR schedule, the animal is rewarded on the *average* of every five responses; thus he might receive two rewards in a row or may make ten or fifteen responses without being rewarded. The VR schedules eliminate the steplike cumulative recording found with the FR schedule and produce the highest response rate of the five schedules we are considering. A cumulative recording produced by an animal under a VR schedule is shown in Figure 5–7.

The VR reinforcement schedule is the one governing the behavior of gamblers at a place like Las Vegas. The faster one pulls the handle of a slot machine, for example, the more frequently one is rewarded.

To summarize, continuous reinforcement yields the least resistance to extinction and the lowest response rate during training. All partial reinforcement schedules produce greater resistance to extinction and higher response rates during training than continuous reinforcement. Generally speaking, the VR schedule produces the highest response rate, FR produces the next highest rate, then VI, followed by FI, and finally CRF.

Verbal Behavior.

Skinner believes that verbal behavior (language) can be explained within the context of reinforcement theory. Talking and listening are responses that are influenced by reward just as any other response. Any utterance, therefore, will tend to be repeated if it is rewarded.

Skinner classified verbal responses in terms of how they were related to reward, that is, in terms of what was being done in order to be rewarded. These classifications are discussed briefly below.

1. Mand.   About the mand, Skinner says (1957):

> A mand is characterized by the unique relationship between the form of the response and the reinforcement characteristically received in a given verbal community. It is sometimes convenient to refer to this relation by saying that a mand "specifies" its reinforcement. *Listen!, Look!, Run!, Stop!,* and *Say yes!* specify the behavior of a listener; but when a hungry diner calls *Bread!,* or *More soup!,* he is specifying the ultimate reinforcement. Frequently both the behavior of the listener and the ultimate reinforcement are specified. The mand *pass the salt!* specifies an action (pass) and an ultimate reinforcement (the salt) [p. 37].

The word *mand* comes from the fact that a demand is being made. When the demand is met, the utterance (mand) is rewarded and next time the need arises, the person is likely to repeat the mand.

2. Tact.   About the tact, Skinner says (1957):

> . . . this type of operant is exemplified when, in the presence of a doll, a child frequently achieves some sort of generalized reinforcement by saying *doll;* or when a teleost fish, or picture thereof, is the occasion upon which the student of zoology is reinforced when he says *teleost fish.* There is no suitable term for this type of operant. "Sign," "symbol," and more technical terms from logic and semantics commit us to special schemes of reference and stress the verbal response itself rather than the controlling relationship. The invented term "tact" will be used here. The term carries a mnemonic suggestion of behavior which "makes contact with" the physical world. A tact may be defined as a verbal operant in which a response of given form is evoked (or at least strengthened) by a particular object or event or property of an object or event. We account for the strength by showing that in the presence of the object or event, a response of that form is characteristically reinforced in a given verbal community [pp. 81–82].

Generally speaking, the tact involves naming objects or events in the environment appropriately, and its reinforcement comes from other people's rewarding the match between the environment and the verbal behavior.

3. *Echoic Behavior*. This is verbal behavior that is rewarded when someone else's verbal response is repeated verbatim. Echoic behavior is often a prerequisite to more complicated verbal behavior; for example, first a child must imitate a word before he can learn how that word is related to other words or other events. Thus, repeating something someone else has said is rewarded, and when this response is learned, it permits the speaker to learn more complex verbal relationships.

4. *Autoclitic Behavior*. According to Skinner (1957), "the term 'autoclitic' is intended to suggest behavior which is based upon or depends upon other verbal behavior" [p. 315]. The main function of autoclitic behavior is to qualify responses, express relations, and provide a grammatical framework for verbal behavior.

The most severe critic of Skinner's explanation of verbal behavior has been Noam Chomsky (1959). Chomsky contends that language is too complex for a child to be able to have learned. Some process other than learning must explain all the verbal utterances that, say, a three-year-old is capable of making. Miller (1965) in fact, points out that there are 10^{20} possible 20-word sentences in the English language, and it would take 1,000 times the estimated age of the earth just to listen to them all. Obviously, says Chomsky, operant conditioning just doesn't explain the complexity of our language capabilities. Chomsky's explanation of language development is that our brain is structured to generate language. The underlying grammatical structure of all human languages reflects an underlying brain structure. That is, we are "wired" to produce grammatical utterances just as a computer can be wired to produce moves in a chess game. Chomsky and Skinner seem to be continuing the nature-nurture debate launched by Plato and Aristotle: Chomsky's deep brain structures theory of language acquisition represents the nature, or Platonic, side and Skinner's view that verbal behavior is shaped by environment represents the nurture, or Aristotelian, side.

Programmed Learning.

Skinner, like Thorndike, was very interested in applying his theory of learning to the process of education. To Skinner, learning proceeds most effectively if (1) the information to be learned is presented in small steps; (2) the learner is given rapid feedback concerning the accuracy of his learning, i.e., he is shown immediately after a learning experience whether he has learned the information correctly or incorrectly; and (3) the learner is able to learn at his own pace.

Skinner learned firsthand that these principles were not being used in the classroom. He reflects upon a visit he made in 1953 to one of his daughter's classes (1967):

> On November 11, as a visiting father, I was sitting in the back of the room in an arithmetic class. Suddenly the situation seemed perfectly absurd. Here were twenty extremely valuable organisms. Through no fault of her own, the teacher was violating almost everything we knew about the learning process [p. 406].

It is interesting to note that the most common teaching technique is the lecture, and the lecture technique violates all three of the above principles. Skinner proposes an alternative teaching technique, programmed learning, which does incorporate all three principles. A device invented to present programmed material has been called a *teaching machine*. The advantages of using a teaching machine are outlined by Skinner as follows (1958):

> The machine itself, of course, does not teach. It simply brings the student into contact with the person who composed the material it presents. It is a labor-saving device because it can bring one programmer into contact with an indefinite number of students. They may suggest mass production, but the effect upon each student is surprisingly like that of a private tutor. The comparison holds in several respects. (i) There is a constant interchange between program and student. Unlike lectures, textbooks, and the usual audio-visual aids, the machine induces sustained activity. The student is always alert and busy. (ii) Like a good tutor, the machine insists that a given point be thoroughly understood, either frame-by-frame or set-by-set, before the student moves on. Lectures, textbooks, and their mechanized equivalents, on the other hand, proceed without making sure that the student understands and easily leave him behind. (iii) Like a good tutor, the machine presents just that material for which the student is ready. It asks him to take only that step which he is at the moment best equipped and most likely to take. (iv) Like a skillful tutor, the machine helps the student to come up with the right answer. It does this in part through the orderly construction of the program and in part with techniques of hinting, prompting, suggesting, and so on, derived from an analysis of verbal behavior. . . (v) Lastly, of course, the machine, like the private tutor, reinforces the student for every correct response, using this immediate feedback not only to shape his behavior most efficiently but to maintain it in strength in a manner which the laymen would describe as "holding the student's interest" [p. 971].

We will have more to say about programmed learning in Chapter 14.

Contingency Contracting.

Contingency contracting is a fairly recent extension of Skinnerian thinking. Briefly, it involves making arrangements so that a person gets something he wants when he acts in a certain way. Some arrangements can be simple and cover simple behavior, such as when a teacher says to a child, "If you sit quietly for five minutes, you can go out and play." Other arrangements can extend over a much longer period of time. For example, if a person has a weight problem, and has difficulty losing weight on his own, he may wish to arrange the environment so that he is rewarded for losing weight. He may, for example, sign over to another person something important to him such as money, a record collection, a stamp collection, or his favorite clothes. Taking money as an example, the person trying to lose weight may put up, say, one hundred dollars and draw up an agreement whereby the other person gives back ten dollars each week if he loses three pounds. Each week that he does not lose at least three pounds, he loses ten dollars. The same kind of arrangement can be made utilizing anything important to the person, and the behavior involved could as easily be smoking as losing weight.

The term "contingency contracting" comes from the fact that an agreement (contract) is made that certain activities will be rewarded that otherwise may not have been. In other words, the contract rearranges the reinforcement contingencies in the environment causing them to be responsive to behavior patterns that one hopes to modify in some way.

Contingency contracting need not involve a second person; one can follow these procedures alone by giving oneself a "treat" of some kind each day one goes without smoking, or drinking, or overeating. For a more detailed discussion of contingency contracting see Homme, Csanyi, Gonzales, and Rechs (1970).

Skinner's Attitude Toward Learning Theory.

Skinner believes that it is unnecessary to formulate complicated theories to study human behavior, and he believes it is unnecessary to know the physiological correlates of behavior. He believes that behavioral events must be described in terms of things that directly affect behavior, and that it is logically inconsistent to attempt to explain behavior in terms of physiological events. For this reason, Skinner's method of research has been called "the empty organism approach."

Skinner thinks that complex theories of learning, such as Hull's (Chapter 6), are time-consuming and wasteful. Some day such theories may be useful in psychology, but not until we have collected much more basic data. Our main concern at this time should be, Skinner believes, to discover basic relationships between classes of stimuli and classes of responses. Therefore, the use of theory in studying the learning process cannot be justified. Skinner says (1950):

> Research designed with respect to theory is also likely to be wasteful. That a theory generates research does not prove its value unless the research is valuable. Much useless experimentation results from theories, and much energy and skill are absorbed by them. Most theories are eventually over-thrown, and the greater part of the associated research is discarded. This could be justified if it were true that productive research requires a theory—as is, of course, often claimed. It is argued that research would be aimless and disorganized without a theory to guide it. The view is supported by psychological texts which take their cue from the logicians rather than empirical science and describe thinking as necessarily involving stages of hypothesis, deduction, experimental test, and confirmation. But this is not the way most scientists actually work. It is possible to design significant experiments for other reasons, and the possibility to be examined is that such research will lead more directly to the kind of information which a science usually accumulates [pp. 194–95].

Skinner's approach to research is to do a *functional analysis* between stimulating events and measurable behavior. Skinner says (1953):

> The external variables of which behavior is a function provide for what may be called a causal or functional analysis. We undertake to predict and control the behavior of the individual organism. This is our "dependent variable"—the effect for which we are to find the cause. Our "independent variables"—the causes of behavior—are the external conditions of which behavior is a function. Relations between the two—the "cause-and-effect relationships" in behavior—are the laws of a science. A synthesis of these laws expressed in quantitative terms yields a comprehensive picture of the organism as a behaving system [p. 35].

Thus, Skinner manipulates hours of food or water deprivation and notes the effect on the rate with which the lever press response is learned; or he observes the effect of schedules of reinforcement on response rate or resistance to extinction. In interpreting the results of his research, Skinner stays very close to the data, that is, if partial reinforcement produces greater resistance to extinction than does 100 percent reinforcement, that is a fact and that is all that can be said. In other words, Skinner does not attempt to explain why this is the case.

Even in deciding *what* to investigate, Skinner claims he is not guided by theoretical notions, but rather uses a hit-and-miss process. He tries first one thing and then another. If he sees one line of research is not producing anything worthwhile, he will shift to something that looks more fruitful and will continue in this trial-and-error fashion until he hits upon something of value. This rather liberal attitude toward scientific investigation is summarized in Skinner's article, "A Case Study in Scientific Method" (1956).

The Need for a Technology of Behavior.

Skinner feels very strongly that a carefully worked out behavior technology could solve many human problems; yet many people would oppose such a technology because it seems to challenge a number of our cherished beliefs about ourselves, especially that human beings are rational, free, and dignified. Skinner believes that these beliefs are now interfering with the solution of our major problems and also preventing the development of the very tool that could solve them. Skinner says (1971):

> What we need is a technology of behavior. We could solve our problems quickly enough if we could adjust the growth of the world's population as precisely as we adjust the course of a spaceship, or improve agriculture and industry with some of the confidence with which we accelerate high-energy particles, or move toward a peaceful world with something like the steady progress with which physics has approached absolute zero (even though both remain presumably out of reach). But a behavioral technology comparable in power and precision to physical and biological technology is lacking, and those who do not find the very possibility ridiculous are more likely to be frightened by it than reassured. That is how far we are from "understanding human issues" in the sense in which physics and biology understand their fields, and how far we are from preventing the catastrophe toward which the world seems to be inexorably moving [p. 5].

Elsewhere, Skinner says (1953):

> . . . the traditional view of human nature in Western culture is well known. The conception of a free, responsible individual is embedded in our language and pervades our practices, codes, and

beliefs. Given an example of human behavior, most people can describe it immediately in terms of such a conception. The practice is so natural that it is seldom examined. A scientific formulation, on the other hand, is new and strange. Very few people have any notion of the extent to which a science of human behavior is indeed possible. In what way can the behavior of the individual or of groups of individuals be predicted and controlled? What are laws of behavior like? What over-all conception of the human organism as a behaving system emerges? It is only when we have answered these questions, at least in a preliminary fashion, that we may consider the implications of a science of human behavior with respect to either a theory of human nature or the management of human affairs [pp. 9–10].

Skinner's theory of learning has had, and is having, a profound influence on psychology. No matter what area of psychology one studies, he is apt to find reference to some aspect of Skinner's work. As we noted in Chapter 2, a characteristic of any good theory is that it generates research, and Skinner's theory has certainly done that. In the next section we shall review the work of an important researcher who has been influenced by Skinner's work.

DAVID PREMACK

Traditionally, reinforcers have been thought of as stimuli. A primary reinforcer is usually thought of as being related to an organism's survival, and a secondary reinforcer is a stimulus that has been consistently paired with a primary reinforcer. Premack, however, has suggested that all responses be thought of as potential reinforcers. Specifically, he suggests that any response that occurs with a fairly high frequency can be used to reinforce a response that occurs with a relatively lower frequency. Using Premack's notion of reward, one would allow an organism to engage freely in whatever activities it wanted to and carefully record what activities were engaged in, and with what frequency. Afterwards, the various activities that the organism engaged in would be arranged in a hierarchy. The activity that was engaged in most frequently would be listed first, the next frequently engaged in activity would be listed next, and so on. By referring to this list, the experimenter would know exactly what could and could not be used to reinforce that particular organism. Say, for example, it was found that in a tweny-four hour period, the activity engaged in most frequently by a rat was eating, then drinking, then running in an activity wheel, then grooming, and finally, gazing out

David Premack

of the cage. According to Premack, allowing the animal to eat could be used to reinforce any of the other activities. For example, if the animal was allowed to eat each time he groomed himself, grooming would increase in frequency. Likewise, allowing the animal to groom himself could be used to reward the animal for looking outside the cage. The opportunity to look outside the cage, however, could not be used to reward any of the other activities, because they all occurred with a greater frequency than the response of looking outside the cage.

According to Premack, the way to find out what can be used as a reinforcer is to observe the organism's behavior while he has the opportunity to engage in any number of activities, and the activities that he engages in most often can be used to reward the activities that he engages in less often.

In summary we can say that if one activity occurs more often than another, it can be used to reinforce the activity that occurs less often. This is called the *Premack principle* and it seems to hold for humans as well as for lower organisms.

In order to test his theory, Premack (1959) allowed thirty-one first-grade children to either play a pinball machine or to operate a candy dispenser as often as they wanted. Some of the children played mainly with the pinball machine, and they were called "manipulators." The children who were primarily interested in the candy dispenser were called "eaters." The first phase of the study merely determined the children's preferences for these two events.

In the second phase of the study, the groups of "manipulators" and "eaters" were each subdivided into two groups. One group was placed on "manipulate-eat" contingencies, where the children had to play the pinball machine before they were allowed to operate the candy dispenser. The other group was placed on "eat-manipulate" contingencies, where they had to operate the candy dispenser before they could play the pinball machine. It was found that for the "manipulators" the "manipulate-eat" arrangement made little difference in their behavior. They simply went right on playing the pinball machine as before. Under the "eat-manipulate" conditions, however, the frequency of eating went way up for the manipulators, since they now had to eat in order to play the pinball machine. Likewise, for the "eaters" the "eat-manipulate" condition made little difference. They simply went on eating candy as before. But under the "manipulate-eat" conditions, their frequency of playing the pinball machine went way up. Thus, Premack found support for his contention that a less frequently engaged in activity can be rewarded by the opportunity to engage in a more frequently engaged in activity.

When preferences change, the reinforcers also change. For example, as long as an animal is hungry, he will eat frequently, and therefore the opportunity to eat can be used to reinforce any number of activities. When the animal is satiated, however, the frequency of his eating will decrease and the opportunity to eat will become ineffective as a reinforcer. Premack demonstrated the reversibility of reinforcement in a study involving a running response and a drinking response (1962). It was found that if animals were deprived of water for a considerable length of time, they will turn an activity wheel in order to gain access to water. But they would not increase their drinking in order to run in the activity wheel. That is, drinking reinforces running, but running did not reinforce drinking. This is what one would predict from traditional reinforcement theory. Premack also found that if an animal was allowed to drink all the water it wanted but was prevented from running in the activity wheel, the situation was reversed. Under these circumstances, drinking activity increased if it resulted in the animal having the opportunity to run, but running did not increase if it allowed the animal to drink. That is, now running could reinforce drinking, but not vice versa.

The implications of Premack's research are far-reaching. For one thing, what can act as a reward becomes a very personal and continuously changing thing. The teacher can apply this knowledge by noticing individual children's preferences in a free choice situation and determining their rewards accordingly. For one child, the opportunity to run and play may be a reinforcer; for another child, playing with clay may be a reinforcer. The idea of recess as a way to improve the performance of the class as a whole will need to be looked at more carefully. For examples of how the Premack principle can be used to control the behavior of school children, see Homme, deBaca, Divine, Steinhorst, and Rickert (1963).

HARRY HELSON

Another approach that shows the relativity of reinforcement is that of Harry Helson. Briefly, Helson's _adaptation-level theory_ states that for any class of experiences, there are two extremes with a neutral point in between them. The neutral point is the adaptation level (AL). For example, if one is asked to judge weights, some weights will be thought of as heavy, some light, and some in between. In fact, those weights falling on one side of the AL will tend to be judged as heavy, and those falling on the other side of AL will tend to be judged as light. The magnitude of the lightness or heaviness is determined by the distance from AL. In other words, a weight falling right on AL will be judged as neither heavy nor light but in between; a weight that falls just to the right of the AL

Harry Helson

will tend to be judged as "slightly heavy"; and a weight that falls way to the right of the AL will tend to be judged as "very heavy." Clearly the extremes for any experience will change and therefore, one's adaptation-level will change. How one interprets a social date, or pain, or a meal, or the difficulty of a test will depend upon one's total experiences with dates, pain, meals, or tests. When reacting to a test, for example, one places it somewhere on a continuum between the easiest test ever taken and the hardest test ever taken. If the test is between the two extremes, that is, at the adaptation-level, the person will say the test was neither easy nor hard. But any test that falls on one side of the adaptation-level will be interpreted as hard, and any test that falls on the other side of the adaptation-level will be interpreted as easy. Thus, according to Helson's theory, what is rewarding and what is not is based to a large extent on the individual's experiences. (See Helson, 1964, for a review of adaptation-level theory.) No doubt, the topic of the relativity of reinforcement will generate considerable research in the future.

DISCUSSION QUESTIONS

1. Outline the procedure you would use while following Skinner's theory to increase the probability of a child's becoming a creative adult.
2. Would you use the same rewards to manipulate the behavior of both children and adults? If not, what would make the difference?
3. Are there some forms of adult human behavior for which you feel Skinner's theory is not applicable? Explain.
4. What would characterize the classroom procedures suggested by Skinner's theory of learning? List a few differences between these procedures and those now being followed in our schools.
5. Assuming the conclusions Skinner reached concerning the effectiveness of punishment are valid, what major change would they suggest in the area of child rearing? Criminal behavior? Religion? Education?
6. What is the partial reinforcement effect? Briefly describe the basic reinforcement schedules that Skinner studied.
7. Propose a theory designed to account for the partial reinforcement effect.
8. What is contingency contracting?

9. From Skinner's point of view, what are the advantages of programmed learning and teaching machines over the traditional lecture technique of teaching?

10. According to Skinner, why have we not developed a more adequate technology of behavior in this country? What would need to be done before man would be willing to utilize such a technology in solving his problems?

11. Discuss the relativity of reinforcement from the point of view of both Premack and Helson.

12. Discuss chaining from Skinner's point of view.

13. Explain language development from Skinner's point of view. Explain Chomsky's opposition to Skinner's explanation of language development.

GLOSSARY

Adaptation-Level Theory. The theory proposed by Helson that between extremes in experience there is a neutral point or what he calls an adaptation level. For example, a weight that corresponds to the individual's adaptation level for weights will be interpreted as neither heavy nor light but in between the two.

Autoclitic behavior. Provides a grammatical framework for verbal behavior.

Chaining. According to Skinner, chaining occurs when one response brings the organism into proximity with stimuli that both reward the last response and cause the next response. That response in turn causes the organism to experience stimuli that both reward the response and cause the next response, and so on.

Contingency contracting. Making arrangements, sometimes with another person, so that certain behavior will be rewarded. For example, each time the person goes a week without smoking he receives ten dollars.

Contingent reinforcement. Reinforcement that only occurs if a specific response is made. If the response is not made, the organism is not rewarded.

Continuous reinforcement (CRF). The condition where the organism is rewarded each time he makes an appropriate response.

Cumulative recording. A special kind of graphing technique used by Skinner. Each time a response is made, the cumulative recording rises one notch and remains at that level until another response is made. The steepness of the line, therefore, indicates rate of responding.

Differential reinforcement. The condition where some responses made by the organism are reinforced and others are not.

Discriminative operant. An operant response that is made selectively to one set of circumstances but not to another set of circumstances.

Discriminative stimulus (S^D). A cue or signal indicating that if a certain operant response is made it will be rewarded.

Echoic behavior. Repeating someone else's verbal utterances.

Extinction of an operant response. In operant conditioning, extinction involves the gradual decrease in the *frequency* with which a conditioned response occurs after it is no longer rewarded, whereas in classical conditioning, the extinction of a conditioned response involves the gradual decrease in *amplitude* of the conditioned response following the removal of reward. When the frequency of an operant response returns to its operant level, it is said to be extinguished.

Fixed interval reinforcement schedule (FI). The condition where only the response made after a certain interval of time has passed is rewarded.

Fixed ratio reinforcement schedule (FR). The condition where only the *n*th response made is rewarded.

Functional analysis. The investigation of how certain stimuli and certain responses vary together. Skinner's approach to research was to avoid theorizing and to deal only with the manipulation of observable stimuli and note how their manipulation affected behavior; sometimes called the "empty organism" approach to research.

Functional autonomy. A term introduced by Gordon Allport to explain behavior that apparently occurs independently of external reward. Such behavior, according to Allport, was originally dependent upon reward, but eventually becomes autonomous or self-rewarding.

Generalized reinforcers. Stimuli that derive their reinforcement properties from being paired with more than one primary reinforcer. Generalized reinforcers have wide application since their effectiveness does not depend on any particular need of the organism.

Magazine training. Training the animal to approach the food cup when he hears the feeder mechanism operate. This way, the click of the feeder mechanism is associated with food and thereby becomes a secondary reinforcer.

Mand. A verbal command that is rewarded when the listener carries out the command. For example, the mand "pass the salt" is rewarded when the person receives the salt.

Noncontingent reinforcement. Reinforcement that occurs independently of the organism's behavior.

Operant behavior. Behavior that is simply emitted by the organism rather than elicited by a known stimulus. Operant behavior is under the control of its consequences.

Operant conditioning. Increasing the rate with which a response occurs or the probability of a response by arranging the situation so that the occurrence of that response is followed by reward. Also called type R conditioning.

Operant level. The frequency with which an operant response occurs before it is systematically reinforced.

Partial reinforcement effect (PRE). The fact that a response that has been rewarded only sometimes takes longer to extinguish than a response that had been rewarded each time it occurred.

Primary negative reinforcer. A stimulus related to the organism's survival which, when removed from the situation following a response, increases the probability of the response's recurring.

Primary positive reinforcer. A stimulus related to the organism's survival which, when added to the situation following a response, increases the probability of the response's recurring.

Programmed learning. A procedure that provides information to the learner in small steps, guarantees immediate feedback concerning whether or not the material was learned properly, and allows the learner to determine the pace with which he goes through the material.

Punishment. The procedure whereby a negative reinforcer is made to be contingent on a response.

Resistance to extinction. The number of nonreinforced responses that occur before an operant response returns to its operant level.

Respondent behavior. Behavior elicited by a known stimulus.

Respondent conditioning. The same as classical conditioning; also called type S conditioning.

Secondary negative reinforcer. A previously neutral stimulus that has taken on reinforcing properties through its pairing with a primary negative reinforcer.

Secondary positive reinforcer. A previously neutral stimulus that has taken on reinforcing properties through its pairing with a primary positive reinforcer.

Shaping. The process whereby a desired response is encouraged through the use of differential reinforcement and successive approximation rather than simply waiting for it to occur.

Skinner box. An experimental test chamber usually consisting of a grid floor, a lever, a light, and a food cup.

Spontaneous recovery of an operant response. The increased frequency with which a conditioned operant response occurs following a delay after extinction and with no further training.

Successive approximation. Rewarding only those responses that become increasingly similar to the response that is finally desired; a component of the process of shaping.

Superstitious behavior. Behavior that looks as if it is governed by the belief that it must be engaged in before reward can be obtained, whereas, in reality, the behavior has nothing to do with the presence or absence of reward. Superstitious behavior results from noncontingent reinforcement.

Tact. The verbal behavior of naming things. Such behavior results in reward when objects or events are named correctly.

Teaching machine. A device used to present programmed material.

Variable interval reinforcement schedule (VI). The condition where only the response made after the passage of some *average* interval of time is rewarded.

Variable ratio reinforcement schedule (VR). The condition where a certain *average* number of responses need to be made before the organism is rewarded.

6

Clark Leonard Hull

Clark L. Hull (1884–1952) received his Ph.D. from the University of Wisconsin in 1918 where he also taught from 1916 to 1929. In 1929 he moved to Yale where he stayed until his death.

Hull's career can be divided into three separate parts. His first major concern was with the testing of aptitudes. He gathered material on aptitude testing while teaching a course on the topic at the University of Wisconsin, and published a book entitled *Aptitude Testing* in 1928. Hull's second major concern was with hypnosis and after a long study of the hypnotic process, he wrote a book entitled *Hypnosis and Suggestibility* (1933b). His third concern, and the work for which he is most famous, was the study of the learning process. Hull's first major book on learning, *Principles of Behavior* (1943), radically changed the study of learning. It was the first attempt to apply comprehensive scientific theory to the study of a complex psychological phenomenon. We saw in Chapter 3 that Ebbinghaus was the first to use an experiment to investigate learning. But it was Hull who first utilized a rigorous theory to study learning. Hull's theory, as presented in 1943, was extended in 1952 in *A Behavior System*. He intended to write a third book on learning, but never did.

For his efforts, Hull received the Warren Medal in 1945 from the Society of Experimental Psychology. The award read:

To Clark L. Hull: For his careful development of a systematic theory of behavior. This theory has stimulated much research and it has been developed in a precise and quantitative form so as to permit predictions which can be tested empirically. The theory thus contains within itself the seeds of its own ultimate verification and of its own possible final disproof. A truly unique achievement in the history of psychology to date.

Hull was a cripple most of his life. He suffered partial paralysis from polio which he had as a child. In 1948, he had a coronary attack and four years later he died. In the last book he wrote (*A Behavior System*), he expressed regret that the third book that he intended to write on learning would never be written.

Even though Hull felt that his theory was incomplete, it has had a profound influence on learning theory throughout the world. Kenneth Spence, one of Hull's many famous students, indicates that 40 percent of all experiments in the *Journal of Experimental Psychology* and in the *Journal of Comparative and Physiological Psychology* during the period

Clark Leonard Hull

between 1941 and 1950 refer to some aspect of Hull's work, and when one looks only at the areas of learning and motivation, this figure rises to 70 percent (Spence, 1952). Ruja (1956) reports that in the *Journal of Abnormal and Social Psychology* between 1949 and 1952 there are 105 references to Hull's *Principles of Behavior,* and the next most popular reference was listed only 25 times. In fact, it is still quite common for the student of learning to come across numerous references to Hull's work while going through the psychological journals. By any measure, Clark Hull was a major contributor to our knowledge of the learning process.

Hull, like most functionalistic learning theorists, was significantly influenced by Darwin's writings. Because learning is adaptive, Hull believed, it is related to survival. The purpose of Hull's theory was to explain this adaptive behavior and to understand the variables affecting it. In fact, it can be said that Hull was interested in developing a theory that explained how bodily needs, the environment, and behavior interact so as to increase the probability of the organism's surviving.

Hull's Approach to Theorizing.

As a first step in developing his theory, Hull reviewed the research on learning up to that time. Next, he attempted to summarize those findings. Finally, he attempted to deduce testable consequences from those summary principles. We will look at this approach to theory construction in somewhat more detail below.

Hull's approach to theory construction has been called *logical-deductive* or *hypothetical-deductive.* His theory has a logical structure of postulates and theorems much like Euclid's geometry. The postulates are general statements about behavior which cannot be directly verified. From the postulates, theorems are generated. The theorems follow logically— that is, they are *deduced*—from the postulates. Although the postulates are not testable, the theorems that they generate can be tested. An experiment is designed to test the theorem and if the results of the experiment are as predicted, the theorem is said to be correct and the postulate from which it is deduced gains in strength. If the experiment does not come out in the predicted direction, the theorem is said to be incorrect, and the postulate from which it is deduced must either be revised or abandoned.

It can be seen that this type of theorizing creates a dynamic, open-ended system. Hypotheses are constantly being generated; some of them are supported by experimental outcomes, some are not. When experiments come out in a predicted direction, the whole theory, including postulates and theorems, is strengthened. When the experiments do not come out as predicted, the theory is weakened and must be revised. A theory such as the one suggested by Hull must continually be updated in accordance with the outcome of empirical investigation.

Hull (1943) says:

> Empirical observation, supplemented by shrewd conjecture, is the main source of the primary principles or postulates of a science. Such formulations, when taken in various combinations together with relevant antecedent conditions, yield inferences or theorems, of which some may agree with the empirical outcome of the conditions in question, and some may not. Primary propositions yielding logical deductions which consistently agree with the observed empirical outcome are retained, whereas those which disagree are rejected or modified. As the sifting of this trial-and-erorr process continues, there gradually emerges a limited series of primary principles whose joint implications are progressively more likely to agree with relevant observations. Deductions made from these surviving postulates, while never absolutely certain, do at length become highly trustworthy. This is in fact the present status of the primary principles of the major physical sciences [p. 382].

It should be recalled, as was mentioned in Chapter 2, that any scientific theory is merely a tool that aids the researcher in synthesizing facts and in knowing where to look for new information. The ultimate value of a theory is determined by how well it agrees with observed facts, or in this case, with the outcome of experiments. The ultimate authority in science is the empirical world. Although a theory such as Hull's can become very abstract, still it must make statements concerning observable events. As was pointed out in Chapter 2, no matter how elaborate and abstract a theory becomes, it must ultimately be reducible to *thing* language, that is, it must generate propositions that are empirically verifiable; Hull's theory does exactly that.

MAJOR THEORETICAL CONCEPTS

Although Hull's 1952 version of his theory is highly complex, it is still simply an extension of his 1943 theory; therefore the best way to summarize Hull's thoughts on learning is to outline the 1943 version of his theory and then to point out the major changes that were made in 1952. Following that plan, we will first discuss Hull's sixteen major postulates as they appeared in 1943 and then, later in the chapter, we will turn to the major revisions Hull made in his theory in 1952.

Postulate 1. Sensing the External Environment and the Stimulus Trace.

External stimulation triggers an afferent (sensory) neural impulse that outlasts the environmental stimulation. Thus, Hull postulates the existence of a stimulus trace that continues for a few seconds after the stimulus event has terminated. Because this afferent neural impulse becomes associated with a response, Hull changes the traditional S–R formula to S–s–R, where s is the stimulus trace. For Hull, the association of interest is between s and R. The stimulus trace ultimately causes an efferent (motor) neural reaction (r) that results in an overt response. Thus we have S–s–r–R, where S is external stimulation, s is the stimulus trace, r is the firing of motor neurons, and R is an overt response.

Postulate 2. The Interaction of Sensory Impulses.

This postulate indicates the complexity of stimulation and, therefore, the difficulties in predicting behavior. Behavior is seldom a function of only one stimulus. Rather, it is a function of many stimuli converging upon the organism at any given time. These many stimuli and their related traces interact with one another and their synthesis determines behavior. We can now refine the S–R formula further as follows:

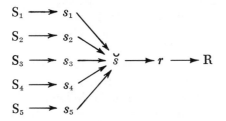

where $\breve{s}$ represents the combined effects of the five stimuli acting upon the organism at the moment.

Postulate 3. Unlearned Behavior.

Hull believed that the organism is born with a hierarchy of responses that is triggered when a need arises. For example, if a foreign object enters the eye, considerable blinking and tear secretion may follow automatically. If the temperature varies from that which is optimal for normal bodily functioning, the organism may sweat or shiver. Likewise, experiencing pain, hunger, or thirst will trigger certain innate response patterns that have a high probability of reducing the effects of those conditions.

The term hierarchy is used in reference to these responses because more than one reaction may occur. If the first innate response pattern does not alleviate a need, another pattern will occur. If the second response pattern does not reduce the need, still another will occur, and so on. If none of the innate behavior patterns is effective in reducing the need, the organism will have to *learn* new response patterns. Thus, according to Hull, learning is required only when innate neural mechanisms and their related responses fail to reduce an organism's need. Generally, as long as either innate responses or previously learned responses are effective in satisfying needs, there is no reason to learn new responses. In this sense, learning depends upon failure.

Postulate 4. Contiguity and Drive Reduction as Necessary Conditions for Learning.

This postulate states that if a stimulus leads to a response, and if the response results in the satisfaction of a biological need, then the association between the stimulus and the response is strengthened. The more often the stimulus and the response that leads to need satisfaction are paired, the stronger the relationship between the stimulus and the response becomes. On this basic point, Hull is in complete agreement with Thorndike's revised law of effect. Hull, however, is more specific about what constitutes a "satisfying state of affairs." Primary reinforcement, according to Hull, must involve need satisfaction, or what Hull called *drive reduction.*

Postulate 4 also describes a secondary reinforcer as (Hull, 1943, p. 178): ". . . a stimulus which has been closely and consistently associated with the diminution of a need." Secondary reinforcement following a response will also increase the strength of the association between that response and the stimulus with which it was contiguous. To summarize, we can say that if a stimulus is followed by a response, which in turn is followed by reinforcement (either primary or secondary), the association between that stimulus and that response is strengthened. It can also be said that the "habit" of giving that response to that stimulus gets stronger. Hull's term, *habit strength,* will be explained below.

Although Hull, like Thorndike and Skinner, was very much a reinforcement theorist, he was more specific about his definition of reinforcement. Skinner simply said that a reinforcer was anything that increased the rate with which a response occurred, and Thorndike talked about a nebulous "satisfying" or "annoying" state of affairs. For Hull, reinforcement was drive reduction, and reinforcers were stimuli that were capable of reducing a drive. Thus, reinforcement was a biological condition, and a reinforcer was anything that reduced that condition. We shall see in the next chapter that although Pavlov used the term *reinforcement,* he was not a reinforcement theorist in the same sense that Hull, Thorndike, and Skinner were. For Pavlov, a reinforcement was used simply because it reliably elicited a certain response. Pavlov was much more interested in the effects of contiguity than in the effects of reinforcement.

Habit Strength ($_sH_R$).

Habit strength is one of Hull's most important concepts, and as stated above, it refers to the strength of the association between a stimulus and a response. As the number of reinforced pairings between a stimulus and a response goes up, the habit strength of that association goes up. The mathematical formula that describes the relationship between $_sH_R$ and number of reinforced pairings between S and R is as follows:

$$_sH_R = 1 - 10^{-0.0305\,N}$$

N is the number of reinforced pairings between S and R. This formula generates a negatively accelerated learning curve, which means early

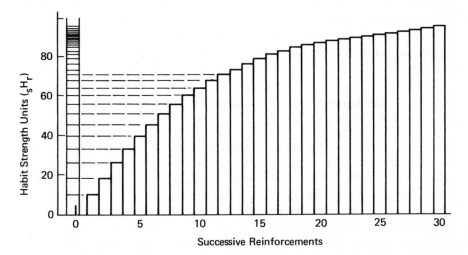

Figure 6–1. The relationship between gains in habit strength ($_sH_R$) and successive reinforcements (from Hull, 1943, p. 116).

reinforced pairings have more of an effect on learning than do later ones. In fact, a point is reached where additional reinforced pairings have no effect on learning. Figure 6–1 shows that early reinforcements have more of an effect on learning than do later ones.

Postulate 5. Stimulus Generalization.

Here Hull is saying that the ability of a stimulus (other than the one used during conditioning) to elicit a conditioned response is determined by its similarity to the stimulus used during training. Thus, $_sH_R$ will generalize from one stimulus to another to the extent that the two stimuli are similar. This postulate also indicates that prior experience will effect current learning, that is, learning that took place under similar conditions will transfer to the new learning situation. Hull called this *generalized habit strength* which he symbolized $_s\overline{H}_R$. This postulate essentially described Thorndike's identical elements theory of the transfer of training.

Postulate 6. Stimuli Associated with Drives.

Biological deficiency in the organism produces a drive state (D) and each drive has specific stimuli associated with it. Hunger pangs that accompany the hunger drive and dry mouth, lips, and throat that accompany the thirst drive are examples. The existence of specific drive stimuli make it possible to teach an animal to behave in one way under one drive and another way under another drive. For example, an animal can be taught to turn right in a T-maze when he is hungry, and to turn left when he is thirsty. As we will see later in the chapter, the concept of drive stimuli became very important in Hull's 1952 revision of his theory.

Postulate 7. Reaction Potential as a Function of Drive and Habit Strength.

The likelihood of a learned response's being made at any given moment is called *reaction potential* and is symbolized $_sE_R$. Reaction potential is a function of both habit strength ($_sH_R$) and drive (D). In order for a learned response to occur, $_sH_R$ has to be activated by D. Drive does not direct behavior; it simply arouses it and intensifies it. Without drive, the animal would not emit a learned response even though there had been a large number of reinforced pairings between a stimulus and a response. Thus, if an animal has learned to press a bar in a Skinner box in order to obtain food, he would press the bar only when he was hungry, no matter how well he was trained. The basic components of Hull's theory that we have covered thus far can be combined into the following formula:

$$\text{Reaction potential} = {}_sE_R = {}_sH_R \times D$$

Thus, reaction potential is a function of how often the response was rewarded in that situation and the extent to which a drive is present. By looking at the above formula, it can be seen that if either ${}_sH_R$ or D were zero, ${}_sE_R$ would necessarily be zero. As we shall see in postulates 13 to 15, in addition to being related to response probability, ${}_sE_R$ is also related to resistance to extinction, latency, and amplitude of response.

Postulate 8. Responding Causes Fatigue which Operates Against the Elicitation of a Conditioned Response.

Responding requires work, and work results in fatigue. Fatigue eventually acts to inhibit responding. *Reactive inhibition* (I_R) is caused by the fatigue associated with muscular activity and is related to the amount of work involved in performing a task. Since this form of inhibition is related to fatigue, it automatically dissipates when the organism stops performing. This concept has been used to explain the spontaneous recovery of a conditioned response after extinction. That is, the animal may stop responding because of the buildup of I_R. After a rest, the I_R dissipates and the animal commences to respond once again. For Hull, extinction is not only a function of nonreinforcement, but it is also influenced by the buildup of reactive inhibition.

I_R has also been used to explain the *reminiscence effect*, which is the improvement of performance following the cessation of practice. For example, if an experimental subject is trained to track a rotating disc with a stylus, his performance will gradually improve until it reaches some asymptotic (maximal) level. If, after his asymptotic level is reached, the subject is allowed to rest for a few minutes and is then asked to track the disc again, his performance will tend to exceed his previous asymptotic level. This is called the reminiscence effect and it is explained by assuming that I_R builds up during training and operates against tracking performance. After a rest, I_R dissipates and performance improves. Figure 6–2 presents an example of the reminiscence effect.

Additional support for Hull's notion of I_R comes from research on the difference between *massed* and *distributed* practice. It is consistently

Figure 6–2. There were three groups of subjects in this experiment which measured ability to track a rotating disc with a stylus. One group received distributed practice; another received massed practice; and a third group was first given massed practice, then a rest period, and then massed practice again. Clearly, the group receiving distributed practice performed much better than the other two groups. The vast improvement of the massed practice-rest group following the rest is an example of the reminiscence effect.

From Gregory A. Kimble and Norman Garmezy, "Principles of General Psychology," 3rd ed. © 1968, The Ronald Press Co., New York, N. Y.

found that when practice trials are spaced far apart (distributed practice), performance is superior to what it is when practice trials are close together (massed practice). On a tracking task, for example, subjects resting between practice trials reach higher asymptotic levels of performance than subjects who go immediately from one practice trial to the next. Figure 6–2 shows the difference in performance under massed and distributed practice conditions.

Postulate 9. The Learned Response of Not Responding.

Fatigue being a negative drive state, it follows that not responding would be rewarding. Not responding allows I_R to dissipate, thereby reducing the negative drive of fatigue. The learned response of not responding is called *conditioned inhibition,* which is symbolized $_sI_R$. Both I_R and $_sI_R$ operate *against* the elicitation of a learned response and are therefore subtracted from reaction potential ($_sE_R$). When I_R and $_sI_R$ are subtracted from $_sE_R$, *effective reaction potential* is the result. Effective reaction potential is symbolized $_s\bar{E}_R$.

$$\text{Effective reaction potential} = {}_s\bar{E}_R = {}_sH_R \times D - (I_R + {}_sI_R).$$

Postulate 10. Factors Tending to Inhibit a Learned Response Change from Moment to Moment.

According to Hull, there is an "inhibitory potentiality," which varies from moment to moment and operates against the elicitation of a learned response. This "inhibitory potentiality" is called the *oscillation effect* and is symbolized $_sO_R$.

The oscillation effect was the "wild card" in Hull's theory—it is his way of taking into consideration the probabilistic nature of predictions concerning behavior. There is, he says, a factor operating against the elicitation of a learned response, whose effect varies from moment to moment but always operates within a certain range of values, that is, although the range of the inhibitory factor is set, the value that may be manifested at any time could vary within that range. The values of this inhibitory factor are assumed to be normally distributed with middle values most likely to occur. If, by chance, a large inhibitory value does occur, it considerably reduces the chances of a learned response's being made. This oscillation effect ($_sO_R$) explains why a learned response may be elicited on one trial but not on the next. Predictions concerning behavior based upon the value of $_s\bar{E}_R$ will always be influenced by the fluctuating values of $_sO_R$ and will thus always be probabilistic in nature. $_sO_R$ must be subtracted from effective reaction potential ($_s\bar{E}_R$) which creates *momentary effective reaction potential,* symbolized $_s\dot{\bar{E}}_R$. Thus we have:

$$\begin{aligned}\text{Momentary effective reaction potential} = \\ {}_s\dot{\bar{E}}_R = [{}_sH_R \times D - (I_R + {}_sI_R)] - {}_sO_R.\end{aligned}$$

Postulate 11. Momentary Effective Reaction Potential Must Exceed a Certain Value Before a Learned Response Can Occur.

The value that $_s\dot{\bar{E}}_R$ must exceed before a conditioned response can occur is called the *reaction threshold,* symbolized $_sL_R$. Therefore, a learned response will be emitted only if: $_s\dot{\bar{E}}_R > {_sL_R}$.

Postulate 12. The Probability of a Learned Response's Being Made Is a Combined Function of $_s\bar{E}_R,$ $_sO_R,$ and $_sL_R$.

In the early stages of training, i.e., after only a few reinforced trials, $_s\bar{E}_R$ will be very close to $_sL_R$ and therefore, due to the effects of $_sO_R$, a conditioned response will be elicited on some trials but not on others. This is because on some trials the value of $_sO_R$ subtracted from $_s\bar{E}_R$ will be large enough to reduce $_s\bar{E}_R$ to a value below $_sL_R$. As training continues, subtracting $_sO_R$ from $_s\bar{E}_R$ will have less and less of an effect since the value of $_s\bar{E}_R$ will become much larger than the value of $_sL_R$. Even after considerable training, however, it is still possible for $_sO_R$ to assume a large value, thereby preventing the occurrence of a conditioned response. How $_s\bar{E}_R$, $_sO_R$, and $_sL_R$ combine to determine the probability of a learned response is shown in Figure 6–3. Hull used p to symbolize the probability of a response occurring.

Postulate 13. The Greater the Value of $_s\dot{\bar{E}}_R$ the Shorter Will Be the Latency Between S and R.

Latency is the time between when a stimulus is presented to the organism and a learned response is made. Latency is symbolized $_st_R$. This postulate simply states that the reaction time between the onset of a stimulus and the elicitation of a learned response goes down as the value of $_s\dot{\bar{E}}_R$ goes up.

Postulate 14. The Value of $_s\dot{\bar{E}}_R$ Will Determine Resistance to Extinction.

The value of $_s\dot{\bar{E}}_R$ at the end of training determines how many nonreinforced responses will need to be made before extinction occurs. The greater the value of $_s\dot{\bar{E}}_R$, the greater the number of nonreinforced responses that have to be made before extinction takes place. Hull used n to symbolize the number of nonreinforced trials that occurred before extinction resulted.

Figure 6–3. The relationship between effective reaction potential $(_s\bar{E}_R)$, the oscillation effect $(_sO_R)$, and reaction threshold $(_sL_R)$. The up-ended normal curve shows the function of $_sO_R$. The area of the normal curve lying above $_sL_R$ indicates the probability of a conditioned response occurring (from Hull, 1943, p. 327).

Postulate 15. The Amplitude of a Conditioned Response Varies Directly with $_s\dot{\bar{E}}_R$.

This postulate deals with the situation where the learned response occurs in degrees, for example, salivation or the galvanic skin response (GSR). When the conditioned response is one that can occur in degrees, the magnitude of the conditioned response will be directly related to the size of $_s\dot{E}_R$, the momentary effective reaction potential. Hull used A to symbolize response amplitude.

Postulate 16. When Two or More Incompatible Responses Tend to Be Elicited in the Same Situation, the One with the Greatest $_s\dot{E}_R$ Will Occur.

This postulate seems self-explanatory.

Summary of the Symbols Used in Hull's Theory.

D = drive
$_sH_R$ = habit strength

$_sE_R$ = reaction potential = $_sH_R \times D$

I_R = reactive inhibition

$_sI_R$ = conditioned inhibition

$_s\bar{E}_R$ = effective reaction potential = $_sH_R \times D - (I_R + {_sI_R})$

$_sO_R$ = oscillation effect

$_s\dot{\bar{E}}_R$ = momentary effective reaction potential = $_s\bar{E}_R - {_sO_R}$ =
    $[_sH_R \times D - (I_R + {_sI_R})] - {_sO_R}$

$_sL_R$ = the value that $_s\dot{\bar{E}}_R$ must exceed before a learned response
    can occur

$_st_R$ = reaction time

p = response probability

n = trials to extinction

A = response amplitude

Major Differences Between Hull's 1943 and 1952 Theories

Incentive Motivation (K)

In the 1943 version of his theory, Hull treated magnitude of reward as a learning variable: the greater the amount of reward the greater the amount of drive reduction, and thus the greater the increase in $_sH_R$. Research showed this notion to be unsatisfactory. Experiments showed that performance was dramatically altered as size of reward was varied *after* learning was complete. For example, when an animal trained to run a straight runway for a small reward was switched to a larger reward, his running speed suddenly went up. When an animal trained on a large reward was shifted to a smaller reward, his running speed went down. Crespi (1942, 1944) and Zeaman (1949) were two early experimenters who found that performance changed radically when the magnitude of reward was changed. The results of Crespi's (1942) experiment are shown in Figure 6–4.

The changes in performance following a change in magnitude of reward could not be explained in terms of changes in $_sH_R$ since they were too rapid. Moreover, $_sH_R$ was thought to be fairly permanent. Unless one or more factors operated against $_sH_R$, it would not decrease in value. Results like those found by Crespi and Zeaman led Hull to reach the conclusion that organisms learn as rapidly for a small incentive as they do for a large one, but they *perform* differently as the size of the incentive varies. The rapid change in performance following a change in re-

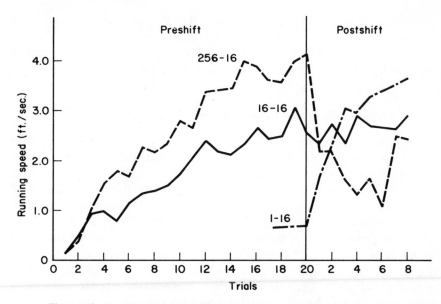

Preshift   Postshift

256-16

16-16

1-16

Running speed (ft./sec.)

4.0

3.0

2.0

1.0

0

0 2 4 6 8 10 12 14 16 18 20 2 4 6 8

Trials

Figure 6–4. The results show that when animals are trained on a large reward (256 pellets of food) and are then switched to a relatively small reward (16 pellets of food), performance drops off rapidly. Likewise, when animals are trained on a small reward (1 pellet of food) and then are switched to a relatively large reward (16 pellets of food), performance improves rapidly

From Robert C. Bolles, "Theory of Motivation" (after Crespi, 1942). Harper & Row, 1967, p. 335.

ward size is referred to as the *Crespi effect,* after Crespi who first observed it.

Stimulus-Intensity Dynamism (V)

According to Hull, this was an intervening variable that varied along with the intensity of the external stimulus (S). Stated simply, the stimulus-intensity dynamism indicates that the greater the intensity of a stimulus, the greater the probability that a learned response will be elicited. Thus, we must revise Hull's earlier formula for momentary reaction potential as follows:

$$_s\dot{E}_R = [_sH_R \times D \times V \times K - (I_R + _sI_R)] - _sO_R.$$

It is interesting to note that since $_sH_R$, D, V, and K are multiplied, if any one had a value of zero, reaction potential would be zero. For example, there could have been many reinforced pairings between S and R ($_sH_R$) but if drive is zero, reward absent, or if the organism cannot detect the stimulus, a learned response will not occur.

Change from Drive Reduction to Drive Stimulus Reduction.

Originally, Hull had a drive reduction theory of learning, but later he revised it to a *drive stimulus reduction theory* of learning. One reason for the change was the realization that if a thirsty animal is given water as a reward for performing some act, it takes a considerable amount of time for the thirst drive to be satisfied by the water. The water goes into the mouth, the throat, the stomach, and eventually into the blood. The effects of ingesting water must ultimately reach the brain, and finally the thirst drive will be reduced. Hull concluded that the drive reduction was too far removed from the presentation of the reinforcer to explain how learning could take place. What was needed to explain learning was something that occurred soon after the presentation of a reinforcer, and that something was the reduction of *drive stimuli* (S_D). As mentioned earlier in this chapter, drive stimuli for the thirst drive include dryness in the mouth and parched lips. Water almost immediately reduces such stimulation, and thus Hull had the mechanism he needed for explaining learning.

A second reason for changing from a drive reduction theory to a drive stimulus reduction theory was provided by Sheffield and Roby (1950), who found that hungry rats were reinforced by nonnutritive saccharine that could not possibly have reduced the hunger drive. About this research Hull (1952) says:

> Sheffield and Roby appear to have presented a critical case in point. . . . They showed that hungry albino rats are reinforced by water sweetened by saccharine which presumably is not at all nourishing, i.e., it does not reduce the need in the least. It may very well be that the ingestion of saccharine-sweetened water reduces hunger tension S_D for a brief period sufficient for a mild reinforcement, much as the tightening of the belt is said to do in hungry men, thus reinforcing that act [p. 153].

S_D symbolizes drive stimulus or drive stimuli.

Fractional Antedating Goal Response (r_G)

You will recall that when a neutral stimulus is consistently paired with primary reinforcement, it takes on reinforcing properties of its own, i.e., it becomes a secondary reinforcer. The concept of secondary reinforcement is vital in understanding the operations of the *fractional antedating goal response* (r_G), which is clearly one of Hull's most important concepts.

Let us suppose we are training a rat to solve a multiple component maze. We place the animal in the start box and eventually he reaches the goal box where he is rewarded with food, a primary reinforcer. All the stimuli in the goal box were experienced just prior to the animal's receiving primary reinforcement (food) and will, therefore, through the process of classical conditioning, become secondary reinforcers. Moreover, following classical conditioning principles, the rat will develop a conditioned response that closely resembles the unconditioned response. In our present example, the unconditioned response would be that of salivation, chewing, and licking caused by presenting food to a hungry animal. The conditioned response, also involving salivation, chewing, or licking, would be elicited by the various stimuli in the goal box as the rat approaches the food. It is this conditioned response to stimuli, experienced prior to the ingestion of food, that is called the fractional antedating goal response (r_G). The development of r_G is shown in Figure 6–5.

In the chapter on Pavlov we will learn that neutral stimuli paired with secondary reinforcers come to have reinforcing properties of their own through the process of higher order conditioning (a process similar to associative shifting). When applied to maze learning, this process would cause stimuli prior to those occurring in the goal box to also become reinforcers, and then the stimuli before them, etc. Gradually the process works backward until even the stimuli in the start box come to have reinforcing properties. When these previously neutral stimuli become secondary reinforcers, they perform two very important functions: (1) they reinforce the overt responses on the part of the organism that bring him into contact with them; and (2) they elicit r_Gs.

Now as the animal leaves the start box, he comes into contact with a variety of stimuli, some with reinforcing properties, others without reinforcing properties. Those responses that bring the animal into close proximity to reinforcing stimuli will tend to be repeated while other responses will extinguish. In this manner the animal learns to make the correct turns in the maze. *Thus, maze learning is thought to involve both classical and instrumental conditioning.* Classical conditioning produces the secondary reinforcers and r_Gs; instrumental conditioning produces the appropriate motor responses that bring the animal into proximity with both the primary and secondary rewards. Thus far, the explanation for maze learning is essentially the same as Skinner's explanation of chaining

Figure 6–5. The development of the fractional antedating goal response (r_G).

(see Chapter 5); but as we shall see below, Hull assigns the r_G a prominent role in the learning of chained responses.

Two characteristics of the r_G must be noted. First, r_G must always be some fraction of the goal response (R_G). If the goal response involves eating, then r_G will be minute chewing movements and perhaps salivation. Secondly, and more important, *the r_G produces stimulation.* Overt responding causes the kinesthetic receptors in the muscles, tendons, and joints to fire, causing what Guthrie (see Chapter 8) called movement-produced stimuli. More technically, the firing of these kinesthetic receptors causes *proprioceptive stimuli.* Like any other response, the r_G has stimulation associated with it. The proprioceptive stimulation caused by the r_G is symbolized s_G. The r_G and s_G are inseparable since whenever r_G occurs, so does s_G. Perhaps the most important aspect of r_G is the fact that it produces s_G.

After a considerable amount of maze learning has taken place the situation that emerges is as follows: the stimuli in the start box will become signals or S^Ds for leaving the start box, since leaving it brings the animal into proximity with secondary rewards. A secondary reward does three things: it rewards the response the animal just made; it acts as an S^D for the next overt response; and it elicits an r_G. When the r_G is elicited, it automatically produces an s_G. The main function of the s_G is to elicit the next overt response. Thus, both the secondary reinforcers, which are external, and the s_Gs, which are internal, tend to elicit overt responses. The response that exposes the animal to the next secondary reinforcer most rapidly will be the one that finally becomes associated with the s_G. When the next secondary reinforcer is experienced, it rewards the overt response made prior to it, it elicits the next overt response, and it elicits the next r_G. When the r_G is elicited, it triggers the next s_G, which triggers the next overt response, and so on. The process continues in this manner all the way to the goal box. The chaining process, as Hull saw it, is diagrammed in Figure 6–6. An example of chaining on the human level is shown in Figure 6–7.

It should be clear that Hull really had two explanations for chaining that he used simultaneously. One explanation, which emphasized external stimuli, was very much like Skinner's explanation of chaining. The other, which emphasized internal events, was very much like Guthrie's explanation of chaining as we shall see in Chapter 8. Hull, then, combined the notions of Skinner and Guthrie, and said that chained behavior is a function of either internal or external cues or, more probably, of both internal and external cues.

One might ask why it is important to postulate the r_G-s_G mechanisms if Skinner's explanation of chaining is adequate. The answer is that the r_G-s_G mechanism is thought to be important because of the other things that it may be related to. For example, the r_G-s_G mechanism can be thought of as the "mental" component of chaining. Generally speaking, the r_G-s_G concept provides an objective means of investigating thought processes. In the example in Figure 6–7, one can say that the time (noon) acted as an S^D, which triggered an r_G, which triggered the thought of food. Or one can say that the "expectation" of food was triggered, which keeps the person moving toward his goal of food. Clearly, at this point, the behavioristic point of view and the cognitive point of view come very close together. In fact, it might be said that the only value of the proposed r_G-s_G is opening up research in the area of cognition. In this regard Hull (1952) said:

> Further study of this major automatic device presumably will lead to the detailed behavioral understanding of thought and reasoning, which constitute the highest attainment of organic evolution. Indeed, the r_G-s_G mechanism leads in a strictly logical

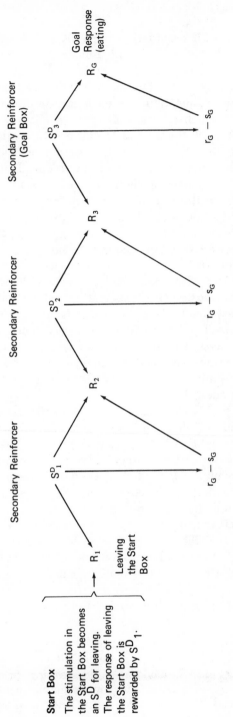

Figure 6-6. How S^D's, overt responses (R) and the r_G-s_G mechanism combine to produce a chained response.

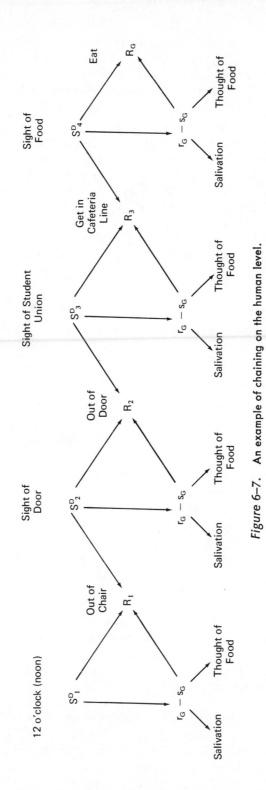

Figure 6–7. An example of chaining on the human level.

manner into what was formally regarded as the very heart of the psychic: interest, planning, foresight, foreknowledge, expectancy, purpose, and so on [p. 350].

Thus Hull, in the tradition of Watson, Pavlov, and Guthrie, concluded that thinking consists of a minute internal representation of things that happen overtly. The "thought" of eating is nothing more than an s_G elicited by an r_G. We will review one of the many theoretical extensions of the r_G-s_G mechanism when we consider Abram Amsel's theory later on in this chapter.

The Habit Family Hierarchy.

Since there are any number of overt responses possible to any particular s_G, there are many alternative ways of reaching a goal. However, the route that is most likely is the one that brings the animal into proximity of reward most rapidly. This fact was originally referred to as the "goal-gradient hypothesis" in Hull's early writings, but appeared as a corollary to one of his postulates in 1952. The corollary concerned the delay of reinforcement (J) and, read (1952, p. 126): "The greater the delay in reinforcement of a link within a given behavior chain, the weaker will be the resulting reaction potential of the link in question to the stimulus traces present at the time."

Here Hull is talking about a single link in a behavioral chain but the same idea can be generalized to whole behavioral chains. Whether one is talking about a single response, or a series of responses, delay of reward has a deleterious effect on reaction potential. Likewise, either individual responses or chains of responses that are followed rapidly by reinforcement have relatively higher value of sE_R and are more likely to occur than those responses or behavioral chains with a longer delay between their occurrence and reward.

The most direct route through a maze, whether a T-maze or a more complicated maze, has the greatest amount of sE_R associated with it because it results in less delay of reinforcement and also because there is less reactive and conditioned inhibition to be subtracted from sE_R. But the shortest route through a maze is only one of many possible routes. The habit family hierarchy simply refers to the fact that in any learning situation, any number of responses are possible and the one that is most likely is the one that brings about reward most rapidly and with the least amount of effort. If that particular way is blocked, the animal will prefer the next shortest route, and if that is blocked, he will go to the third route, etc.

There is a close relationship between the habit family hierarchy and how the fractional antedating goal response (r_G) and the stimulus it gives rise to (s_G) operate in chaining. We noted earlier that any number of overt responses can follow the occurrence of an s_G. Some of these responses will result immediately in exposure to a secondary reinforcer, and others will not. Eventually the responses that bring the animal into contact with the secondary reinforcers most rapidly will be the ones made, since they will have the highest values of $_sE_R$ associated with them. Remember, the greater the delay of reinforcement (J), the lower the value of $_sE_R$. Thus, there is a hierarchy of possible responses associated with every s_G and, therefore, there is a large number of routes through a maze. If the route consisting of the responses with the highest values of $_sE_R$ is blocked, the next one in the hierarchy will be chosen, etc. The situation can be diagrammed as follows:

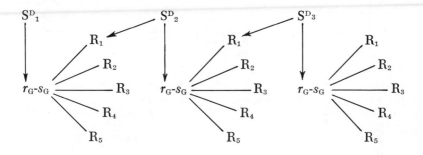

Hull's Final System Summarized.

There are three kinds of major events in Hull's theory:

1. **Independent variables,** which are stimulus events systematically manipulated by the experimenter.
2. **Intervening variables,** which are processes thought to be taking place within the organism but are not directly observable. All the intervening variables in Hull's system are operationally defined (see Chapter 2).
3. **Dependent variables,** which are some aspect of behavior that is measured by the experimenter in order to determine whether the independent variables had any effect.

Figure 6–8 updates our summary of Hull's 1943 system by considering the main components of his 1952 theory as consisting of the three kinds

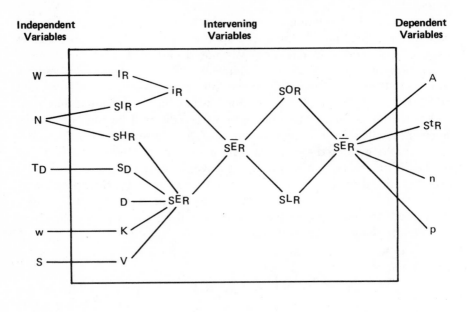

W = Work
N = Number of Prior Reinforcements
T_D = Total Drive
w = Amount of Reward
S = Stimulus Intensity
I_R = Reactive Inhibition
S^IR = Conditioned Inhibition
$\dot{I}_R$ = Combined Inhibitory Potential
S^HR = Habit Strength
S_D = Drive Stimulus
D = Drive

K = Incentive Motivation
V = Stimulus Strength
S_ER = Reaction Potential
$S\bar{E}R$ = Effective Reaction Potential
S^OR = Behavioral Oscillation
$S\dot{L}R$ = Response Threshold
$S\dot{\bar{E}}R$ = Momentary Reaction Potential
A = Response Amplitude
S^tR = Response Latency
n = Trials to Extinction
p = Probability of a Response

Figure 6–8.   Summary of Hull's Theory of Learning after 1952.

of variables listed above. It should be noted that Hull's 1952 system comprised 17 postulates and 133 theorems. The present review of Hull in this chapter should be regarded as a brief introduction to a theory known for its thoroughness and complexity.

HULL'S CONTRIBUTION TO PSYCHOLOGY

As mentioned above, Hull's learning theory has made an enormous impact on psychology. Marx and Hillix (1963) put the matter aptly:

Hull's most important contribution to psychology was his demonstration of the possibility of setting one's sights upon the ultimate
goal of a thoroughly scientific and systematic behavior theory. He
lived his own scientific life in pursuit of that goal and thereby
influenced even those who disagreed most vehemently with the
substantive and methodological details of his work. No other
psychologist has had so extensive an effect on the professional
motivation of so many researchers. He popularized the strictly
objective behavioristic approach as it had never been popularized
previously [p. 252].

After Hull's death the main spokesman for the Hullian point of view
was Kenneth W. Spence (1907–1967) who both expanded and significantly modified Hull's original theory (see Spence, 1956, 1960). We will
encounter some of Spence's ideas in the next chapter. Other important
followers of Hull include Neal E. Miller, who extended Hull's theory into
the areas of personality, conflict, social behavior, and psychotherapy
(e.g., Miller and Dollard, 1941; Dollard and Miller, 1950); Robert R.
Sears, who translated a number of Freudian concepts into Hullian terms
and who also worked extensively in the area of experimental child psychology (e.g., Sears, 1944; and Sears, Whiting, Nowlis, and Sears, 1953);
and O. Hobart Mowrer, who followed many of Hull's ideas while studying such areas as personality dynamics and the special characteristics of
learning where fear or anxiety are involved. Mowrer has always been a
courageous theorist who has been willing to use terms such as sin, hope,
and fear while attempting to explain human motivation and learning. For
example, Mowrer (1960) says:

A conditioned stimulus not only makes the subject salivate: it
also makes him *hopeful,* just as surely as a stimulus which has been
associated with the onset of pain makes the subject *fearful* [p. 3].

Spence, Miller, Sears, and Mowrer have all made significant contributions to the psychology of learning and the advanced student of psychology will encounter their research often.

Abram Amsel was another theorist whom Hull greatly influenced. We
offer Amsel's theory below as one example of how Hull's r_G-s_G mechanism
has been extended by neo-Hullian theorists.

Amsel's Theory of Frustrative Nonreward

Hull's concept of the r_G-s_G mechanism has been used by various theorists to help explain a variety of phenomena. One example is Abram

Abram Amsel

Amsel's use of the mechanism to explain behavior associated with non-reward (Amsel, 1958, 1962). In general, Amsel assumes that after an organism is rewarded a number of times in a given situation, he learns to expect reward in that situation. An organism experiences frustration when its expectation of reward is unfulfilled. This frustration has motivational properties similar to those of punishment. For example, it has been found that animals will learn to perform a response that terminates a stimulus which was present when the animal experienced frustration (Daly, 1969; Wagner, 1963).

Further evidence for the motivational properties of frustration is provided by an experiment run by Amsel and Roussel (1952). In this experiment two straight alley runways were linked together. For the first 84 trials, the animals were rewarded at the end of each runway. After this preliminary training, however, the animals were run under conditions where they were rewarded at the end of runway 1 on only 50 percent of the trials, while they continued to be rewarded at the end of runway 2 on each trial. It was found that running speed in runway 2 was significantly faster following nonreward in runway 1 than it was following reward in runway 1. This increased vigor following nonreward is called the *frustration effect* (FE). This finding supports the contention that nonreward causes frustration and that frustration is motivating or drive inducing.

Further support for the above contention was provided by a study by Bower (1962). Bower reasoned that amount of frustration should be related to amount of reward reduction. To test his assumption, he used a two-runway apparatus similar to that used by Amsel and Roussel. In Bower's experiment, however, the rats were given four pellets of food at the end of each runway. The training phase of the experiment consisted of 6 trials a day for 24 days, or a total of 144 trials. After training, the conditions were changed so that the number of food pellets found at the end of the first runway was either 4, 3, 2, 1, or zero. The 4 food pellets found at the end of the second runway remained constant throughout the experiment. Bower found that running speed in runway 2 was inversely related to the number of food pellets present in runway 1 (fewer food pellets, faster running). That is, the animals ran fastest in runway 2 when they received no reward in runway 1; next fastest when they received only 1 pellet, then 2, then 3, and slowest after receiving 4 food pellets in runway 1. This experiment supports Bower's hypothesis that amount of frustration is related to the amount of reward reduction. Thus it appears that nonreward causes frustration and frustration has behavioral consequences.

Next we turn to the relationship between frustration and Hull's r_G-s_G mechanism. First, Amsel assumes that when nonreward occurs after a prolonged period of reward, the organism experiences *primary frustration* (R_F). Thus, if an animal is rewarded a number of times for running down a straight alley and then is not rewarded after running down that same alley, he will experience primary frustration in the goal box where he had been previously rewarded.

We learned earlier in this chapter that when the animal experiences primary reinforcement in a goal box, the stimuli in the goal box take on secondary reinforcing properties, that is, they develop the capacity to elicit r_Gs, which in turn elicit s_Gs. We also saw that through stimulus generalization and/or higher order conditioning, these r_Gs slowly develop associations all the way back to the start box. After this happens, when the animal leaves the start box, his behavior is guided to the goal box by these r_Gs and these s_Gs which they elicit. According to Amsel, the same backward conditioning process is associated with primary frustration. That is, stimuli associated with primary frustration will develop the capacity to elicit a fractional anticipatory frustration reaction, or r_F, which is associated with an s_F, just as r_G necessarily is associated with an

s_G. The r_G-s_G and the r_F-s_F mechanisms have different behavior patterns associated with them, however. Whereas the r_G-s_G mechanism causes locomotion toward the goal box, r_F-s_F tends to cause avoidance of the goal box. In general, we can say that r_G is related to the expectancy of reward, while r_F is related to the expectancy of frustration.

During extinction, the animal experiences nothing but frustration, which gradually generalizes backward to the start box, through the r_F-s_F mechanism. When this happens, the animal experiences stimuli that elicit r_Fs either in the start box, or shortly after leaving the start box, and they cause him to stop running. At that point we say extinction has occurred.

Now we come to what is perhaps the most important aspect of Amsel's theory: its proposed explanation of the *partial reinforcement effect* (PRE). The PRE refers to the fact that it takes longer to extinguish a response that was intermittently rewarded during training than if it was continuously rewarded. In other words, PRE means that partial reinforcement yields greater resistance to extinction than does 100 percent reinforcement. A number of theories have been offered to explain the PRE and Amsel's is one of the most widely accepted.

Amsel explains PRE as follows. First, the animal is trained to make a response, such as running down a straight alley. During this training, the animal usually experiences primary reinforcement (R_G) in the goal box on 100 percent of the trials. Under these circumstances, all the stimuli in the runway will eventually become associated with R_G through the r_G-s_G mechanism. Next, the animal is placed on a partial reinforcement schedule where he is rewarded on, say, only 50 percent of the trials. Since the animal had developed a strong expectancy for reward, he will experience primary frustration (R_F) on those trials when he does not receive reward. As we saw above, the stimuli just prior to the experience of primary frustration will come to elicit r_Fs which give rise to s_Fs. After several nonreward trials, a conflict develops, because the same stimuli tend to elicit conflicting habits. When an r_G-s_G is elicited, the animal tends to run toward the goal box, but when an r_F-s_F is elicited, the animal tends to avoid the goal box. Since the animal had already developed a strong habit of running toward the goal during training prior to being switched to a partial reinforcement schedule and perhaps because positive reinforcement is more influential than frustration, the animal continues to approach the goal box while under the partial reinforcement schedule. In other words, although there is an approach-avoidance conflict associated with the goal box, the approach tendency wins out.

Since the animal continues to approach the goal box even though he is not rewarded on some trials, eventually all the stimuli in the apparatus become associated with the running response, even those stimuli associated with frustration. Perhaps you have already anticipated Amsel's next step in his explanation of the PRE. When subjects trained on a continuous or 100 percent reinforcement schedule are switched to extinction, they experience frustration for the first time. For them, the effects of this frustration associate backward to the start box and normal extinction occurs. Subjects trained on a partial reinforcement schedule, however, have already experienced frustration during training and have learned to run in the presence of the stimuli associated with frustration. The partial reinforcement subjects will therefore take much longer to extinguish, thus the PRE.

One could deduce from Amsel's proposed explanation of the PRE that great variation in behavior would accompany the conflict stage of partial reinforcement training. That is, when the same stimuli in the apparatus are eliciting both approach and avoidance tendencies, running speed should vary from trial to trial. At the same time, when the stimuli become associated with the running response later in training, the running response should stabilize. Amsel (1958) found support for both deductions. One could also deduce from Amsel's theory that the PRE will occur only when there are a substantial number of preliminary training trials. This is because his explanation depends on frustration and the animal will not experience frustration unless he has learned to expect a reward. Evidence supporting this contention was also found by Amsel (1958). It was found that the PRE resulted if animals had 84 preliminary training trials before being switched to a partial reinforcement schedule, but did not if they had only 24 preliminary training trials.

Amsel's theory of frustrative reward is but one of the many creative extensions of Hull's r_G-s_G mechanism. The student of psychology or education will experience a number of others in advanced courses. In fact, a review of the many uses of the r_G-s_G mechanism to explain various psychological phenomena would make an excellent independent study project.

DISCUSSION QUESTIONS

1. How would one overcome or minimize the negative contribution of work (I_R and $_sI_R$) in a learning situation?

2. In Hull's system, what effect would increasing the size of the reward have on learning? Explain.

3. Describe a situation that would allow one to differentiate between learning and performance.

4. What would characterize classroom procedures designed in accordance with Hull's principles of learning?

5. According to Hull's theory, who do you think would learn faster: high anxious students or low anxious students? Explain.

6. On what basic points would Skinner disagree with Hull? Where would the two most closely agree?

7. In your opinion, what do you think Hull means when he says "psychic phenomena" will someday be explained in terms of the r_G-s_G mechanism?

8. Explain chaining from Hull's point of view.

9. What is a habit family hierarchy?

10. Describe Hull's approach to theory construction. What is meant by the statement that Hull's theory is "open-ended"?

11. Diagram Hull's final version of his theory as it was presented in this chapter.

12. You drive around a corner and see the house of the good friend you are about to visit and you begin to smile. How would Hull explain this smiling behavior?

13. Summarize Amsel's explanation of the partial reinforcement effect.

GLOSSARY

Conditioned inhibition ($_sI_R$). A learned response of not responding. Since responding produces fatigue (I_R) and fatigue is a negative drive state, not responding is reinforcing; hence conditioned inhibition.

Crespi effect. The rapid change in performance level as size of reward is varied.

Distributed practice. Learning a skill under the conditions where practice trials are separated by a considerable length of time.

Drive (D). The condition that exists when there is a biological deficiency in the body. For all practical purposes, the terms *drive* and *need* mean the same thing.

Drive reduction.   The satisfaction of a biological deficiency. Originally Hull thought it to be a necessary condition for learning. Hull later turned to a drive stimulus reduction theory of learning.

Drive stimuli.   The stimuli that characteristically accompany a certain drive, such as the dryness of the mouth, lips, and throat that accompany the thirst drive.

Drive stimulus reduction.   The reduction or removal of the stimuli that accompany a drive. This usually occurs before the drive itself is actually reduced; for example, the dryness of the mouth, lips, and throat are eliminated before the effects of drinking water can reach the brain and thereby reduce the thirst drive.

Effective reaction potential $(_s\bar{E}_R)$.   Reaction potential $(_sE_R)$ minus the effects of I_R and $_sI_R$.

Fractional antedating goal response (r_G).   A response that is conditioned to the stimuli present prior to the ingestion of a primary reward. The conditioned response (r_G) is always some fraction of the goal response (R_G). For example, if the goal response is eating, then r_G would consist of minute chewing responses. Each r_G automatically produces a stimulus, which is symbolized s_G. The r_G-s_G mechanism plays an important role in Hull's explanation of chained behavior.

Fractional anticipatory frustration reaction (r_F).   Stimuli that precede primary frustration will develop the capacity to elicit some portion of the primary frustration response. These fractions of the primary frustration response that occur prior to the goal are called fractional anticipatory frustration reactions or r_Fs.

Frustration effect *(FE)*.   The increased vigor of responses following nonreward. For example, it has been found that rats will run faster following nonreward than following reward.

Generalized habit strength $(_s\bar{H}_R)$.   Habit strength from previous learning experiences that generalizes to a new learning experience because of the similarity between the new learning experience and older ones.

Habit family hierarchy.   A hierarchy of responses arranged according to their values of $_sE_R$. When a particular response is thwarted, the animal makes the next response available in his response repertory. Responses that result in an organism's being reinforced most rapidly have the greatest value of $_sE_R$ associated with them and are, therefore, most likely to occur. If a response with the highest value of $_sE_R$ is blocked, however, the response with the next highest value of $_sE_R$ will occur, etc.

Habit strength $(_sH_R)$.   A measure of the strength of association between a stimulus and a response. The magnitude of the $_sH_R$ depends on the number of reinforced pairings between the stimulus and the response. In the final version of Hull's theory, $_sH_R$ was the only learning variable; the other factors were performance variables. In other words, Hull believed that the only thing that affected learning directly was the number of reinforced trials.

Hypothetical-deductive theory (also called logical-deductive). A theory consisting of posulates and theorems. Postulates are assumptions that cannot be verified directly; theorems are deduced from the postulates and they can be verified experimentally. If an experiment designed to test a theorem comes out in the predicted direction, its postulate is indirectly verified and the theory gains strength. If the experiment does not come out in the predicted direction, the theory loses strength. A hypothetical-deductive theory is constantly changing in light of experimental evidence.

Incentive motivation (K). Size of reward. Originally (1943), Hull felt that K affected learning, but he later (1952) concluded that it only affected performance.

Interaction of sensory impulses $(\breve{s})$. Behavior is usually the result of many stimuli impinging on sensory receptors at any given time. The afferent (sensory) neural impulses caused by these stimuli interact with each other and it is their combined effect that causes an efferent (motor) neural impulse and finally an overt response (R).

Latency $(_st_R)$. The time between the presentation of a stimulus and the occurrence of a learned response.

Massed practice. Learning a skill under the conditions where practice trials are separated by only a very short interval of time.

Momentary effective reaction potential $(_s\dot{E}_R)$. Reaction potential $(_sE_R)$ minus the effects of I_R, $_sI_R$, and $_sO_R$.

Oscillation effect $(_sO_R)$. An "inhibitory potentiality" that opposes the emission of a conditioned response and whose value changes from moment to moment. The values of $_sO_R$ are normally distributed and therefore the value that manifests itself at any given moment can be large or small, but will most likely be a value that is neither very large nor very small.

Partial reinforcement effect (PRE). The fact that a response that has been rewarded only sometimes takes longer to extinguish than a response that has been rewarded each time it occurred.

Primary frustration (R_F). The response that occurs when an organism experiences nonreward after it had learned to expect reward.

Primary need. A deviation from the optimal conditions of air, water, food, temperature, or sex which are necessary for survival.

Proprioceptive stimuli. The stimuli that result from the firing of the kinesthetic receptors in the muscles, joints, and tendons of the body. Also called movement-produced stimuli.

Reaction potential ($_sE_R$). Directly influences four response measures. As reaction potential goes up, the probability of a learned response being elicited by a stimulus goes up, resistance to extinction goes up, the amplitude of a conditioned response goes up, and latency goes down.

Reaction threshold ($_sL_R$). The minimal value that the momentary effective reaction potential ($_s\dot{E}_R$) must exceed before a learned response can occur.

Reactive inhibition (I_R). The fatigue caused by responding, which operates against the emission of a conditioned response.

Reinforcer. Anything that causes either drive reduction or drive stimulus reduction.

Reinforcement. Drive reduction or drive stimulus reduction.

Reminiscence effect. The improvement of performance on a skill following a rest after cessation of practice.

Resistance to extinction. See entry in Glossary for Chapter 5.

Stimulus generalization. See Generalization *in Glossary for Chapter 7.*

Stimulus-intensity dynamism (V). The internal result of varying the magnitude of an external stimulus. A larger external stimulus will result in a larger stimulus trace, thereby increasing the probability of a learned response's being elicited.

Stimulus trace (s). The afferent (sensory) neural impulse that is caused by an external stimulus and continues for a short while after the external stimulus has ceased.

Unlearned behavior. Associations between stimuli and responses that are genetically determined and therefore do not depend upon experience for their development.

part **3**

Predominantly Associationistic Theories

7

Ivan Petrovich Pavlov

Pavlov was born in Russia in 1849 and died there in 1936. His father was a priest and originally Pavlov himself studied to become a priest. He changed his mind, however, and spent most of his life studying physiology. In 1904 he won a Nobel Prize for his work on the physiology of digestion. He did not begin his study of the conditioned reflex until he was fifty years of age.

With Thorndike we saw that scientists are obliged to change their views when the data require it, an important characteristic of the scientific enterprise. With Pavlov, we see the importance of serendipity, or accidental discovery, in science. Pavlov's method of studying digestion involved a surgical arrangement on a dog that allowed gastric juices to flow through a fistula to the outside of the body where it was collected. This arrangement is shown in Figure 7–1.

Pavlov was measuring stomach secretions as the dog's response to such things as meat powder when he noticed that the mere sight of the food caused the dog to salivate. In addition, the mere sight of the experimenter or the sound of his footsteps would cause salivation. Originally Pavlov called such responses "psychic" reflexes. Being an extremely objective scientist and at heart a physiologist, Pavlov originally resisted investigating the "psychic" reflex. After a long personal struggle, however, and contrary to the advice of some of his colleagues, he finally decided to delve into the issue. He decided to study it, however, as a purely physiological problem to guard against any subjective element entering into

Figure 7–1. The figure shows a dog with esophageal and gastric fistulae. Such an arrangement allowed the dog to be fed, but prevented the food from reaching the stomach. Also, gastric juices flowing from the stomach could be measured (from Kimble, Garmezy & Zigler 1974, p. 208).

From G. A. Kimble, N. Garmezy, and E. Zigler, "Principles of General Psychology," © 1974, The Ronald Press, Co. New York, N. Y.

his research. The apparatus used by Pavlov to study the "psychic" reflex is shown in Figure 7–2.

Just as Pavlov started a second career at age fifty when he turned to the study of the psychic reflex, he started a third career at age eighty when

Figure 7–2. The figure shows a dog with a tube entering its cheek. When the dog salivates, the saliva is gathered in the test tube and its quantity is recorded on the rotating drum on the left.

From Garrett, H. E., "Great Experiments in Psychology," New York: Appleton-Century-Croft, 1951.

he turned to the application of his work on conditioning to mental illness. This work resulted in a book entitled *Conditioned Reflexes and Psychiatry* (1941), which many consider a monumental contribution to psychiatry.

At the time Thorndike was developing his theory, American psychology was struggling to be objective. Structuralism, with its introspective method, was losing influence. In fact, consciousness per se was becoming a highly questionable subject matter. With his blending of associationism, Darwinism, and experimental science, Thorndike represented the best in American objective psychology. He was an important part of the functionalist movement which, as we have seen, was the first major psychological movement in America. Under the influence of Darwin, the functionalist's main concern was survival which, of course, involved adapting to the environment. The functionalists tried to discover how human actions as well as thought processes contribute to adaptation and survival.

At the time Thorndike was doing his major research, Pavlov was also investigating the learning process. He, too, was impatient with subjective psychology, and in fact, had almost decided not to study the conditioned reflex because of its "psychic" nature. Although Pavlov did not have a high opinion of psychologists, he had considerable respect for Thorndike and acknowledged him as the first to do systematic research on the learning process in animals (Pavlov, 1928):

> Some years after the beginning of the work with our new method I learned that somewhat similar experiments on animals had been performed in America, and indeed not by physiologists but by psychologists. Thereupon I studied in more detail the American publications, and now I must acknowledge that the honour of having made the first steps along this path belongs to E. L. Thorndike. By two or three years his experiments preceded ours, and his book must be considered as a classic, both for its bold outlook on an immense task and for the accuracy of its results [pp. 38–40].

Thorndike and Pavlov, although traveling two different paths in many respects, shared an enthusiasm toward science and a belief in its ultimate ability to solve man's major problems (Pavlov, 1928):

> Only science, exact science about human nature itself, and the most sincere approach to it by the aid of the omnipotent scientific method, will deliver man from his present gloom, and will purge him from his contemporary shame in the sphere of interhuman relations [p. 28].

Pavlov never waivered from his scientific outlook and in 1936 at the age of 87 he wrote the following letter to the young scientists of his country (Babkin, 1949):

> This is the message I would like to give to the youth of my country. First of all, be systematic. I repeat—be systematic. Train yourself to be strictly systematic in the acquisition of knowledge. First study the rudiments of science before attempting to reach its heights. Never pass on to the next stage until you have thoroughly mastered the one on hand. Never try to conceal the defects in your knowledge even by the most daring conjectures and hypotheses. Practice self-restraint and patience. Learn to do the drudgery of scientific work. Although a bird's wing is perfect, the bird could never soar if it did not lean upon the air. Facts are the air on which the scientist leans. Without them you will never fly upward. Without them your theories will be mere empty efforts. However, when studying, experimenting or observing, try not to remain on the surface of things. Do not become a mere

Ivan Petrovich Pavlov

collector of facts but try to penetrate into the mystery of their origin. Search persistently for the laws which govern them.

The second important requisite is modesty. Never at any time imagine that you know everything. No matter how highly you are appreciated by others, have the courage to say to yourself, "I am ignorant." Do not let pride possess you.

The third thing that is necessary is passion. Remember that science demands of a man his whole life. And even if you could have two lives, they would not be sufficient. Science calls for tremendous effort and great passion. Be passionate in your work and in your search for truth [p. 110].

MAJOR THEORETICAL NOTIONS

Development of a Conditioned Reflex.

Exactly what is meant by a psychic or conditioned reflex is indicated by the following statement by Pavlov (1955):

> I shall mention two simple experiments that can be successfully performed by all. We introduce into the mouth of a dog a moderate solution of some acid; the acid produces a usual defensive reaction in the animal: by vigorous movements of the mouth it ejects the solution, and at the same time an abundant quantity of saliva begins to flow first into the mouth and then overflows, diluting the acid and cleaning the mucous membrane of the oral cavity. Now let us turn to the second experiment. Just prior to introducing the same solution into the dog's mouth we repeatedly act on the animal by a certain external agent, say, a definite sound. What happens then? It suffices simply to repeat the sound, and the same reaction is fully reproduced—the same movements of the mouth and the same secretion of saliva [p. 247].

The ingredients necessary to bring about conditioning include (1) an *unconditioned stimulus* (UCS), which elicits a natural and automatic response from the organism; (2) an *unconditioned response* (UCR), which is the natural and automatic response elicited by the UCS; (3) a *conditioned stimulus* (CS), which is a neutral stimulus in that it does not elicit a natural and automatic response from the organism. When these ingredients are mixed in a certain way, a *conditioned reflex* (CR) occurs. In order to produce a CR, the CS and the UCS must be paired a number of times. First the CS is presented and then the UCS. The order of presentation is very important. Each time the UCS occurs, a UCR occurs.

Eventually the CS can be presented alone and it will elicit a response similar to the UCR. When this happens, a CR has been demonstrated. The procedure can be diagrammed as follows:

Training procedure: CS → UCS → UCR
Demonstration of conditioning: CS → CR

In Pavlov's example above, the UCS was acid, the UCR was salivation (caused by the acid), and the CS was a sound. The sound, of course, would not ordinarily cause the dog to salivate, but by being paired with the acid, the sound developed the capability to elicit salivation. Salivation as the result of hearing the sound was the CR.

The UCR and the CR are always the same kind of response; if the UCR is salivation, then the CR must also be salivation. The magnitude of the CR, however, is always less than that of the UCR. For example, Pavlov, who measured the magnitude of a response by counting drops of saliva, found that the UCS elicited more drops of saliva than did the CS.

Experimental Extinction.

A CR depends upon a UCS for its existence and that is precisely why Pavlov referred to the UCS as a *reinforcer*. Obviously, without the UCS, a CS would never develop the capability of eliciting a CR. Likewise, if after a CR has been developed, the CS is continually presented without the UCS's following the CR, the CR gradually disappears. When the CS no longer elicits a CR, experimental extinction is said to have occurred. Again, extinction results when the CS is presented to the organism and is not followed by reinforcement. In classical conditioning studies, reinforcement is the UCS. The terms Pavlovian conditioning and classical conditioning are synonomous.

Spontaneous Recovery.

After a period of time following extinction, if the CS is again presented to the animal, the CR will temporarily reappear. The CR has "spontaneously recovered" even though there had been no further pairings between the CS and the UCS. Again, if there is a delay following extinction and the CS is presented to the organism, it will tend to elicit a CR. The extinction and spontaneous recovery of a CR are shown in Figure 7–3.

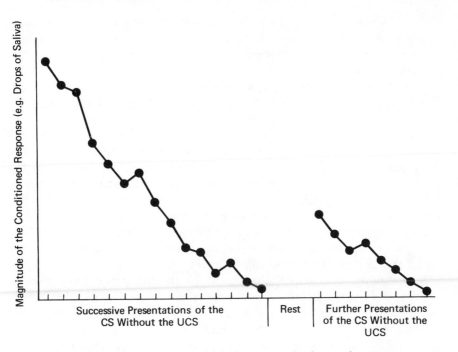

Figure 7–3. Typical curves showing the extinction and spontaneous recovery of a conditioned response.

Higher Order Conditioning.

After a CS has been paired with a UCS a number of times, it can be used much like a UCS. That is, through its pairing with the UCS, the CS develops reinforcing properties of its own and it can be paired with a second CS to bring about a CR. Let us pair, for example, a blinking light (CS) with the presentation of food powder (UCS). Food powder will cause the animal to salivate and after a number of pairings between the CS and the UCS, the blinking light presented alone will cause the animal to salivate. That the animal salivates to the blinking light is, of course, a conditioned response.

Now that the blinking light can elicit salivation, it can be paired with a second CS, say, a buzzer. The direction of the pairing is the same as in the original conditioning: first the new CS (buzzer) is presented and then the old one (blinking light). Note that food is no longer involved. After a number of such pairings, the buzzer, when presented alone, causes the animal to salivate. In this example, the first CS was used much like a UCS is used to bring about a conditioned response. This is called *second order conditioning.* We also say that the first CS developed *secondary reinforcing properties* since it was used to condition a response to a new stimulus. Therefore the CS is called a secondary reinforcer. Since secondary reinforcement cannot develop without the UCS, the UCS is called a *primary reinforcer.*

This procedure can be carried one more step. The second CS (buzzer) can be paired with one more CS, such as a 2000 cps tone. The direction of the pairing is the same as before: first the tone, then the buzzer. Eventually, the tone presented alone will cause the animal to salivate. Thus, through its pairing with the blinking light, the buzzer too became a secondary reinforcer and therefore could be used to condition a response to another new stimulus, the 2000 cps tone. This is *third order conditioning.* Both second and third order conditioning come under the general heading of higher order conditioning.

Since higher order conditioning must be studied during the extinction process, it is very difficult, if not impossible, to go beyond third order conditioning. In fact, such studies are quite rare. As one goes from first to third order conditioning, the magnitude of the CR becomes smaller and the CR lasts only for a few trials. In this example, the tone would only elicit a few drops of saliva and do so only the first few times it was presented to the animal.

Generalization.

To illustrate generalization, we return to the basic conditioning procedure. We will use a 2000 cps tone for our CS and meat powder for our UCS. After a number of pairings, the tone alone causes the animal to salivate; thus we have developed a CR. Once this has been accomplished, we enter the extinction phase of the experiment, only this time we will expose the animal to tones other than the one it was trained on. Some of the new tones will have a frequency higher than 2000 cps and some will have a lower frequency. Using the number of drops of saliva as our measure of the magnitude of the CR, we find the CR has its greatest magnitude when the 2000 cps tone is presented, but CRs are also given to other tones. The magnitude of the CR given to the other tones depends on their similarity to the tone the animal was actually trained on; in this case, the greater the similarity to the 2000 cps tone, the greater the magnitude of the CR. An example of generalization is shown in Figure 7–4.

There is a relationship between Pavlov's concept of generalization and Thorndike's concept of the transfer of training. With generalization, as the

Figure 7–4. Idealized stimulus generalization curve showing that as stimuli become increasing dissimilar to the one used as the CS during training the magnitude of the CR goes down.

training and testing situations have more in common, there is a greater probability that the same response will be made to both. This could easily be subsumed under Thorndike's "identical elements" theory of transfer. Likewise, both generalization and transfer explain how we can have a learned reaction to a situation we have never encountered before; that is, we respond to a new situation as we would respond to a similar situation that we are familiar with.

It is important to note the distinction between Thorndike's spread of effect and Pavlov's generalization. The spread of effect refers to the influence of reinforcement on responses neighboring the reinforced response, regardless of their similarity to the reinforced response. With the spread of effect, proximity is the important thing. Generalization describes the increased capability of producing a CR of stimuli related to the stimulus which actually preceded reinforcement. With generalization, similarity and not proximity is the important thing.

Discrimination.

The opposite of generalization is discrimination. As we saw above, generalization refers to the tendency to respond to a number of stimuli that are related to the one actually used during training. Discrimination, on the other hand, refers to the tendency to respond to a very restricted range of stimuli or to only the one used during training.

Discrimination can be brought about in two ways: prolonged training, and differential reinforcement. If a CS is paired with a UCS many times, the tendency to respond to stimuli related to the CS, but not identical to it, goes down. In other words, if the minimum number of pairings between the CS and UCS necessary to develop a CR is used, there is a relatively strong tendency to respond to stimuli related to the CS during extinction; that is, there is considerable generalization. However, if training is prolonged, there is a reduced tendency to respond to stimuli related to the CS during extinction. Thus, it is possible to control generalization by controlling training level: the greater the amount of training, the less generalization.

The second way of bringing about discrimination is through differential reinforcement. This procedure involves, using the above example, presenting the 2000 cps tone along with a number of other tones that will occur during extinction. Only the 2000 cps tone is followed by reinforcement. After such training, when the animal is presented with tones other than the 2000 cps tone during extinction, he tends not to respond to them. Thus, discrimination is demonstrated. Pavlov's attempt at providing a physiological explanation for generalization and discrimination will be considered later in this chapter.

Relationship Between the CS and the UCS.

Two general considerations about classical conditioning must be mentioned. First, there appears to be an optimal interval of presentation between the CS and UCS for conditioning to take place most rapidly. A number of investigators have found that if the CS comes on a half-second before the UCS, conditioning proceeds most efficiently. The most common procedure is to have the CS come on and stay on until the UCS comes on. If the time between these two events is greater or less than .5 seconds, conditioning is relatively more difficult to establish. This should be looked upon as an oversimplification, however, since the optimal interval of time between the onset of the CS and the onset of the UCS for conditioning to occur depends upon many factors, and it is the subject of a considerable amount of research.

The second important matter is related to the first. If the CS comes on *after* the UCS is presented, conditioning is extremely difficult, if not impossible, to establish. This is referred to as *backward conditioning*. Recently it has been found that a CS must be "informative" to the organism before conditioning will occur. Clearly, a CS that comes on after the UCS has already been presented cannot be used by the organism to predict occurrence of the UCS. This would be true not only of the backward conditioning situation, but would also be true of redundant CSs and unreliable CSs. Evidence for this point of view is supplied by Egger and Miller (1962, 1963) who found that (1) if two CSs reliably predict a UCS, the first one presented will become a secondary reinforcer, and the second one, which is redundant, does not; and (2) if two signals precede a UCS but one is always followed by the UCS and the other only sometimes followed by the UCS, the more reliable signal becomes a more powerful secondary reinforcer than the unreliable signal. Stimuli that occur after the UCS or stimuli that are either redundant or unreliably correlated with the UCS cannot be used by the organism to predict the occurrence of primary reinforcements; that is, they have no *information value*. In general, Egger and Miller conclude that for classical conditioning to take place, the organism must be able to use the CS to predict whether or not reinforcement will occur. It appears that if a CS is not informative about major events in the environment, conditioning will not take place.

Pavlov's Physiological Explanations of Conditioning Phenomena

Pavlov considered himself to be an experimental physiologist and he therefore sought to explain his observations in physiological terms. Many of his physiological explanations were highly speculative and most have since been found erroneous, but correcting for the time and conditions under which they were made, his explanations were quite remarkable. It was obvious to Pavlov that a CS and UCS became associated through the consistent pairings of the two. The question was, "What is the physiological basis for this association?" Pavlov answered this question as follows: The unconditional stimulus sets up a dominant activity in some area of the cerebral cortex.. All other stimuli present at the time also cause cerebral activity, but this activity is weaker and is drawn toward the area of dominant activity caused by the UCS. The weaker activity is drawn toward the stronger activity and a temporary connection is formed between these various centers in the brain. In this way, all the stimuli preceding the onset of the UCS become associated with it. Thus, when one of the stimuli that accompanied the UCS is presented to the organism, it causes activity in the area of the brain associated with it. If it is a visual stimulus, it will cause activity in the visual part of the brain. The activity in this area in turn causes activity in the area corresponding to the unconditioned stimulus because of the temporary connection between the two. The result is that the organism emits a response to the visual stimulus that is associated naturally with the UCS; that is, we have a conditioned response. To summarize, Pavlov is simply saying that brain centers that are repeatedly active together form temporary connections, and the arousal of one will cause the arousal of the others. Thus, if a tone is consistently presented to a dog just before it gets fed, the area of the brain aroused by the tone will form a temporary connection with the area of the brain which responds to food. When this connection is formed, the presentation of the tone will cause the animal to act as if food was present. At that point, we say a conditioned reflex has been developed.

Excitation and Inhibition.

According to Pavlov, the two basic processes governing all central nervous system activity were excitation and inhibition. Babkin says (1949):

> The fundamental theoretical conception of Pavlov concerning the functional properties of the nervous system, and of the cerebral cortex in particular, was that they were based on two equally important processes: the process of excitation and the process of inhibition. Very often he compared the nervous system with the ancient Greek god Janus, who had two faces looking in opposite directions. The excitation and the inhibition are only sides of one and the same process; they always exist simultaneously, but their proportion varies in each moment, at times the one prevailing, at times the other. Functionally the cerebral cortex is, according to Pavlov, a mosaic, consisting of continuously changing points of excitation and inhibition [p. 313].

Pavlov believed that each environmental event corresponded to some point on the cortex and that as these events were experienced they tended to either excite or inhibit cortical activity. Thus, the cortex is constantly being excited or inhibited depending on what the organism is experiencing. This pattern of excitation and inhibition that characterizes the brain at any given moment is what Pavlov called the *cortical mosaic*. The momentary cortical mosaic determines how an organism will respond to his environment. As either the external environment or the internal environment changes, the cortical mosaic changes and behavior changes accordingly.

The Dynamic Stereotype.

When events consistently occur in the environment, they come to have neurological representation and they become increasingly easy to respond to. Thus, responses to a familiar environment become rapid and automatic. When this happens, a *dynamic stereotype* is said to have been developed. Roughly, the dynamic stereotype is a cortical mosaic that has become stable because the organism has been in a highly predictable environment for a considerable length of time. As long as this cortical mapping accurately reflects the environment and produces appropriate responses, everything is fine. If, however, the environment is radically changed, the organism may find it difficult to change a dynamic stereotype. Pavlov (1955) puts the matter as follows:

> The entire establishment and distribution in the cortex of excitatory and inhibitory states, taking place in a certain period under the action of external and internal stimuli, become more and more fixed under uniform, recurring conditions and are effected with ever-increasing ease and automatism. Thus, there appears a dynamic stereotype (systematization) in the cortex, the maintenance of which becomes an increasingly less difficult nervous task; but the stereotype becomes inert, little susceptible to change and resistant to new conditions and new stimulations. Any initial elaboration of a stereotype is, depending on the complexity of the system of stimuli, a difficult and often an extraordinary task [p. 259].

Pavlov is saying that certain environmental events tend to be followed by certain other environmental events, and as long as this continues to be true, the association between the two on the neural level continues to grow stronger. (Note the similarity here to Thorndike's early thinking concerning the effect of exercise on a neural bond.) If the environment abruptly changes, new neural paths must be formed, and that is no easy matter.

Irradiation and Concentration.

Pavlov used the term "analyser" to describe the path from a sense receptor to a certain area of the brain. An analyser consists of sense receptors, the sensory tract in the spinal cord, and the area of the brain onto which the sensory activity is projected. Sensory information projected onto some area of the brain causes excitation in that area. Initially, this excitation spills over into neighboring brain areas; in other words, there is an *irradiation of excitation*. It is this process that Pavlov used to explain generalization. In our example of generalization described above, we noted that when an animal was conditioned to respond to a 2000 cps tone, he responded not only to that tone but to other related tones. The magnitude of the response was determined by the similarity between the tone being presented and the actual CS used during training. As the similarity increased, the CR's magnitude increased.

Pavlov's explanation for generalization was that neural impulses travelled from the sense receptors—in this case from the ear—to a specific area of the cortex that reacted to a 2000 cps tone. The activity caused by the 2000 cps tone irradiates from this location out into the neighboring regions. Pavlov assumed that tones closest to the 2000 cps tone would be represented in brain regions close to the area corresponding to the one for the 2000 cps tone. As tones become dissimilar, the brain regions representing them will be farther away from the area representing the 2000 cps tone. In addition, Pavlov assumed that excitation diminished with distance: it was strongest at the point corresponding to the CS and weaker farther away. Therefore an association was made not only between the CS and the UCS but with a number of stimuli related to the CS that had representation in neighboring brain regions. In addition to his hypothesis that excitation irradiated or spread to neighboring regions of the cortex, Pavlov found that inhibition also irradiated.

Pavlov also found that concentration, a process opposite to irradiation, can govern both excitation and inhibition. He found that under certain circumstances both excitation and inhibition can be concentrated at specific areas of the brain. As the process of irradiation is used to explain generalization, so is the process of concentration used to explain discrimination.

At first the organism has a generalized tendency to respond to a CS during conditioning. For example, if a signal is followed by a reinforcer, there is a learned tendency to respond to that and related signals. Likewise, if a signal is presented and is not followed by a reinforcer, there is a learned tendency not to respond to that and related signals. We say, therefore, that both excitation and inhibition have irradiated. With prolonged training, however, the tendencies to respond and not to respond become less general and increasingly specific to a narrow range of stimuli. In the latter case, we say the excitation and inhibition have been concentrated.

As we noted earlier in this chapter, discrimination, or the ability to respond differentially to related stimuli, can be brought about by prolonged training or differential reinforcement. If a large number of pairings are made between the CS and the UCS the excitation begins to concentrate. After such training, one would find that the organism tends to respond only to the CS or to stimuli very similar to the CS. In other words, because excitation has been concentrated, very little generalization would take place.

Summary of Pavlov's Views on Brain Functioning.

Pavlov saw the brain as a mosaic of points of excitation and inhibition. Each point on the brain corresponded to an environmental event. Depending on what was being experienced at the moment, a different pattern of excitation and inhibition would occur in the brain and that pattern would determine behavior. Some connections in the brain are between unconditioned stimuli and their associated responses, and some are between conditioned stimuli and their associated responses. The former are permanent and the latter are temporary and change with varied environmental conditions.

When a temporary connection is first being formed in the brain, there is a tendency for a conditioned stimulus to have a very general effect in the brain. That is, the excitation caused by a conditioned stimulus irradiates over a relatively larger portion of the cortex. The same thing is true when an organism is learning not to respond to, or to avoid, a stimulus. The inhibitory effects of such a stimulus also irradiates over a fairly large portion of the brain in the early stages of learning. As learning proceeds, however, the excitation caused by a positive stimulus and the inhibition caused by a negative stimulus become concentrated in specific areas of the cortex. As the organism develops the connections between environmental events and brain processes that allow it to survive, a dynamic stereotype develops, which is a kind of neural mapping of the environment. The dynamic stereotype makes it easier to respond to a highly predictable environment but makes it difficult to adjust to a new environment.

Pavlov never explained how all these processes interact to produce the smooth, coordinated behavior we see from organisms, but he did express amazement that systematic behavior did result from such a large number of influences. Pavlov puts the matter as follows (1955):

> Countless stimuli, different in nature and intensity, reach the cerebral hemispheres both from the external world and the internal medium of the organism itself. Whereas some of them are

merely investigated (the orienting reflex), others evoke highly diverse conditioned and unconditioned effects. They all meet, come together, interact, and they must, finally, become systematized, equilibrated, and form, so to speak, a dynamic stereotype. What truly grandiose work [p. 454]!

The "orienting reflex" to which Pavlov refers is the tendency for organisms to attend to and explore novel stimuli that occur in their environment. The orienting reflex has been the topic of considerable research in recent years.

First and Second Signal Systems.

Pavlov believed that human behavior was much more complex than that of other animals because humans have a language, which Pavlov called a second signal system. The first signal system consists of the organism's reactions—both learned and unlearned—to environmental stimuli. Our discussion of learning up to this point has been concerned with the first signal system. Even though words are only symbols of reality, they too can have responses conditioned to them and, therefore, words can govern our behavior. For example, actual objects associated with previous pain or anxiety will be avoided but so will things labelled dangerous or harmful.

One example of how language complicates classical conditioning is found in the area of *semantic generalization* (sometimes called mediated generalization). Semantic generalization studies have shown that a response can be conditioned to the *meaning* of a stimulus rather than to the concrete stimulus itself. For example, if a response is conditioned to the number 4, the human subject will emit a conditioned response when he is confronted with such stimuli as $\sqrt{16}$; $2\overline{)8}$; 2×2; $10\overline{)40}$, etc. In other words, the number 4 elicits a conditioned response, but so will a variety of other stimuli that result in 4 after mental operations have been performed. The conclusion to be drawn is that for human subjects the true CS is the concept of "fourness." (See Razran, 1961, for additional examples of semantic conditioning.)

Semantic generalization also seems to vary as a function of age. In his work with children of different ages, Reiss (1946) found that after initial training which involved visually presenting a word such as "right" as a CS, children generalized by giving conditioned responses according to their level of language development. He found that eight-year-olds generalized to visually presented homophones (e.g., *rite*); eleven-year-olds generalized to antonyms (e.g., *wrong*); and fourteen-year-olds generalized to synonyms (e.g., *correct*).

Although the second signal system is clearly more complex than the first signal system, Pavlov felt that the same laws of conditioning govern both and therefore they both could be studied objectively. In other words, the process by which we develop a reaction to an environmental event is the same process by which we develop a reaction to a word or a thought.

A COMPARISON BETWEEN CLASSICAL AND INSTRUMENTAL CONDITIONING

The kind of conditioning that Thorndike studied is now called instrumental conditioning because the response being observed was instrumental in getting the animal something it wanted (reward). In the case of the cat in the puzzle box, the cat had to learn to perform a certain response which released him from the box and rewarded him with a piece of fish. If the appropriate response did not occur, the animal was not rewarded. To summarize, we can say that in instrumental conditioning, any response that leads to reward tends to be repeated, and a reward is something the animal wants.

Classical conditioning elicits a response from the animal, and instrumental conditioning depends on the animal's emitting the response. The former can be said to be involuntary and automatic; the latter to be voluntary and under the animal's control.

The function of reinforcement (reward) is also quite different for classical and instrumental conditioning. With instrumental conditioning reward is presented to the animal *after* the response of interest has been made. With classical conditioning, however, the reward (UCS) is presented in order to *elicit* the response of interest. The two situations can be diagrammed as follows:

Instrumental Conditioning

Environmental situation →   Effective behavior   →   Reward
   (e.g., puzzle box)   (e.g., behavior which   (e.g., being re-
                    releases the animal   leased from con-
                    from confinement)   finement and/or
                                            receiving a piece
                                              of fish)

Association of interest

Classical Conditioning

Conditioned stimulus →Reward (Unconditioned → Unconditioned
   (e.g., a tone)   stimulus e.g., food)   response
                                                              (e.g., salivation)

Conditioned
   response
Association of Interest   (salivation)

Pavlov felt that he had discovered the physiological bases for the associations that philosophers and psychologists had been talking about for so many years. To him, conditioned reflexes could explain how the mind works. Pavlov placed himself squarely among the associationists with the following statement (1955):

> Are there any grounds . . . for distinguishing between that which the physiologist calls the temporary connection and that which the psychologist terms association? They are fully identical; they merge and absorb each other. Psychologists themselves seem to recognize this, since they (at least, some of them) have stated that the experiments with conditioned reflexes provide a solid foundation for associative psychology, i.e., psychology which regards association as the base of psychical activity [p. 251].

The two kinds of conditioning reflect basic differences in outlook between Pavlov and Thorndike. Pavlov was basically an experimental physiologist who was interested in learning how the brain functioned. Thorndike was an early functionalist who was strongly influenced by Darwin. Thorndike's main concern was how learning was involved in man's adaptation to his environment. He was more concerned with the *function* of learned behavior than was Pavlov. This may be why Thorndike did little more than acknowledge associative shifting, a kind of learning based strictly on contiguity between stimuli and response, whereas Pavlov developed a physiological model to explain this phenomena in detail.

Despite basic differences between the classical and instrumental conditioning paradigms, they have many similarities. Most importantly, both kinds of conditioning are dependent upon reward. In classical conditioning the UCS is the reward and if it is removed from the experimental arrangement, extinction occurs. In instrumental conditioning the reward is the "satisfying state of affairs" that *follows* an appropriate response. If reward no longer follows a certain response, the probability of that response goes back to the point where it was before reward was introduced. To summarize, classical and instrumental conditioning not only have in common the necessity of reward (extinction follows when it is removed), but also the phenomena of spontaneous recovery, generalization, discrimination, and secondary reinforcement.

John B. Watson

One cannot conclude a discussion of Pavlov without reviewing briefly the work of John Broadus Watson (1878–1958), upon whom Pavlov had a great influence. We noted earlier that psychologists were becoming increasingly dissatisfied with the study of consciousness. Structuralism, with its search for the elements of thought through the use of introspection, was abandoned and the new school of functionalism took its place. The functionalist studied both behavior and consciousness to discover how the organism adapted to the environment. Gradually psychologists developed the idea that there was no need to study consciousness at all; that in order to be completely objective, psychology had to make behavior its only subject matter. Watson embraced this idea enthusiastically and founded the school of *behaviorism*.

In order to be a science, psychology had to have a subject matter that

John Broadus Watson

could be measured reliably. That subject matter, said Watson, was behavior. Explanations of behavior that involved mental processes were not admitted in the science of behaviorism since such processes were unobservable and therefore unmeasurable. Thorndike's "pleasurable state of affairs" and "annoying state of affairs" was also mentalistic and therefore had no place in the new psychology. No more introspection, no more talk of instinctive motivation, and no more attempts to study man's conscious or unconscious mind. Behavior is what we can see and therefore behavior is what we study. According to Watson (1913):

> Psychology as the behaviorist views it is a purely objective experimental branch of natural science. Its theoretical goal is the prediction and control of behavior. Introspection forms no essential part of its methods, nor is the scientific value of its data dependent upon the readiness with which they lend themselves to interpretation in terms of consciousness. The behaviorist, in his efforts to get a unitary scheme of animal response, recognizes no dividing line between man and brute. The behavior of man, with all its refinement and complexity, forms only a part of the behaviorist's total scheme of investigation . . . [p. 158].

Elsewhere Watson says (1929):

> . . . The behaviorist cannot find consciousness in the test tube of his science. He finds no evidence anywhere for a stream of consciousness, not even for one so convincing as that described by William James. He does, however, find convincing proof of an ever-widening stream of behavior [p. 26].

Personality was, to Watson, a collection of conditioned reflexes. Human emotion was a product of both heredity and experience. According to Watson, we inherit three emotions—fear, rage, and love. Through the conditioning process, these three basic emotions become attached to different things for different people. Speech was behavior that resulted from the movement of the muscles in the throat. Thinking was implicit or subvocal speech. During overt speech, the vocal apparatus responded with vigor; during thinking, the same apparatus is involved but its movements are minute. Speech could indeed be studied but it had to be studied as behavior and not as a tool used to investigate "inner experience."

Watson was an extreme environmental determinist. He held the position that all we come equipped with at birth is a few reflexes and a few basic emotions, and through classical conditioning, these reflexes become paired with a variety of stimuli. He emphatically denied that we are born with any mental abilities or predispositions. In this, Watson's thinking followed that of John Locke, who said that the mind was a blank slate at birth. The extreme to which he was willing to carry this position is exemplified by his following famous statement (1926):

> Give me a dozen healthy infants, well-formed, and my own specified world to bring them up in and I'll guarantee to take any one at random and train him to become any type of specialist I might select—doctor, lawyer, artist, merchant, chief, and yes, even beggarman and thief, regardless of his talents, penchants, tendencies, abilities, vocations, and race of his ancestors [p. 10].

Experiment with Albert.

To demonstrate how inborn emotional reflexes become conditioned to neutral stimuli, Watson and Rosalie Rayner (1920) performed an experiment on an eleven-month-old infant named Albert. In addition to Albert, the other ingredients in the experiment were a white rat, a steel bar, and a hammer. At the onset of the study, Albert showed no fear of the rat. In fact, he reached out and tried to touch it. During the initial part of the experiment, when Albert saw the rat and reached for it, the experimenter took the hammer and struck the steel bar behind the infant, making a loud noice. In response to the noise, Albert "jumped violently and fell forward." Again Albert saw the rat and reached for it, and again, just as his hand touched the rat, the bar was struck making a loud noise. Again Albert jumped violently and began to whimper. Because of Albert's emotional state, the experiment was suspended for one week so Albert would not become too disturbed.

After a week, the rat was again presented to Albert. This time Albert was very cautious of the animal and watched him very carefully. At one point, when the rat came into contact with his hand, Albert withdrew his hand immediately. There were several more pairings between the rat and the sound and eventually Albert developed a strong fear of the rat. Now when the rat was presented to Albert again, he began to cry and "almost instantly he turned sharply to the left, fell over, raised himself on all fours and began to crawl away . . . rapidly" [1920, p. 5].

It was also shown that Albert's fear generalized to a variety of objects that were not feared at the onset of the experiment: a rabbit, a dog, a fur coat, cotton, and a Santa Claus mask. Thus, Watson showed that our emotional reactions can be rearranged through classical conditioning. In the experiment above, the loud noise was the UCS, fear produced by the noise was the UCR, the rat was the CS, and the fear of the rat was the

CR. Albert's fear of all white and furry objects showed that generalization also took place.

Watson was enthusiastic about his work and its implications. He saw behaviorism as a means of stripping ignorance and superstition from human existence, thereby paving the way for a more rational, meaningful life. Understanding the principles of behavior, he thought, was the first step toward that kind of life. He said (1925):

> I think behaviorism does lay a foundation for saner living. It ought to be a science that prepares men and women for understanding the first principles of their own behavior. It ought to make men and women eager to rearrange their own lives, and especially eager to prepare themselves to bring up their own children in a healthy way. I wish I had time more fully to describe this, to picture to you the kind of rich and wonderful individual we should make of every healthy child; if only we could let it shape itself properly and then provide for it a universe unshackled by legendary folk lore of happenings thousands of years ago; unhampered by disgraceful political history; free of foolish customs and conventions which have no significance in themselves, yet which hem the individual in like taut steel bands [p. 248].

Clearly, Watson was a rebel. He took the various objective approaches to the study of psychology that were appearing here and there, and through his forceful writing and speaking, organized them into a new school of psychology. Unfortunately, Watson's career as a professional psychologist was cut short when he was asked to leave the Johns Hopkins University because of marital troubles leading to divorce. The same year he left the Johns Hopkins University he married Rosalie Rayner, with whom he did the study with Albert, and went into the advertising business. From that point on, instead of writing in professional journals, Watson published his ideas in *McCall's*, *Harper's*, and *Collier's* magazines.

Watson never waivered from his behaviorist outlook, and in 1936 he had the following to say about the position he took in 1912 (1936):

> I still believe as firmly as ever in the general behavioristic position I took overtly in 1912. I think it has influenced psychology. Strangely enough, I think it has temporarily slowed down psychology because the older instructors would not accept it wholeheartedly, and consequently they failed to present it convincingly to their classes. The youngsters did not get a fair presentation, hence they are not embarking wholeheartedly upon a behavioristic career, and yet they will no longer accept the teachings of James, Titchener, and Angell. I honestly think that psychology has

been sterile for several years. We need younger instructors who will teach objective psychology with no reference to the mythology most of us present-day psychologists have been brought up upon. When this day comes, psychology will have a renaissance greater than that which occurred in science in the Middle Ages. I believe as firmly as ever in the future of behaviorism—behaviorism as a companion of zoology, physiology, psychiatry, and physical chemistry [p. 231].

DISCUSSION QUESTIONS

1. Design a cigarette commercial utilizing the principles of classical conditioning. How would this commercial differ from one based upon the principles of instrumental conditioning?
2. Differentiate between classical conditioning and Thorndike's notion of associative shifting.
3. Give a few examples of your own conditioned reflexes.
4. Give a few examples of how classical conditioning might operate in a classroom situation.
5. Can you think of where a knowledge of classical conditioning would be useful in child rearing? Give examples.
6. Briefly describe the following: acquisition of a conditioned response, extinction, spontaneous recovery, generalization, discrimination, and higher order conditioning.
7. Briefly describe Pavlov's physiological explanation of conditioning, generalization, and discrimination.
8. According to Pavlov, what determines how we respond to the environment at any given time?
9. Discuss the major differences and similarities between instrumental and classical conditioning.
10. How is classical conditioning related to survival?
11. Describe the conditions necessary for a stimulus to become a secondary reinforcer. How can one tell if a stimulus has become a secondary reinforcer?
12. Explain emotional development from J. B. Watson's point of view.

GLOSSARY

Backward Conditioning. An experimental arrangement where the conditioned stimulus is presented to the organism after the unconditioned stimulus is presented.

Behaviorism. The school of psychology started by J. B. Watson. The behaviorist believes that the proper subject matter for psychology is behavior, not mental events.

Conditioned Response (also called conditioned reflex). A response that is made to a stimulus not originally associated with the response. For example, salivation to the sound of a tone is a conditioned response because an organism would not ordinarily salivate to the sound of a tone.

Conditioned Stimulus. A stimulus that, before conditioning, does not cause an organism to respond in any particular way. Before conditioning, the stimulus is a neutral stimulus. After conditioning, however, the conditioned stimulus elicits a conditioned response.

Cortical Mosaic. The pattern of excitation and inhibition that constitutes the activity of the cortex at any given moment.

Discrimination. Learning to respond to one stimulus but not to other stimuli although they may be related to the first. For example, through discrimination training a tone of 500 cps elicits a conditioned response, whereas a tone of 490 cps does not.

Dynamic Stereotype. A cortical mapping of events consistently occurring in the environment. A stable environment comes to have neurological representation on the cortex.

Excitation. An increase in brain activity. A stimulus that causes excitation is called a positive stimulus.

Extinction. The procedure whereby a conditioned response is elicited but is not followed by reinforcement. Under these circumstances, the magnitude of the conditioned response gradually becomes smaller. When a conditioned response is no longer elicited by a conditioned stimulus, the conditioned response is said to have been extinguished.

First Signal System. Physical events in the environment and the stimuli they produce.

Generalization. The tendency for an organism to respond not only to the specific stimulus it was trained on, but also to other related stimuli. For example, if an organism was trained with a 500 cps tone as a conditioned stimulus, such tones as 600, 550, and 490 cps will also tend to elicit conditioned responses.

Higher Order Conditioning. After classical conditioning has taken place, a second conditioned stimulus is paired with the first conditioned stimulus. After a number of such pairings, the second conditioned stimulus can also elicit a conditioned response. This is called second order conditioning. Once the second conditioned stimulus has the power to elicit a conditioned response, it can be paired with a third conditioned stimulus to produce third order conditioning.

Information Value of a Stimulus. The ability of a stimulus to act as a signal to an organism that a significant event is about to occur. For example, a stimulus that signals the occurrence of food for a hungry animal has information value.

Inhibition. A decrease in brain activity. A stimulus that causes inhibition is called a negative stimulus.

Irradiation. The tendency for excitation or inhibition in a specific area of the brain to spill over into neighboring brain regions.

Orienting Reflex. The tendency for an organism to attend to and explore a novel stimulus as it occurs in his environment.

Primary Reinforcer. Something related to survival such as food, water, or sex. All conditioning ultimately depends upon primary reinforcement. In classical conditioning, the primary reinforcer is the unconditioned stimulus.

Secondary Reinforcer. A previously neutral stimulus that takes on reinforcing properties through its close association with primary reward. After conditioning has taken place, a conditioned stimulus must necessarily be a secondary reinforcer.

Second Signal System. Language. The symbols man uses in communication. Since responses can be conditioned to symbols, they can influence man's behavior. The second signal system, which is peculiarly human, makes human behavior much more complex than the behavior of other animals.

Semantic Generalization. Generalization to symbols that have a meaning similar to the meaning of the conditioned stimulus used during training, although the physical characteristics of symbols may be totally dissimilar to those of the conditioned stimulus. For example, if a human subject is taught to salivate when he sees the number 10, he will also salivate when he sees $8\overline{)80}$ or $\sqrt{100}$. In semantic generalization, it is meaning that determines how much generalization occurs rather than the physical similarity between stimuli.

Spontaneous Recovery. When a conditioned response is no longer elicited by a conditioned stimulus, extinction is said to have taken place. Following a delay after extinction, the conditioned stimulus again elicits conditioned responses, although there were no further pairings between the conditioned stimulus and the unconditioned stimulus. The reappearance of the conditioned response after extinction has taken place is called spontaneous recovery.

Unconditioned Response. The natural and automatic response that is elicited when an unconditioned stimulus is presented to an organism. Withdrawing when stuck by a pin, salivating at the sight of food, and the constriction of the pupil of the eye when light is shone into it, are all examples of unconditioned responses.

Unconditioned Stimulus. A stimulus that causes a natural and automatic response from the organism. An object that causes pain to a certain part of the body will cause the organism to automatically withdraw from the source of pain. Pain, therefore, is an unconditioned stimulus. Shining a light into the pupil of the eye will cause the pupil to automatically constrict; the light, therefore, is an unconditioned stimulus.

Watson, J. B. The founder of the school of behaviorism. Watson relied heavily on Pavlov's theory of learning in his explanation of human behavior. Watson believed that, except for a few basic emotions, human behavior was learned. Therefore, he believed that by controlling the learning process it is possible to control human personality. For this reason, Watson was considered an extreme environmental determinist.

8

Edwin Ray Guthrie

Guthrie was born in 1886 and died in 1959. He was professor of psychology at the University of Washington from 1914 until his retirement in 1956. His most basic work was *The Psychology of Learning*, published in 1935 and revised in 1952. His style of writing is easy to follow, humorous, and involves many homespun anecdotes to exemplify his ideas. There are no technical terms or mathematical equations, and he firmly believed that his theory—or any scientific theory for that matter—should be stated so that it would be understandable to college freshmen. He placed a great emphasis on practical application of his ideas and in this regard was very much like Thorndike. He was not really an experimentalist himself, although he certainly had an experimental outlook and orientation. He, along with Horton, performed only one experiment related to his theory of learning, and we will discuss that experiment later on. He was, however, clearly a behaviorist. As a matter of fact, he felt theorists like Thorndike, Pavlov, and Watson were too subjective, and that by carefully applying the law of parsimony, it was possible to explain all learning phenomena by using only one principle. As we shall see below, this one principle was one of Aristotle's laws of association. It is for this reason that we place Guthrie's behavioristic theory within the associationistic paradigm.

MAJOR THEORETICAL NOTIONS

The One Law of Learning.

In general, most learning theories can be thought of as attempts to determine the rules by which stimuli and responses become associated. Guthrie felt that the rules that had been generated by theorists like Thorndike and Pavlov were unnecessarily complicated and in their place he proposed one law of learning, the *law of contiguity*, which he stated as follows (1952):

> A combination of stimuli which has accompanied a movement will on its recurrence tend to be followed by that movement. Note that nothing is here said about "confirmatory waves" or reinforcement or pleasant effects [p. 23].

There is nothing new about the law of contiguity as a principle of learning. In fact, as we noted in Chapter 3, it goes all the way back to Aristotle's laws of association. Guthrie, however, made the law of contiguity the cornerstone of his unique theory of learning.

Edwin Ray Guthrie

Another way of stating the law of contiguity is to say that if you did something in a given situation, the next time that you are in that situation, you will tend to do the same thing. In his last publication before he died, Guthrie (1959) revised his law of contiguity to read, "What is being noticed becomes a signal for what is being done" [p. 186]. This was Guthrie's way of recognizing the enormous number of stimuli that confront an organism at any given time and the fact that the organism cannot possibly form associations with all of them. Rather, the organism responds selectively to only a small proportion of the stimuli confronting him and it is that proportion that becomes associated with whatever response is being made. One can note the similarity between Guthrie's thinking and Thorndike's concept of "prepotency of elements" which also stated that organisms respond selectively to different aspects of the environment.

Guthrie explains why, although the law of contiguity may be true, prediction of behavior will always be probabilistic, as follows (1952):

> Although the principle as it has just been stated is short and simple, it will not be clear without a considerable amount of elaboration. The word "tend" is used because behavior is at any time subject to a great variety of conditions. Conflicting "tendencies" or incompatible "tendencies" are always present. The outcome of any one stimulus or stimulus pattern cannot be predicted with certainty because there are other stimulus patterns present. We may express this by saying that the final behavior is caused by the total situation, but we may not, in making this statement, flatter ourselves that we have done more than offer an excuse for a failure to predict. No one has recorded and no one ever will record any stimulus situation in its totality, or observed any total situation, so that to speak of it as a "cause" or even as the occasion of a bit of behavior is misleading [p. 23].

One-Trial Learning.

Another of Aristotle's laws of association was the law of frequency which stated that the strength of an association depends upon the frequency with which it has occurred. If the law of frequency is modified to refer to the association between a response which leads to a "satisfying state of affairs" and the stimulating conditions preceding the response, Thorndike would accept it. The more often a response is rewarded in a given situation the greater the probability of that response's being made when that situation recurs. If the association is between a CS and a UCS, Pavlov would accept the law of frequency. The greater the number of pairings between the CS and the UCS the greater is the magnitude of the conditioned response elicited by the CS.

Guthrie completely rejected the law of frequency as a learning principle. He says (1942): " . . . *A stimulus pattern gains its full associative strength on the occasion of its first pairing with a response*" [p. 30]. Thus, to Guthrie learning is the result of contiguity between a pattern of stimulation and a response, and learning is complete (the association is at full strength) after only one pairing between the stimuli and the response.

The Recency Principle.

The principles of contiguity and one-trial learning necessitate the recency principle, which states: that which was done last in the presence of a set of stimuli will be that which will tend to be done when that stimulus combination next recurs. In other words, whatever we did *last* under a given set of circumstances will be what we will tend to do again if those circumstances are reencountered.

Movement-Produced Stimuli.

Although Guthrie reasserted his belief in the law of contiguity throughout his career, he felt it would be misleading to think of the learned association to be exclusively between environmental stimuli and overt behavior. For example, an environmental event and the response that it produces sometimes are separated by a fairly large interval of time, and it would be difficult, therefore, to think of the two as contiguous. Guthrie solves this problem by postulating the existence of movement-produced stimuli, which, as the name implies, are caused by the movement of the body. If we hear a sound and turn toward it, for example, the muscles, tendons, and joints produce stimuli that are distinctly different from the external stimulation that caused us to move. The important fact about movement-produced stimuli is that they can have responses conditioned to them. That is, after a response has been initiated by an external stimulus, the body itself can produce the stimulus for the next response and that response can furnish the stimulus for the next one, etc. Thus, the interval between the occurrence of an external stimulus and the response finally made to it is filled with movement-produced stimuli. Conditioning is still between contiguous events, but in some cases the contiguity is between movement-produced stimuli and behavior rather than between external stimuli and behavior. Guthrie gave the following example of how he believed movement-produced stimuli function (1935):

> Such a movement as listening or looking is not over like a flash or an explosion. It takes time. The movement, once started, maintains itself by the stimuli it furnishes. When the telephone bell rings we rise and make our way to the instrument. Long before we have reached the telephone the sound has ceased to act as a stimulus. We are kept in action by the stimuli from our own movements toward the telephone. One movement starts another, then a third, the third a fourth, and so on. Our movements form series, very often stereotyped in the form of habit. *These movements and their movement-produced stimuli make possible a far-reaching extension of association or conditioning* [p. 54].

A simplified version of the situation described in Guthrie's example could be diagrammed as follows:

External stimulation → Overt response → Movement-produced stimuli →
(telephone ringing)   (e.g., turning
                        toward telephone)

Overt response → Movement-produced stimuli → Overt response →
 (e.g., rising   (e.g., walking toward
 from chair)   telephone)

Movement-produced stimuli → Overt response
                           (e.g., picking up
                               telephone)

Guthrie's contention that a response can provide stimulation for the next response is very popular among learning theorists today and comes under the general heading of *chaining*.

As we have seen in Chapter 5, Skinner's explanation of chaining emphasized external stimuli and their secondary reinforcing properties. In this chapter we have seen that Guthrie's explanation of chaining emphasized internal stimuli. Hull's explanation of chaining, covered in Chapter 6, can be looked upon as a combination of Skinner's and Guthrie's views since it maintains that both internal and external stimulation are involved in chaining.

Why Does Practice Improve Performance?

To answer this question Guthrie differentiated between *acts* and *movements*. Movements are simple muscle contractions; acts are made up of a large number of movements. Acts are usually defined in terms of what they accomplish, that is, what change they make in the environment. As examples of acts, Guthrie lists such things as typing a letter, eating a meal, throwing a ball, reading a book, or selling a car. Guthrie and Horton explained improvement as the result of practice as follows (1946):

> We have taken the position that acts are made up of movements that result from muscular contraction, and that *it is these muscular contractions that are directly predicted by the principle of associa-tion.* We are assuming that such movements are subject to condi-tioning or associative learning and that this conditioning is in itself an "all or none" affair, and its degree is not dependent on practice. One experience is sufficient to establish an association.
>
> But the learning of an act does take practice. We assume that the reason for this is that the act names an end result that is at-tained under varied circumstances and by movements varied to suit the circumstances. Learning an act as distinguished from a movement does require practice because it requires that the proper movement has been associated with its own cues. Even so simple an act as grasping a rattle requires different movements according to the distance and direction and position of the object. One successful experience is not sufficient to equip the infant with an act because the one movement acquired on that occasion might never again be successful [pp. 7–8].

Thus, learning a skill such as playing golf or driving a car consists of learning thousands of associations between specific stimuli and specific movements. For example, learning to putt a golf ball into the cup from ten feet away from a certain angle under specific conditions (wind com-ing from a certain direction at a certain velocity, temperature is 85°, etc.), is only one of thousands of responses that constitute the game of golf. Practice allows more and more of these specific associations to be made. The same is true of driving, typing, and all other skills. Elsewhere Guthrie says (1942):

> Learning occurs normally in one associative episode. The rea-son that long practice and many repetitions are required to estab-lish certain skills is that these really require many specific move-ments to be attached to many different stimulus situations. A skill is not simple habit, but a large collection of habits that achieve a certain result in many and varied circumstances [p. 59].

To summarize, a skill is made up of many acts, and acts are made up of many movements. The relationship between one set of stimuli and one movement is learned at full strength in one trial, but this does not bring about proficiency at a skill. For example, driving a car, typewriting, or playing baseball are all very complicated skills consisting of a large number of stimulus-response associations, and any one of these bonds or associations is learned at full strength in one trial. But it takes time and practice for all the necessary associations to be made. Learning to type the letter *A* while looking at an *A* on a written sheet of paper alongside the typewriter might be considered a specific stimulus-response (S-R) association. Looking at the letter *B* and typing the letter *B* is another specific association, as is looking at and typing the letter *C*. These specific associations must be built up for the entire alphabet, and then for the numbers, and then for the capital letters, and finally for the various symbols that occur on the typewriter. Also, the typist must learn to make these responses under a wide variety of circumstances, such as, under varying lighting and temperature conditions, from different angles of seeing the material, and on different kinds of paper. When all these responses have been learned, we say the person has become a proficient typist. In summary, the skill of typing involves an enormously large number of specific S-R connections each of which is learned in a single trial.

The reason Thorndike found systematic improvement through successive trials was that he was studying the learning of a skill, not the learning of individual movements. Guthrie and Horton say (1946):

> We believe that when the puzzle-box situation varies indefinitely, as it did in the Thorndike box with the hanging loop, it is necessary for the cat to establish a large repertoire of specific escape movements adjusted to the specific differences in the situation. In other words, the cat establishes a skill, rather than a stereotyped habit. But the skill is made up of many specific habits. The gradual reduction of time reported by Thorndike is a consequence of the varied situation confronting the cat [p. 41].

Whether or not learning occurs after one experience, as Guthrie believed, or in small increments, as Thorndike believed, is still a controversial issue and one which we will discuss in more detail in the next chapter.

Nature of Reward.

What is the place of reward, or reinforcement, in Guthrie's theory? At this point Guthrie took issue with Thorndike, who, as you remember, made the revised law of effect the cornerstone of his theory. Learning depended upon the outcome of an action. When a response led to a satisfying state of affairs, its probability of recurring increased. Guthrie felt the law of effect was completely unnecessary. For Guthrie, reward was merely a mechanical arrangement which he felt could be explained by his one law of learning. According to Guthrie, *reward changes the stimulating conditions and thereby prevents unlearning.* For example, in a puzzle box, the last thing the animal does before receiving a reward is to move a pole or pull on a ring, which allows him to escape from the box. Therefore, the response that allowed the animal to escape—moving the pole, in this case—changed the entire pattern of stimuli that the animal experienced. According to the recency principle, when the animal is placed back into the puzzle box, he will tend to move the pole again. In other words, being released from the puzzle box after moving the pole preserves the association between being in the puzzle box and moving the pole. In fact, the last response that was made in the puzzle box will be the response the animal makes when he is again placed into the box, *regardless of what that response was.* Guthrie and Horton (1946) say:

> In our opinion the second occasion tends to repeat the behavior of the first, errors and all, except in so far as remaining in the puzzle box for a long time tends to establish new responses to the puzzle-box situation. *The reason for the remarkable preservation of the end action leading to escape is that this action removes the cat from the situation and hence allows no new responses to become attached to the puzzle-box situation.* Escape protects the end action from relearning [p. 39].

Elsewhere (1940) he says:

> The position taken in this paper is that the animal learns to escape with its first escape. This learning is protected from forgetting because the escape removes the animal from the situation which has then no chance to acquire new associations.
> . . . what encountering the food does is not to intensify a previous item of behavior but to protect that item from being unlearned. The whole situation and action of the animal is so changed by the food that the pre-food situation is shielded from new associations. These new associations can not be established in the absence of the box interior, and in the absence of the behavior that preceded latch-opening [pp. 144–45].

The Guthrie-Horton Experiment.

Guthrie and Horton carefully observed approximately eight hundred escapes by cats from a puzzle box. Their observations were reported in

Figure 8-1. A pictorial record of a series of escape responses made by one of Guthrie's cats. The pictures were taken automatically when the cat moved the pole. Note that the cat tended to move the pole in the same way on each trial. (From Guthrie and Horton, "Cats In a Puzzle Box." New York: Holt, Rinehart & Winston, Inc., 1946, pp. 53–55. Reprinted by permission).

a small book entitled *Cats in a Puzzle Box* (1946). The puzzle box they used was very similar to the apparatus that Thorndike used in his selecting and connecting experiments. Guthrie and Horton used a large number of cats as subjects but they noted that each cat learned to escape from the puzzle box in his own peculiar way. The particular response learned by a particular animal was the one the animal had hit upon just prior to being released from the box. Since that exact response tended to be repeated the next time the animal was placed into the puzzle box, it was referred to as *stereotyped behavior*. For example, Cat A would hit the pole by backing into it, Cat B would push it with his head, or Cat C would move it with his paw. Guthrie would say that in each case the door's flying open was an abrupt change in the stimulating conditions. By changing the stimulating conditions, the response of backing into the pole, for example, is protected from unlearning. The last thing that the animal did before the chamber was opened was to back into that pole, and because he backed into the pole the stimulating conditions changed. Thus, applying the law of recency, the next time we put that animal in, he should respond by backing into the pole, and this is exactly what Guthrie and Horton observed. A pictorial record of a typical cat's performance is shown in Figure 8–1.

Guthrie and Horton observed that very often the animal, after escaping from the puzzle box, would ignore a piece of fish that was offered to him. Even though the animal ignored the so-called reward, he was just as proficient at leaving the box the next time he was placed in it. This observation, according to Guthrie, added further support to his contention that reward is merely a mechanical arrangement that prevents unlearning. Guthrie concluded that any event following the desired response from an animal would change the stimulating conditions and thereby preserve that response under the preceding stimulating conditions.

Forgetting.

Not only does learning occur in one trial, but so does forgetting. All forgetting occurs, according to Guthrie, by merely causing an alternative response to occur in the presence of a stimulus pattern. After a stimulus pattern results in the alternative response, that stimulus pattern will thereafter tend to bring about the new response. *All forgetting must involve new learning.* This is an extreme form of *retroactive inhibition,* which refers to the fact that old learning is interfered with by new learning. To demonstrate retroactive inhibition, let us suppose someone learns task A and then he learns task B. Then he is tested for retention on task A. Another person learns task A, does *not* learn task B, and is tested on task

A. It is generally found that the first person remembers less of task A than does the second person. Thus, it is demonstrated that learning something new (task B) has interfered with the retention of what was learned previously (task A.)

As we have mentioned, Guthrie accepts an extreme form of retroactive inhibition. His position is that whenever something new is learned it must completely "knock out" something old. In other words, all forgetting is due to interference. *No interference, no forgetting.*

About forgetting, Guthrie says (1942):

> The child who has left school at the end of the seventh grade will recall many of the details of his last year for the rest of his life. The child who has continued on in school has these associations of the schoolroom and school life overlaid by others, and by the time he is in college may be very vague about the names and events of his seventh-grade experience.
>
> When we are somehow protected from established cues we are well aware that these may retain their connection with a response indefinitely. A university faculty member's wife recently visited Norway, the original home of her parents. She had not spoken Norwegian since the death of her grandmother when she was five and believed that she had forgotten the language. But during her stay in Norway, she astonished herself by joining in the conversation. The language and atmosphere of her childhood revived words and phrases she could not remember in her American home. But her conversation caused much amusement among her relatives because she was speaking with a facile Norwegian "baby talk." If her family in America had continued to use Norwegian, this "baby talk" would have been forgotten, its association with the language destroyed by other phrases.
>
> Forgetting is not a passive fading of stimulus-response associations contingent upon the lapse of time, but requires active un-learning, which consists in learning to do something else under the circumstances [pp. 29–30].

Summary of Guthrie's Theory as Presented Thus Far.

Associations between stimulating conditions and movements are constantly being made. An association between a stimulus and a response is made simply because the two occur together. The association can be between either external stimuli and overt responses, or between movement-produced stimuli and overt responses. This association will continue until the same response occurs in the presence of other stimuli or until the same stimuli occur and the response is prevented from occurring.

In a structured learning situation, such as a puzzle box, the environment is arranged so that there is an abrupt change in stimulation after a certain response is made. For example, if the cat hits the pole, the door opens and he is allowed to escape. Guthrie would say that after the cat hit the pole the stimulus situation abruptly changed and whatever association existed before that time will be preserved. The most recent association before the abrupt change was between the stimulation in the puzzle box and the response that allowed the animal to escape. According to the recency principle, when the animal is again placed in the puzzle box, he will tend to repeat that same response (he will tend to hit the pole again) and we say that the cat has learned how to escape from the box.

How to Break Habits.

A habit is a response that has become associated with a large number of stimuli. The more stimuli that elicit the response, the stronger the habit. Smoking, for example, can be a strong habit because the response of smoking has taken place in the presence of so many cues. Each cue present as a person smokes will tend to elicit smoking when next it is encountered. Guthrie indicates the complexities of a habit in the following quote (1952):

> The chief difficulty in the way of avoiding a bad habit is that the responsible cues are often hard to find, and that in many bad habit systems, they are extremely numerous. Each rehearsal is responsible for a possible addition of one or more new cues which tend to set off the undesired action. Drinking and smoking after years of practice are action systems which can be started by thousands of reminders, and which become imperative because the absence of the object of the habit, the drink or the smoke, results in a block to action and so in restlessness and tension. The desire, which includes tension in the muscles used in drinking or smoking, disrupts other action. The writer who "wants a smoke" is disturbed in his writing and the disturbed state will continue until the aroused action tendency is allowed to go through. The original wakening of the desire may be caused by any of the chance accompaniments of previous smoking—the smell of smoke, the sight of another person smoking, or of a cigar, the act of sitting back in the office chair, sitting down to a desk, finishing a meal, leaving the theater, and a thousand other stimulus patterns. Most smokers, while busily engaged in activities not associated with smoking, can go for long periods with no craving. Others find that the craving is strictly associated with such things as the end of a meal, if it has been their practice to smoke at that time. I once had a caller to

whom I was explaining that the apple I had just finished was a splendid device for avoiding a smoke. The caller pointed out that I was smoking at that moment. The habit of lighting a cigarette was so attached to the finish of eating that smoking had been started automatically [p. 116].

Threshold method. To break a habit, the rule is always the same: find the cues that initiate the bad habit and practice another response in the presence of those cues. Guthrie lists three ways in which an organism can be made to make a response, other than an undesirable one, to a certain pattern of stimuli. The first technique is referred to as the threshold method. According to Guthrie (1938), this method involves:

> ...introducing the stimulus at such weak strengths that it will not cause the response and then gradually increasing the intensity of the stimulus, always taking care that it is below the "threshold" of the response. A gradual introduction to the motion of a ship which, unfortunately, cannot be controlled by human means, but depends on the gradualness of change in the weather, can bring about tolerance of a considerable storm. Most children react to the taste of green olives by spitting them out. But if they begin with small nibbles, not enough to cause rejection, whole olives will eventually be taken with pleasure.
>
> . . . members of families learn to make use of this type of associative inhibition in dealing with their housemates. The proposal to send the daughter to an expensive school is "broken gently" to the father. Casual mention of the school's advantages without directly submitting the issue, criticism of the present school, at first so mild that it will not stir defense, prepare the father so that when the question is at last put squarely before him he does not make a scene over the expense. He is by this time used to the idea and there will be no violent reaction [pp. 60–61].

The threshold method can also be exemplified by what is ordinarily done when a horse is being broken. If you walk up to a horse that has never worn a saddle and attempt to throw a saddle on its back, he will no doubt start kicking and run away. He will do whatever he can to prevent you from putting that saddle on his back. If, instead of the saddle, you put a very light blanket on his back, chances are that he will not react violently. If he remains calm, you can gradually increase the weight on his back by using heavier and heavier blankets. You can then go from blankets to a light saddle and finally to the regular saddle itself. There is a process akin to this in psychotherapy. If the therapist is trying to help a patient overcome a phobia of some kind, he may use the method of approximation described above. If the patient has a terrible fear of a relative, for example his mother, the therapist may first start out talking about people in general, then women, and then women who are related to the patient, and in this way, gradually build up to the point where they are talking about the mother without the patient being fearful.

Fatigue method.   The second method proposed by Guthrie is referred to as the fatigue method. Again, to take horse-training as an example, the fatigue method would correspond to bronco-busting where a saddle is thrown on the horse, the rider climbs on, and the horse is ridden until he gives up. That is, he is ridden until his fatigue causes him to do something other than buck while the saddle and the rider are on his back. Then, according to Guthrie, the response of riding calmly will replace the bucking response to the stimulus provided by the saddle and the rider. Once you get the animal to act calmly in the presence of the saddle and rider, then forevermore he will act calmly in their presence.

To break a dog of the habit of chasing chickens, all you have to do is to tie a chicken around the dog's neck and let him run around and try to get rid of it. When the dog eventually becomes fatigued he will, therefore, be doing something other than chasing in the presence of the chicken. The chicken has then become a cue for doing something other than chasing.

Another example that Guthrie uses in describing the fatigue method involves a little girl who upsets her parents by lighting matches. Guthrie's advice is to allow the girl (or perhaps force her) to continue to light matches to the point where it is no longer fun. Under these conditions matches become a cue for avoidance rather than for lighting.

Incompatible response method.   The third method of breaking a habit is called the incompatible response method. With this method, the stimuli for the undesired response are presented along with other stimuli that produce a response which is incompatible with the undesired response. For example, a young child receives a panda bear as a gift, and her first reaction is fear and avoidance. On the other hand, the child's mother elicits a warm relaxed feeling in the child. Using the incompatible response method, you would pair the mother and the panda bear; hopefully the mother will be the dominant stimulus. If she is the dominant stimulus, the child's reaction to the mother-panda bear combination will be one of relaxation. Once this reaction has been elicited in the presence of the bear, the bear can be presented alone, and it will produce relaxation in the child. With the incompatible response method, both stimuli are presented to the learner: the one that causes the undesired response, and a stronger stimulus that causes a response incompatible with the undesired response. The learner then tends to make a response other than the undesired one in the presence of the stimuli that previously elicited the undesired response. Because of this pairing, the stimuli that used to elicit the undesired response will now elicit the response associated with the stronger stimulus.

All three of these methods for breaking a habit have equivalent results. Guthrie (1938) said:

> All three of these methods are, of course, only one method. All of them consist in presenting the cues of an undesirable action and seeing to it that the action is not performed. Since there is always other behavior going on when we are awake, the cues we present become stimuli for this other behavior and are alienated from the obnoxious response [p. 62].

The three examples we gave of breaking a habit can be summarized as follows:

Threshold Method

1. Regular saddle ⟶ kicking
2. Light blanket ⟶ calm
3. Heavier blanket ⟶ calm
4. A still heavier blanket ⟶ calm
5. Light saddle ⟶ calm
6. Regular saddle ⟶ calm

Fatigue Method

1. Saddle ⟶ kicking
2. Passage of time
3. Saddle ⟶ calm

Incompatible Response Method

1. Panda bear ⟶ fear
2. Mother ⟶ relaxation
3. Panda bear and mother ⟶ relaxation
4. Panda bear ⟶ relaxation

We noted in our discussion of Thorndike's theory (Chapter 4) that he believed associative shifting to be a second kind of learning, one based on contiguity alone and not governed by the law of effect. Since Guthrie believes learning is dependent on contiguity alone, one would expect to find a great deal of similarity between Thorndike's concept of associative shifting and Guthrie's views about learning. In fact, Guthrie's entire theory can be looked upon as an effort to describe how a response that is associated with one stimulus shifts over and becomes associated with another stimulus.

The incompatible response method of breaking a habit seems to represent one kind of associative shifting. Stimulus 1, the mother, elicits relaxation. Stimulus 2, the panda bear, elicits fear. When stimulus 1 is presented along with stimulus 2, the response previously associated with stimulus 1 now is elicited by stimulus 2, simply because the two stimuli are contiguous. Now the panda bear elicits the response that was previously associated with the mother.

The threshold method of breaking a habit also appears to represent a kind of associative shifting. Using the threshold method to eliminate the child's fear of the panda bear would involve *gradually* associating the bear with the mother. To begin with something only indirectly related to the bear, perhaps another of the child's toys, would be paired with the mother. Then the objects paired with the mother would become increasingly similar to the panda bear on successive pairings, and finally, the panda bear itself is presented with the mother. Again, the end result is that the response once associated with the mother "shifts over" to the panda bear.

Sidetracking a Habit.

There is a difference between breaking a habit and sidetracking a habit. Sidetracking a habit can be accomplished by avoiding the cues that elicit the undesirable behavior. If you have accumulated a large number of behavior patterns that are not effective or for other reasons cause concern and anxiety, probably the best thing to do would be to leave the situation altogether. Guthrie would advise going to an environment that would give you a fresh start, since you would not have as many associations built up in a new environment. Going to a new environment would release you to develop new behavior patterns. This would only be a partial escape, however, since many of the stimuli causing your undesired behavior are internal and you would, therefore, be taking them with you to the new environment. Also, as we shall see below, stimuli in the new environment identical or similar to stimuli in the old environment will tend to elicit the responses previously attached to them.

Punishment.

Guthrie says the effectiveness of punishment is determined by what it causes the punished organism to do. Punishment works, not because of the pain experienced by the individual, but because it changes the way

he responds to certain stimuli. Punishment is effective only when it results in a new response to the same stimuli. Punishment succeeds in changing the undesired habit because it elicits behavior incompatible with the
punished behavior. Punishment fails because the behavior caused by the
punishment is not incompatible with the punished behavior.

Let's say that you have a dog that chases cars and you want him to stop.
Guthrie would say, get in your car and allow the dog to chase it. As he is
running along the side of the car, reach down and slap his nose. This is
likely to be effective. On the other hand, slapping his rear as he is chasing
the car is not likely to be effective, although it can be assumed that a
slap in the nose and a slap in the rear are equally painful to the dog. The
difference is that the slap on the nose tends to make him stop and jump
backward in the presence of the car, whereas the slap on the rear tends
to make him continue forward, perhaps even a little more energetically.
Thus one form of punishment causes incompatible behavior and is effective, and the other does not and is ineffective.

Guthrie (1952) says:

> . . . what is learned will be what is done—and what is done in
> intense feeling is usually something different from what was being
> done. Sitting on tacks does not discourage learning. It encourages
> one in learning to do something else than sit. It is not the feeling
> caused by punishment, but the specific action caused by punish-
> ment that determines what will be learned. In training a dog to
> jump through a hoop, the effectiveness of punishment depends on
> where it is applied, front or rear. It is what the punishment makes
> the dog *do* that counts, or what it makes a man do, not what it
> makes him feel. The mistaken notion that it is the feeling that
> determines learning derives from the fact that often we do not
> care what is done as a result of punishment, just as long as what is
> done breaks up or inhibits the unwanted habit.
>
> . . . as the outcome of this discussion punishment and reward
> are not summarily to be ejected from the place they hold in public
> favor. No doubt whatever has been thrown on their general effec-
> tiveness. Children may still be spanked or caressed. But we shall
> have a much better insight into the uses of punishment and reward
> if we analyze their effects in terms of association and realize that
> punishment is effective only through its associations. Punishment
> achieves its effects not by taking away strength from the physio-
> logical basis of the connection . . . but by forcing the animal or the
> child to do something different and thus establishing inhibitory
> conditioning of unwanted habit. Punishment is effective *only in
> the presence of cues for the bad habit.*

Furthermore, when the effect of punishment is only emotional excitement, punishment facilitates the stereotyping of the un-desired habit. Punishment and reward are essentially moral terms, not psychological terms. They are defined not in terms of their effects on the recipient, but in terms of the purposes of the indi-vidual who administers them. Theory stated in their terms is bound to be ambiguous [pp. 132–33].

Guthrie talks about a ten-year-old girl who threw her hat and coat on the floor whenever she came home (1935, p. 21). Each time she did so, her mother scolded her and made her hang her hat and coat up. The situation continued until the mother guessed that her nagging had be-come the cue for the child to hang her clothes up. Realizing this, the next time the child threw her hat and coat on the floor, the mother made her pick them up and go back outside. Now as the girl came in the door, the mother insisted that she hang her coat and hat up immediately. This procedure was repeated a few times and soon the girl learned to hang up her hat and coat upon entering the house. Now the response of hang-ing up her clothes was attached to the stimuli present as she entered the house rather than to her mother's nagging. In this case, punishing the girl after her hat and coat were already on the floor could have no effect on the habit, except perhaps to strengthen it.

Guthrie and Powers also advise that a command never be given if it could be disobeyed. They say (1950):

> The skilled animal trainer never gives a command that he does not expect to be obeyed. In this he is like the army officer and the experienced teacher. If a teacher makes a request for silence in the room and it is disregarded, the request actually becomes a signal for disturbance [p. 129].

Summary of Guthrie's Views on Punishment.

Everything that Guthrie says about punishment is directly in accor-dance with his one law of learning—the law of contiguity. When stimuli and responses are paired, they become associated and remain associated unless the stimuli occur in the presence of another response, at which time they will become associated with the new response. While discuss-ing ways of breaking a habit, we saw three mechanical arrangements that could be used to rearrange the associations between stimuli and re-sponses. Punishment is another such arrangement. Punishment, when used effectively, causes stimuli that previously elicited an undesired re-sponse to elicit an acceptable response. Guthrie's views about punishment can be listed as follows:

1. The important thing about punishment is not the pain it may cause, but what it makes the organism do.
2. In order to be effective, punishment must cause behavior that is incompatible with the punished behavior.
3. In order to be effective, punishment must be applied in the presence of the stimuli that elicited the punished behavior.
4. If the conditions specified in 2 and 3 are not met, punishment will be ineffective or may even strengthen the undesired response.

Thus, when punishment is effective, it causes the organism to do something other than what it was punished for doing while the stimuli that elicited the punished behavior are still present. This, of course, causes a new association to be formed and the next time those stimuli appear, they will tend to elicit a favorable response instead of an unfavorable one.

Drives.

Physiological drives provide what Guthrie called *maintaining stimuli* that keep the organism active until a goal is reached. For example, being hungry produces internal stimulation that continues until food is consumed. When food is obtained, the maintaining stimuli are terminated and therefore the stimulating conditions have changed, thus preserving the response that led to the food. It should be emphasized, however, that physiological drives are only one source of maintaining stimuli. Any persistent source of stimulation, whether it be internal or external, can provide maintaining stimuli. Guthrie (1938) says:

> To explain this requires that we first understand what a problem is. What makes the puzzle box or an unyielding parent a problem? The answer to this is that problems are persistent stimulus situations of such a nature that they keep the animal or the person disturbed and excited until some act is hit upon which removes the "maintaining stimuli" and allows the excitement to subside.
> Such persistent and disturbing stimuli are sometimes called "drives." In a hungry animal, the recurring spasms of the stomach serve to make the animal disturbed and to produce excitement. . . .
> The same behavior could be produced by some artificial and external stimulation. A paper bag fastened to the cat's foot with a rubber band will similarly activate the cat, and it will become disturbed and excited and this state will continue until some one of its movements eventually removes the bag [p. 96].

Guthrie goes on to say (1938):

And here is a point very apt to be overlooked. The next time that the disturbers are present, they will tend to call out, by virtue of their last association, the act that removed them. Other acts associated with them have been dissociated or unconditioned each by the next act. But after successful removal of the disturber, it is no longer there to be associated with a new act. The drive remains faithful to the act that removed it because that was its last association. After that no new associations could be established because the drive is gone [p. 98].

Guthrie explains the habitual use of alcohol and other drugs in a similar way. Let's say, for example, a person feels tense or anxious. In this case, tension or anxiety provide maintaining stimuli. If, under these circumstances, the person takes a drink or two, his tension may be reduced. According to Guthrie, this assures the relationship between tension and drinking. Therefore, the next time the person feels tense, he will tend to have a drink. Gradually tension will tend to elicit drinking (or drug taking) under a wider range of circumstances, with the result that the person becomes a habitual drinker or a drug addict.

Intentions.

Responses that are conditioned to maintaining stimuli are called *intentions*. They are called intentions because maintaining stimulation from a drive usually lasts for a period of time (until the drive is reduced). Thus the *sequence of behavior* preceding the drive reducing response is repeated next time the drive with its related stimuli occurs. The sequence of behavior associated with maintaining stimuli seems to be interrelated and logical and is, therefore, referred to as intentional. If an animal is hungry and is allowed to eat, he will do so. If, however, the direct satisfaction of the hunger drive is not possible, he will tend to perform whatever behaviors led to food last time he was hungry: he may turn in a certain direction in a maze, press a lever, or move a pole. If a person is hungry and has a sandwich in his office, he will eat it; if, however, he forgot his lunch, he will get up, put on his coat, get into his car, find a restaurant, enter the restaurant, place an order, and so on. Different reaction patterns have been associated with the maintaining stimuli from hunger plus the stimuli from environmental circumstances, e.g., having one's lunch or not. Behavior triggered by maintaining stimuli may look purposive or intentional but Guthrie felt it too could be explained by the law of contiguity.

Transfer of Training.

It should be clear that Guthrie would expect very little transfer of training. He would say that if a child learns to add 2 and 2 at the blackboard, there is no guarantee that that child is going to know how to add 2 and 2 when she returns to her seat. The stimulating conditions under which that association was made is much different than those prevailing at her seat. So the child really must learn the response of adding 2 and 2 at the blackboard, at her seat, at home, and wherever she hopes to practice that response.

Guthrie would say to the college student, if you want to get the most from your studies, you should practice in exactly the same situation in which you're going to be tested. The best place to study, according to Guthrie, is in the room where you're going to be tested because all the stimuli in that room will be associated with the information that you're studying. If you learn something in your dorm room, there is no guarantee that this knowledge will transfer into the classroom. This is how Guthrie would explain why a student may say after taking a test, "I don't know what happened to me; I went over that material a hundred times; I knew it quite well, and yet, it didn't come to me during the test." Guthrie would say that there simply was not enough similarity between the conditions under which the student studied and the conditions under which he was tested.

Guthrie's advice is to always practice the exact behaviors that are going to be demanded of us; in addition we should practice them in the exact conditions under which we are going to be tested or evaluated. If you want to utilize this information beyond the testing situation, you must go beyond the classroom and associate other stimuli with the behavior that the book or the class or the lecture caused you to do. Guthrie's advice to the student preparing for an essay examination is the same: in preparing for an essay test, write essay questions. Guess what the questions will be and anwer them. Force yourself to respond to the questions under the time conditions that you are going to be exposed to during the test. Guthrie would give the same advice to the automobile mechanic, or the electrician. If you want to learn how to fix motors or engines, work on motors and engines, and work on them under conditions similar to those that will prevail in real life situations. This will maximize transfer.

Essentially, Guthrie accepted Thorndike's identical elements theory concerning the transfer of training. The probability of making the same response to two different situations is determined by the similarity between the two situations. Like Thorndike, Guthrie rejected the formal discipline theory of transfer and felt that acceptance of such a position would generate unfortunate classroom practices. Guthrie and Powers say (1950):

> The teacher's acceptance or rejection of the formal discipline theory of transfer, the identical elements or generalization explanation, will be reflected in numerous day-to-day teaching practices. *The subject-matter* teacher no doubt would give evidence of an actual, if not verbal, acceptance of the formal discipline doctrine. Exposure to the content of certain courses becomes in itself, then, the objective of education, methods of teaching and the attempt to link content and the needs of the learner are of relatively secondary importance. The student must conform to subject matter requirements and must develop a docile, submissive role.
>
> A challenging or questioning attitude on the part of the teacher as regards the validity of the formal discipline doctrine paves the way for educational experimentation. The teacher will ask what values, direct and indirect, are being served by pupil participation in given curricular areas. He will be willing to revise content and method as facts regarding transfer are uncovered. The child will be viewed as a growing and developing organism constantly organizing and reorganizing experience into more or less efficient patterns of behavior. The discovery of the child's interests and wise use of effective incentives in order to motivate participation become primary tasks of instruction [p. 256].

Elsewhere Guthrie has said (1942): ". . . it is essential that the student be led to do what is to be learned . . . a student does not learn what was in a lecture or in a book. He learns only what the lecture or book caused him to do" [p. 55]. According to Guthrie, *we learn what we do.* The notions of insight, understanding, and thinking have little or no meaning to Guthrie. The only law of learning is the law of contiguity which states that when two events occur together, they are learned. All learning, whether it be subhuman or human, simple or abstract, is subsumed under the law of contiguity and its related principles. There is no reference to conscious events in Guthrie's theory, nor is there any special interest in the survival value of learned behavior. According to Guthrie, incorrect responses are learned just as readily as correct ones, and the acquisition of both is explained by the same law of learning.

The reader should not conclude that Guthrie's theory of learning is of historical interest only. As we shall see in the next chapter, one trend in modern learning theory is toward the greater use of mathematical models in explaining the learning process. It was Guthrie's theory of learning that formed the bases for the early mathematical models of learning and continues to be at the heart of most of them. Indeed, Guthrie's theory of learning is, to many, the most viable learning theory available today.

DISCUSSION QUESTIONS

1. What suggestions does Guthrie offer for breaking a bad habit? Choose one of the suggestions and show how it could be used to break the smoking habit.
2. How would Guthrie explain the phenomenon of regression i.e., the tendency to act as you did at a younger age under certain conditions, like when you visit the house or room you grew up in?
3. How would Guthrie explain the tendency for someone to act like a "different person" under various conditions?
4. How would you revise your study habits so that they are in accordance with Guthrie's theory?
5. What would characterize a classroom designed in accordance with Guthrie's theory?
6. How might Guthrie explain the development of drug addiction?
7. Describe Guthrie's use of the term "reward."
8. According to Guthrie, under what circumstances would punishment be an effective technique in modifying behavior? Do you feel punishment is usually used as Guthrie says it should be? Explain.
9. What was Guthrie's purpose in introducing the notion of "movement-produced stimuli"?
10. Design an experiment to test Guthrie's contention that anything that disrupts a stimulus pattern will preserve the last response made to that stimulus pattern.

GLOSSARY

Acts. Complicated behavior patterns usually involving some goal accomplishment. Acts are made up of many individual movements.

Chaining. The process whereby the stimulation caused by one response acts as a stimulus for another response and that response in turn triggers another, and so on. Chaining, according to Guthrie, depends on movement-produced stimuli.

Drive. Maintaining stimuli usually caused by some physiological need, such as hunger or thirst.

Fatigue method of breaking a habit. Forcing an organism to continue to respond to a source of stimulation until he is fatigued. When he is fatigued he will respond to the source of stimulation in a way different from the way he originally responded to it.

Forgetting. All forgetting, according to Guthrie, involves the blocking out of old associations by the formation of new ones. This is an extreme form of retroactive inhibition.

Incompatible response method of breaking a habit. The stimulus for an undesired response is presented along with another stimulus that will cause a response incompatible with the undesired one. Because of this pairing, the stimulus that originally elicited the undesired response will no longer do so.

Intentions. Behavior patterns that are conditioned to maintaining stimuli.

Law of contiguity. Guthrie's one law of learning, which states that when a pattern of stimuli is experienced along with a response, the two will become associated so that when that pattern of stimuli next recurs, it will tend to elicit that response. In 1959, Guthrie revised the law of contiguity to read, "What is being noticed becomes a signal for what is being done."

Maintaining stimuli. Any source of stimulation that persists until some specific act is performed. For example, putting a rubber band around an animal's nose provides maintaining stimuli until it is removed, and the hunger drive provides maintaining stimuli until the animal is fed.

Movement-produced stimuli. Stimulation caused by the receptors found in the muscles, tendons, and joints of the body. As the body moves these receptors fire, thereby providing a source of stimulation, or what Guthrie called movement-produced stimuli.

Movements. Specific responses to specific stimuli. Acts are made up of many specific movements.

One trial learning. The contention that the association between a pattern of stimuli and a response develops at full strength as a result of just one pairing between the two.

Punishment. The presentation of an aversive stimulus in order to modify behavior. According to Guthrie, two conditions must be met before punishment will be effective: (1) the punishment must produce behavior that is incompatible with the undesired response, and (2) the punishment must be applied in the presence of the stimuli that elicit the undesired response.

Recency principle.   The principle that states that the response that was last made in a situation is the response that will be made when that situation next recurs.

Retroactive inhibition.   The interference of old learning by new learning.

Reward.   According to Guthrie, one of many events that can change a stimulus pattern, thus allowing the association between the previous stimulus pattern and the last response made to it to remain intact. Reward, to Guthrie, is nothing more than a mechanical arrangement that prevents unlearning.

Threshold method of breaking a habit.   A change in stimulating conditions is introduced so slowly that the organism does not notice it. Finally, the organism is reacting to the changed conditions in a manner other than it would have if the change had not occurred so slowly.

Stereotyped behavior.   The tendency to repeat exactly the behavior patterns that were previously made to a situation.

9

William Kaye Estes

One current trend in learning theory today is to move away from the broad, comprehensive theory and toward miniature systems. Researchers are marking off an area of interest and exploring it thoroughly. Breadth is sacrificed for depth. Exemplifying this trend are the so-called statistical learning theorists who attempt to build a rigorous minisystem from which a restricted range of learning phenomena can be deduced. The most influential of these, and one of the earliest, was developed by Estes (1950). Estes, born in 1919, is now at Rockefeller University in New York. In Chapter 5, we encountered some of the research on punishment that Estes performed while he was a student of Skinner at the University of Minnesota. It is for his development of statistical learning theory, however, that Estes is best known. Estes' theory can be thought of as an attempt to quantify Guthrie's theory of learning. Guthrie's theory appears deceptively simple, but when one asks about the nature of a stimulus in more detail, for example, one soon realizes that his theory is much more complex than it appeared to be at first. Estes investigates this complexity and offers a model that effectively deals with it.

ESTES' STIMULUS SAMPLING THEORY (SST)

Before giving a concrete example of how his theory works, we will first look at a number of assumptions made by Estes. First, he looks upon the learning situation as being comprised of a large but finite number of stimulus elements. These elements consist of the many things that the experimental subject experiences at the onset of a learning trial. They include the experimental conditions themselves, such as a light, a buzzer, verbal material presented in a memory drum, the sight of a bar in a Skinner box, or the runway in a T-maze. They also include the experimenter, the room temperature, extraneous noises inside and outside the room, and conditions within the experimental subject, such as fatigue, or a headache. All these stimulus elements taken collectively are symbolized S. S, therefore, is the total number of stimuli that accompany a trial in a learning situation.

Further, all responses made in the experimental situation fall into one of two categories. If the response is one that the experimenter is looking for (e.g., salivation, an eye blink, a bar press, turning right in a T-maze, or reciting a nonsense syllable correctly), it is called an A_1 response. If the response is anything other than what the experimenter wants, it is wrong and is labeled A_2. Thus, Estes divides all responses that may occur in a learning experiment into two classes: correct (A_1) or incorrect (A_2). There are no gradations in between: either an animal makes a condi-

William Kaye Estes

tioned response or he does not; either a student recites a nonsense syllable correctly or he does not.

Next, Estes assumes that all elements in S are attached to either A_1 or A_2. Again this is an all-or-nothing situation: all stimulus elements in the experimental situation are either conditioned to (attached to) A_1 or to A_2. As we will see below, elements conditioned to A_1 tend to elicit A_1 responses, and elements conditioned to A_2 tend to elicit A_2 responses. It can be seen that in certain experiments, such as those involving the bar press, almost all the stimulus elements will be conditioned to A_2 responses (not pressing the bar) at the beginning of the experiment. Therefore, in the early stages of such an experiment, the animal will tend not to press the bar.

The next assumption that Estes makes is that the experimental subject does not experience all of the elements in S on any given trial, but only a small proportion of them. The proportion of elements experienced, or sampled, on any given trial remains constant throughout the experiment, and is symbolized θ (theta). *Theta is a proportion of stimulus elements from S that the subject experiences at the onset of a learning trial.* After the trial, the sample of elements θ is returned to S.

Next, Estes assumes that if an A_1 response terminates a trial, then θ proportion of S will become conditioned to the A_1 response. Following Guthrie, Estes accepts a contiguity explanation of learning. Since an A_1 response occurs, an association is formed between that response and the stimuli that preceded it. In other words, since θ proportion of the stimulus elements in S were sampled at the beginning of the trial, those elements will become conditioned to A_1 through the principle of contiguity. Thus, when an A_1 response terminates a learning trial, the number of stimulus elements conditioned to A_1 goes up. As the number of elements in S that are conditioned to A_1 goes up, the tendency for an A_1 response to be elicited at the onset of a learning trial also goes up. In this manner, the attachment of stimulus elements to A_1 and A_2 responses gradually changes, and this is what Estes calls learning. The *state of the system* at any given moment is the proportion of elements attached to A_1 and A_2 responses.

What determines which response will occur on any given trial? The answer to this question indicates why Estes' theory is called a statistical learning theory. The probability of an A_1 response occurring is equal to the proportion of stimulus elements in θ conditioned to A_1 at the beginning of a learning trial. If all the stimulus elements in θ are conditioned to A_1, then an A_1 response has a 100 percent chance of occurring. If, however, only 75 percent of the stimulus elements in θ are conditioned to A_1, then we would expect to get an A_2 response about 25 percent of the time.

The proportion of elements in θ conditioned to A_1 reflects the proportion of elements in S that are conditioned to A_1, since θ is a random sample of elements from S. It can be seen that the probability of getting an A_1 response on any given trial changes as the state of the system changes.

The following formula summarizes the learning process as it is seen by Estes:

$$P_n = 1 - (1 - P_1)(1 - \theta)^{n-1}$$

where:

$\quad\quad\quad\quad n$ = any particular trial in a learning experiment.

$\quad\quad\quad\quad P_n$ = the probability of an A_1 response occurring on trial n.

$\quad\quad (1 - P_1)$ = the probability of an A_1 response *not* occurring on trial 1 (i.e., the proportion of elements *not* conditioned to A_1 at the beginning of the experiment).

$\quad\quad (1 - \theta)$ = the proportion of stimulus elements in S that are not sampled on trial n.

Since the expression $(1 - P_1)(1 - \theta)^{n-1}$ must necessarily get smaller as n increases (i.e., as the number of successive learning trials goes up), this formula generates a negatively accelerated learning curve with an asymptote of 1. The learning curve generated by Estes' formula is essentially the same as the one generated by Hull's formula which was described in Chapter 6 (see Figure 6–1). Both Estes and Hull assume that more learning takes place in the early stages of a learning experiment than in the later stages.

The negatively accelerated curve occurs, according to Estes, because trials in a learning experiment usually end with an A_1 response, and as a result, an increasing number of elements become conditioned to A_1. But there are diminishing returns. Taking as an example the situation where, at the onset of an experiment, an A_1 response is highly unlikely (such as with eye blink conditioning), we see that almost all elements in S would be conditioned to A_2 (not blinking when a light is presented). Suppose, however, that blinking occurs at the end of trial 1. This results in all the elements sampled on that trial (θ) switching from A_2 to A_1, since they were all conditioned to A_2 to begin with. On the next trial, a few elements will be conditioned to A_1, but most will still be conditioned to A_2. Therefore, it is now possible that some elements conditioned to A_1 will be sampled along with those conditioned to A_2. This means the rate of changeover (from A_2 to A_1) will not be as great on trial 2 as it was on trial 1, since only those elements conditioned to A_2 can be transferred to A_1. As we saw earlier, this changeover from A_2 to A_1 is what constitutes learning. In the later trials, more and more elements are already conditioned to A_1 and therefore, the number of elements conditioned to A_2 responses contained in θ on any given trial is small. It can be seen then that as learning trials progress, the rate of learning goes down. When all the elements in S are conditioned to A_1, no further learning can occur and the probability of an A_1 response occurring is 1. Thus, we have a negatively accelerated learning curve which again simply indicates that learning progresses more rapidly in the early stages of learning than it does in the later stages. This negatively accelerated rate of changeover of the stimulus elements is diagrammed in Figure 9–1.

Generalization.

Generalization from the original learning situation to other situations is easily taken care of by stimulus sampling theory. Estes takes the same position on transfer as did Thorndike. That is, transfer takes place to the extent that two situations have stimulus elements in common. If many of the elements previously conditioned to an A_1 response are present in a new learning situation, the probability is high that an A_1 response will be elicited in the new situation. If no elements are conditioned to A_1 at the onset of new learning situations, then the probability of an A_1 response being given is zero. In a new situation, as with original learning, the probability of an A_1 response occurring is equal to the proportion of stimulus elements in S conditioned to it.

Extinction.

Estes handles the problem of extinction essentially the same way as Guthrie did. Since in extinction, a trial usually ends with the subject doing something other than A_1, the stimulus elements previously conditioned to A_1 gradually switch back to A_2. The laws for acquisition and for extinction are the same. In fact, in Estes' system, it doesn't make sense to speak of extinction. What is called extinction results whenever conditions are arranged so that stimulus elements are switched from response A_1 back to response A_2.

Spontaneous Recovery.

As you may remember from Chapter 7, spontaneous recovery refers to the reappearance of a conditioned response after that response has undergone extinction. In order to explain spontaneous recovery, Estes expands

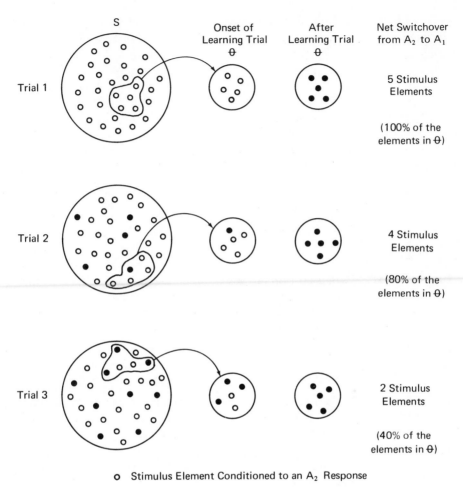

Figure 9–1. Estes' model of how stimulus elements change from the unconditioned state to the conditioned state.

slightly on his notion of S. Earlier in this chapter, S was defined as the
total number of stimulus elements present at the beginning of a trial in a
learning experiment. We also noted that these stimulus elements included
transitory events such as extraneous noises from the outside (e.g., car
backfiring, thunder, loud voices), and temporary body states of the experimental subject (e.g., indigestion, headache, anxiety). Since these and
many other events are transitory, they may be part of S on one occasion
but not on others. Likewise, when they are part of S, they are available to

be sampled by the subject; when they are not part of S, they cannot be sampled. In other words, only those elements present in S can be sampled as part of θ.

Under the above conditions, it is possible that during training, A_1 responses become conditioned to many of these transitory elements. If it turns out that these elements are not available during extinction, then the A_1 response conditioned to them cannot be switched to A_2 responses. Switching can only occur for stimulus elements actually sampled; thus if certain elements had been conditioned to A_1 responses during training and are subsequently not available during extinction, their status remains the same, i.e., attached to A_1.

Now the importance of these transitory elements for spontaneous recovery becomes evident. It is entirely possible that many elements that were conditioned to A_1 during acquisition are not available during extinction, but may reappear some time after extinction has taken place. Thus, if the subject is placed back into the experimental situation some time after extinction, a portion of these elements may now be present and would therefore tend to elicit an A_1 response. Spontaneous recovery is explained then by assuming the extinction process (switching elements from A_1 to A_2) was never complete in the first place.

Probability Matching.

For years, behaviorists puzzled over the phenomenon of *probability matching*. The traditional probability matching experiment involves a signal light that is followed by one of two other lights. When the signal light comes on, the subject is to guess which of the other two lights will come on. The experimenter arranges the situation so that the lights come on in any pattern he wishes, e.g., left light 75 percent of the time, right light 25 percent of the time; left light 100 percent of the time, right light 0 percent of the time. The results of such an arrangement are usually that the subject ends up guessing the frequencies at which the lights come on almost exactly as the experimenter had arranged them, e.g., if the right light comes on 80 percent of the time, the subject will predict that light will come on about 80 percent of the trials. This is referred to as probability matching.

To handle these results, we need to add symbols for the two new stimulus events to Estes' theory:

E_1 = left light going on
E_2 = right light going on

In this case, an A_1 response is predicting E_1, and A_2 is predicting E_2. In Estes' analysis of probability matching, the subject's actual guess is irrelevant. It is assumed that when E_1 occurs, it evokes in the subject an implicit A_1 response, and when E_2 occurs, it evokes an implicit A_2 response. Thus, for Estes, the event itself acts as a "reinforcer" (see Estes and Straughan, 1954 for greater detail). The experimental situation can be diagrammed as follows:

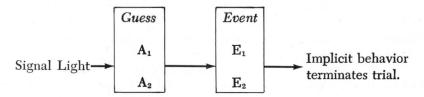

Two additional symbols are necessary for Estes' analysis of probability matching:

$$\pi = \text{the probability of } E_1 \text{ occurring}$$
$$1 - \pi = \text{the probability of } E_2 \text{ occurring}$$

On a trial in which E_1 occurs, all elements sampled from S on that trial become conditioned to A_1, and on a trial on which E_2 occurs, the sample of elements will become conditioned to A_2.

As before, the probability of an A_1 response on any given trial is equal to the proportion of elements in S that are conditioned to A_1 (P_n) and the probability of an A_2 response is equal to the proportion of those elements not conditioned to A_1 or $(1 - P_n)$. As before, θ equals the proportion of elements sampled on each trial, and again, this value remains the same throughout the experiment.

The probability of an A_1 response after n trials is given by the following formula:

$$P_n = \pi - (\pi - P_1)(1 - \theta)^{n-1}$$

Since $(1 - \theta)$ is less than 1, with n getting larger, this equation yields a negatively accelerated curve with an asymptote of π. Thus, whatever the value of π, this theory predicts that the proportion of A_1 responses made by the subject will eventually match the proportion of E_1 occurrences set by the experimenter. In other words, Estes predicts probability matching by the subject, and this is what occurs. For more detail concerning the application of Estes' theory to probability matching, see Estes and Straughan (1954) or Estes (1964b).

ESTES' MARKOV MODEL OF LEARNING

All statistical learning theories are probabilistic, that is, the dependent variable that they study is response probability. There is, however, a difference in opinion over what these changing response probabilities tell us about the nature of learning. The classic argument is over whether learning is gradual or complete in one trial. Thorndike concluded that learning was gradual, that it increased in small increments from trial to trial. Hull and Skinner went along with Thorndike on this matter. Guthrie differed by saying that learning occurred in an all-or-none fashion and only looked gradual because of the complexity of the task being learned. We shall see in Chapter 10 that Gestalt theorists, with their insight studies, also felt they demonstrated that the learner went from the un-learned state to the learned state very rapidly and not bit by bit.

Estes' early stimulus sampling theory accepted both an incremental (gradual) and an all-or-none point of view concerning the learning process. You will remember that only a small proportion of the total number of stimulus elements present during an experiment is sampled on any given trial. The sampled elements were conditioned in an all-or-none fashion to whatever response terminated the trial. However, since only a small portion of elements is conditioned on any given trial, learning proceeds bit by bit and this is how the characteristic negatively accelerated learning curve is generated. To repeat, Estes' early position was that those stimulus elements that were sampled on a given trial were conditioned in an all-or-none manner; but since only a small number of them were sampled on a trial, learning proceeded in an incremental or gradual fashion. The probability of making an A_1 response changed gradually from one trial to the next, and if the total number of stimulus elements present in the experiment was large enough, the all-or-none nature of learning could not be detected. That is, with a large number of stimulus elements present in an experiment, there would be very small changes in response probabilities from one learning trial to the next, and when those probabilities were plotted, it would look *as if* learning was incremental rather than all-or-none in nature.

More recently, Estes has designed a number of studies that allow the learning process to be observed in more detail (for example, Estes, 1960; Estes, 1964a; Estes, Hopkins and Crothers, 1960). These studies have shown that when the number of elements to be sampled is very small, learning clearly occurs in an all-or-none fashion; in fact, it can be said that learning occurs completely on one trial or it does not occur at all—there appears to be no in-between. This rapid change from the unlearned state to the learned state is said to correspond to a *Markov process,* which is characterized by an abrupt, stepwise change in response probabilities rather than a relatively slow, gradual change from trial to trial.

In his 1964a study, Estes used *paired associates* to show the stepwise nature of learning. In paired associate learning, subjects learn pairs of items so that when they are shown the first member of the pair, they can respond with the other. Estes used a variation of paired associate learning where, when the subject was shown the first member of the pair, he had four responses to choose from and only one of the four was correct. Thus, after the subject sees the first member of the pair, the probability of his choosing the correct response by chance alone was .25 (1 in 4). Estes found that if a subject guessed correctly on one trial, the probability of his guessing correctly on the next trial went to 1 and stayed there. In other words, after guessing correctly, the subject would be correct on 100 percent of the subsequent trials. Subjects who did not guess correctly went on guessing at chance level until they guessed correctly, at which time their subsequent probability of being correct jumped to 1. The most important fact here is that different subjects learned the correct response at different points in the experiment; that is, when subjects learn, they learn completely, but this occurred on different trials for different subjects. This fact is shown in Figure 9–2.

What happens when the individual instances of going from the un-

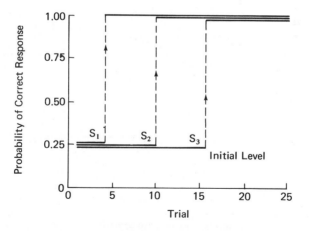

Figure 9–2. The figure shows that subjects go from chance level performance to perfect performance in just one trial, but this process occurs at different times for different subjects (from Estes, 1964a, p. 19).

From W. K. Estes, "All-or-None Processes in Learning and Retention," in *American Psychologist,* 1964, 19: 16–25.

learned to the learned state are overlooked and the data from all subjects are pooled together? Under these circumstances, the probabilities of making a correct response for the subjects in the unlearned state would be combined with those in the learned state and *average* probabilities would be plotted. For example, if there were five subjects in an experiment and three were in the unlearned state (probability of making a correct response = .25), and two were in the learned state (probability of making a correct response = 1), the average probability of making a correct response for the group would be .55. As more learning trials occur, more subjects will enter the learned state, and the average probability for the group would increase. This is demonstrated in Figure 9–3.

$P(C_{n+1}|N_n)$ is read "the probability that subjects will be correct on trial $n + 1$, given that they were incorrect on trial n." $P(C_n)$ is the probability that subjects will be correct on trial n.

It is important to note that because the data were combined, one gets the impression that learning is gradual and improves slightly from trial to trial. When one looks at individual performance the illusion of gradual learning disappears.

In an earlier study, Estes (1960) used another paired associate situation with a nonsense syllable and a number. He ran 48 subjects on an 8-item paired associate list; that means there were eight pairs of nonsense syllables and numbers. Each subject was presented with each of the eight

Figure 9–3. The figure shows that even though individual subjects learn completely in one trial, when the data from a number of individual subjects are pooled, a negatively accelerated learning curve is generated. This gives the erroneous impression that learning is continuous and does not occur in an all-or-none fashion.

From W. K. Estes, "All-or-None Processes in Learning and Retention," in *American Psychologist*, 1964, 19: 16–25.

syllable-number pairs once, and then tested by seeing the syllable alone and guessing the number that was associated with it. This time there was not a multiple choice as there was in the other paired associate study mentioned above.

To differentiate between the point of view that says learning is gradual and the one that says it is all-or-none, Estes hypothesizes four subjects who start the experiment with zero probability of being correct. These four hypothetical subjects see a syllable and a number paired once. When tested, one of the four anticipates the number correctly after seeing the nonsense syllable. Estes supposes that the probability of being correct on subsequent tests is raised from 0 to .25 for the group. But this increase in the probability of being correct can occur in two ways: (1) those who believe in the gradual nature of learning would say that the "associative strength" is increased in all four subjects and therefore on subsequent tests all members of the group have a probability of being correct of .25 and a probability of being wrong of .75; (2) the alternative explanation is

Figure 9–4. The diagram shows what the effects of a single reinforcement is thought to be according to the "associative strength" (upper part of diagram) and all-or-none (lower part of diagram) points of view. N=an incorrect response; C=a correct response; R=the response made on a test trial following one reinforcement. For example, R=N means the subject made an incorrect response on the test trial.

From W. K. Estes, Learning Theory and the "New Mental Chemistry," in *Psychological Review*, 67: 207–23. Copyright 1960, by the American Psychological Association. Reprinted by permission.

that one member of the group formed the correct association while the other three did not. According to the principle of all-or-none learning, one person will always be correct on subsequent tests and the other three will always be wrong. The difference between the "associative strength" point of view and the all-or-none point of view is diagrammed in Figure 9–4.

Now we return to the real experiment involving 48 subjects. Estes indicates that according to the "associative strength" point of view, how subjects perform on a second test, in the situation described above, should have little to do with whether or not they were correct on the first test. In other words, if the performance of subjects who were wrong on the first test was compared with the performance of subjects who were correct on the first test, it should show that they do about as well on the second test. The all-or-none point of view, on the other hand, would say that all or most of the subjects who were correct on the first test should

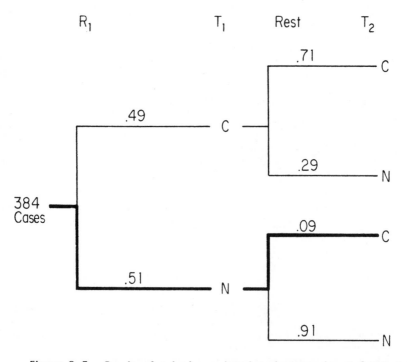

Figure 9–5. Results of paired associate learning experiment. See text for explanation.

From W. K. Estes, Learning Theory and the "New Mental Chemistry," in Psychological Review, 67: 207–23. Copyright 1960, by the American Psychological Association. Reprinted by permission.

also be correct on the second test, and most of the subjects who were wrong on the first test should also be wrong on the second test. Estes ran such a test and the results are summarized in Figure 9–5.

It can be seen in Figure 9–5 that of the 384 possibilities of being correct (48 subjects × 8 paired associates), 49 percent of the responses on test 1 were correct and 51 percent were incorrect. Seventy-one percent of the items that were responded to correctly on test 1 were also responded to correctly on test 2, whereas only 9 percent of the items that were responded to incorrectly on test 1 were responded to correctly on test 2. This lends support to the notion that when something is learned, it is learned completely; if it is not learned completely, it is not learned at all. Estes ran some trials with control groups which showed that the 51 percent of the items missed were just as difficult as the 49 percent not missed, and that the subjects missing the 51 percent had the same average learning ability as the other subjects.

As with most notions in learning theory today, Estes' work has not gone uncriticized. Underwood and Keppel (1962), for example, find fault with many aspects of the experiment we have just discussed. Among other things, they wonder, if the all-or-none point of view is correct, why all the items that were correct on the first test were not also correct on the second test instead of only 71 percent of them. Underwood and Keppel feel that Hull's incremental learning theory is better able to handle the data than Estes' all-or-none theory. They say (1962):

> . . . it could be said that if an item were incorrect on the first test trial then it was below the performance threshold; there is no reason why it should be correct on the second test with no intervening study. Likewise, an item above threshold on the first test trial has a high probability of being correct on the second. Items which were correct on the first test trial but not on the second, and those which were not correct on the first but correct on the second, would be handled by some incremental theories via the notion of *oscillation* [pp. 3–4].

As you may recall, the oscillation effect ($_sO_R$) was part of Hull's theory of learning (see Chapter 6). According to Hull, the oscillation effect operated against a learned response in varying amounts from trial to trial and in a random fashion. When the value of $_sO_R$ happened to be high, the probability of a learned response being made on that particular trial was low. When the value of $_sO_R$ was low, it had little effect on the elicitation of a learned response. Hull used the oscillation effect to explain why a learned response may occur on one trial but not on a subsequent trial.

LEARNING TO LEARN

The controversy over the incremental versus the all-or-none position of learning (sometimes called the continuity-noncontinuity controversy) is still very much alive and promises to be for some time to come. As with most extreme positions, however, the truth will probably be found somewhere between the two. An example that seems to be satisfactory to both sides of the debate is Estes' earlier position that, with a complex learning environment, learning proceeds in an all-or-none fashion, only it does so a little bit at a time. In fact, logically, all incremental theories of learning can be reduced to all-or-none theories. What the theorists are really arguing over is the size of the "chunk" of material that is learned on any given trial.

Indeed, there is considerable evidence showing that the incremental and all-or-none positions are both correct. One example comes from the famous work of Harry Harlow. Using the Wisconsin General Test Apparatus shown in Figure 9–6, Harlow presented monkeys with a large number of discrimination problems to solve.

In an early study, Harlow (1949) confronted monkeys with a total of

Harry F. Harlow

Figure 9–6. The Wisconsin General Test Apparatus.

From Harlow, H. F., "The Formation of Learning Sets." *Psychological Review*, 56: 52. Copyright 1949, by the American Psychological Association. Reprinted by permission.

344 discrimination problems, including 32 practice problems. On each problem, they were to pick the one of two objects that had a reward placed underneath it. Each of the 344 problems involved a different set of objects. Harlow's remarkable finding was that the more discrimination problems the monkeys solved, the better they became at solving them. It appeared that the animals were *learning how to learn,* or forming what Harlow called a *learning set.* In the early discrimination problems, the monkeys tended to make a large number of errors and improvement from problem to problem was fairly slow. The later problems, however, tended to be solved either with only one error or with none. On the last block of 56 problems, the monkeys chose the correct object 95 percent of the time by the second trial. It was as if they had developed the strategy of "win-stay, lose-shift." That is, if they picked the correct object on the first trial, they stayed with it on the next; if their first choice was incorrect, however, they switched to the other object on the next trial. The percentage of correct responses for the first 6 trials of each of the discrimination problems is shown in Figure 9–7.

Figure 9–7. The figure shows the gradual improvement in the ability to solve discrimination problems found by Harlow. Although performance is relatively poor on early discrimination problems, later problems tend to be solved in just one trial.

From H. F. Harlow, "The Formation of Learning Sets," Psychological Review, 56: 51–65. Copyright 1949, by the American Psychological Association. Reprinted by permission.

The gains from the early learning trials were slow and incremental in nature. Later learning, however, was very rapid and more like the all-or-none variety. Harlow (1949) said:

> Before the formation of a discrimination learning set, a single training trial produces negligible gain; after the formation of a discrimination learning set, *a single training trial constitutes problem solution.* These data clearly show that *animals can gradually learn insight* [p. 56].

In order to explain his results, Harlow used the concept of *error factors* (Harlow, 1950; 1959). Error factors were erroneous strategies that had to be extinguished before a discrimination problem could be solved. In other words, error factors are response tendencies that lead to incorrect responses. One error factor could be the tendency to always choose the object on the left (position preference); another might be the tendency to continue to choose the same object although it is incorrect (stimulus preservation). For Harlow, learning is more a matter of eliminating incorrect strategies (error factors) than it is a matter of strengthening a correct response. Thus, early learning is slow, since it involves the elimination of error factors; later learning is rapid since it is based upon a strategy that can be effectively applied to all two-choice discrimination problems.

Another theorist who accepts both the slow incremental and rapid all-or-none interpretations of learning is Donald Hebb. According to Hebb, learning that occurs very early in life is of the incremental variety, whereas later learning is cognitive, insightful, and more all-or-none in nature. We will have more to say about Hebb's views of learning in Chapter 13.

THE CURRENT STATUS OF MATHEMATICAL MODELS OF LEARNING

Although we have minimized the mathematics in our coverage of Estes in this chapter, his approach is often referred to as a mathematical model of learning because he attempts to show how the learning process can be described in terms of various mathematical formulations. Mathematical models of learning are relatively new in psychology, and their newness is evident. Psychologists have always wanted to be scientific, and the language of science is mathematics. Therefore, when an opportunity came along to use mathematics in a new way in psychology, it was met with considerable enthusiasm and optimism. Since then, however, it has been found that one of the main contributions of the mathematical study of learning has been to allow a precise description of phenomena that have been studied for years without being described in terms of mathematical models. Outside of this cleanup operation mathematical models have provided little new information concerning the nature of the learning process. Currently, there are a large number of mathematical formulations to describe different learning phenomena without any unifying theme running through the various formulations. In that sense, mathematical models are at about the same level as the search for the neurophysiological correlates of learning to which we will turn in Chapter 13. Both are a hodgepodge of minisystems to explain some specific aspect of learning. The lack of synthesis is not a criticism of either mathematical models or neurophysiological explanations of learning; rather, it characterizes any new approach to the field.

DISCUSSION QUESTIONS

1. Categorize each of the following theorists as accepting either an incremental explanation of learning or an all-or-none explanation: Thorndike, Pavlov, Watson, Guthrie, Skinner, and Hull. Briefly explain your reason(s) for categorizing each theorist as you did.
2. Design an experiment that would allow one to clearly determine whether learning is incremental or all-or-none.
3. List some advantages and disadvantages of statistical learning theory as you see them.
4. From your everyday experience do you feel that learning is incremental or all-or-none? What place do personal feelings of this kind have in science? Explain.
5. Do you feel that a process similar to "learning to learn" occurs in the life of the student? Explain becoming "testwise" in terms of learning to learn.
6. How does Harlow's error factor theory of learning compare to most of the other theories of learning you have covered in this book? For example, does his theory emphasize the "stamping in" of correct responses?
7. Regarding the learning process, briefly describe the incremental (continuity) position, the all-or-none (noncontinuity) position, and the compromise position that would accept both at different times or for different reasons.
8. Do you feel the size of θ would influence the learning process as Estes views it? List some factors that you feel might influence the size of θ.

GLOSSARY

Continuity-noncontinuity controversy. Another label for the debate over whether learning occurs gradually and in small increments, or in large steps in an all-or-none fashion.

Error factors. False strategies that operate against the solution of a problem. According to Harlow, learning is more a matter of eliminating error factors than it is a matter of strengthening correct responses.

Learning to learn.   The tendency to become increasingly effective at solving problems as more problems are solved. Also called learning set.

Learning set.   *See* Learning to learn.

Markov process.   The situation where probabilities of response increase and decrease in a stepwise fashion rather than in small, steady amounts.

Negatively accelerated learning curve.   A learning curve that shows the rate of learning to be more rapid during the early trials in a learning situation than it is in the later trials. In other words, as the number of successive learning trials increases, the rate of learning decreases.

Paired associate learning.   The learning of pairs of stimuli so that when a subject sees the first member of the pair, he can respond by reporting the second member.

Probability matching.   In a situation where a subject is asked to guess whether or not an event will occur, the proportion of the trials where he predicts the event will occur comes to approximately match the proportion of the trials that it does actually occur. For example, if a light is illuminated on 60 percent of the trials, the subject will come to predict that it will be illuminated on about 60 percent of the trials.

State of the system.   The proportion of stimulus elements in S that are conditioned to A_1 and A_2 responses at any given point in a learning experiment.

Stimulus sampling theory (SST).   A theory such as the one developed by Estes that attempts to show how stimuli are sampled and attached to responses.

Theta (θ).   The proportion of stimulus elements sampled from S at the onset of a trial in a learning experiment.

part 4

Predominantly Cognitive Theories

10

Gestalt Theory

After J. B. Watson, behaviorism became the rage among American psychologists, and since his time most eminent learning theorists, such as Guthrie, Skinner, and Hull, have been behaviorists. The behavioristic attack on the introspective method of Wundt and Titchener resulted in introspectionism's almost completely being abandoned. At about the same time the behaviorists were attacking introspection in America, a group of psychologists began attacking its use in Germany. This small group of German psychologists called themselves *Gestalt psychologists*. While the behavioristic movement is thought to have been launched by Watson's article "Psychology as the Behaviorist Views It" which appeared in 1913, the Gestalt movement is thought to have been launched by Wertheimer's article on apparent motion which appeared in 1912.

Although Max Wertheimer (1880–1943) is considered the founder of Gestalt psychology, from its very inception he worked closely with two men who can be considered cofounders of the movement, Wolfgang Köhler (1887–1967) and Kurt Koffka (1886–1941). Köhler and Koffka acted as subjects in the first experiments performed by Wertheimer. Although all three men made significant and unique contributions to Gestalt psychology, their ideas were always in close agreement.

Apparently the entire Gestalt movement started as the result of an insight Wertheimer had while riding a train heading for the Rhineland for a vacation. It occurred to him that if two lights blink on and off at a

235

Max Wertheimer

certain rate, they give the observer the impression that one light was moving back and forth. He left the train and bought a toy stroboscope (a device that is used to present visual stimuli at various rates) with which he conducted numerous simple experiments in his hotel room. He substantiated the notion he had on the train that if the eye sees stimuli in a certain way, they give the illusion of motion. Wertheimer called this apparent motion the *phi phenomenon.* Wertheimer's discovery was to have a profound influence on the history of psychology.

The importance of the phi phenomenon was that it was different from the elements that caused it. The sensation of motion could not be explained by analyzing each of the two lights flashing on and off; somehow the experience of motion emerged from the combination of the elements. For this reason, the members of the Gestalt school believed that although psychological experiences resulted from sensory elements they were different from the sensory elements themselves. In other words, they believed that phenomenological experience (for example, apparent motion) resulted from sensory experience (for example, flashing lights) but could not be understood by analyzing the phenomenal experience into its components. That is, *the phenomenological experience is different from the parts that make it up.* This, of course, is what John Stuart Mill had said many years before.

Thus, the Gestaltists believed that the organism added something to experience that is not contained in sensory data, and that something is organization. *Gestalt* is the German word for *configuration* or *organization.* The members of this school believed that we experience the world in meaningful wholes. We do not see isolated stimuli but stimuli gathered together into meaningful configurations or *Gestalten* (plural for *Gestalt*). We see people, chairs, cars, trees, and flowers. We do not see lines and patches of color. Our perceptual field is broken up into organized wholes or Gestalten, and these are the basic subject matter of psychology.

The battle cry of the Gestaltists became "the whole is more than the sum of its parts" or "to dissect is to distort." You cannot really get the full impact of the "Mona Lisa" by looking at first one arm and then another, then the nose, then the mouth, and then trying to put all these experiences together. You cannot understand the experience of listening to a symphony orchestra by analyzing the separate contributions of each of the musicians. The music emanating from the orchestra is more than the sum of the various notes being played by the various musicians. The melody has an *emergent quality* which is something different from the sum of the parts.

Opposition to Both Behaviorism and Structuralism.

The structuralists had used the introspective method in order to discover the chemistry of the mind. Influenced by the success of physical chemistry, they attempted to isolate the elements of thought that they believed were combined to produce our complex mental experiences. Since they were interested in studying the mental analog to sensation, they instructed their experimental subjects to avoid naming things and otherwise reading things into their experience. Instead, they were instructed to describe their raw experiences. The structuralists were associationists in that they believed complex ideas were made up of simpler ideas which were combined in some way. Their main concern was to discover these simpler ideas that supposedly were the building blocks of more complicated thoughts.

The functionalist movement, under the influence of Darwinian thought, was gaining momentum in America and began to challenge structuralism.

The functionalist was primarily concerned with how human behavior or thought processes were related to survival, and attacked the structuralists for the irrelevance of their approach. Thus, the structuralists were suspect even before the behaviorists came along.

The behaviorists attempted to make psychology completely scientific, and being scientific necessarily involved measurement. They concluded that the only psychological subject matter that could be reliably and publicly measured was overt behavior. The description of conscious elements, as in structuralism, was unreliable because it was influenced by, among other factors, the verbal ability of the reporter. Because it can only be studied indirectly, the behaviorists found consciousness a dubious subject matter for a science.

The Gestalt psychologists maintained that both the structuralists and the behaviorists were making the same basic error in using a reductionistic approach. Both attempted to divide up their subject matter into elements in order to understand it; the structuralists reduced thoughts into their basic elements, and the behaviorists reduced behavior into habits, conditioned responses, or more generally, into stimulus-response combinations. Gestalt psychologists opposed reductionism of any kind.

The Gestaltists saw nothing wrong with the introspective method in general, but they felt the structuralists had misused it. Rather than using the introspective method to divide experiences, it should be used to investigate whole, meaningful experiences. It should be used to investigate how people perceive the world. When the technique is used in this way, it is found that a person's perceptual field consists of events that are organized and meaningful. It is these organized and meaningful events that the Gestaltists believed should be the subject matter of psychology. When these Gestalten are divided up in any way, they lose their meaning. Therefore, perceptual phenomena are to be studied directly and without further analysis. Because of this aproach of studying perceptual phenomena directly, the Gestalt psychologist has sometimes been called a phenomenologist. A phenomenologist studies meaningful, intact mental events without dividing them up for further analysis. Following is a list of terms that have been used to describe both the Gestalt and the behavioristic approaches:

Gestalt	Behavioristic
holistic	atomistic, reductionistic, elementistic
molar	molecular
subjective	objective
nativistic	empiricistic
cognitive, phenomenological	behavioral

The only terms on the list whose meaning may not be obvious are molar and molecular. In general, *molar* means large and *molecular* means small; when describing behavior, however, molar means a large segment of behavior that is goal directed and purposive, and molecular behavior is a small segment of behavior, such as a conditioned reflex, that is isolated for analysis. Obviously, the former would be of more interest to the Gestalt psychologist than the latter. We will have more to say about molar behavior in our discussion of Tolman in Chapter 12.

Major Theoretical Concepts

Field Theory.

Gestalt psychology can be thought of as an attempt to apply field theory from physics to the problems of psychology. Roughly speaking, a *field* can be defined as a dynamic interrelated system, any part of which influences every other part. The important thing about a field is that nothing in it exists in isolation. Gestalt psychologists utilize the concept of field on many levels. Gestalten themselves, for instance, can be thought of as a small field; the perceived environment can be looked upon as a field; and the person himself can be thought of as a dynamic interrelated system. Gestalt psychologists believe that whatever happens to a person influences everything else about him; for example, the world simply does not look the same if one has a sore toe or an upset stomach. For the Gestalt psychologist, the emphasis is always on a totality or whole and not on individual parts.

Kurt Lewin (1890–1947) another early Gestalt psychologist, used field theory and developed a theory of human motivation around it. He said that human behavior at any given time is determined by the total number of psychological facts being experienced at the time. A psychological fact, according to Lewin, is anything that has an effect on behavior, including being hungry, a memory of a past event, being in a certain physical location, the presence of certain other people, or having a certain amount of money. All of these psychological facts make up the person's *life space*. Some of these facts will exert a positive influence on the person's behavior and some a negative influence. It is the totality of these events that determines behavior at any given time. For Lewin, only those things consciously experienced could influence behavior; therefore, before anything experienced in the past can influence current behavior, the person must be conscious of it. A change in any psychological fact rearranges the entire life space. Thus, the causes of behavior are continually chang-

Kurt Lewin

ing; they are dynamic. The person exists in a continually changing field of influences, and a change in any one of them affects all the others. This is what is meant by a psychological field theory.

Nature versus Nurture.

The behaviorists tended to look upon the brain as the passive receiver of sensations that, in turn, produced responses. The brain to them was a complex switchboard. Human nature, said the behaviorists, is determined by what we experience. The content of the "mind" is therefore looked upon as the synthesis of our experiences, and little else. The Gestaltists assigned a more active role to the brain. The brain, to them, was not a passive receiver and storer of information from the environment. The brain acted upon incoming sensory information in such a way as to make it more meaningful and organized. This is not a learned function but is the result of the brain's structure. The organizational abilities of the brain are genetically determined and occur in every normal, healthy, human brain. Thus, like Plato, Descartes, and Kant, the Gestalt psychologists can be considered nativists, since they all believed important attributes of the mind exist independently of experience. This belief, of course, is diametrically opposed to the behaviorist's notion of the passive mind.

We can say, therefore, that according to the Gestalt psychologists, the tendency to divide our perceptual field into meaningful units is inherited. Note that the Gestalt psychologists are not saying that *ideas* are inherited, but only the tendency to organize incoming sensory information in certain lawful ways. In summary, we can say that the Gestaltists, stressing the importance of genetic influences on perception, are nativistic; that is, they stress the importance of abilities that the organism comes equipped with at birth. The behaviorists, on the other hand, say that even the tendency to organize experience comes from experience, thus stressing nurture rather than nature in explaining perception and learning. As we shall see later in this chapter, however, the Gestaltists did not neglect the role of experience altogether.

Law of Prägnanz.

The Gestalt psychologists' main concern has always been with perceptual phenomena. Through the years, well over a hundred perceptual principles have been studied by Gestalt theorists. However, one overriding principle applies to all mental events, including the principles of perception, and that is the law of *Prägnanz* (*Prägnanz* is the German word for pregnant). Koffka (1935) defined the law of *Prägnanz* as follows: "Psychological organization will always be as good as the controlling circumstances permit" [p. 110]. By "good," Koffka meant such qualities as simple, concise, symmetrical, or harmonious. In other words, there is a tendency for every psychological event to be meaningful, complete, and simple. A good figure, or a good perception, or a good memory, cannot be made simpler or more orderly through any kind of perceptual shift; that is, there is nothing more we can do mentally that would make the conscious experience any more organized. The law of *Prägnanz* was used by the Gestaltists as their guiding principle while studying perception, learning, and memory. Later the law of *Prägnanz* was also applied to the areas of personality and psychotherapy.

GESTALT PRINCIPLES OF PERCEPTION

Figure-Ground Relationship.

The most basic organization in perception is the separation of the perceptual field into two parts: the *figure*, which is dominant, unified, and is the focus of attention; and the *ground,* which is more homogeneous, diffuse, and provides the setting for the figure. When we attend to something in the environment, it becomes the figure, and everything we are not attending to becomes the ground. While we attend to one aspect of the environment, we can clearly see its detailed characteristics, while the details of other aspects of the environment are lost. Which aspect of a perceptual field is the figure and which is the ground is a matter of attention and the two can be switched by switching one's attention. Looking at Figure 10–1, it will be noted that when you look at the older woman it is very difficult to see the younger one, and vice versa. Likewise, while attending to the vase it is difficult to see the two faces, and vice versa.

Gestalt principles of perception have been invoked to describe how a particular arrangement of stimuli stand out from their background and are perceived as a unified figure. Although the Gestaltists have isolated over a hundred of these principles, we will briefly discuss only a few of the more important ones.

Figure 10–1. While attending to the profile of the young woman, it is difficult to see the older woman in the picture. The older woman's mouth is the younger woman's necklace and the younger woman's ear is the older woman's eye. Once both women are seen, it is possible to switch from one woman to the other at will (from Leeper, 1935). Likewise, in figure 10-1B, the viewer can either see two faces or a vase depending on what is attended to.

Principle of Continuity (also called the principle of direction, or the principle of good continuation). This principle says that those stimuli that have continuity with one another will stand out from the background and will be organized as a whole. In other words, elements that seem to flow in the same direction or follow the same pattern will be perceived as a figure. Wertheimer used such phrases as "intrinsic togetherness" and "imminent necessity" in explaining why stimuli that follow the same pattern are seen as a perceptual unit. Examples of the principle of continuity are seen in Figure 10–2.

Principle of Proximity. The principle of proximity states that when stimuli are close together, they tend to be grouped together in our perceptual field. Examples of this principle are seen in Figure 10–2.

Principle of Inclusiveness. This principle states that the figure we are most likely to see is the one that includes the greatest number of stimuli. For example, if a small figure is embedded in a larger figure, and both are distinctly different, we will tend to perceive the larger figure rather than the smaller one. Camouflage, for instance, works by destroying the configuration of an object that would be readily perceived otherwise. That is, incorporating a smaller figure within a larger one makes the smaller one difficult to perceive. Painting a ship blue or a fawn having a speckled coat as it hides among the leaves would be examples of camouflage. Figure 10–2 illustrates other examples of the principle of inclusiveness.

Principle of Similarity. This principle simply says that similar objects tend to be grouped together in our perceptual field. Examples of the principle of similarity are shown in Figure 10–2.

Principle of Common Fate (also called the law of joint destiny, the law of common movement, or the law of uniform destiny). This principle states that elements are grouped together if they move simultaneously or in a similar manner. When we see a group of lights moving together down a river, we organize them into a unit just as we do with the lights of an airplane against the stars. Katz (1950) gives another example:

> Two projectors can be used to demonstrate the effectiveness of movement in creating forms. Groups of dots—one group from each projector—are projected onto the same part of a screen, so that they form one haphazard collection, one sum total. However, when one projector is moved, the dots projected by it combine immediately and are set apart from the other, motionless, set of dots. As long as motion continues, the two groups do not merge. As soon as

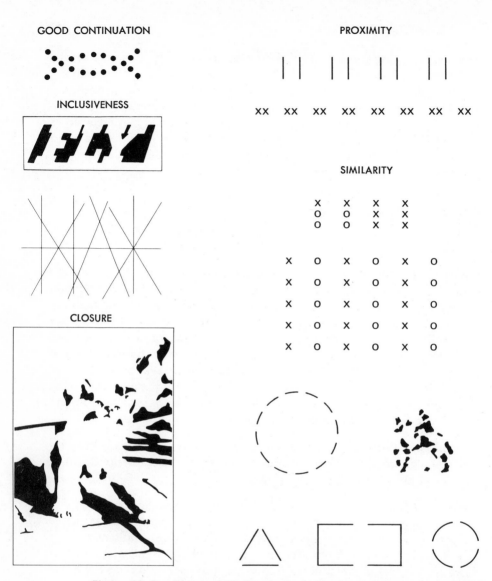

Figure 10–2. The word "fly" under inclusiveness tends not to be perceived because so much of the word blends into the background (a). Likewise, the word "may" is not seen in the second figure (b) because it is encompassed by more inclusive stimuli. Seeing the patches of black and white as a cat exemplifies the principle of closure (c).

Source: (a) Brown and Gilhousen, College Psychology. Englewood Cliffs, N. J.: Prentice-Hall, 1950, p. 330. (b) Mussen, P. and Rosenzweig, R., Psychology: An Introduction. Lexington, Mass.: D. C. Heath and Co., 1973. Reprinted by permission of the publisher, (c) Sartain, Q., North, J., Strange, R., and Chapman, M. Psychology: Understanding Human Behavior. New York: McGraw-Hill, 1973, p. 229.

the moving group comes to a standstill in its former position, all the dots again blend into a single chaotic group [p. 27].

Again, according to the principle of common fate, objects that move together in a common direction or in a common pattern tend to be grouped together in our perceptual field. The major difference between the principle of continuity and the principle of common fate is that the latter involves real movement, the former does not.

Principle of Closure. The principle of closure states that we have a tendency to complete incomplete experiences. For example, if one looks at a line that is almost circular except for a small gap in it, the person will tend to fill in the gap perceptually and respond to the figure as if it were a complete circle. This principle, like all the others, follows the general law of *Prägnanz* which says that we respond to the world so as to make it maximally meaningful under existing conditions. Because responding to a complete geometric form is more meaningful than responding to what is really physically present (an incomplete circle), we tend to fill in the gap perceptually. Examples of closure are shown in Figure 10–2. We will discuss a possible explanation for closure later in this chapter and again when we discuss Hebb's theory in Chapter 13.

The Perceptual Constancies

Perceptual constancy refers to the fact that we see an object as the same object under a variety of circumstances. We say a door is a door regardless of what position the door is in. We identify a person as the same person whether he is standing in front of us or a block away. The Gestaltists point out that in each case, the actual stimulation has changed radically; what has remained constant is the *meaning* of the object. Thus, the meaning an object conveys is much more important than the actual physical stimulation involved. Köhler (1929) says:

> The man approaching us on the street does not grow larger, as for simple optical reasons he should. The circle observed on the oblique plane does not become an eclipse; it seems to remain a circle after its retinal image has become a very flat eclipse. The white object in the shadow remains white, the black paper remains black in full light, though the first may reflect much less light than the second. These three examples have one common property: the physical object *as such* remaining constant, while actual stimulation varies according to more or less accidental conditions (of distance, of position, of illumination), our experience

agrees with the constancy of the physical object much better than with the varying stimulation produced by it [p. 80].

The reductionistic approach of the behaviorist which emphasizes either basic sensations or the nature of the stimulating environment would probably, according to the Gestaltists, miss the most important point involved in perceptual constancies—the object's *meaning* remains constant. Once again we have an example of how the brain organizes sensory information to make it more meaningful. The fact that the brain recognizes the same object under a wide variety of circumstances makes our conscious experiences much more harmonious than if we had to learn to recognize an object anew each time it was presented to us in a slightly different way. The behaviorist would say, however, that the notion of stimulus generalization could handle this problem quite easily.

The Brain and Conscious Experience

Every major psychological theory must in some way deal with the mind-body problem. The problem can be stated in many ways, for example, "How can something purely physical cause something purely mental?" or "What is the relationship between the body and consciousness?" No matter how reductionistic one's answer becomes—even studying how individual brain cells respond to various forms of stimulation—the question as to how the external world is translated into conscious experience still remains.

The behaviorists solved the mind-body problem by ignoring it. In fact, they concentrated their investigations on behavior in order to avoid the mind-body problem. The structuralists implied a direct relationship between the body (sensation) and the content of the mind. In fact, it can be said that they studied the content of the mind to discover what had been sensed. The structuralist's view of the mind-body relationship was that the two were parallel, that is, the contents of the mind (consciousness) varied as a function of sensory experience. Such a view is referred to as a *psychophysical parallelism.*

The Gestaltists took a much different approach to solving the mind-body problem than did the structuralists or the behaviorists. They assumed an *isomorphism* between psychological experience and the processes that exist in the brain. External stimulation causes reactions in the brain and we experience those reactions *as they occur in the brain.* The main difference between this point of view and the one held by the structuralists is that the Gestaltists believed *the brain actively transformed sensory stimulation.* The brain, they thought, organized, simplified, and made meaningful incoming sensory information. We experience the information only after it has been transformed by the brain in accordance with the law of *Prägnanz*. Köhler says (1947): "Experienced order in space is always structurally identical with a functional order in the distribution of underlying brain processes" [p. 61]. Koffka says (1935):

> Thus, isomorphism, a term implying equality of form, makes the bold assumption that the "motion of the atoms and molecules of the brain" are not "fundamentally different from thoughts and feelings" but in their molar aspects, considered as processes in extension, identical [p. 62].

Over and over, the Gestalt psychologists state their belief that the phenomenal world (consciousness) is an accurate expression of the circumstances that exist in the brain.

With their concept of psychophysical isomorphism, the Gestaltists felt they solved a major problem that the more mechanistic theories had not solved, that is, "How does the *mind* organize sensory information and make it meaningful?" The Gestalt psychologist answered this question by saying that the content of thought (consciousness) comes to us already organized; it is organized by the brain before we experience it or as we are experiencing it. Therefore, to the Gestaltists, *the activities of the brain correspond dynamically with the content of thought*. It should be made clear that from this point of view the brain is much more than a complex switchboard. According to the Gestaltists, the brain actively transforms incoming sensory information according to the law of *Prägnanz* and this transformed information is what we are "conscious" of. The relationship among external stimulation, the brain, and conscious experience can be diagrammed as follows:

$$S_1, S_2, S_3, S_4, S_5, S_6, S_7$$

External Stimulation $\longrightarrow$ Brain transforms sensory data in accordance with the law of *Prägnanz*. $\longrightarrow$ Conscious experience determined by the characteristics of brain activity and not by the external environment.

Because of their strong belief in an "active mind," the Gestaltists are clearly rationalists, and because they believe the "powers of the mind" are genetically determined, they are clearly nativists. These beliefs place them in the tradition of Plato, Descartes, and Kant.

Gestalt Principles of Learning

The most famous work on learning by a member of the Gestalt school was done by Köhler at the University of Berlin Anthropoid Station on Tenerife, one of the Canary Islands. Köhler did his work between 1913 and 1917 and summarized his findings in *The Mentality of Apes* (1925). While on Tenerife, Köhler also studied the problem solving ability of chickens, although this work is rarely mentioned.

Since Gestalt psychologists were primarily field theorists interested in perceptual phenomena, it is no surprise to find them looking at learning as a special problem in perception. They assumed that when an organism is confronted with a problem, a state of cognitive disequilibrium is set up and continues until the problem is solved. Therefore, to the Gestalt psychologist, cognitive disequilibrium had motivational properties that caused the organism to attempt to regain the balance in his mental system. According to the law of *Prägnanz*, cognitive balance is more satisfying than cognitive disbalance. On this point the Gestaltists are in close agreement with both Guthrie and Hull. It can be said that problems provide maintaining stimuli (or drive, to use Hull's term) which persist until the problem is solved, at which point the maintaining stimuli terminate (the drive is reduced). Support for this point of view was provided by the work of Bluma Zeigarnik who found that incompleted tasks were remembered longer and in greater detail than completed ones. She explained this phenomenon in terms of the motivational properties of a problem that persist until the problem is solved. The tendency to remember incompleted tasks better than completed ones has come to be called the *Zeigarnik effect*.

Learning, to the Gestaltist, is a cognitive phenomenon. The organism "comes to see" the solution after pondering a problem. The learner thinks about all the ingredients necessary to solve a problem and puts them together (cognitively) first one way and then another until the problem is solved. When the solution comes, it comes suddenly, that is, the organism gains an *insight* into the solution of a problem. The problem can exist in only two states, (1) unsolved and (2) solved; there is no state of partial solution in between. As we saw in Chapter 4, Thorndike believed that learning was continuous in that it increased systematically in small amounts as a function of reinforced trials. The Gestaltists believed that either a solution is reached or it is not; learning to them was discontinu-

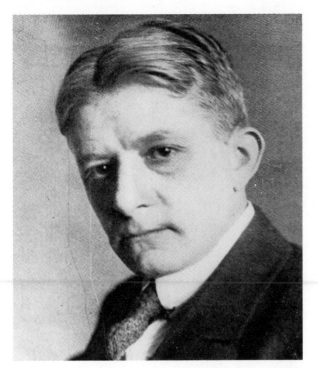

Wolfgang Köhler

ous. As we saw in Chapter 9 the continuity-noncontinuity controversy is still very much alive today.

In order to test his notions about learning, Köhler used a number of creative experimental arrangements. One arrangement involved detour problems. In a detour problem, the animal can clearly see his goal but is unable to reach it directly. He must turn away from the sight of the ob-

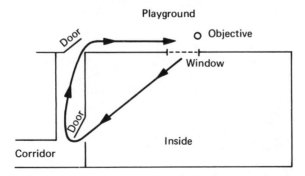

Figure 10–3.   **A typical detour problem (from Köhler, 1925, p. 21).**

ject he wants and take an indirect route to reach it. A typical detour problem is diagrammed in Figure 10–3 on page 249. With this type of problem, Köhler found that chickens had great difficulty in reaching a solution, but apes did so with relative ease.

A second kind of arrangement utilized by Köhler necessitated the animal's using an implement of some kind in reaching a goal. For example, a banana was placed just out of the reach of an ape so that he must either use a stick to reach it or put two sticks together so that they were long enough for him to reach it. In either case, the animal had all the ingredients necessary to solve the problem available to him; it was just a matter of putting them together in an appropriate manner. Figure 10–4 shows the ape named Chica using a pole to obtain the fruit. Figure 10–5 shows

Figure 10–4. An ape named Chica using a pole to obtain food (from Köhler, 1925, p. 72a).

Figure 10–5. An ape named Grande using a stack of boxes to obtain food as Sultan watches (from Köhler, 1925, p. 142a).

Figure 10–6. Grande creating an even more elaborate structure (from Köhler, 1925, p. 144a).

Figure 10–7.   Chica beating down her objective with a pole.

Figure 10–8.   Sultan putting two sticks together (from Köhler, 1925).

the ape named Grande using a stack of boxes that he arranged in order
to reach some bananas. Figure 10–6 shows Grande putting together an
even more complex structure. Figure 10–7 shows Chica using both boxes
and a pole to obtain the fruit. Figure 10–8 shows Sultan, Köhler's most
intelligent ape, putting together two sticks in order to reach fruit that
otherwise would be inaccessible.

The Presolution Period.

Usually a rather lengthy period of time transpires before an insightful
solution to a problem is reached. Describing what happens during this
period, the Gestalt psychologist comes fairly close to the concept of trial
and error learning, but the trial and error learning they refer to is cognitive rather than behavioral. The organism, they say, runs through a number of "hypotheses" concerning an effective way to solve the problem.
The animal *thinks* about different possible solutions until he hits upon
one that works and then he acts upon that solution behaviorally. When
the correct strategy is discovered, insight is said to have occurred. Of
course, for insightful learning to occur, the organism must be exposed to
all elements of the problem; if he is not, his behavior will seem to be
blind and groping. This, say the Gestaltists, was the problem with Thorndike's research. Thorndike found what appeared to be incremental learning because important elements of the problem were hidden from the
animal, thus preventing insightful learning. The reader can experience
the "aha" experience that usually accompanies insightful learning by trying to find the hidden bear in Figure 10–9.

Typically one searches through a good portion of the picture before the

Figure 10–9. Can you find the hidden bear (From Munn, Fernald and Fernald, 1972).

hidden shape is found. The problem creates a cognitive disequilibrium whose mild tension lasts until the problem is solved. In this case, discovering the bear restores cognitive equilibrium, relaxes the tension, and may make one feel like saying "aha."

Insightful Learning Summarized.

Insightful learning is usually regarded as having four characteristics: (1) the transition from presolution to solution is sudden and complete; (2) performance based upon a solution gained by insight is usually smooth and free of errors; (3) a solution to a problem gained by insight is retained for a considerable length of time; and (4) a principle gained by insight is easily applied to other problems. We shall see an example of this last characteristic of insightful learning in our discussion of transposition below.

Transposition.

When a principle learned in one problem solving situation is applied to the solution of another problem, the process is referred to as transposition. Köhler's early work on transposition was done with chickens and apes. The typical experiment involved training an animal to approach one of two shades of gray paper; for example, chickens were fed on a dark shade of gray paper, but not on a lighter shade. After such training, when the animal was given a choice between the two shades of gray, he approached the darker one. If the experiment was to end at this point, the behaviorists would be delighted, since that is exactly how the animal should react acording to their point of view. It is the second part of the experiment, however, that the Gestaltists felt was most revealing.

After the preliminary training, the animal was given a choice between the dark paper on which it was trained and a still darker sheet of gray paper. The situation is diagrammed in Figure 10–10.

How will the animal respond to the new situation? The answer to that

Stimuli: Used During Preliminary Training

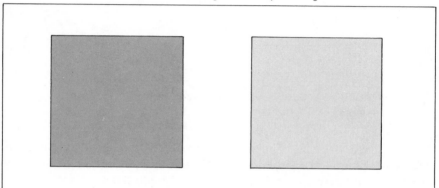

Stimuli: Used During the Transposition Test

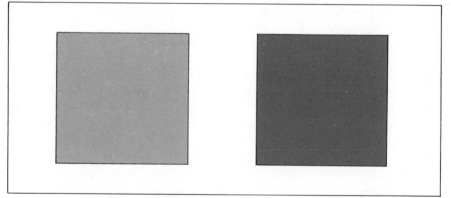

Figure 10–10. First the animal is taught to approach the dark grey stimulus and then is offered a choice between the dark grey stimulus and a still darker grey stimulus. If the animal chooses the darker of the two, transposition is said to have been demonstrated.

question depends on how one views the learning process. The Gestaltists felt that the behaviorists would have to predict that the animal would approach the lighter of the two shades of gray in the new situation since it is the exact one that had been rewarded in the first phase of the experiment. The Gestaltists, however, did not view learning as the development of specific habits or S–R connections. To them what was learned in this kind of a situation was a relational principle, i.e., they felt the animal learned the principle of approaching *the darker of the two objects* in the first phase of the experiment and that same principle would be applied in the second phase of the experiment. The Gestaltists would predict, therefore, that the animal would choose the darker of the two objects in phase two, although they had been rewarded for choosing the other object in phase one. Generally speaking, the prediction made by the Gestalt psychologists in this situation is an accurate one.

The Behaviorists' Explanation of Transposition.

In the kind of learning situation described above, the behaviorist tends to talk about the learning of specific S–R connections. As a result, his views on learning have been referred to as an *absolute* theory. On the other hand, since the Gestalt view of learning emphasizes the comparison between the two stimuli, has been referred to as a *relational* theory. Köhler's research created some problems for the absolute position until Spence came up with his now famous explanation of the transposition phenomenon based on S–R concepts (Spence, 1937).

Suppose, says Spence, that an animal is rewarded for approaching a box whose lid measures 160 sq cm, and not rewarded for approaching a box whose lid measures 100 sq cm. Soon the animal will learn to approach the larger box exclusively.

In phase two of this experiment, the animal chooses between the 160 sq cm and a box whose lid is 256 sq cm. The animal will usually choose the larger box (256 sq cm) even though he had been rewarded specifically for choosing the other one (160 sq cm) during phase one. Again, this finding seems to support the relational learning point of view.

Spence's behavioristic explanation of transposition is based on generalization. First, he says, it must be assumed that the tendency to approach the positive stimulus (160 sq cm) generalizes to other related stimuli. Second, it must be assumed that the tendency to approach the positive stimulus (and the generalization of this tendency) is stronger than the tendency to avoid the negative stimulus (and the generalization of this tendency). What behavior occurs will be determined by the algebraic summation of the positive and negative tendencies. Spence's explanation is diagrammed in Figure 10–11.

STIMULUS SIZE - SQ.CMS.

Figure 10–11. According to Spence's explanation of transposition, the tendency to avoid a stimulus (dashed curve) must be subtracted from the tendency to approach a stimulus (solid curve). It is the net value that results when these positive and negative influences are added algebraically that determines which of the two stimuli will be approached (from Spence, 1942).

Whenever there is a choice between two stimuli, the one eliciting the greatest net approach tendency will be chosen. In the first phase of Spence's experiment, the animal chose the 160 sq cm box over the 100 sq cm box because the net positive tendency was 51.7 for the former and 29.7 for the latter. In phase two, the 256 sq cm box was chosen over the 160 sq cm box because the net positive tendency was 72.1 for the former and still 51.7 for the latter.

Spence's explanation has the advantage of making some unexpected predictions of transpositional phenomena. For example, his theory would predict that transposition should break down at some point and, in the example above, the animal would choose the smaller object in a pair of test stimuli. This would happen if the animal were presented with a choice between a 256 sq cm box and any box larger than 409 sq cm. In all choices involving a 256 sq cm box and a box 409 sq cm or larger, the animal will choose the *smaller of the two,* thereby reversing the principle the animal was supposed to have learned. Likewise, if given a choice between a 160 sq cm box and one slightly larger than 409 sq cm, choices will be about equally divided, since the net positive tendency for each box is about the same.

Since Spence's theory could predict both the successes and failures of the transposition phenomenon, his point of view became more popular than the Gestalt point of view. Research on various aspects of transposition, however, has demonstrated that both S–R and Gestalt predictions fail under certain circumstances, and the matter is still very much unsettled. A third explanation, based on Helson's adaptation-level theory, is currently gaining acceptance and is closer to the Gestalt point of view than the behavioristic one (see Herbert and Krantz, 1965).

THE MEMORY TRACE

We mentioned above that Gestalt psychologists tended to be nativists in that they stressed inherited abilities in their explanation of learning and perception. Although they mainly stressed genetic factors, they also took into account the effects of experience. There was too much substantial evidence for the effects of prior experience on present experience to be ignored. Koffka (1935) attempted to link the past with the present through his concept of the *memory trace*. Koffka's treatment of the memory trace is long and complicated and only a rudimentary sketch of it can be presented here. (The interested reader is referred to Koffka, 1935, pp. 425–647 for greater detail.)

Koffka assumed that a current experience gave rise to what he called a *process*. The process is the activity in the brain caused by an environmental experience. This process could be simple or complex, depending on the experience it was based on. When a process is terminated, a trace of its effect remains in the brain. This trace, in turn, will influence all similar processes that occur in the future. According to this point of view, a process, which is caused by an experience, can occur only once in "pure" form; thereafter similar experiences result from the interaction between

Kurt Koffka

the process and the memory trace. Thus, each time a process is aroused, it modifies the organism and that modification influences future experiences. In fact, Koffka says, if one defines learning as a modification in behavior that results from experience, each elicitation of a process can be looked upon as a learning experience.

What is the nature of the influence of the trace on the process? Koffka (1935) answers that a trace "exerts an influence on the process in the direction of *making it similar to the process which originally produced the trace*" [p. 553]. The stronger the memory trace, the stronger will be its influence on the process; therefore, one's conscious experience will tend to be more in accordance with the trace than with the process.

According to this point of view, if the last thing a person did in a problem-solving situation was to solve the problem, the solution becomes "etched" in his mind. The next time he is in a similar problem-solving situation, a process will occur that will "communicate" with the trace from the previous problem-solving situation. The trace then will influence the ongoing process in the direction stated above, making the problem easier to solve. With repetition the trace becomes more and more influential over the process. In other words, as the animal solves more problems that are similar, he becomes a better problem-solver. Koffka explains improvement in a skill as the result of the increasing influence of the trace on the process.

At this point in Gestalt theorizing, we see considerable agreement with Guthrie. It seems, for example, that Koffka accepts the recency principle, which states that what an organism did last in a situation is what he will do if the situation recurs. Likewise, as we shall see below, the Gestaltists are in essential agreement with Guthrie's explanation as to how repetition results in improvement of a skill.

Individual Trace versus Trace System.

Solving an individual problem is but a specific occurrence of problem-solving behavior, and learning to type the letters *A*, *B*, and *C* are but specific occurrences of the more general behavior we call typing. Every complex skill can be looked upon as consisting of many processes and their corresponding traces, and yet each of the individual traces have in common that they are related to the same skill. Numerous interrelated individual traces are referred to as a *trace system*. Koffka assumes that through repetition the trace system becomes more important than the individual traces that make it up. The "wholeness" quality of the skill comes to dominate the individual traces, thereby causing them to lose their individuality. This phenomenon may at first seem paradoxical; that is, repetition can benefit learning although it tends to destroy the traces of individual experiences. Koffka (1935) says:

> There is loss of consolidation of the *single individual* traces which we are apt to overlook because it is accompanied by a gain in the stability of the *trace system*. When we learn to type, the clumsy movement which we originally executed will at a later stage be impossible; i.e., the traces of the first lesson have become changed by the aggregate of traces which has been produced by the many repetitions and is responsible for the improvement of the skill. Similarly, when we stay in a room for any length of time, we get a great number of impressions of it by moving about or merely letting our eyes roam. But only a few of them can be recalled [p. 545].

Just as the individual trace exerts a greater influence on future processes as it becomes more fixed, so does the trace system exert greater influence on related processes as it becomes more fixed. This contention has very interesting implications. For example, it is assumed that through the years we develop trace systems that correspond to similar experiences. Thus we develop trace systems that correspond to chairs, dogs, trees, males, females, or pencils. These trace systems will be a kind of neurological summation of all our experiences with objects in a certain class, e.g., cows, or clowns. Since these trace systems become firmly established, they will have a profound effect on any individual experience we may have. For example, if we look at an individual elephant, the process aroused by that elephant will be influenced by the trace system that resulted from all our other experiences with elephants. The resulting experience will be a combination of the two influences, with the trace system being the most important. Our memory of that event, then, will be one of "elephantness" that has little to do with any particular elephant but has more to do with what they have in common. This also serves to explain the phenomenon of closure. The individual experience of a partial circle is dominated by the trace system of "circleness" and the resulting experience is one of a complete circle.

Memory, like perception and learning, follows the law of *Prägnanz*. Memories tend to be complete and meaningful, even when the original experience was not. Irregular experiences tend to be remembered as regular, unique events are remembered in terms of something familiar (e.g., a catlike object will be remembered as a cat), and minor flaws or discrepancies in a figure will tend to be forgotten. It is the enduring features of past experience, rather than uncommon occurrences, that guide our behavior. Again, the emphasis is on the pattern, the Gestalt, the wholeness of experience and the recollection of experience. This is contrasted with the association theory of memory accepted by the behaviorists. The associationists accept the "bundle hypothesis" which states that complex thoughts are made up of simple ideas bound together by continuity, similarity, or contrast. Memory occurs when one element in the bundle causes the recall of the other elements. The Gestaltists rejected association theory in favor of the law of *Prägnanz* in explaining all aspects of human experience, including perception, learning, and memory.

Behaviorism had nothing to say about perception and early Gestalt theory had little or nothing to say about learning. But when the Gestaltists fled to America from Nazi Germany, they began to address the problem of learning because it was a major interest of American psychologists. Gestalt theory was clearly better able to handle problems in perception, mostly because behaviorism, in excluding mental events from its domain of study, ignored the topic of perception. So on the one hand we had the Gestalt theorists attempting to expand their perceptual theory to cover learning, and on the other hand, we had the behaviorists ignoring perceptual learning. As usual, accepting a paradigm as an ideology blinded both the Gestaltists and the behaviorists to important aspects of the learning process. Fortunately, later thinkers have attempted to utilize the best of both paradigms. The best example of an effort to combine the two paradigms is Tolman's theory of learning, to which we turn in Chapter 12.

The healthy debate between the Gestalt psychologists and the behaviorists resulted in each point of view's being modified because of criticism from the other. Both positions were extreme and both have left an indelible mark on psychology. Thanks to the Gestalt psychologists the study of cognitive processes is no longer taboo. However, cognitive processes currently are being studied under rigorous laboratory conditions under such headings as risk-taking, problem solving, and concept formation. For the insistence on operationally defining these concepts and on empirically verifying any statement made about them, we can thank the behavioristic influence.

DISCUSSION QUESTIONS

1. What were the main sources of disagreement between the Gestalt psychologists and the behaviorists? Were they in agreement on any matter? Explain.

2. List and describe as many Gestalt principles of perception as you can.
3. What is meant by the statement, "The law of *Prägnanz* was used by the Gestalt psychologists as an overriding principle in their explanation of perception, learning, memory, personality, and psychotherapy"?
4. Discuss the term *isomorphism* as it is used in Gestalt theory.
5. Discuss the topic of memory from the point of view of a Gestalt psychologist. Include in your answer the concepts of process, individual trace, and trace system.
6. Explain transposition from both a Gestalt and a behavioristic point of view.
7. Summarize the characteristics of insightful learning.
8. What is meant by the statement, "For the Gestalt psychologist, learning is basically a perceptual phenomenon"?
9. List some differences between classroom procedures developed according to Gestalt principles and those developed according to S–R principles. In general, do you feel American public schools are based on a Gestalt model or a behavioristic model? Explain.
10. How might a behaviorist explain the "perceptual constancies"?

GLOSSARY

Absolute theory.   The contention of the behaviorists that what an organism learns are specific responses to specific stimuli.

Closure, principle of.   Tendency to complete incomplete experiences, thereby making them more meaningful.

Common fate, principle of.   The tendency to see objects moving in the same direction as a perceptual unit.

Continuity, principle of.   The tendency to respond to trends and themes running through a series of objects and to perceive all objects corresponding to that trend or theme as being part of the same perceptual unit.

Field theory.   The belief that the environment consists of interdependent events. In psychology, field theory assumes that behavior and/or cognitive processes are a function of many variables that exist simultaneously, and a change in any one of them changes the effect of all the others.

Figure-ground relationship.   The fact that the perceptual field is divided into an object of attention (the figure) and a diffuse background (the ground).

Gestalt.   A German word meaning pattern or configuration.

Inclusiveness, principle of.   The tendency to respond to objects in the environment that contain the largest number of stimuli.

Individual memory trace.   The memory trace left by a specific experience.

Insightful learning.   Learning that occurs very rapidly, is remembered for a considerable length of time, and transfers readily to situations related to the one in which the insightful learning took place.

Isomorphism.   As the term is used by the Gestalt psychologists, it means the relationship that exists between brain activity and consciousness.

Law of Prägnanz.   The overriding principle in Gestalt psychology which states that all mental events tend toward completeness, simplicity, and meaningfulness.

Life space.   A concept employed by Kurt Lewin to describe the simultaneous influences on a person at a given time. Anything that could affect behavior was called a "psychological fact" and the total number of "psychological facts" influencing a person at any given moment was his life space.

Memory process.   The brain activity that is caused by environmental stimulation.

Memory trace.   The remnants of an environmental experience after the experience is terminated.

Molar behavior.   A large segment of behavior that is goal-directed and therefore purposive.

Molecular behavior.   A small segment of behavior, such as a conditioned reflex, that is isolated for detailed study.

Nativist.   See Glossary, Chapter 3.

Nature-versus-nurture controversy.   The debate as to whether genetics or experience is more important in determining the characteristics of such cognitive processes as perception and reasoning.

Perceptual constancy.   The tendency to respond to an object as the same object although it is experienced under varying circumstances.

Phenomenology.   The study of intact, meaningful mental events. These intact, meaningful mental events are called phenomenological experiences. It is these phenomenological experiences that the structuralists wanted their subjects to actively avoid and that the Gestalt psychologists felt were the basic subject matter of psychology.

Phi phenomenon.   The experience of apparent motion that is caused by lights flashing on and off at a certain frequency. Wertheimer's discovery of apparent motion launched the Gestalt school of psychology.

Proximity, principle of.   Objects that are close together are seen as a perceptual unit.

Psychophysical parallelism.   The position taken on the mind-body question which states that the contents of the mind varies directly with sensory experience.

Relational theory.   The contention of the Gestalt psychologists that the organism learns in terms of a principle of relationship and not in terms of specific responses to specific stimuli.

Similarity, principle of.   Objects that are similar to one another are organized into one perceptual unit.

Trace system.   A number of interrelated individual memory traces.

Transposition.   The Gestalt version of transfer of training which states that a principle that works in solving a problem will tend to be applied to the solution of similar problems.

Zeigarnik effect.   The tendency to remember uncompleted tasks longer than completed ones.

11

Jean Piaget

Jean Piaget was born on August 9, 1896 in Neuchâtel, Switzerland. His father was a historian whose specialty was medieval literature. Piaget showed early interest in biology and when only eleven years old he published a one-page article on a partially albino sparrow he had seen in a park. Between fifteen and eighteen, he published a number of articles on mollusks. Piaget notes that because of his many publications, he was accidentally offered the position of curator of the mollusk collection in the Geneva Museum while he was still a secondary school student.

As an adolescent, Piaget vacationed with his godfather who was a Swiss scholar. It was through this visit with his godfather that Piaget developed an interest in philosophy in general and in epistemology in particular. (Epistemology is a branch of philosophy that is concerned with the nature of knowledge.) Piaget's interests in biology and epistemology have continued throughout his life and are clearly evident almost everywhere in his theoretical writings.

Piaget received his Ph.D. in biology at the age of twenty-one and by the time he was thirty, he had published over twenty papers, mainly on mollusks, but on other topics as well. For example, at the age of twenty-three, he published an article on the relationship between psychoanalysis and child psychology. After receiving his doctorate, Piaget held a variety of jobs, among them was a position with the Binet Testing Laboratory in Paris where he helped to standardize intelligence tests. The Binet Laboratory's approach to testing was to develop a number of test questions which were then presented to children of different ages. It was found, in general, that older children could answer more questions correctly than younger children, and that some children could answer more questions correctly than other children of the same age. The former children were considered to be more intelligent than the latter children. Thus, the child's intelligence quotient was derived from the number of questions a child of a certain age could answer correctly. It was during his employment at the Binet Laboratory that Piaget developed his interest in the intellectual abilities of children. This interest in the intellectual abilities of children, as well as his interests in biology and epistemology, have permeated all of Piaget's work.

Jean Piaget

While working on the standardization of intelligence tests, Piaget noted something that was to have a major influence on his later theory of intellectual development. He discovered that a child's *incorrect* answers to test questions were more informative than the child's correct answers. He observed that the same kind of mistakes were made by children of approximately the same age, and that the kind of mistakes generally made by children of one age was *qualitatively* different from the kind of mistakes made by children of different ages. Piaget observed further that the nature of these mistakes could not be explored adequately in a highly structured testing situation where the child either answered a question correctly or he did not. Instead, Piaget employed the *clinical method,* which was an open-ended form of questioning. Using the clinical method, Piaget's questions were determined by the child's answers. If the child would say something of interest, Piaget would formulate a number of questions designed to explore further that item of interest. This method of gathering data is used by Piaget and his followers to this day.

It was during his employment at the Binet Laboratory that Piaget began to realize that "intelligence" could not be equated with the number of test items that a child answers correctly. To Piaget, the more basic question was *why* some children were able to answer some questions correctly and other children were not, or why a child could answer some items correctly but miss other items. Piaget began his search for the variables influencing the test performance of children. His search was to result in a view of intelligence which was as revolutionary as Freud's view of human motivation.

Piaget left Binet's laboratory to become director of research at the Jean-Jacques Rousseau Institute in Geneva, Switzerland, where he was able to pursue his own interests using his own methods. Soon after his affiliation with the institute, his first major works on developmental psychology began to appear. Piaget, who never had a course in psychology, soon became an internationally known authority on child psychology. He continued his work using his own three children as subjects. He and his wife (a former student of his at the Rousseau Institute) made careful observations about their children over a long period of time and summarized their findings in several books. The fact that Piaget's own children were used as sources of information in the development of his theory has often been criticized. The fact that more elaborate observations, involving large numbers of other children, have been in agreement with Piaget's earlier observations has tended to still this criticism however.

Piaget has published about thirty books and over two hundred articles, and he continues doing productive research at the University of Geneva. His theory of intellectual development in the child is extensive and complicated and in this chapter we merely will summarize its essential features. It will also become apparent that Piaget's approach to the learning process is different from all the other approaches covered in this text.

The information in this chapter was compiled from several sources. The secondary sources utilized were Beard, 1969; Flavell, 1963; Furth, 1969; and Ginsberg and Opper, 1969. The primary sources utilized were Inhelder and Piaget, 1958; Piaget, 1966, 1970a, 1970b; and Piaget and Inhelder, 1969.

MAJOR THEORETICAL NOTIONS

Intelligence.

We noted above that Piaget was opposed to defining intelligence in terms of the number of items answered correctly on a so-called intelligence test. To Piaget, an intelligent act is one that causes an approximation to the conditions optimal for an organism's survival. In other words, intelligence allows an organism to deal effectively with its environment. Since both the environment and the organism are changing constantly, an "intelligent" interaction between the two must also change constantly. An intelligent act always tends to create optimal conditions for the organism's survival *under the existing circumstances*. Thus, for Piaget, intelligence is a dynamic trait since what is available as an intelligent act will change as the organism matures biologically and as it gains experience. Intelligence, according to Piaget, is an integral part of any living organism since all living organisms seek those conditions conducive to their survival, but how intelligence manifests itself at any given time will necessarily vary as conditions vary. Piaget's theory has often been referred to as *genetic epistemology* since it attempts to trace the development of intellectual capabilities. It should be clear that the term *genetic* refers to developmental growth rather than biological inheritance. Piaget's views on how intellectual potential develops will be summarized in the remainder of this chapter.

Schemas.

A child is born with a few highly organized reflexes such as sucking, looking, reaching, and grasping. Rather than discussing individual occurrences of any one of these reflexes, Piaget chooses to talk about the general potential to do such things as suck, look, reach or grasp. These potentials to act in certain ways Piaget labelled *schemas*. For example, the grasping schema refers to the general ability to grasp things. The schema is more than a single manifestation of the grasping reflex. The grasping schema can be thought of as the cognitive structure that makes all acts of grasping possible.

When any particular instance of grasping is being observed or described, one must talk in terms of a specific response to specific stimuli. These aspects of any particular manifestation of a schema are called *content*. Again, schema refers to a general potential to perform a class of behaviors and content describes the conditions that prevail during any particular manifestation of that general potential.

Schema is an extremely important term in Piaget's theory. A schema can be thought of as an element in the organism's cognitive structure. The schemas available to an organism will determine how it can respond to the physical environment. Schemas can manifest themselves in overt behavior, as in the case of the grasping reflex, or they can manifest themselves covertly. Covert manifestations of a schema can be equated roughly with thinking. We will have more to say about covert manifestations of a schema later in this chapter. In both the case of overt behavior and of thinking, the term *content* refers to the specifics of a particular manifestation of a schema.

Obviously, the way a child is able to deal with its environment changes as he grows older. In order for new organism-environment interactions to occur, the schemas available to the child must change. We will examine the circumstances under which schemas change next.

Assimilation and Accommodation.

As we saw above, the number of schemas available to an organism at any given time constitutes that organism's cognitive structure. How an organism interacts with his environment will depend on the kind of cognitive structures he has available. In fact, how much of the environment can be understood, or even responded to, is determined by the various schemas available to the organism. In other words, the cognitive structures determine what aspects of the physical environment can even "exist" for the organism.

The process of responding to the environment in accordance with one's cognitive structures is called *assimilation*. Assimilation refers to a kind of matching between the cognitive structures and the physical environment. The cognitive structures that exist at any given moment set bounds on what can be assimilated by the organism. For example, if only the sucking, looking, reaching, and grasping schemas are available to a child, then everything he experiences will be assimilated into those schemas. As cognitive structures change it becomes possible for the child to assimilate different aspects of the physical environment.

Clearly, if assimilation were the only cognitive process, there would be no intellectual growth since an organism would simply go on assimilating his experiences into his existing cognitive structures. However, a second equally important process provides a mechanism for intellectual growth. The second process is called *accommodation*. Accommodation is the process by which cognitive structures are modified.

Optimally, every experience a person has involves both assimilation and accommodation. Events for which the organism has corresponding cognitive structures are readily assimilated, but events for which the organism had no existing cognitive structures would necessitate accommodation. Thus, most experiences involve two equally important processes: recognition, or knowing, which corresponds to the process of assimilation, and accommodation which results in the modification of cognitive structures. Such modification can be roughly equated with learning. To put the matter still another way, we respond to the world according to our previous experience (assimilation) but each experience contains aspects unlike anything we had experienced before. These unique aspects of experience cause minor changes in our cognitive structures (accommodation). Accommodation, then, provides a major vehicle for intellectual development.

Assimilation and accommodation are referred to as *functional invariants* because they occur at all levels of intellectual development. It should be clear, however, that early experiences tend to involve more accommodation than later experiences, since more and more of what is experienced will correspond to existing cognitive structures making substantial accommodation less necessary as the individual matures.

Equilibration.

One might ask what the driving force behind intellectual growth is. For Piaget, the answer would be found in his concept of *equilibration*. Piaget assumes that all organisms have an innate tendency to create a harmonious relationship between themselves and their environment. In other words, all aspects of the organism are geared toward optimal adaptation. Equilibration is this innate tendency to organize one's experiences so as to assure maximal adaptation. Roughly, equilibration can be defined as the continuous drive toward equilibrium or balance.

The concept of equilibration is for Piaget what the concept of hedonism was for Freud or self-actualization was for Maslow or Jung. It is his major motivational concept which, along with assimilation and accommodation, is used to explain the steady intellectual growth observed in children. Next we will describe how these three processes interact.

As we have seen, assimilation permits the organism to respond to a present situation in accordance with previous knowledge. Because the unique aspects of the situation cannot be responded to on the basis of previous knowledge, these novel or unique aspects of an experience cause a slight cognitive disbalance. Since there is an innate need for harmony (equilibrium), the organism's mental structures change in order to incorporate these unique aspects of the experience, thus causing the sought-after cognitive balance. As with the Gestalt psychologists, lack of cognitive balance has motivational properties that keep the organism active until a balance is attained. In addition to restoring the balance, however, this adjustment paves the way for new and different interactions with the environment. The accommodation described above causes a change in mental structures so that if those previously unique aspects of the environment were again encountered they would not cause a disbalance, i.e., they would be readily assimilated into the organism's existing cognitive structure. In addition, this new cognitive arrangement forms the basis for new accommodations, since accommodation always results from a disbalance and what causes a disbalance must always be related to the organism's current cognitive structures. Gradually, through this adaptive process, information that could not at one time be assimilated eventually can be. It is the dual mechanisms of assimilation and accommodation, along with the driving force of equilibration, that provides for slow, but steady intellectual growth. The process can be diagrammed as follows:

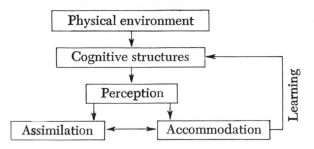

Interiorization.

The child's early interactions with the environment are strictly sensorimotor, that is, he responds directly to environmental stimuli with reflex motor reactions. The child's early experiences, then, involve the use and elaboration of his innate schemas such as grasping, sucking, looking, and reaching. The results of these early experiences are registered in the cognitive structures and gradually transform them. With increasing experience, the child expands his cognitive structures, thereby making it possible for him to adapt more readily to an ever increasing number of situations.

As more elaborate cognitive structures develop, the child is capable of responding to more complex situations. Also, the child is less dependent on the here and now. For example, he is capable of "thinking" of objects that are not before him. Now, what the child experiences is a function of both the physical environment and his cognitive structures which reflect his cumulative prior experiences. This gradual decreasing dependence on the physical environment and the increased utilization of cognitive structures is called *interiorization*.

As the cognitive structures develop, they become increasingly important in the adaptive process. For example, elaborate cognitive structures make more complex problem solving possible. As more experiences are interiorized, thinking becomes a tool in adapting to the environment. Earlier the child's adaptive responses were direct and simple and without thought. The child's early adaptive responses were mainly overt. As the process of interiorization continues, however, the child's adaptive responses become more covert: they involve internal actions rather than external ones. Piaget called these internal covert actions *operations* and the term operation can be roughly equated with "thinking." Now, rather than manipulating the environment directly, the child can do so mentally through the use of operations.

The most important characteristic of any operation is that it is *reversible*. Reversibility means that once something is thought, it can be "unthought"; i.e., an operation, once performed, can be mentally undone. For example, one can first mentally add 3 and 5 making a total of 8 and then mentally subtract 3 from 8 making a total of 5.

As we have seen, first the child's adjustment to the environment is direct and involves no thinking (operations). Next, as the child develops more complex cognitive structures, thinking becomes more important. The early use of operations depends upon those events the child can experience directly; that is, the child can think about those things that he can see. Piaget calls these *concrete operations* since they are applied to concrete environmental events. Later operations, however, are completely independent of physical experience and they therefore allow the child to solve purely hypothetical questions. Piaget calls the latter *formal operations*. Unlike the concrete operation, the formal operation is not bound to the environment.

Interiorization, then, is the process by which adaptive actions become increasingly covert rather than overt. In fact, operations can be thought of as interiorized actions. Adaptive behavior, which first involves only sensorimotor schemas and overt behavior, evolves to the point where formal operations are utilized in the adaptive process. The use of formal operations characterizes the highest form of intellectual development.

Although intellectual growth is continuous, Piaget found that certain mental abilities tend to appear at certain stages of development. It is important to note the word *tend*, however. Piaget and his colleagues found that although mental abilities appear around a certain age level, some children will show the ability earlier and some later than other children. Although the actual age at which an ability appears may vary from child to child or from culture to culture, the order in which mental abilities appears does not vary since mental development is always an extension of what preceded. Thus, although children of the same age may have different mental abilities available to them, the order with which the abilities emerge is constant. Below we will summarize the various stages of intellectual development suggested by Piaget.

STAGES OF DEVELOPMENT

1. *Sensorimotor stage* (birth to 2 years). This stage is characterized by the absence of language. Because the child has no words for things, they cease to exist when he is not dealing directly with them. His interactions with the environment are strictly sensory-motor and deal only with the here and now. The child at this stage is egocentric. Everything is seen with himself as a frame of reference and his psychological world is the only one that exists. Toward the end of this stage, the child develops the concept of object permanence. In other words, he comes to realize that objects go on existing even when he is not experiencing them.

2. *Preoperational thinking* (2 to 7 years). This stage has two subdivisions:

(a) Preconceptual thinking (about 2 to 4 years). During this part of preoperational thinking, the child begins rudimentary concept formation. He begins to classify things in certain classes because of their similarity, but makes a number of mistakes because of his concepts; e.g., all men are "Daddy", and all women are "Mommy," and all toys he sees are "mine." Rather than his logic being either inductive or deductive, it is *transductive*. An example of transductive reasoning would be "cows are big animals with four legs. That animal is big and has four legs; therefore, it is a cow."

(b) Period of intuitive thought (4 to 7 years). During this part of preoperational thinking, the child solves problems intuitively, instead of in accordance with some logical rule. The most striking characteristic of the child's thinking during this stage is his failure to develop *conservation*. Conservation is defined as the ability to realize that number, length, substance, or area remains constant even though these things may be presented to the child in a number of different ways. For example, a child is shown two containers filled to some level with some liquid.

Next, the contents of one container are poured into a taller, thinner container.

At this stage of development, the child, who observed that the first containers contained an equal amount of liquid, will now tend to say that the taller container has more liquid because the liquid is higher in the container. The child at this stage cannot mentally reverse cognitive operations, which means he cannot mentally pour the liquid from the tall container back into the shorter one and see that the amount of liquid is the same in both.

For Piaget, conservation is an ability that comes about as a result of the child's cumulative experiences with the environment and it is not an ability that can be taught until the child has had these preliminary experiences. As with all stage theories, teachability is a central issue. Do various capabilities come about because of certain experiences (e.g., learning), or do they unfold as a function of maturation along some genetically determined path? For Piaget it is both. Maturation provides the necessary sensory apparatus and brain structures but it takes experience to develop the ability. The question as to whether conservation can be taught before "its time has come" is still open; some say yes (for example, LeFrancois, 1968), and some say no, thus agreeing with Piaget (for example, Smedslund, 1961).

3. *Concrete operations* (about 7 to 11 or 12 years). The child now develops the ability to conserve, along with the abilities to deal adequately with classes, with seriation (i.e., he can arrange things from smallest to largest, and vice versa), and with number concepts. During this stage, however, the thought processes are directed to real events observed by the child. The child can perform rather complex operations on problems as long as the problems are concrete and not abstract.

The diagram on pg. 276 represents a typical problem given to children who are about eleven years old in order to study their thought processes. Their task is to determine what letter should go into the empty section of the circle. Perhaps you would like to try to solve the problem yourself.

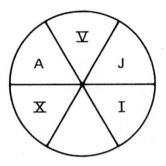

In order to solve the problem, one must realize that the letter of the alphabet opposite the Roman numeral I is *A*, the first letter of the alphabet. Also, the letter across from Roman numeral X is *J*, the tenth letter of the alphabet. Thus, the letter across from Roman numeral V must be the fifth letter of the alphabet, or *E*. At least two concepts must be utilized in solving such a problem: "one-to-one correspondence" and "opposite to." That is, it must be realized that Roman numerals and letters of the alphabet can be placed so that they correspond and it must also be realized that the corresponding numerals and letters are placed opposite one another. If the child does not have these concepts available, he cannot solve the problem. Likewise, if he can solve the problem, he must have the concepts available.

4. *Formal operations* (about 11 or 12 to 14 or 15 years). The child can now deal with hypothetical situations and his thought processes are not tied down exclusively to what is immediate and real. Thinking at this stage is as logical as it will ever become. This means that the mental apparatus that a person has is as sophisticated as it will ever be, but this apparatus can be directed toward the solution of a never ending array of problems throughout one's life.

Optimal Conditions for Learning.

It should be clear that if something cannot be at least partially assimilated into an organism's cognitive structure, it cannot act as a biological stimulus. It is in this sense that the cognitive structures create the physical environment. As the cognitive structures become more elaborate, the physical environment becomes better articulated. Likewise, if something is so far from an organism's cognitive structure that it cannot be accommodated, no learning will take place. For optimal learning to take place, information must be presented that can be assimilated into present cognitive structures, but at the same time, be different enough to necessitate a change in those structures. If the information cannot be assimilated, it simply cannot be understood. If it is completely understood, however, no learning is necessary. In fact, in Piaget's theory, assimilation and understanding mean about the same thing. This is about what Dollard and Miller meant by their term *learning dilemma,* which points out that all learning depends upon failure. According to Piaget, failure of previous knowledge to allow for assimilation of an experience causes accommodation, or new learning. Experiences should be moderately challenging in order to stimulate cognitive growth. Again, no such growth will occur if only assimilation occurs.

One must determine for each individual learner what kind of cognitive structures they have available and slowly change these structures one small step at a time. It is for this reason that Piaget would favor a one-to-one relationship between teacher and pupil. It should be obvious, however, that he would favor such a relationship for much different reasons than a theorist like Skinner, who also favors such a relationship.

Often Piaget is thought of as a pure nativist who believes intellectual development occurs as the result of biological maturation. Clearly this is not the case. Piaget believes that maturation provides only the framework for intellectual development, but in addition to this framework, both physical and social experience are indispensable for mental development. Inhelder and Piaget (1958) put the matter as follows:

> The maturation of the nervous system can do no more than determine the totality of possibilities and impossibilities at a given stage. A particular social environment remains indispensable for the realization of these possibilities. It follows that their realization can be accelerated or retarded as a function of cultural and educational conditions [p. 337].

Elsewhere Piaget says (1966):

> The human being is immersed right from birth in a social environment which affects him just as much as his physical environment. Society, even more, in a sense, than the physical environment, changes the very structure of the individual, because it not only compels him to recognize facts, but also provides him with a ready-made system of signs, which modify his thought; it presents him with new values and it imposes on him an infinite series of obligations [p. 156].

Into What Camp Does Piaget's Theory Fall?

Clearly, Piaget is not an S–R theorist. As we have seen, S–R theorists attempt to determine the relationship between environmental events (S) and responses to those events (R). Most S–R theorists assume a passive organism which builds up response capabilities by accumulating habits. Complex habits, according to this point of view are merely combinations of simpler habits. Certain S–R relationships are "stamped in" either by reinforcement or by contiguity. Knowledge, according to such a point of view, represents a "copy" of conditions that exist in the physical world. In other words, through learning, relationships that exist in the physical world come to be represented in the organism's brain. Piaget refers to this epistemological position as a copy theory of knowledge.

Piaget's theory is diametrically opposed to the S–R conception of knowledge. As we have seen, Piaget equated knowledge with cognitive structures which provide potential to deal with the environment in certain ways. The cognitive structures provide a framework for experience; that is, they determine what can be responded to and how it can be responded to. In this sense, the cognitive structures are projected onto the physical environment and thus create it. In this way the environment is constructed by the cognitive structures. But it also is correct to say that the environment plays a large part in creating the cognitive structures. As we have seen, the interaction between the environment and the cognitive structures through the processes of assimilation and accommodation is of primary importance in Piaget's theory. Piaget differentiates his views of intelligence and knowledge from those of the empiricists as follows (1970b):

> In the common view, the external world is entirely separate from the subject, although it encloses the subject's own body. Any objective knowledge, then, appears to be simply the result of a set of perceptive recordings, motor associations, verbal descriptions, and the like, which all participate in producing a sort of figurative copy or "functional copy" (in Hull's terminology) of objects and the connections between them. The only function of intelligence is systematically to file, correct, etc., these various sets of information; in this process, the more faithful the critical copies, the more consistent the final system will be. In such an empiricist prospect, the content of intelligence comes from outside, and the coordinations that organize it are only the consequences of language and symbolic instruments.

> But this passive interpretation of the act of knowledge is in fact contradicted at all levels of development and, particularly, at the

sensorimotor and prelinguistic levels of cognitive adaptation and intelligence. Actually, in order to know objects, the subject must act upon them, and therefore transform them: he must displace, connect, combine, take apart, and reassemble them.

From the most elementary sensorimotor actions (such as pushing and pulling) to the most sophisticated intellectual operations, which are interiorized actions, carried out mentally (e.g., joining together, putting in order, putting into one-to-one correspondence), knowledge is constantly linked with actions or operations, that is, with *transformations* [pp. 703–4].

There is both agreement and disagreement between Piaget's theory and Gestalt theory. Both agree that experiences are organized. Both believe that there is an innate need for a psychological balance and that a disbalance has motivational properties. Both believe that prior experience influences present experience. As we noted in the last chapter, the Gestalt theorists contended that as the memory trace becomes more fully established, it has an increasing influence on experience. Thus, when the memory trace of "circleness" is firmly established, an incomplete circle is experienced as a complete circle. The memory trace therefore "constructed" an experience that was not in accordance with physical reality. In a way, we can say that experiences are assimilated into existing memory traces, just as they are assimilated into existing cognitive structures. Just as cognitive structures are slowly changed by cumulative experiences, so are memory traces.

The major source of disagreement between the Gestalt theorists and Piaget is over the developmental nature of one's organizational ability. The Gestalt theorists believed that humans are born with a brain that organizes experiences according to the law of *Prägnanz* (see previous chapter). They believed that sensory data is experienced in an organized fashion at all stages of development. Piaget, on the other hand, believes that the organizational abilities of the brain develop as the cognitive structures develop. To him, experience is always organized in terms of the cognitive structures, but the cognitive structures are always changing as a function of both biological maturation and sensory experience. Thus, Piaget uses the term *progressive equilibrium* to describe the fact that the balance or organization that is sought is optimal under existing circumstances, and that those circumstances are constantly changing.

The difference between Piaget and the Gestalt theorists on the matter of innate organizational abilities would result in a difference in educational practices. The teacher attempting to utilize Gestalt principles in his teaching practices would tend to emphasize the "Gestalt" at all levels of education; seeing the total picture would be all-important. Such a teacher would accept group discussions or even the lecture system. The Piagetian teacher, in attempting to utilize Piaget's theory in his teaching practices, as we mentioned earlier, would be very concerned about the individual student. Such a teacher would first attempt to determine what stage of development a particular student was at before deciding what information to present. He would realize that knowing something about the student's cognitive structures would enable him to present the student with information that he would be ready to assimilate. There is considerable difference, then, in assuming that the brain is constantly organizing experiences and in assuming that organizational ability varies at different stages of development.

One can see that Piaget's theory is hard to classify in the traditional categories. It is empirical in the sense that knowledge depends upon experience, but clearly it is not empirical in the same way that an S–R theory is. One is tempted to compare Piaget's theory of knowledge with that of Kant (see Chapter 3), but Kant's categories of the mind were innate whereas Piaget's are the result of cumulative experience. Piaget's theory is not entirely empirical, however. The concept of equilibration provides a nativistic component to his theory. It is this innate drive toward harmony between the internal and external environment that provides the basis of all intellectual growth. We see in Piaget's theory, then, a creative mixture of many points of view; for that reason his theory is similar to that of Tolman to which we turn in the next chapter.

Summary of Piaget's Theory.

According to Piaget, the child is born with a few sensorimotor schemas which provide the framework for his initial interactions with the environment. The child's early experiences are determined by these sensorimotor schemas. In other words, only those events that can be assimilated into these schemas can be responded to by the child, and they therefore set limits on his experience. Through experience, however, these initial schemas are modified. Each experience contains unique elements that the child's cognitive structure must accommodate. Through this interaction with the environment, the child's cognitive structure changes, allowing for an ever growing number of experiences. This is a slow process, however, since new schemas always evolve from those that existed previously. In this way, intellectual growth that starts out with the child's responding reflexively to the environment, develops to the point where the child is able to ponder potential events and to explore mentally probable outcomes.

Interiorization results in the development of operations that free the child from needing to deal directly with the environment by allowing him to deal with symbolic manipulations. The development of operations (interiorized actions) provides the child with a highly complex means of dealing with the environment and he is, therefore, capable of more complex intellectual actions. Since his cognitive structure is more articulated, so is his physical environment; in fact, his cognitive structures can be said to construct the physical environment. It should be remembered that the term *intelligent* is used by Piaget to describe all adaptive activity. Thus, the behavior of a child grasping a rattle is as intelligent as an older child's solving a complex problem. The difference is in the cognitive structures available to each child. According to Piaget, an intelligent act always tends to create a balance between the organism and its environment under the existing circumstances. The ever present drive toward this balanced state is called equilibration.

Although intellectual development is continuous during childhood, Piaget chooses to refer to stages of intellectual development. He describes four major stages: (1) sensorimotor, where the child deals directly with the environment by utilizing his innate reflexes; (2) preoperational, where the child begins rudimentary concept formation; (3) concrete operations, where the child uses interiorized actions or thought to solve problems in his immediate experience; and (4) formal operations, where the child can ponder completely hypothetical situations.

Piaget's theory is currently having a great effect on educational practice in this country. Many educators have attempted to formulate specific policies based on his theory (e.g., Furth, 1970; Athey and Rubadeau, 1970; Ginsberg and Opper, 1969). Others have attempted to develop an intelligence test in accordance with his theory (e.g., Goldschmid and Bentler, 1968).

Clearly Piaget's theory opens new avenues of research that were either unnoticed or ignored by those accepting an associationistic point of view. As we noted in Chapter 2, one characteristic of a good scientific theory is that it be heuristic and Piaget's theory is certainly that. We also saw in Chapter 2 that scientific revolutions occur when old theories are continuously confronted with data they cannot explain. Under such circumstances, a new theory eventually emerges that explains what the other theories could explain and, in addition, resolves the anomalies that previous theories could not resolve. Piaget's theory offers a promise of revolution that may some day "overthrow" the firmly established doctrine of associationism and resolve some of its many anomalies.

DISCUSSION QUESTIONS

1. Discuss Piaget's view of intelligence.
2. Explain what Piaget means when he says the cognitive structures "construct" the physical environment.
3. Discuss the nature of knowledge from both the empiricist's point of view and from Piaget's point of view.
4. Discuss Piaget's concept of progressive equilibrium.
5. Describe the educational implications of Piaget's theory.
6. Compare and contrast Piaget's theory of learning with any other theory of learning.
7. Describe the kind of life style that you feel would provide an optimal balance between assimilation and accommodation. For example, do you feel that living in the same environment all of one's life would facilitate or inhibit accommodation?
8. What do you suppose Piaget's views on the transfer of training would be? In other words, according to Piaget, what makes it possible to utilize what was learned in one situation in other situations?
9. Discuss Piaget's concept of interiorization.
10. Outline the major stages of intellectual development as they are viewed by Piaget.

GLOSSARY

Accommodation. The modification of cognitive structures as the result of having an experience that could not be assimilated into existing cognitive structures. Accommodation can be roughly equated with learning.

Assimilation. Responding to the physical environment in accordance with existing cognitive structures. Assimilation refers to a kind of matching between the cognitive structures and the physical environment. Assimilation can be roughly equated with recognition or knowing.

Clinical method. An open-ended form of questioning in which the researcher's questions are guided by the child's answers to previous questions.

Cognitive structure. The schema that an organism has available at any given time with which to interact with the physical environment. Cognitive structure results from both biological maturation and cumulative experience. The cognitive structure is not only affected by experience but also determines what can be experienced. If a physical event cannot be at least partially assimilated into the organism's cognitive structure, then that physical event cannot constitute a biological stimulus. The dual processes of assimilation and accommodation must always occur with the existing cognitive structure as a point of departure.

Concrete operations. The stage of intellectual development where the child can deal logically with only those events that he can experience directly.

Conservation. The realization that number, length, substance, or area has not changed although it may be presented in a number of different ways. The ability to conserve requires the use of reversible operations.

Content. The ingredients that accompany a specific manifestation of a schema.

Epistemology. The study of knowledge.

Equilibration. Piaget's major motivational concept; the innate need for balance between the organism and its environment and within the organism itself. Disbalance has motivational properties that cause the organism to do whatever is necessary to regain a balance. Equilibration is an invariant because it is present at all stages of intellectual development. In fact, it is responsible for continuous intellectual development.

Formal operations. The stage of intellectual development where the child can deal logically with hypothetical events in addition to those events that he can experience directly.

Functional invariants. Processes that are not stage specific but are present at all stages of development. Examples would include assimilation, accommodation, and equilibration.

Genetic epistemology. A term often used to describe Piaget's theory. The term *genetic* means *developmental* rather than having anything to do with inheritance. Epistemology refers to the study of knowledge; thus the term *genetic epistemology* is used to describe the study of knowledge as a function of maturation and experience.

Intelligence. Intelligence is a complex term in Piaget's theory, but in general it can be said that an intelligent act always tends to create optimal conditions for an organism's survival under existing circumstances. Intelligence is always related to an organism's adaptation to his environment.

Interiorization. The increased tendency to rely more and more on mental operations in adjusting to the environment as the cognitive structure becomes more articulated. An operation is referred to as an "interiorized" action since it is an adaptive response that occurs mentally rather than overtly.

Learning dilemma. Dollard and Miller's contention that in order for learning to occur, previously learned behavior and innate behavior patterns must be ineffective in solving a problem. In this sense failure is a prerequisite for learning.

Operation. Cognitive action. As a sensorimotor schema manifests itself in overt behavior, an operation manifests itself in covert behavior or thinking. An operation can be thought of as interiorized action.

Preoperational thinking. The stage of intellectual development where the child begins to classify objects and events into crude categories.

Progressive equilibrium. Living organisms constantly seek a balance between themselves and their environment. But, according to Piaget, the cognitive structures of an organism are always changing as the result of maturation and experience. Therefore, a balance can never be absolute but must rather be a progressive equilibrium which is a balance that is the best under the prevailing circumstances. As circumstances change, what an optimal balance would consist of must change accordingly.

Reversibility. An important characteristic of mental operations that refers to the process of reversing a thought. For example, one can mentally pour liquid from one container into another, and then reverse the process by mentally pouring the liquid back into the original container. Reversibility of mental operations is a necessary condition for *conservation* (*see above*) to occur.

Schema. The general potential to engage in a class of overt or covert actions. A schema can also be thought of as an element in an organism's cognitive structure.

Sensorimotor stage. The initial stage of intellectual development where the child responds directly to events as they occur in the environment. During this stage of development, the child adjusts to the environment in terms of his innate schemas such as grasping, looking, sucking, and reaching.

12

Edward Chace Tolman

Tolman (1886–1959) was born in Newton, Massachusetts, and received his B.S. degree from the Massachusetts Institute of Technology in electrochemistry in 1911. His M.A. (1912) and Ph.D. (1915) degrees were earned at Harvard University in psychology. He taught at Northwestern University from 1915 to 1918, at which time he was released for "lack of teaching success"; but, more likely it was because of his pacifism during wartime. From Northwestern, he went to the University of California where he remained until his retirement. His stay at the University of California was interrupted, however, when he was dismissed for refusing to sign a loyalty oath. He led a fight against the loyalty oath as an infringement on academic freedom, and was reinstated at the University of California when the professors won their case.

Tolman was raised in a Quaker home and his pacifism was a constant theme running through his career. In 1942, he wrote *Drives Toward War* in which he suggested several changes in our political, educational, and economic systems that would increase the probability of continued world peace. In the preface of that book, he states his reasons for writing it:

> As an American, a college professor, and one brought up in the pacifist tradition, I am intensely biased against war. It is for me stupid, interrupting, unnecessary, and unimaginably horrible. I write this essay within that frame of reference. In short, I am

driven to discuss the psychology of war and its possible abolition because I want intensely to get rid of it [p. xi].

Tolman spent much of his life being a rebel. Above, we saw that he opposed war when the war was an extremely popular cause, and below, we shall see that he opposed Watsonian behaviorism when behaviorism was an extremely popular school of psychology.

As we mentioned at the conclusion of Chapter 10, Tolman's theory of learning can be looked upon as a blending of Gestalt theory and behavior-

Edward Chace Tolman

ism. While still a graduate student at Harvard, Tolman travelled to Germany and worked for a short time with Koffka. The influence of Gestalt theory on his own theorizing had a profound and lasting effect. His favorable attitude toward Gestalt theory did not, however, preclude a favorable attitude toward behaviorism. Like the behaviorists, Tolman saw little value in the introspective approach, and he felt psychology had to become completely objective. His main disagreement with the behaviorists was over the unit of behavior to be studied. Behaviorists such as Guthrie, Hull, Watson, and Skinner represented, according to Tolman, the psychology of "twitchism," because they felt that large segments of behavior could be divided into smaller segments, such as reflexes, for further analysis. Tolman felt that, by being reductionistic, the behaviorists were throwing away the baby with the bathwater. He believed that it was possible to be objective while studying molar behavior (large, intact, meaningful behavior patterns). Unlike the other behaviorists, Tolman chose to systematically study molar behavior. It can be said that Tolman was methodologically a behaviorist, but metaphysically a cognitive theorist. In other words, he studied behavior in order to discover cognitive processes.

Molar Behavior.

The chief characteristic of molar behavior is that it is purposive; that is, it is always directed toward some goal. Perhaps now the reader can better understand the title of Tolman's major work, *Purposive Behavior in Animals and Men* (1932).* Tolman never contended that behavior could not be divided into smaller units for the purposes of study; rather, he felt that whole behavior patterns had a meaning that would be lost if studied from a reductionistic viewpoint. Thus, for Tolman, molar behavior constituted a Gestalt that was more than the individual "twitches" that made it up. In other words, purposive behavior patterns can be looked upon as behavioral Gestalten. He says (1932):

> It will be contended by us (if not by Watson) that "behavior-acts," though no doubt in complete one-to-one correspondence with the underlying molecular facts of physics and physiology, have, as "molar" wholes, certain emergent properties of their own. And it is these, the molar properties of behavior-acts, which are of prime interest to us as psychologists. Further, these molar properties of behavior-acts cannot in the present state of our knowledge, i.e., prior to the working-out of many empirical correlations between behavior and its physiological correlates, be known even inferentially from a mere knowledge of the underlying, molecular facts of physics and physiology. For, just as the properties of a beaker of water are not, prior to experience, in any way envisageable from the properties of individual water molecules, so neither are the properties of a "behavior-act" deducible directly from the properties of the underlying physical and physiological processes which make it up. Behavior as such cannot, at any rate at present,

* Tolman, E. C. *Purposive Behavior in Animals and Men.* Reprinted by permission of Irvington Publishers, Inc. New York.

be deduced from a mere enumeration of the muscle twitches, the mere motions *qua* motions, which make it up. It must as yet be studied first hand and for its own sake [pp. 7–8].

The type of behavior that Tolman labels as molar is exemplified in the following passage (1932):

A rat running a maze; a cat getting out of a puzzle box; a man driving home to dinner; a child hiding from a stranger; a woman doing her washing or gossiping over the telephone; a pupil marking a mental-test sheet; a psychologist reciting a list of nonsense syllables; my friend and I telling one another our thoughts and feelings—*these are behaviors (qua molar)*. And it must be noted that in mentioning no one of them have we referred to, or, we blush to confess it, for the most part even known, what were the exact muscles and glands, sensory nerves, and motor nerves involved. For these responses somehow had other sufficiently identifying properties of their own [p. 8].

Purposive Behaviorism.

Tolman's theory has been referred to as a purposive behaviorism because it attempts to explain goal directed behavior. It must be emphasized that Tolman used the term *purpose* as a purely descriptive term. He noted, for example, the searching behavior of a rat in a maze will persist until food is found; therefore it looks "as if" his behavior is goal directed or purposive. For Tolman, the term *purposive* was used to describe behavior just as the terms slow, fast, correct, incorrect, or right turn might be used to describe behavior. There is some similarity between Guthrie and Tolman on this point. For Guthrie, behavior persisted as long as maintaining stimuli were being provided by some need state. For Tolman, behavior will look "as if" it is goal directed as long as the organism is seeking something in the environment. In both cases, the behavior will look purposive. Tolman (1932) says:

. . . it must . . . be emphasized that purposes and cognitions which are thus immediately, immanently, in behavior are wholly objective as to definition. They are defined by characters and relationships which we observe out there in the behavior. We, the observers, watch the behavior of the rat, the cat, or the man, and note its character as a getting to such and such by means of such and such a selected pattern of commerces-with. It is we, the independent neutral observers, who note these perfectly objective characters as immanent in the behavior and have happened to choose the terms *purpose* and *cognition* as generic names for such characters [pp. 12–13].

Although Tolman is a little freer with the terms he is willing to employ in his theory than most behaviorists, he remains a behaviorist, and an objective one. As we shall see below, Tolman develops a cognitive theory of learning, but in the final analysis, he is dealing with what every other behaviorist deals with—observable stimuli and overt responses. Tolman (1932) says:

> . . . For a Purposive Behaviorism, behavior, as we have seen, is purposive, cognitive, and molar, i.e., "Gestalted." Purposive Behaviorism is a molar, not a molecular, behaviorism, but it is none the less a behaviorism. Stimuli and responses and the behavior-determinants of responses are all that it finds to study [p. 418].

The Use of Rats.

Some may think it strange for a cognitive theorist to use rats as experimental subjects, but Tolman had a special fondness for them. He stimulated the use of rats in psychological experiments at the University of California, and he dedicated his 1932 book to the white rat. Throughout Tolman's writings, one finds humor and wit, as exemplified by his following thoughts on the use of rats as experimental subjects (1945):

> . . . let it be noted that rats live in cages; they do not go on binges the night before one has planned an experiment; they do not kill each other off in wars; they do not invent engines of destruction, and if they did, they would not be so inept about controlling such engines; they do not go in for either class conflicts or race conflicts; they avoid politics, economics, and papers on psychology. They are marvelous, pure, and delightful [p. 166].

Elsewhere (1938) Tolman says:

> . . . I believe that everything important in psychology (except perhaps such matters as the building up of a super-ego, that is, everything save such matters as involve society and words) can be investigated in essence through the continued experimental and theoretical analysis of the determiners of rat behavior at a choice-point in a maze. Herein I believe I agree with Professor Hull and also with Professor Thorndike [p. 34].

MAJOR THEORETICAL CONCEPTS

Tolman introduced the use of intervening variables into psychological research and Hull borrowed the idea from Tolman. Both Hull and Tolman used intervening variables in a similar way in their work. Hull, however, developed a much more comprehensive and elaborate theory of learning than did Tolman. We will consider the formal aspects of Tolman's theory later in this chapter, but first we will turn to a few of his general assumptions about the learning process.

What Is Learned?

In answering the question, the behaviorists, such as Watson, Guthrie, Skinner, and Hull, would say that stimulus-response associations are learned and that complex learning involves complex S–R relationships. Tolman, however, taking his lead from the Gestalt theorists, said that learning is essentially a process of discovering what leads to what in the environment. The organism, through exploration, discovers that certain events lead to certain other events, or that one sign leads to another sign. For example we learn that when it's five o'clock (S_1), dinner (S_2) will soon follow. For that reason, Tolman was called an S–S rather than an S–R theorist. Learning, for Tolman, was an ongoing process that required no motivation. On this matter Tolman is in agreement with Guthrie and in opposition to Thorndike, Skinner, and Hull.

It should be pointed out, however, that motivation was important in Tolman's theory because it determined which aspects of the environment would be attended to by the organism. For example, the hungry organism would attend to food-related events in the environment, and the sexually deprived organism would attend to sex-related events. In general, an organism's drive state determines which aspects of the environment will be emphasized in his perceptual field. Thus, for Tolman, motivation acted as a perceptual "emphasizer."

According to Tolman, what is learned is "the lay of the land"; the organism learns what is there. He learns that if he turns to the left, he will find one thing, and if he turns to the right, he will find another thing. Gradually he develops a picture of the environment that he can use to get around in it. Tolman called this picture a *cognitive map*. On this point, Tolman was diametrically opposed to the other behaviorists. According to him, it is meaningless to look at individual responses or even individual routes to a goal. Once the organism has developed a cognitive map, he can reach a particular goal from any number of directions. If one commonly used route is blocked, the animal simply takes an alternate route, just as the human takes a detour on the way home from work. The organism will, however, always choose the shortest route or the one requiring the least amount of work. This is referred to as the *principle of least effort*.

There is a great deal of similarity between Tolman's principle of least effort and Hull's notion of the habit family hierarchy. Both theorists conclude that, after training, an organism can reach a goal using alternate routes. Tolman would say that the organism's first choice is the route requiring the least amount of effort. Hull would say that the organism prefers the shortest route because it has the shortest delay of reinforcement (J) and therefore, the greatest amount of $_sE_R$ associated with it. Furthermore, the response that has the greatest amount of $_sE_R$ associated with it will tend to occur in any given situation.

Later in this chapter, we shall see some of Tolman's ingenious experimentation designed to show that animals respond according to cognitive maps, rather than according to simple S–R processes.

Confirmation versus Reward.

As with Guthrie, the concept of reinforcement was unimportant to Tolman, but there is some similarity between what Tolman calls confirmation and what the other behaviorists call reward. During the development of a cognitive map, expectations are utilized by the organism. Expectations are hunches concerning what leads to what. Early tentative expectations are called *hypotheses* and they are either confirmed by experience or not. Hypotheses that are confirmed are retained and those that are not are abandoned. Through this process, the cognitive map develops.

An expectancy that is consistently confirmed develops into what Tolman referred to as a *means-end readiness*, or what is commonly referred to as a belief. When an expectation is consistently confirmed, the organism ends up "believing" that if he acts in a certain way, a certain result will follow, or if he sees a certain sign (stimulus), another sign will follow. Thus, the confirmation of expectancies in the development of a cognitive map is similar to the notion of reward, as other behaviorists may use the term. It should be noted, however, that the production, acceptance, or rejection of hypotheses is a cognitive process that need not involve overt behavior. Also, the hypotheses-testing process, so important to the development of a cognitive map, does not depend on any physiological need state of the organism. As mentioned above, learning is taking place constantly and does not depend on any motivational state of the organism.

Vicarious Trial and Error.

Tolman noted a characteristic of rats learning a maze that he took as support for his cognitive interpretation of learning. He noted that very often a rat would pause at a choice-point and look around as if he were thinking about the various alternatives available to him. This pausing and looking around at the choice-point, Tolman called *vicarious trial and error*. Instead of behavioral trial and error, where first one response is tried and then another until a solution to a problem is reached, with vicarious trial and error the testing of different approaches is done cognitively rather than behaviorally.

Learning versus Performance.

We saw in Chapter 6 that Hull distinguished between learning and performance. In Hull's final theory, number of reinforced trials was the only learning variable; the other variables in his system were performance variables. Generally speaking, performance can be thought of as the translation of learning into behavior. Although the distinction between learning and performance was important for Hull, it was even more important for Tolman.

According to Tolman, we know many things about our environment but only act upon this information when we need to do so. As mentioned above, this knowledge, which comes about through reality testing, lies dormant until a need arises. In a state of need, the organism utilizes what he has learned through reality testing to bring him into proximity to those things that will alleviate the need. For example, there may be two drinking fountains in your building and you may have passed them both many times without having paused for a drink; but if you became thirsty, you would merely walk over to one of them and take a drink. You knew for some time how to find a drinking fountain, but you did not need to translate that knowledge into behavior until you became thirsty. We will discuss the learning-performance distinction in more detail when we consider latent learning below.

The points that we have made so far can be summarized as follows:

1. The organism brings to a problem solving situation various hypotheses that he may utilize in attempting to solve the problem. These hypotheses are based largely on prior experience, but, as we shall see later, Tolman believed that some problem solving strategies may be innate.
2. The hypotheses which survive are those that correspond best with reality; that is, those that result in goal achievement.

3. After awhile a clearly established cognitive map develops which can be used under altered conditions. For instance, when his preferred path is blocked, the organism simply chooses, in accordance with the principle of least effort, an alternative path from his cognitive map.
4. When there is some sort of demand or motive to be satisfied, the organism will make use of the information in its cognitive map. The fact that information can exist but only be utilized under certain conditions is the basis for the very important distinction between learning and performance.

Latent Learning.

Generally speaking, latent learning can be thought of as learning that is not translated into performance. In other words it is possible to have learning remain dormant for a considerable length of time before it is manifested in behavior. The concept of latent learning was very important to Tolman and he felt he succeeded in demonstrating its existence. The now famous experiment that Tolman and Honzik (1930) ran involved three groups of rats learning to solve a maze. One group was never rewarded for correctly traversing the maze, one group was always re-

Figure 12–1. The results of the Tolman and Honzik experiment showing that when animals are rewarded after a period of non-reward, their performance very rapidly equals or exceeds that of animals that had been rewarded from the onset of the experiment (after Tolman and Honzik, 1930).

warded, and one group was not rewarded until the eleventh day of the experiment. It was the last group that was of greatest interest to Tolman. His theory of latent learning predicted that this group would be learning the maze just as much as the group that was being regularly rewarded, and that when reward is introduced on the eleventh day, this group should soon perform as well as the group that had been continually rewarded. The results of the experiment are shown in Figure 12–1.

By examining Figure 12–1, three things become apparent: (1) there is slight improvement in performance even in the group never receiving reward; (2) the rewarded group showed steady improvement throughout the seventeen days of the experiment; and (3) when reward was introduced on the eleventh day to the group not previously receiving reward, their performance vastly improved. In fact, the latter group performed even better than the group that was rewarded throughout the experiment. Tolman took the results to support his contention that reward was a performance variable and not a learning variable.

The S–R theorists insisted that reward was, in fact, not removed from the situation; why, they asked, would the group never receiving food show slight improvement? They pointed out that simply being removed from the apparatus after reaching the goal box could act as a reward for reaching the goal box. At present, the issue is far from settled.

Place Learning versus Response Learning.

Tolman maintained that animals learn where things are, while the S–R theorists maintained that specific responses are learned to specific stimuli. Tolman and his collaborators performed a series of experiments designed to determine whether animals were place learners, as Tolman suggests, or response learners as S–R theory suggests. A typical experiment in this area was done by Tolman, Ritchie, and Kalish (1946b). The apparatus they used is diagrammed in Figure 12–2.

Two groups of rats were utilized. Members of one group were sometimes started at S_1 and sometimes at S_2, but no matter where they started from, they always had to turn in the same direction to be rewarded. For example, if the group was learning to turn right, it was fed at F_1 if they started at S_1, and were fed at F_2 if they started at S_2. This was the response learning group. Members of the other group were always fed at the same place, e.g., F_2. If a member of this group started at S_1, he had to turn left to be rewarded. If he started at S_2, he had to turn right. This was the place learning group.

The animals were given 6 trials a day for 12 days, or 72 trials. The criterion for learning was 10 successive errorless trials. At the end of the

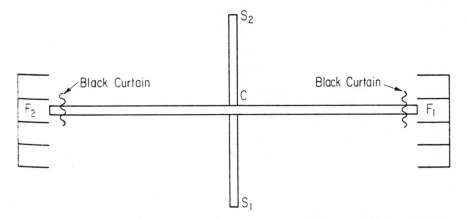

Figure 12–2. Apparatus used in the Tolman, Ritchie and Kalish experiment on place vs response learning. S_1 and S_2 are starting points, F_1 and F_2 are food boxes, and C is the center point of the maze (from Tolman, Ritchie, and Kalish 1946b, p. 223).

experiment, only 3 of the 8 rats in the response learning group had reached criterion, whereas all 8 rats in the place learning group reached criterion. In fact, the mean trials to criterion for the latter group was only 3.5 whereas it was 17.33 for the 3 response learners that reached criterion.

Figure 12–3. The figure shows the average number of errors made on successive trials by place learning and response learning groups of rats (from Tolman, Ritchie, and Kalish 1946b, p. 226).

The place learners solved their problem much faster than the response learners solved theirs. It appeared, therefore, that it was more "natural" for animals to learn places than specific responses and this was taken as support for Tolman's theory. The results of the experiment are shown in Figure 12–3.

In another study by Tolman, Ritchie, and Kalish (1946a), animals were first trained in the apparatus shown in Figure 12–4. The animals had to learn to follow the route A, B, C, D, E, F, and G. H indicates the place where a five-watt bulb was located, the only illumination in the room during the experiment. After preliminary training, the apparatus shown in Figure 12–4 was removed and was replaced with the apparatus shown in Figure 12-5.

The path the animals were trained to take in the first phase of the experiment was now blocked, but the animals could choose among 18 alternative paths. On the basis of S–R theory, one might expect that when the original path was blocked, the animals would choose the unblocked path closest to the original. This, however, was not the case. The most frequently picked was alley number 6, the one pointing directly to where

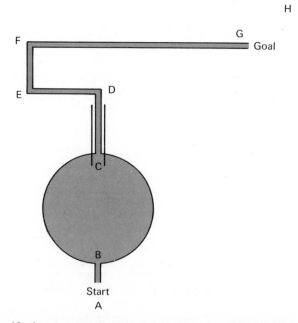

Figure 12–4. Apparatus used for preliminary training in the experiment by Tolman, Ritchie and Kalish on place vs. response learning (after Tolman, Ritchie, and Kalish, 1946b).

Figure 12–5. After preliminary training on the apparatus shown in Figure 12–4, the animals were allowed to choose one of the 18 alleys shown in the top figure above. The lower figure shows the apparatus used for preliminary training superimposed over the test apparatus so that the relationship between the two can be seen (after Tolman, Ritchie and Kalish 1946b).

the goaľ was during the first phase of the experiment. In fact, the alleys closest to the original alley were only infrequently chosen (alley 9 by 2 percent of the rats and alley 10 by 7½ percent). Tolman, Ritchie, and Kalish reported that the first pathway, the one chosen with the second greatest frequency, was the alley pointing to the place in the room where the animals had been fed in their home cages. The results of the experiment are shown in Figure 12–6.

Once again it looked as if the animals were responding in terms of where something was, rather than in terms of specific responses. The S–R theorists felt that such experiments did not support place learning, since it was entirely possible that the animals simply learned the response of running toward the light. The cognitive theorists refuted this interpretation by saying that if that were true, the animals would have chosen alleys 5 and 7 at least as often as alley 6, and this of course was not the case.

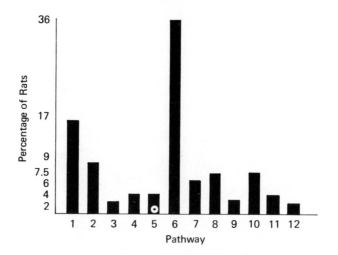

Figure 12–6. The results of the experiment diagrammed in Figures 4 and 5 above. It can be seen that the most frequently chosen path on the test trial was the one pointing directly to the goal. Tolman, Ritchie and Kalish also pointed out that the second most frequently chosen path was the one that pointed to the animals' home cages where they were fed (after Tolman, Ritchie and Kalish, 1946a).

Reward Expectancy.

According to Tolman, when we learn, we come to know the "lay of the land." The term "understanding" is not foreign to him as it is to the behaviorists. In a problem solving situation, we learn where the goal is and we get to it following the shortest possible route. We learn to expect certain events to follow other events. The animal expects that if he goes to a certain place, he will find a certain reward. The S–R theorist would expect that changing rewards in a learning situation would not disrupt behavior as long as the rewards were appropriate to the animal's drive state, and as long as the quantity of reward was not changed drastically. Tolman, however, predicted that if rewards are changed, behavior will be disrupted, since a particular reward becomes a part of what is expected.

Tolman reported an experiment by Elliott (Tolman, 1932, p. 44), who trained one group of rats to run a maze for bran mash and another group to run a maze for sunflower seeds. On the tenth day of training, the group that had been trained on bran mash was switched to sunflower seeds. The results of Elliott's experiment are shown in Figure 12–7.

Figure 12–7. The results of an experiment by Elliott (reported by Tolman, 1932, p. 44), showing the disruption in behavior that occurs when a reward other than the one which is expected is experienced.

We see that switching reward considerably disrupted performance, thus supporting Tolman's prediction. It should be noted, however, that the group trained on bran mash performed consistently better than the group trained on sunflower seeds before the switch. The Hullians could say that because the bran mash had a larger incentive value (K) than did the sunflower seeds, reaction potential would be greater. After the switch to sunflower seeds, K would go down accordingly. The Hullian explanation can only partially account for the results, however, since the group that switched to sunflower seeds performed much worse than the group consistently trained on sunflower seeds. Even correcting for the differences in incentive value, there still seems to be considerable disruption of performance that can be explained by the departure from what was expected.

The reader can certainly recall situations where there has been a discrepancy between what was expected and what was experienced. Examples might include a good friend or relative's acting "totally unlike himself," a familiar house torn down while you've been on vacation, seeing a parent intoxicated for the first time, or receiving a raise in pay either larger or smaller than what you expected. In each case, the expected events were not the ones that actually occurred. If a person has important expectations, their failure in being realized could be traumatic. Leon Festinger (1957) has constructed theory of personality around this notion. According to Festinger, when a person's beliefs do not conform to what actually occurs, the person experiences a psychological state called *cognitive dissonance*. Cognitive dissonance is a negative drive state and the person experiencing it seeks ways to reduce it, just as the person experiencing hunger seeks to reduce the hunger drive.

THE FORMAL ASPECTS OF TOLMAN'S THEORY

As an example of Tolman's more abstract theorizing, we will summarize his article "The Determiners of Behavior at a Choice Point" (1938). In this example, the choice point is where the rat decides to turn either right or left in a T-maze. Some of the symbols we will be using are seen in the diagram of the T-maze shown in Figure 12–8.

In an experiment where a rat was being trained to turn left in a T-maze, Tolman's dependent variable was a behavior ratio as follows:

$$\frac{B_L}{B_L + B_R}$$

This gives the percentage tendency to turn left at any stage of learning. If, for example, an animal turned left 6 out of 10 times, we would have:

$$\frac{6}{6 + 4} = 60\%$$

Tolman felt that the behavior ratio was determined by the collective experiences that come from the animal's having turned both ways at the choice point on various trials. This allows the animal to learn what leads to what. The cumulative nature of these experiences was diagrammed by Tolman as follows:

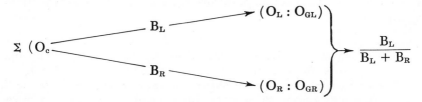

Rather than repeating this cumbersome diagram, Tolman abbreviated it ΣOBO, which stands for the accumulated knowledge that comes from making both B_L and B_R responses and seeing what they lead to. Thus, learning in a T-maze can be summarized simply as (assuming turning left is rewarded):

$$\Sigma OBO \longrightarrow \frac{B_L}{B_L + B_R}$$

O_C = the choice point
O_R = the complex of stimulus objects that are met after making a right turn
O_L = the complex of stimulus objects that are met after making a left turn
B_R = the behavior of turning right at the choice point
B_L = the behavior of turning left at the choice point
O_{GR} = the goal on the right
O_{GL} = the goal on the left

Figure 12–8. A diagram of a T-Maze (from Tolman, 1938, p. 1).

Environmental Variables.

Unfortunately, the situation is not as simple as suggested above. Tolman thought of ΣOBO as an independent variable since it directly influenced the dependent variable (e.g., trials to criterion), and it was under the control of the experimenter who determined the number of training trials. In addition to ΣOBO a number of other independent variables could have an effect on performance. Tolman suggested the following list:

> M = maintenance schedule. This refers to the animal's deprivation schedule; for example, the number of hours since he has eaten.
> G = appropriateness of goal object. The reward must be related to the animal's current drive state. For example, one does not reward a thirsty animal with food.
> S = types and modes of stimuli provided. This refers to the vividness of the cues or signals available to the animal in the learning situation.
> R = types of motor responses required in the learning situation; for example, running, jumping, sharp turns, etc.
> P = pattern of succeeding and preceding maze units. The pattern of turns that need to be made to solve a maze as determined by the experimenter.
> ΣOBO = the number of trials and their cumulative nature (see above).

It should be clear that Tolman was no longer talking only about the learning of T-mazes but about the learning of more complex mazes as well.

Individual Difference Variables.

In addition to the independent variables described above, there are the variables that the individual subjects bring into the experiment with them. The list of individual difference variables suggested by Tolman is as follows (note their initials create the acronym HATE, a somewhat strange word for Tolman to use):

H = Heredity
A = Age
T = Previous training
E = Special endocrine, drug, or vitamin conditions

Each of the individual difference variables interacts with each of the independent variables, and a combination of all these variables working together is what produces behavior. This can be seen in Figure 12–9.

Intervening Variables.

Up to this point, we have been discussing the effects of observed stimulus variables (independent variables) on observed behavior (dependent variables). It would be possible, as Skinner suggests, to conduct thousands of experiments showing how those variables are related to each other in various combinations. The functional analysis suggested by Skinner, however, is not appealing to Tolman, who wants to move beyond the facts. He says (1938):

> But why, you may ask, can we not be satisfied with just experiments and the "facts" resulting from them? I find that there are two reasons. In the first place, an entirely factual, empirical establishment of the complete functional relation, f_1, to cover the effects

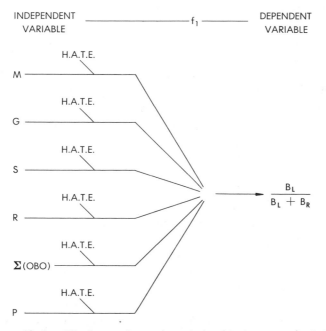

Figure 12–9. The figure shows the relationship between the independent variables, the individual difference variables and behavior (from Tolman, 1938, p. 8).

on $(B_L/B_L + B_R)$ of all the permutations and combinations of M, G, S, etc., etc., would be a humanly endless task. We have time in this brief mortal span to test only a relatively limited number of such permutations and combinations. So, in the first place, we are forced to propose theories in order to use such theories to extrapolate for all these combinations for which we have not time to test.

But I suspect that there is another reason for theories. Some of us, psychologically, just demand theories. Even if we had all the million and one concrete facts, we would still want theories to, as we would say, "explain" those facts. Theories just seem to be necessary to some of us to relieve our inner tensions [pp. 8–9].

Tolman defines a theory as a set of intervening variables. An intervening variable is a construct created by the theorist to aid in explaining the relationship between an independent variable and a dependent variable. The example given in Chapter 2 was that of hunger. It has been found that performance on a learning task varies with hours of food deprivation, and that is an empirical relationship. If one says, however, that *hunger* varies with hours of deprivation and in turn influences learning, the concept of hunger is being used as an intervening variable. As Tolman says, such a concept is used to fill in the blanks in a research program.

For similar reasons, Tolman creates an intervening variable to go along with each of his independent variables. In each case, the intervening variable is systematically tied to both an independent variable and a dependent variable. In other words, each of Tolman's intervening variables is operationally defined. Maintenance schedule, for example, creates a *demand* which in turn is related to performance. Appropriateness of the goal object is related to *appetite,* which in turn is related to performance. Types of stimuli provided are related to the animal's capacity for *differentiation,* etc. A summary of Tolman's system showing his use of intervening variables is shown in Figure 12–10.

One can now see the similarity between Tolman and Hull in the use of intervening variables. Hull, as we have mentioned, borrowed the approach from Tolman, who introduced the use of intervening variables into psychology. The part of the system shown in Figure 12–10 that relates most closely to the main theme in Tolman's theory is the intervening variable of "hypotheses." As the result of previous experience (ΣOBO) hypotheses are developed which affect behavior $(B_L/B_L + B_R)$. As these hypotheses are confirmed by experience, they become means-end readinesses, or beliefs. The function of an intervening variable is seen clearly at this point. It is an empirical fact that performance improves as a function of the number of learning trials, but the intervening variables are created in an effort to explain why this is the case. According to those who use intervening variables, the facts would be the same without their use, but our understanding of the facts would be severely limited.

Six Kinds of Learning

In his 1949 article, "There Is More Than One Kind of Learning," Tolman proposed six kinds of learning. Each is briefly summarized below.

Cathexes (singular, cathexis).

This refers to the learned tendency to associate certain objects with certain drive states. For example, certain foods might be available to satisfy the hunger drive of individuals who live in a particular country. A hungry person who lives in a country where fish is usually eaten will tend to seek fish to satisfy his hunger. The same person may avoid beef or

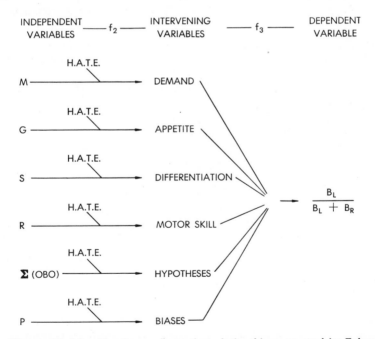

Figure 12–10. The figure shows the relationship suggested by Tolman between independent variables, individual difference variables, intervening variables, and the dependent variable (from Tolman 1938, p. 16).

spaghetti because, for him, those foods had not been associated with the satisfaction of the hunger drive. Since certain stimuli have been associated with the satisfaction of a certain drive those stimuli will tend to be sought out when the drive recurs. Tolman (1949) says:

> . . . when a type of goal has been positively cathected it means that when the given drive is in force the organism will tend to apprehend, to approach, and to perform the consummatory reaction upon any instance of this type of goal which is presented by the immediate environment [p. 146].

When the organism has learned to avoid certain objects while in a certain drive state, a negative cathexis is said to have occurred. There is little difference between Tolman and the S–R theorists concerning this kind of learning.

Equivalence Beliefs.

When a "subgoal" has the same effect as the goal itself, the subgoal is said to constitute an equivalence belief. Although this is extremely close to what the S–R theorists call secondary reinforcement, Tolman felt that this kind of learning more typically involved the "social drives" rather than the physiological drives. He gives the following example (1949):

> In so far as it can be demonstrated that with the reception of the high grades there is some temporary reduction in this student's need for love and approbation even without his going on to tell others about his grade, then we would have evidence for an equivalence belief. The A's would then be accepted by him as equivalent to the love or approbation to which they were originally a mere means [p. 148].

Here again, there is little difference between Tolman and the S–R theorists, except for the fact that Tolman talks about "love reduction" as the reinforcement, and the S–R theorists would prefer to remain with the reduction of drives such as hunger or thirst.

Field Expectancies.

These are developed in the same way a cognitive map is developed: the organism learns what leads to what. Upon seeing a certain sign, for instance, he expects that a certain other sign will follow. This general knowledge of the environment is used to explain latent learning, place learning, and the use of shortcuts. This is not S–R learning but rather, S–S or sign-sign learning, i.e., when the animal sees one sign, he learns to expect another to follow. The only "reward" necessary for this kind of learning to take place is the confirmation of an hypothesis. His belief in this kind of learning places Tolman in the cognitive camp.

Field-Cognition Modes.

This is the kind of learning about which Tolman was least confident. A field-cognition mode is a strategy, or a way of approaching a problem-solving situation. It is a tendency to arrange the perceptual field in certain configurations. Tolman suspected that these tendencies were innate and could be modified by experience. In fact, the most important thing about a strategy that works in solving a problem is that it will be tried in similar situations in the future. Thus, effective field-cognition modes, or problem solving strategies, transfer to related problems. In that way they are similar to means-end readinesses (beliefs) which also transfer to similar situations. Tolman summarized his thinking about this kind of learning as follows (1949):

> In a word, I am trying to summarize under this fourth category all those principles as to the structure of environmental fields which are relevant to all environmental fields, and which (whether innate or learned) are carried around by the individual and applied to each new field with which he is presented [p. 153].

Drive Discriminations.

This simply refers to the fact that organisms can determine their own drive state and therefore can respond appropriately. It has been found, for example, that animals can be trained to turn one way in a T-maze when they are hungry, and the other way when they are thirsty (Hull, 1933a; Leeper, 1935). Since Tolman implies a belief in social as well as physiological drives, drive discrimination was an important concept to him. Unless an organism can clearly determine his own drive state, he will not know how to read his cognitive map. If an organism's needs are not clear, his goals are not clear and therefore his behavior may be inappropriate. How one will act when he needs love, for example, will be different from how he will act when he needs water.

Motor Patterns.

Tolman pointed out that his theory is mainly concerned with the association of ideas and is not overly concerned with the manner in which those ideas become associated with behavior. Motor pattern learning is an attempt to resolve this difficulty. Of all people, Tolman accepted Guthrie's interpretation of how responses become associated with stimuli. He did accept Guthrie reluctantly, however, which is exemplified by the following quote (1949):

> . . . in default of other experimental theories about the learning of motor patterns I am willing to take a chance and to agree with Guthrie that the conditions under which a motor pattern gets acquired may well be those in which the given movement gets the animal away from the stimuli which were present when the movement was initiated [p. 153].

Tolman was truly an eclectic. Somewhere among the six kinds of learning he described, there is agreement with every other major theory of learning. Combining the ideas of Hull, Gestalt theory, and Guthrie in one system would have confused a lesser mind. As for his reason for postulating many kinds of learning rather than one or two kinds, Tolman said the following (1949):

> Why do I want thus to complicate things; why do I not want one simple set of laws for all learning? I do not know. But I suppose it must be due to some funny erroneous equivalence belief on my part to the effect that being sweeping and comprehensive though vague, is equivalent to more love from others than being narrow and precise. No doubt, any good clinician would be able to trace this back to some sort of nasty traumatic experience in my early childhood [p. 155].

Tolman's Attitude Toward His Own Theory.

Tolman presented the final version of his theory in *Psychology: A Study of a Science,* edited by Sigmund Koch, which appeared the year Tolman died, 1959. There is probably no better indication of how Tolman felt toward his own theory and toward science in general than the first and last paragraphs of his chapter in that volume. They are presented below. First, Tolman's opening statement (1959):

> I would like to begin by letting off steam. If in what follows I have not done a very clear or useful job, I would plead some half-

dozen reasons. First, I think the days of such grandiose, all-covering systems in psychology as mine attempted to be are, at least for the present, pretty much passé. I feel therefore, that it might have been more decent and more dignified to let such an instance of the relatively immediate dead past bury its dead. Secondly, I don't enjoy trying to use my mind in too analytical a way. Hence, I have found it frustrating and difficult to try to subject my system to the required sorts of analyses. Thirdly, I suppose I am personally antipathetic to the notion that science progresses through intense, self-conscious analysis of where one has got and where one is going. Such analyses are obviously a proper function for the philosopher of science and they may be valuable for many individual scientists. But I myself become frightened and restricted when I begin to worry too much as to what particular logical and methodological canons I should or should not obey. It seems to me that very often major new scientific insights have come when the scientist, like the ape, has been shaken out of his up-until-then approved scientific rules such as that food can be reached only by the hand and discovers "out of the blue," and perhaps purely by analogy, . . . the new rule of using a stick (or a sign-Gestalt). Fourthly, I have an inveterate tendency to make my ideas too complicated and too high-flown so that they become less and less susceptible to empirical tests. Fifthly, because of increasing laziness, I have not of late kept up, as I should have, with the more recent theoretical and empirical discussions which bear upon my argument. If I had, the argument would have been different and better and also I would have given more credit to those to whom credit is due. Finally, to talk about one's own ideas and to resort frequently to the use of the first person singular, as one tends to do in such an analysis, bring about a conflict, at least in me, between enjoying my exhibitionism and being made to feel guilty by my superego . . . [p. 93–94].

And Tolman's last statement about his theory was as follows (1959):

I started out, as I indicated in the introduction, with considerable uneasiness. I felt that my so-called system was outdated and that it was a waste of time to try to rehash it and that it would be pretentious now to seek to make it fit any accepted set of prescriptions laid down by the philosophy of science. I have to confess, however, that as I have gone along I have become again more and more involved in it, though I still realize its many weak points. The system may well not stand up to any final canons of scientific procedure. But I do not much care. I have liked to think about psychology in ways that have proved congenial to me. Since all the sciences, and especially psychology, are still immersed in such tremendous realms of the uncertain and the unknown, the best that any individual scientist, especially any psychologist, can do seems to be to follow his own gleam and his own bent, however inadequate they may be. In fact, I suppose that actually this is what we all do. In the end, the only sure criterion is to have fun. And I have had fun [p. 152].

Tolman may have lost many skirmishes with the S–R behaviorists, but with the current emphasis in psychology on the study of cognitive processes, his theory may end up winning the war.

DISCUSSION QUESTIONS

1. Why can Tolman's theory be considered a combination of Gestalt psychology and behaviorism?
2. What is purposive behaviorism?
3. Why is Tolman's theory called an S–S theory rather than an S–R theory?
4. Describe a situation that would allow you to determine whether or not an animal is utilizing a cognitive map to solve a problem. Do not use any of the specific studies discussed in this chapter.
5. For Tolman, is reward a learning or a performance variable? Explain.
6. Describe briefly the six kinds of learning proposed by Tolman.
7. Summarize the study performed by Tolman and Honzik on latent learning. What conclusions can be drawn from the results of their study?
8. Describe, according to Tolman, what events take place as an animal is learning to solve a maze. Incorporate as many of Tolman's theoretical terms into your answer as possible.
9. What would characterize classroom procedures designed in accordance with Tolman's theory?
10. Give instances from your own personal life that would either support or refute Tolman's theory of learning.

GLOSSARY

Cathexis. The formation of an association between a certain drive state, such as hunger, and certain stimuli, such as the foods one is accustomed to eating. When a drive occurs, one actively seeks out the stimuli that have been previously associated with its satisfaction. Cathexis is one of Tolman's six proposed kinds of learning.

Cognitive dissonance. A psychological state experienced when there is a discrepancy between what is expected and what actually occurs.

Cognitive map. A mental picture of the environment.

Confirmation of an expectancy. When the prediction made about some future event is found to be accurate.

Demand. The intervening variable that corresponds to maintenance schedule. As number of hours without eating goes up, for example, demand is thought to increase.

Drive discriminations. The fact that organisms can discriminate between various drive states and can therefore adjust their behavior so that appropriate goal objects can be experienced. Drive discrimination is one of Tolman's six proposed kinds of learning.

Emphasizer. A role that motivation played in Tolman's theory. The motivational state of an organism determines which environmental events will be emphasized in that organism's perceptual field.

Equivalence beliefs. Similar to the notion of secondary reinforcement, in that a previously neutral event develops the capability of satisfying a need. One of Tolman's six proposed kinds of learning.

Expectancy. A hunch or hypothesis about the occurrence of a future event.

Field-cognition modes. Learned or inherited strategies that are utilized while attempting to solve a problem. Field-cognition modes is one of Tolman's six proposed kinds of learning.

Field expectancies. Similar to a cognitive map in that the organism comes to know which events in a given environment lead to other events. Field expectancies is one of Tolman's six proposed kinds of learning.

Hypothesis. An expectancy that occurs in the early stages of learning.

Latent learning. Learning that occurs but is not translated immediately into performance. Rather, it is learning that remains dormant until there is some reason for utilizing it, at which time it is translated into behavior.

Maintenance schedule. The feeding schedule arranged by the experimenter for an organism during a learning experiment.

Means-end readiness. An expectancy that is consistently confirmed; sometimes referred to as a belief.

Molar behavior. See Glossary for Chapter 10.

Motor patterns. The learning of the overt behavior that the organism must utilize in reaching a desired goal. Motor patterns is one of Tolman's six proposed kinds of learning.

Place learning. Learning where an object is located. According to Tolman, once the location of an object is known, it can be reached by any number of alternate routes.

Principle of least effort. The contention that a task will always be done in a manner that requires the least amount of effort or work.

Purposive behavior. Behavior directed toward some goal, such as going to the store, cooking a meal, or solving a maze.

Purposive behaviorism. A behavioristic approach that studies purposive behavior as such and does not attempt to reduce such behavior into smaller elements for further analysis.

Response learning. The learning of specific responses that are effective in solving a problem and thereby providing reward.

Reward expectancy. The fact that an organism learns to expect a certain reward if he engages in certain behaviors. It has been found that performance is disrupted when the original reward used in a learning situation is replaced with a different reward.

Vicarious trial and error. The hesitation at a choice point in a learning situation where it looks "as if" the animal is weighing the alternatives before he decides what to do.

part 5

Some Final Thoughts

13

Neurophysiological Explanations of Learning

In recent years, the interest in traditional behaviorism has diminished and interest in cognitive and neurophysiological processes has increased. The purpose of this chapter is to give the student an idea of the kind of research that is taking place in physiological psychology, presently one of psychology's most active areas of research.

Two periods in history involved considerable research in physiological psychology—now, and the nineteenth century. It is not our purpose here to review the early work in physiological psychology, but only to point out that the search for neurophysiological explanations for mental events was very much in the air. For example, William James, frequently referred to as the greatest American psychologist, often spoke of underlying neurophysiological correlates of psychological phenomena. In 1892, he said, "The immediate condition of a state of consciousness is an activity of some sort in the cerebral hemispheres" (p. 5). James even anticipated Pavlov by claiming the laws of association are really laws describing neuronal activity. He said (1892), "When two elementary brain processes have been active together or in immediate succession, one of them, on recurring, tends to propagate its excitement into the other" [p. 256]. This, of course, would also explain associative shifting based solely on the law of contiguity.

Although physiological conceptions were an integral part of psychology at the beginning of the twentieth century, they have played only a minor role in learning theory until recently. In the peroid between 1900 and 1950 when most of the major theories of learning were being developed, physiological explanations of learning were either minimized or actively avoided.

There were at least three reasons for the avoidance of physiological explanations of learning. First, as the philosophy of science developed and as more was learned about the logic of science, many researchers felt that explaining observable behavior in terms of physiological events was like mixing apples and oranges. Using physiological mechanisms to explain overt behavior involved a change in the level of discourse and drawing conclusions from one level to the other violated the canons of scientific logic. In other words, it was believed that physiological events, like overt behavior, constitute a self-contained system, and the relationship between the two systems remained indeterminate.

A second reason that physiological explanations were not very important in the development of the major theories of learning involved the very nature of the behavioristic movement, which was mainly a reaction against introspection. To the behaviorist, the only legitimate subject matter for psychology was something tangible that everyone could see and investigate. This was not true for the experiences reported on introspectively, and it was not true for physiological events. In concentrating on overt, measurable behavior the behaviorists excluded neurophysiology.

The third reason for the lack of "physiologizing" among early learning theorists was the fact that there simply was not much known about the nervous system at the time, and more importantly, there were no adequate techniques available for thorough neurological investigations.

Looking back on the various theories we have covered in this text, we can find a few reasonable attempts to discover physiological correlates of learning phenomena; for instance, Hull's stimulus trace notion, his emphasis on physiological drives, and the r_G-s_G mechanism. Guthrie spoke on movement-produced stimuli. Pavlov talked rather extensively about the neurological substratum of learning by using such notions as irradiation, inhibition, excitation, and concentration. Although his brain physiology was not very well developed, it reflected the state of knowledge in physiology at that time. This was also true of the Gestalt theorists with their notions of the memory trace and isomorphism. The Gestalt theorists attempted to support their theorizing with tangible physiological events inside the organism, but, as with Pavlov, their attempts showed how little was known about the central nervous system at that time. Skinner was really the only theorist who actively avoided physiological conceptions and encouraged other theorists to do the same. Skinner's approach, as we have seen, was to do a functional analysis between stimulus events and overt responses. He was content to look upon the organism as conceptually empty, and felt that physiological explanations just confused the issue.

Present Attitude Toward the Neurophysiology of Learning.

One reason for the present popularity of neurophysiological research is related to technical advances. For example, the development of the microelectrode has made it possible both to record from and/or stimulate various parts of the brain in order to determine their function. The development of small cannulae (tiny hollow cylinders) has made it possible to stimulate various parts of the brain with drugs and chemicals to see how they influence behavior. The electroencephalogram (EEG) permits the study of gross electrical waves emitted by the brain during various states such as problem solving, resting, sleeping, simple learning, and emotionality. The development of new drugs has also added new approaches to research on the neurophysiology of learning.

Another factor involved in the renewed interest in physiological explanations is the *Zeitgeist,* or the spirit of the times. Attempts to develop all-encompassing theories of learning appear to have given way to research on a much more limited scale. When a problem arises, present researchers are apt to either develop a minitheory to explain just that problem, or to pick and choose aspects from existing theories to help explain the problem. The physiological approach to explaining learning is compatible with this new spirit of eclecticism. Since we are no longer expecting the total answer concerning the learning process to come from any single source, we are more likely to accept bits of information from a variety of sources; neurophysiological research on learning promises to be a very fruitful source of information.

S–R versus Gestalt Approaches on the Neural Level.

Often the difference between the S–R mechanistic approach to explaining learning and the Gestalt approach maintains itself in neurophysiological research. The S–R point of view in neurophysiological research is sometimes referred to as the switchboard approach. The emphasis with the switchboard approach is on finding specific neural circuits that connect sensory events with overt responses. It is assumed that certain sensory events trigger certain areas of the brain, causing specific reactions. According to the switchboard approach, learning involves some change in circuitry so that sensory events come to cause other responses than those they originally caused. Although the input-output notion of the S–R point of view is maintained, it is supplemented with neuronal circuitry and pathways.

The Gestalt approach is more apt to involve a search for patterns of neuronal impulses that emerge from many sensory inputs. According to the Gestalt point of view, learning is more than simply a matter of input and output mediated by neural pathways and relay points. It is more a matter of the pattern of brain activity caused by multiple inputs interacting with the remnants of past experience. Roughly speaking, the S–R theorist would tend to look upon the central nervous system as a passive switchboard that is made up of billions of tiny switches (neurons). These switches respond to sensory inputs and finally produce an overt response. The Gestalt theorist would emphasize the organizational abilities of the brain, and would claim that the brain acts upon sensory information somehow to make it more meaningful before an overt response is made (see Chapter 10).

The distinction between the simple switchboard approach and an approach emphasizing the organizational aspects of the brain has been complicated by the kind of research done by Lettvin, Maturana, McCullock, and Pitts (1959). These researchers used microelectrodes to record activity in single optic nerve fibers in a frog while he was confronted with a variety of different environmental stimuli. The results of their experiment were truly startling. They found that some fibers responded to certain environmental events and not to others. In all, they found five separate groups of nerve fibers in the optic nerve of the frog which were described as follows:

1. **sustained edge detectors.**   These cells fire only if an edge of an object is moved into the visual field and left there. The cells continue firing as long as the edge remains in the visual field.
2. **convex edge detectors.**   These cells fire when a small dark object moves around in the visual field.
3. **changing contrast detectors.**   These cells fire when an object that is either lighter than or darker than its background moves across the visual field.
4. **dimming detectors.**   These cells fire when the visual field of the frog is darkened. They respond to the darkening process rather than the dark itself.
5. **dark detectors.**   The frequency of discharge in these cells is inversely proportional to light intensity.

If the findings of Lettvin et al. are found to apply to organisms other than the frog, it would mean that both the switchboard and the Gestalt viewpoints regarding the functioning of the nervous system would need to be modified. Their work shows that information comes to the frog's brain in an already highly organized form. The organizational abilities that some would attribute to the brain were found to take place at the sensory level. The senses, therefore, were found to perform at least part of the function that had traditionally been assigned to the brain. The frog seems to be maximally responsive to bug-like objects independent of any learning or interpretation of stimulation by the brain. It should be pointed out, however, that this organization of information at the receptor level may not be characteristic of higher vertebrates. For example, Hubel and Wiesel (1961) found that for cats, information coding processes occur in the *cortical* visual cells rather than at the receptor level. It should be exciting to watch this line of research develop over the coming years.

Probably the person who is most responsible for casting doubt on the simple switchboard interpretation of brain functioning is Karl Lashley, whose work we turn to next.

The Work of Karl Lashley.

Lashley, one of the main opponents of the switchboard interpretation of learning, was a student of John B. Watson, a main advocate of the

Karl Lashley

switchboard interpretation of learning. This kind of radical departure in thinking between teacher and student is common in science. We saw another example of it with Skinner and Estes. Skinner, who of course is a major reinforcement theorist, was the teacher of Estes, who became a major advocate of Guthrie's contiguity theory.

Lashley's own research on the relationship between brain damage and learning ability drove him from the behavioristic camp. His research was summarized in a monograph entitled *Brain Mechanisms and Intelligence* (1929). Lashley's procedure involved destroying various areas of a rat's brain before and after learning so that it could be determined what function the ablated portion of the brain had in learning and retention. To measure learning, Lashley used mazes with three levels of difficulty. Maze 1 had one blind alley, maze 2 had three blind alleys, and maze 3 had eight blind alleys.

The most startling outcome of Lashley's research was his finding that the *location* of the destroyed portion of the brain was not as important as the *amount* of destruction. This consistent finding became Lashley's principle of *mass action,* which stated that the disruption of learning and retention goes up as the amount of cortical destruction goes up, regardless of the location of the destruction. The major findings from Lashley's work can be summarized as follows: (1) a rat's ability to learn does not depend upon any particular area of the cortex; (2) loss in the ability to learn or remember is proportional to the amount of cortical destruction; and

Figure 13–1. The results of Lashley's research showing the relationship between amount of cortical destruction, maze difficulty and the disruption of learning (after Lashley, 1929, p. 74).

(3) the disruption in learning caused by cortical destruction is related to the complexity of the learning task. The greater the complexity of the learning task, the greater the disruption caused by cortical destruction. The combined effect of learning complexity and the amount of cortical damage on learning ability is shown in Figure 13–1.

Lashley concluded that the cortex functioned as a whole during learning, and if one part of the cortex was destroyed, other parts of the cortex could take over the destroyed portion's function. This ability of one portion of the cortex to take over the function of another was referred to by Lashley as *equipotentiality*. Thus, mass action indicated that the amount of learning and memory disruption is a function of the amount of the cortical area destroyed, and equipotentiality indicated that the location of the cortical ablation was unimportant.

Subsequent research has shown that the principles of mass action and equipotentiality only apply to learning situations where many sensory cues are utilized. For example, if visual, auditory, tactual, and olfactory cues can all be used during learning, the ablation of that portion of the brain which corresponds to any particular sense modality will not necessarily interfere with learning or retention. If, however, a learning task is made to be specifically dependent upon visual cues, and the visual area of the brain is ablated, then the ability to perform the task will be lost.

Next, we turn to the theory of Donald Hebb who worked with Lashley at the University of Chicago. The kind of research described above converted Hebb from an ardent supporter of Pavlov, who tended to look upon the brain as a complex switchboard, to a Gestalt-type physiological psychologist.

DONALD OLDING HEBB

Donald Hebb, who is now at McGill University, was born in Chester, Nova Scotia, in 1904. He received his B.A. from Dalhousie University in 1925, his M.A. from the University of Chicago in 1932, and his Ph.D. from Harvard University in 1936. The student may be interested in knowing that Hebb graduated from Dalhousie with the lowest course average anyone could have without actually failing. Like Skinner, Hebb first tried to write novels for a living, but when this failed, he went back to school as a part-time graduate student. Because of his low academic standing as an undergraduate, he went to the University of Chicago and later to Harvard without financial assistance. Since Hebb is one of psychology's most creative researchers and theorists, undergraduate gradepoint average, in his case, had no predictive value.

Hebb went to the University of Chicago believing strongly in Pavlov's views, but a series of experiences he had while working with Lashley at the University of Chicago changed his mind. For example, he found that in one case, a person who had 20 percent of his cortex removed had no detectable mental defect. This fact was very difficult to reconcile with an associationistic or switchboard view of the functioning of the brain. This and other experiences steered him away from the associationistic point of view. Hebb says (1959): "I had all the fervor of the reformed drunk at a temperance meeting; having been a fully convinced Pavlovian, I was now a fully convinced Gestalter-cum-Lashleyan" [p. 625]. Once again, we are reminded of an important characteristic of good scientists: they are able to change their minds.

Once converted, Hebb launched an attack on the behaviorists that he has continued until the present time. His first major book was *The Organization of Behavior* (1949). The initials of that book, OOB, bore a strange resemblance to the initials of Skinner's major book *The Behavior of Organisms* (1938), which was affectionately known as BOO. A later publication, "Drives and the C.N.S. (Conceptual Nervous System)" (1955) showed Hebb's willingness to "physiologize" about psychological processes. His very readable *Textbook of Psychology* (1972) provides an excellent overview of his theory. A more technical account of his theory appears in Koch's *Psychology: A Study of a Science* (1959). Hebb's approach is diametrically opposed to Skinner's method of functional analysis, where relationships between stimuli and responses are determined without any reference to internal events. Fortunately, the student need not decide which approach is right or which is wrong; instead, he can take the best from both. Some of Hebb's more important theoretical concepts are reviewed below.

Cell Assemblies.

According to Hebb, each environmental object we experience fires a complex package of neurons called a cell assembly. For example, as we look at a house, we will shift our attention from the windows, to the door, to the roof. As our attention shifts, different neurons are stimulated. However, the entire package of neurons stimulated at the time corresponds to one environmental object—a house. All aspects of this complex neural package will, at first, be independent. For example, as one looks at the door of a house, a group of neurons will fire. They will not, however, initially influence the neurons that fire while one is looking at the windows or roof. Eventually, however, because of the closeness in time between the firing of the neurons corresponding to the door and those corresponding to other parts of the house, the various parts of the neurological package become interrelated. Hebb puts the matter as follows (1959):

> If a neuron, *A*, is near enough to another, *B*, to have any possibility of firing it, and if it does take part in firing it on one occasion (it often requires two or more neurons working together to trigger the response in another), the probability is increased that when *A* fires next *B* will fire as a result. In other words, "synaptic resistance" is decreased, by a microscopic growth at the synapse or some chemical change in one of the two cells. The assembly might be made up of perhaps 25, 50, or 100 neurons, and building it up in the first place would be a very slow process, requiring many repetitions of the stimulating conditions [p. 628].

A cell assembly can be large or small, depending upon the environmental object or event it represents. For example, the cell assembly associated with *door knob* would consist of a relatively small number of neurons, but the cell assembly for *house* would consist of a relatively large number of neurons. The entire cell assembly is an interrelated neurological package that can be fired by either external stimulation; internal stimulation, or a combination of the two when any portion is stimulated. When a cell assembly fires, we experience the thought of the event the assembly represents. To Hebb, the cell assembly is the neurological basis of an idea or thought. In this way, Hebb explains why a house, or a cow, or a loved one need not be present for us to think of them.

Phase Sequences.

Just as different aspects of the same object become neurologically interrelated to form cell assemblies, so do cell assemblies become neurologically interrelated to form *phase sequences*. A phase sequence is ". . . a temporarily integrated series of assembly activities; it amounts to one current in the stream of thought" [Hebb, 1959, p. 629]. Once developed, a phase sequence, like a cell assembly, can be fired internally, externally, or by a combination of internal and external stimulation. When any single cell assembly or combination of assemblies in a phase sequence is fired, the entire phase sequence tends to fire. When a phase sequence fires, we experience a stream of thought, that is, a series of ideas arranged in some logical order. This explains how a whiff of perfume, or a few strains from a favorite song may trigger memories of a previous girlfriend.

Hebb has the following to say about the development of phase sequences (1972):

. . . cell-assemblies that are active at the same time become interconnected. Common events in the child's environment establish assemblies, and then when these events occur together the assemblies become connected (because they are active together). When the baby hears footsteps, let us say, an assembly is excited; while this is still active he sees a face and feels hands picking him up, which excites other assemblies—so that "footsteps assembly" becomes connected with the "face assembly" and the "being-picked-up assembly." After this has happened, when the baby hears footsteps only, all three assemblies are excited; the baby then has something like a perception of a mother's face and the contact of her hands before she has come in sight—but since the sensory stimulations have not yet taken place, this is ideation or imagery, not perception [p. 67].

For Hebb, there are two kinds of learning. One involves the slow buildup of cell assemblies early in life. The buildup of cell assemblies can probably be explained by one of the S–R theories of learning, such as Guthrie's. This kind of learning is straight associationism. Likewise, the development of phase sequences can be explained using associationistic terminology. After cell assemblies and phase sequences are developed, however, subsequent learning is more cognitive. Adult learning, for example, often characterized by insight and creativity, probably involves the rearrangement of phase sequences.

Hebb feels psychologists have avoided the physiological study of cognitive processes too long and gives the following advice (1959):

How are we to learn more about these ideational or mediating processes, and the limits of their role in behavior, except by forming hypotheses (as explicit as we can reasonably make them) and then seeing what implications they have for behavior, and whether these implications are borne out in experiment? By all means, if you will, call these central events mediating processes instead of ideas or cell assemblies, but let us get busy and investigate them [p. 630].

It is fortunate for psychology that many investigators are currently following Hebb's suggestion.

Arousal Theory.

Arousal theory involves the functioning of the reticular activating system (RAS), an area about the size of a finger which is located in the brain stem just above the spinal cord and just below the thalamus and hypothalamus. The RAS has been found to be involved in the processes of sleep, attention, and emotional behavior.

According to Hebb (1955), a neural impulse generated by the stimulation of a sense receptor has two functions. One function is referred to as the *cue function*. The sensory stimulus causes an impulse to travel from the sense receptor, up the sensory tract of the spinal cord, to various projection areas, and finally to some area of the cortex. This function of a stimulus allows the organism to gain information about the environment.

The second function of a sensory impulse is its *arousal function*. It has been found that there are collaterals that spill off the sensory track of the spinal cord into the RAS. As sensory information is on its way to the cortex, it influences the RAS through these collaterals and causes it to increase its activity. This tendency for sensory impulses to increase activity in the RAS is referred to as the arousal function of a stimulus.

Amount of activity in the RAS is used as an index of arousal; the greater the amount of RAS activity, the higher the level of arousal. The EEG is generally accepted as a measure of arousal and is therefore thought to reflect RAS activity. As we shall see later in this chapter, a very slow EEG pattern (delta waves) indicates sleep. This also indicates a period of relative inactivity in the RAS. The EEG pattern of a very relaxed person is characterized by rhythmic waves of about 8 to 10 cycles per second, and the excited person shows very fast brain wave activity, or relatively high arousal.

It is generally believed that the RAS stimulates the cortex and thus creates a background of electrical activity without which the cue function of an incoming sensory impulse would be lost. For a number of years, it was believed that the arousal function of a stimulus caused the RAS to bombard the entire cortex with nonspecific electrical activity. Now, however, it is believed that certain stimuli stimulate certain parts of the RAS to stimulate certain parts of the cortex. A visual stimulus, for instance, may cause the RAS to increase the electrical activity only in the occipital lobe of the brain. In general, what seems to happen is that the RAS prepares higher centers of the brain to receive and act upon information from the environment.

A number of studies have implicated the RAS in states of alertness. Lindsley, Schreiner, Knowles, and Magoun (1950) showed that if the RAS was ablated, a cat would sleep permanently even though all his sensory pathways to the brain were left intact. Moruzzi and Magoun (1949), by directly stimulating the RAS, could produce a wakeful EEG pattern even in anesthetized cats. Lindsley (1958) found that with long intervals between flashes, a monkey's brain would show an *evoked potential* (electrical activity in the brain caused by the onset of an external stimulus) each time a light was flashed. With short intervals between flashes, however, the cortex responded to the two flashes as if they were one. Lindsley found that if he stimulated the RAS of the monkey just prior to the presentation of the two flashes within a very short time, the monkey's EEG showed an evoked potential for each of the flashes. The RAS stimulation apparently made it possible for the brain to process information in more detail. Fuster (1958) tested the same notion by training monkeys to discriminate between two objects; they were rewarded with a peanut if they chose the correct object. Next, the animals were placed in the dark and a light was flashed on very briefly (e.g., 20 milliseconds), during which time they had to choose between the two objects they were trained on. On half the trials, the animal received stimulation to his RAS prior to the onset of the flash of light, and on the other half he did not. Results showed that the animals performed much better following stimulation of their RAS, again showing the brain is better able to process detailed information if the RAS is stimulated just prior to the exposure to such information.

Hebb (1955) theorized about the relationship between arousal level and performance. He felt that for the cue function of a stimulus to have its full effect, there must be an *optimal level of arousal* provided by the RAS. When arousal level is too low, such as when the organism is asleep, sensory information transmitted to the brain cannot be utilized. Likewise, when arousal is too high, too much information is being analyzed by the cortex and often conflicting responses or irrelevant behavior results. This suggests that a level of arousal that is neither too high nor too low is necessary for optimal cortical functioning and therefore optimal per-

Donald O. Hebb

formance. The proposed relationship between arousal level and performance is shown in Figure 13–2. This curvilinear relationship between
arousal and performance, first observed in 1908 by R. Yerkes and J.
Dodson, is called the Yerkes-Dodson law.

Hebb speculated that different tasks have different levels of arousal
associated with their optimal performance. For example, a simple, well-
practiced habit may be performed optimally across a wide range of
arousal levels, whereas a highly skilled task may be performed optimally
only within a minimal range of arousal levels. Gross behavioral skills may
be performed best under extremely high arousal. The proposed relationship between optimal performance on various tasks and arousal level is
seen in Figure 13–3.

Relationship Between Arousal Theory and Reinforcement Theory.

According to Hebb, if arousal level is too high for the organism to
attend to existing conditions optimally, he will operate on the environment in such a way as to reduce the arousal level. For example, if a student is trying to study while people are talking and the television is on,
he may have to tell the people to keep quiet and turn off the TV, or he
will simply have to find an environment more compatible with studying.
On the other hand, if it is too quiet and there is not enough sensory input to maintain an optimal level of arousal, the student may turn on the
radio, talk out loud, or perform some kind of motor task such as fidgeting

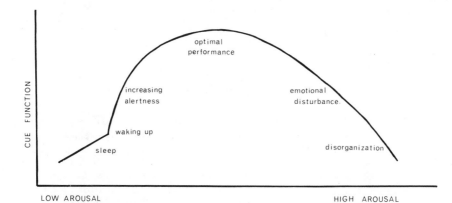

Figure 13–2. The relationship suggested by Hebb between arousal level
and performance.
Source: Hebb, D. O. "Textbook of Psychology," 3rd ed. Philadelphia, Pa.:
W. H. Saunders, 1972, p. 199.

or rubbing his feet together. Generally speaking, when arousal level is too high, decreasing it is rewarding, and when the arousal level is too low, increasing it is rewarding. Unlike Hull's theory, which equates drive reduction with reinforcement, Hebb's theory equates reinforcement with either an increase or decrease in drive, depending on the circumstances. According to Hebb, seeking excitement is a significant motive in human behavior. He says (1955):

> When you stop to think of it, it is nothing short of extraordinary what trouble people will go to in order to get into more trouble at the bridge table, or on the golf course; and the fascination of the murder story, or thriller, and the newspaper accounts of real-life adventure or tragedy, is no less extraordinary. This taste for excitement *must* not be forgotten when we are dealing with human motivation. It appears that, up to a certain point, threat and puzzle have positive motivating value, beyond that point negative value [p. 250].

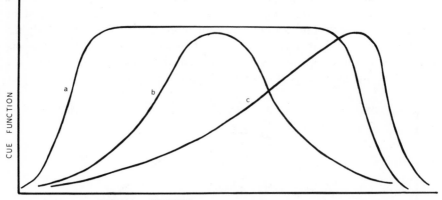

Figure 13–3. The figure shows the relationship suggested by Hebb between arousal level and the performance on three different kinds of tasks. Task a is a well-practiced habit such as giving one's name. Such a task is performed optimally over a wide range of arousal levels. Task b is a complex skill such as typing. Such a task is performed optimally only when arousal is neither too high nor too low. Task c is the kind of task that is relatively uncomplicated but requires the expenditure of a great deal of energy, such as weight-lifting or running a race. Such a task is performed optimally when arousal level is high.
Source: Hebb, D. O. "Textbook of Psychology," 3rd ed. Philadelphia, Pa.: W. H. Saunders, 1972, p. 200.

Long-Term and Short-Term Memory.

Although Müller and Pilzecker originally suggested that there are two distinct kinds of memory as early as 1900, the idea has just recently received wide attention. Currently, it is generally believed that there are two kinds of memory: *long-term memory* and *short-term memory*. (Short-term memory is also called either *immediate memory* or *primary memory;* long-term memory is also called *secondary memory*.) Short-term memory is triggered by sensory stimulation and continues for some time after the stimulation has ceased. Exactly how long the activity continues is not known, but it seems that the information stored in short-term memory is available for less than a minute. For example, Peterson and Peterson (1959) read their subjects a consonant trigram (e.g., *QHJ*) and then instructed them to immediately start counting backwards by 3s or 4s from a three-digit number they were given. Different subjects had their counting interrupted at different times and were asked to repeat the consonant trigram that was read to them. The recall intervals were 3, 6, 9, 12, 15, and 18 seconds. It was found that the best retention was at a recall interval of 3 seconds, with 6 seconds next best, etc. The worst recall ocurred after 18 seconds. Thus, short-term memory seems to decay as a function of time, but its decay is much faster than that of long-term memory.

It is generally believed that sensory experience sets up neural activity that outlasts the stimulation that caused it. Hebb (1949) referred to this as *reverberating neural activity*. It appears that as long as the reverberating neural activity continues after an experience, the memory of that experience can be retrieved.

It is obvious that we retain some information much longer than a few seconds, so there must be some relationship between short-term memory and long-term memory. It is believed that long-term memories develop from short-term memories. Somehow, during the neural activity following an experience, long-term memories consolidate, or become fixed. The short-term memory, which involves continuous neural activity, somehow causes a structural change in the nervous system, which corresponds to the long-term or secondary memory. The contention that short-term memory is somehow translated into long-term memory is referred to as *consolidation theory*. Through the years, Hebb has been a major proponent of the consolidation theory of memory.

Since long-term memory is thought to depend on short-term memory, it follows that anything that disrupts short-term memory should also disrupt long-term memory. Based on this contention, Duncan (1949) trained rats to jump a barrier to avoid an electric shock. If they jumped from one side of an experimental chamber to the other side within ten seconds after they were placed in the apparatus, they could avoid being shocked. If they did not cross over to the "safe" side, they were shocked until they did. The animals were given one learning trial per day. Following each trial, each animal was given an electroconvulsive shock (ECS) through two electrodes clipped to the rat's ears. The ECS causes convulsions much like those of an epileptic seizure. Depending on what group the animal was in, the shock occurred 20 seconds, 40 seconds, 60 seconds, 4 minutes, 15 minutes, 1 hour, 4 hours, or 14 hours after his learning trial. A control group received no ECS after learning. Training continued for 18 days. Figure 13–4 shows the mean number of correct anticipations of the shock for all groups; i.e., jumping to the safe side upon being placed in the apparatus.

It can be seen that the more closely the ECS followed a learning trial, the more it tended to disrupt the memory of the learning experience. For example, animals receiving ECS 20 seconds after a learning trial continued being shocked—they never learned the avoidance response. When the ECS was administered within an hour of the learning trial, it interfered with memory. After an hour, ECS apparently had no effect on mem-

Figure 13–4. The results of Duncan's study showing that as the delay between a learning experience and an electroconvulsive shock becomes longer, the disruptive effect of the shock on the retention of the learning experience goes down.

Source: Duncan, C. P. "The retroactive effect of electroshock on learning," *Journal of Comparative and Physiological Psychology,* 42: 35. Copyright © 1949 by the American Psychological Assoc. Reprinted by permission.

ory. The animals receiving ECS an hour or more after their learning trial performed as well as the control group that received no ECS. The results of Duncan's experiment lent support to consolidation theory and suggests that the consolidation period lasts about an hour. However, the moments immediately following a learning experience seem to be more important for consolidation than those after about the first minute.

Further evidence is provided for consolidation theory by the phenomenon called *retrograde amnesia*. Retrograde amnesia refers to the loss of memory for those events just prior to a traumatic experience, such as an automobile accident or a combat injury. This memory loss for events prior to a traumatic event may involve hours, days, or even months. Usually the memory of such events will slowly return except for those immediately prior to the traumatic event. It is assumed that the traumatic event had the same effect as Duncan's ECS; that is, it interfered with the reverberating neural activity that is necessary for consolidation to take place, thereby making long-term memory impossible.

Some researchers have speculated that one difference between "bright" and "dull" organisms is their rate of consolidation. For example, Thomson, McGaugh, Smith, Hudspeth, and Westbrook (1961) found that ECS can be delayed relatively longer for "dull" rats and still have an effect on memory. "Bright" rats appeared to finish consolidating within about 45 minutes, whereas "dull" rats did not. Likewise, it has been found that the administration of drugs such as strychnine and picrotoxin, believed to increase the rate of consolidation, increases the rate of learning (e.g., McGaugh and Petrinovich, 1959; Breen and McGaugh, 1961). In fact, when such a drug was administered to maze-dull rats (rats that have been inbred with rats that learned to solve a maze very slowly), their performance was equated with that of maze-bright rats. In one study, the maze-dull rats even outperformed the maze-bright rats after both groups received injections of picrotoxin (Breen and McGaugh, 1961).

It is important to note that improvements in learning are found whether a drug such as strychnine or picrotoxin is injected before or after a learning experience. If improvement was shown only when the drug was injected before learning, the results could be attributed to increased motivation or alertness. Consistent with the findings described above, McGaugh, Westbrook, and Burt (1961) found that the closer the injection of a stimulant followed the learning trial, the better was the performance on the next trial.

The results of these and other experiments make it tempting to assume that differences between "bright" and "dull" organisms can be explained in terms of differences in rate of consolidation. Such speculation should be made cautiously, however, since this area of research is fairly new and many alternative explanations for the results must be explored.

Consolidation and the Brain.

A number of interrelated brain structures, collectively referred to as the *limbic system,* are believed to be important for the experience of various emotions. One of these limbic structures is the hippocampus. Peter Milner, one of Hebb's students at McGill University, found that patients with their hippocampus destroyed have no trouble recalling events that took place before the destruction of their hippocampus, but it is impossible for them to form new long-term memories (Milner, 1965). Such a patient performs well on intelligence tests and does very well on motor skills that were acquired before the damage to his hippocampus. Also, Milner reports no apparent personality change resulting from the brain damage. The remarkable thing about such a patient is that he simply cannot retain any new information. As soon as his attention is distracted from an experience, the memory of it is lost. Such an individual looks as if his short-term memory is functioning normally but his long-term memory is not.

Milner speculates that in the early stages of learning, there is an interplay between the sensory input, the hippocampus, and the cortex. Through this interrelated activity, the information finally comes to be stored in the cortex as long-term memory. The hippocampus is thus believed to be responsible for consolidation.

In this section, we have seen the breadth of Hebb's theory. In fact, his can be considered the most comprehensive neurophysiological theory available today. By utilizing such diverse concepts as cell assemblies, phase sequences, arousal theory, and consolidation theory, Hebb offers a refreshingly different account of learning, retention, motivation, and perception. We have organized this book around three paradigms within which most of the research on the learning process has occurred; namely, the functionalistic, associationistic and cognitive paradigms. Perhaps it is now necessary to add a *neurophysiological* paradigm, with Hebb's theory representing such a paradigm. Although we see aspects of other paradigms in his theory, such as that of cognition, his main goal is to determine the neurophysiological correlates of mental processes.

We ended our discussion of Hebb's theory by summarizing the research done by Peter Milner, one of Hebb's students. In the next section we will look at some additional work done by Milner along with James Olds, another of Hebb's students.

REWARD CENTERS IN THE BRAIN

In the chapter on Pavlov, we noted that his discovery of the conditioned reflex was quite accidental. Serendipity, the finding of one thing while

James Olds

looking for another, has led to the discovery of important phenomena whose investigations sometimes resulted in scientific breakthroughs. Another example of serendipity in science is the discovery of *reward centers* in the brain by Olds and Milner (1954). Olds, who was working in Hebb's laboratory at McGill University, describes how the discovery was made (1955):

> In the fall of 1953, we were looking for more information about the reticular activating system. We used electrodes permanently implanted in the brain of a healthy behaving rat. . . . Quite by accident, an electrode was implanted in the region of the anterior commissure.
>
> The result was quite amazing. When the animal was stimulated at a specific place in an open field, he sometimes moved away but he returned and sniffed around that area. More stimulations at that place caused him to spend more of his time there.
>
> Later we found that this same animal could be "pulled" to any spot in the maze by giving a small electrical stimulus *after* each response in the right direction. This was akin to playing the "hot"

and "cold" game with a child. Each correct response brought electrical pulses which seemed to indicate to the animal that it was on the right track [pp. 83–84].

Since Olds and Milner's accidental discovery of reward centers in rats, reward centers have been found in cats, dogs, goldfish, monkeys, porpoises, pigeons, and humans. When a human being's reward center is stimulated, the person sometimes reports erotic sensations and thoughts, or simply a feeling of pleasure.

Olds and Milner originally felt that the septal region of the brain housed most of the reward centers. Since then, however, such centers have been found scattered throughout the limbic system of the brain. The limbic system, which is involved in motivated and emotional behavior, contains part of the lower cortex, the hippocampus, the amygdala, the septum, and parts of the thalamus and hypothalamus.

These brain areas are called reward centers because when they are stimulated, the animal tends to repeat what it was doing before the stimulation. Because of this, an animal with an electrode implanted in a reward center can be trained to run a maze or to press a bar in a Skinner box simply by stimulating that area of the brain with a mild electrical current when the animal performs the appropriate response.

Reinforcement by direct brain stimulation, however, has been found to have some unusual characteristics and is therefore thought to operate differently from the more traditional reinforcers such as food or water. The unusual characteristics of reinforcement by direct brain stimulation are summarized below:

1. No deprivation needed before training. Unlike training involving the use of food or water as a reward, generally no deprivation schedule is needed when direct brain stimulation is used as a reward. The animal does not need to be in a "drive state." There are exceptions to this, however, and occasionally reward centers are found that do seem to be dependent on the drive state of the organism. For example, it has been found that the stimulation of some brain sites is rewarding only if the animal is hungry; stimulation of other sites is rewarding only if the animal is thirsty, and still others if he is sexually aroused.

2. Satiation does not occur. When food or water is used as a reward, the animal will eventually satiate; that is his need for food or water will be satisfied and he will stop responding. With direct brain stimulation, however, the animal will go on responding at an extraordinarily high rate (for example, bar-press rates as high as 7000 per hour have been reported) until he becomes physically exhausted.

3. *Takes priority over other drives.*   Animals continue to press a bar for direct brain stimulation even when food is available and they have not eaten for a considerable length of time. Also, animals will often withstand a greater shock in order to obtain brain stimulation to a reward center than to obtain food even if they have not eaten for twenty-four hours.

4. *Rapid extinction.*   Although rate of responding is extremely high, as long as the animal is being rewarded by brain stimulation, he stops responding very rapidly when the brain stimulation stops. In other words, rather than the gradual extinction process observed when food or water are the rewards, extinction takes place almost immediately when direct brain stimulation reward is terminated. Although extinction is rapid, response rate reoccurs at full strength when the animal is again rewarded.

5. *Most schedules of reinforcement do not work.*   Since extinction occurs very rapidly when brain stimulation is terminated, any schedule of reinforcement that produces some amount of delay between responding and reward will cause the animal to stop responding. Cats, for example, will stop responding if the delay between a response and a reward is longer than about 15 seconds. Therefore, only schedules of reinforcement that provide frequent reward can be used with direct brain stimulation.

As yet, these observations about the rewarding effects of direct brain stimulation have not been explained in a way that is widely accepted by researchers in the field. The situation is complicated further by the fact that *punishment areas* are often found only millimeters away from a reward area. An animal will quickly learn to perform a response that terminates stimulation to such an area, or will learn a response that prevents it from occurring. Humans receiving stimulation in a punishment area report feelings of anxiety or panic.

RESEARCH ON THE SPLIT BRAIN

The *corpus callosum* is a large mass of fibers that connects the two halves of the cortex. For years, the function of the corpus callosum was unknown, but recently it has been found to be instrumental in transferring information from one side of the cortex to the other. In a series of experiments, Sperry (1961) attempted to determine under what circumstances information is transferred from one side of the cortex to the other. He noted that there were two possible routes for such transfer— the corpus callosum and the optic chiasm. The optic chiasm is the point in the optic nerve where information coming from one eye is projected to the side of the cortex opposite to that eye. Realizing this, Sperry taught intact cats to make a visual discrimination with a patch over one eye.

Roger W. Sperry

Following discrimination training, he tested for transfer by switching the patch from one eye to the other, and found that the animal was able to perform just as well with either eye. In other words, complete interocular transfer was found.

Now Sperry began a search for the mechanism by which information was transferred from one side of the brain to the other. His first step was to ablate (cut) the optic chiasm, both before and after training, and again he found complete transfer of training from one eye to the other. Next, in addition to ablating the optic chiasm, he ablated the corpus callosum *after* the discrimination training, and again he found no interference with the transfer of information from one eye to the other. His next step was to ablate *both* the optic chiasm and the corpus callosum *before* training and he found that such a preparation prevented transfer from one eye to the other. Cutting both the optic chiasm and the corpus callosum created two separate brains with one eye going to each, and with no exchange of information between them. Sperry's split-brain preparation is seen in Figure 13–5.

When the cat's brain was split, as shown in Figure 13–5, and the cat was taught to make a visual discrimination with a patch over one eye, it had no recollection of that learning when tested with the other eye. The two halves of the split brain appeared to learn independently. In fact, with a patch over one eye, the animal could be taught to do one thing, such as approach a door with a cross on it, and with a patch over the other eye, it could be taught to approach the adjoining door with a circle on it; thus the two brains in the same skull have learned contradictory habits. It is also possible to teach an animal to approach a stimulus (e.g., a circle) with a patch over one eye, and to avoid the same stimulus with a patch over the other eye. The science fiction implications of the split brain are numerous. For example, it is possible to imagine a person who is maximally attentive at all times, because he alternately uses one-half of his brain and then the other in six- or eight-hour intervals. It is also

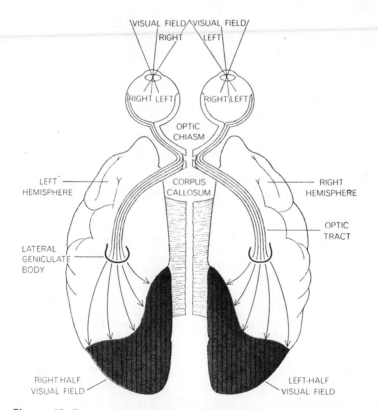

Figure 13–5. A diagram of Sperry's split-brain preparation.
Source: Sperry, R. W. "The Great Cerebral Commissure," Copyright ©
1964 by Scientific American, Inc. All rights reserved.

possible, since personality is thought to be mainly learned behavior, to have two distinct personalities housed in the same body—perhaps like Dr. Jekyll and Mr. Hyde.

Chemically Induced Split Brains.

Leão (1947) and more recently, Bureš and Burešoviá (1960) have described a method of depressing electrical activity of the cortex for a matter of several minutes. By applying a small amount of potassium chloride through a small hole in the skull to one of the two cerebral hemispheres, that hemisphere is rendered temporarily inactive. Under these conditions, one-half of the cortex operates normally, while the other does not. Since the depression of electrical activity caused by the potassium chloride spreads slowly over the hemisphere to which it is applied, the phenomenon is called *spreading depression*.

If an animal is taught a simple habit with its right hemisphere depressed, and is tested the next day with its right hemisphere depressed, it will retain the habit. If, however, it is tested the next day with its left hemisphere depressed, there will be no retention of the habit. An interesting aspect of this research is that after the drug wears off, there is no exchange of information across the corpus callosum. A habit learned with one hemisphere depressed remains specific to the nondepressed hemisphere. It is found, however, that only a few trials are needed to train the hemisphere that was depressed while the other hemisphere was learning.

Drug-specific Habits. Overton (1964) has used sodium pentobarbital to produce a somewhat different learning phenomenon. An animal injected with sodium pentobarbital goes to sleep, but when it awakens, it is capable of learning simple habits, although it is still under the influence of the drug. When the drug wears off, however, the learning that occurred while the animal was in the drugged state is not retained. If the animal is again given sodium pentobarbital, however, he is again able to perform the learned response. Likewise, habits that are learned while in the undrugged state are not available to the animal when he is drugged; this means that the habits were *drug specific*. For example, Overton found he could teach an animal to turn right to avoid a shock while drugged, and to turn left to avoid a shock while undrugged. One tentative interpretation of these results is that the drug causes the animal to use different neural circuits while learning than he would ordinarily use. This is related to Lashley's notion of equipotentiality, which states that one area of the brain can take over for another area that is incapacitated in some way. A Guthrian might say that the stimulating conditions in the drugged

and undrugged states are altogether different and therefore separate response systems could become conditioned to them.

RESEARCH ON BRAIN WAVES

In 1929, Hans Berger discovered that the human brain was continuously
emitting waves of electrical energy and that by placing electrodes on the
scalp, it is possible to record these waves. Such a recording is called an
electroencephalogram or *EEG*. The most important aspect of EEG waves
is that they vary according to a person's conscious state. When a person
has his eyes closed and is relaxed, he will emit brain waves with a frequency of 8 to 10 cycles per second, called *alpha waves* or alpha rhythms.
The brain activity of the person who is sleeping lightly is characterized
by a mixture of slow waves and fast waves, and a person in deep sleep
emits very slow waves called *delta waves,* which are between 2 and 5
cycles per second. When a person is awake and attending to something
or is engaged in problem solving, brain activity is characterized by rapid
desynchronized rhythms called *beta waves.* When a resting, relaxed individual solves a problem mentally, such as dividing one number by another, alpha waves are blocked and replaced by beta waves. When the
problem is solved, the alpha waves return. As we saw when we discussed
arousal theory earlier in this chapter, EEG patterns have also been used
to measure level of emotional excitement. The faster the electrical activity
of the brain, the greater is the emotional excitement. Various brain wave
patterns are shown in Figure 13–6.

Figure 13–6. Electroencephalograms showing Beta, Alpha and Delta
brain activity (from Jasper, 1941).

Brain Wave Conditioning.

One kind of brain wave conditioning that has received considerable attention recently is that of alpha wave blocking. In such an experiment, the subject is first made to relax so that he is emitting alpha waves. While he is relaxed, he is stimulated with a flash of light that causes the alpha waves to block and be replaced by beta waves. A tone is introduced to the subject and it, too, originally causes alpha blocking. Gradually, however, the response to the tone habituates (the person no longer responds to it), and therefore no longer blocks his alpha waves. Next, the tone and the light are paired in accordance with the principles of classical conditioning. First, the tone is presented and then the light. The light, of course, still causes alpha blocking. Eventually the tone alone causes alpha waves to block. In this situation, the light acts as an unconditioned stimulus; the tone acts as the conditioned stimulus; the alpha blocking in response to the light is the unconditioned response; and the alpha blocking in response to the tone is the conditioned response. One of the most interesting things about the conditioning of alpha blocking is that it apparently takes place without any overt responding by the organism. Indeed, Black (1971) has recently trained dogs to control their brain waves while under the influence of a drug that causes total muscle paralysis.

A second kind of brain wave conditioning is called *alpha wave driving*. In this situation, a flickering light is presented to the subject at a frequency slightly above or slightly below a normal alpha rhythm (about 8 to 10 cycles per second). Usually the brain waves will track, or copy, the frequency of the flickering light; that is, if the frequency of the light is 12 cps, the frequency of the brain wave will be 12 cps. This is generally referred to as *photic driving*. If a tone to which the subject has been habituated is consistently presented prior to the flashing light, the tone alone will eventually cause the brain to respond with waves of the same frequency as the flashing light. In other words, the brain wave frequency corresponding to the flashing light can now be elicited by simply presenting the tone. See Morrell (1961) for a review of both brain wave conditioning and photic driving studies.

Learning in the Single Neuron.

We have been talking about gross EEG activity from large areas of the brain and found that such activity can be conditioned. This finding has been met with considerable interest and excitement, but even more interesting was the finding by Morrell (1963) that single neurons in the brain are also conditionable. Using a tiny microelectrode, Morrell measured the electrical activity in a single neuron in the visual cortex as the animal was being stimulated with flashes of light. It was found that the neuron responded in a pattern similar to that of the flashing light, that is, there was photic driving. In other words, if the flashes of light were presented at a rate of 3 per second, the nerve cell would respond with bursts of activity at a rate of about 3 per second. Most interesting, however, was the finding that eventually the cell would respond about 3 times per second even when it was presented with only one flash of light. Furthermore, the cell continued its rate of about 3-per-second responses for about 20 minutes after the cell was actually driven by 3-per-second flashes of light. Although there are many unanswered questions about this phenomenon, it appears to indicate that processes similar to learning and memory take place in the single cortical cell.

The Willful Control of Brain Activity.

Recently, it has been found that not only is brain activity conditionable, but it can also be voluntarily controlled (see, for example, Nowlis and Kamiya, 1970). In the typical test situation, the subject is asked to guess in which one of two states he is—alpha or non-alpha—and then he is told whether or not he was correct. Under these conditions, most subjects learn to detect accurately which of the two states they are in. Once they can discriminate between the two states, they somehow are able to think themselves into one state or the other. For example, if a circuit is arranged so that a light or a tone comes on when an alpha wave is being produced, the subject can turn the light or tone on at will. Exactly how individuals control their own brain waves is yet unknown.

VISCERAL CONDITIONING

The individual's control over his own internal environment is currently being expanded into such areas as heart-rate control, blood pressure control, and skin temperature control. Until recently, it was believed that operant conditioning was possible only for responses that involve the skeletal or striped muscles and that responses involving the smooth muscles and glands could not be operantly conditioned. The smooth muscles and glands are controlled by the autonomic nervous system and, generally, it was believed that responses mediated by the autonomic nervous system could not be operantly conditioned.

To demonstrate that autonomic responses could be operantly conditioned, Miller and Carmona (1967) gave one group of thirsty dogs water whenever they salivated spontaneously. Another group of thirsty dogs

Neal E. Miller

was given water for going for long intervals of time without salivating. The rate of salivation went up for the former group and down for the latter group. Thus, it was demonstrated that salivation, which is governed by the autonomic nervous system, was modifiable through operant conditioning procedures.

In other studies, Miller has taught curarized rats to raise or lower their heart rate, to raise or lower their blood pressure, to modify the functioning of their kidneys, and even to vary the amount of blood in their left and right ears. Curare is a drug that paralyzes the skeletal muscles so their involvement could not have been a factor in this research. Miller used direct stimulation of the reward areas of the brain as reinforcement for his curarized animals.

Shapiro, Tursky, Gerson, and Stern (1969) taught twenty male college students to raise or lower their blood pressure by showing them a picture of a nude female from *Playboy* magazine whenever the student's blood pressure was altered in the direction desired by the experimenter. At the conclusion of the experiment, the students, with only two exceptions, were unaware of the fact that their blood pressure had been systematically altered by the experimenter.

In other studies, heart patients have been taught to control their cardiac abnormalities, epileptics have learned to suppress abnormal brain activity, and individuals suffering from migraine headaches have learned to avoid them by controlling the degree of dilatation of blood vessels surrounding the brain. In cases such as these, a device is used to display to the patient the changes in the internal events that he is trying to control, e.g., high blood pressure or irregular heart activity. Such a display is called *biofeedback* because it provides the patient with information about some internal biological event. Usually after monitoring the biofeedback for a period of time, the patient becomes aware of his internal state and can respond accordingly —either raise or lower his blood pressure—without the aid of biofeedback. Obviously, this whole area of research, sometimes called *visceral conditioning,* has vast implications for the practice of medicine in the future. For a more detailed review of visceral conditioning research see DiCara, 1970; Jonas, 1973; Kimmel, 1974; and Miller, 1969.

Although research using the neurophysiological paradigm is diffuse and unrelated, with the exception of Hebb's work, it is beginning to contribute to our further understanding of the learning process. In Chapter 3, it was said that our understanding of the learning process is enhanced when viewed from different angles. The neurophysiological paradigm provides us with one additional viewing angle.

DISCUSSION QUESTIONS

1. Why have physiological explanations of learning been unpopular until recently?
2. According to Hebb, what are the main differences between adult learning and childhood learning?
3. What are the main differences between the reinforcement that comes from a direct brain stimulation and "natural" reinforcement? What are some implications of direct brain stimulation for human behavior modification?
4. Briefly summarize consolidation theory.
5. How might Guthrie explain "drug specific habits"? How might he explain drug addiction?
6. How might Hebb explain dreams? For example, why might a backfiring car cause a person to have a crime-related dream?
7. How might Hebb explain the Gestalt principle of closure?

8. Briefly summarize arousal theory.

9. In your opinion, have the switchboard or the Gestalt interpretations of brain functioning received the greatest amount of experimental support? Explain.

10. Discuss the possible implications of visceral conditioning for the practice of medicine.

GLOSSARY

Alpha wave blocking.   The disruption of alpha waves by the presentation of an external stimulus or by asking the subject to engage in some mental operation, such as working out an arithmetic problem. In both cases, alpha waves are blocked and are replaced by beta waves.

Alpha wave driving.   Changing the frequency of alpha waves by presenting an external stimulus, such as a light, at a certain frequency. For example, if a light is flashed 12 times per second, the alpha waves will tend to occur at a frequency of 12 per second.

Alpha waves.   A brain wave pattern of about 8 to 10 cycles per second produced by a relaxed organism.

Arousal function of a stimulus.   That function of a stimulus that increases the activity of the reticular activating system, thereby increasing the electrical activity in certain higher centers of the brain.

Arousal theory.   The contention that brain wave activity ranges from very fast to very slow with a rate in between that allows for the optimal performance of certain tasks.

Beta waves.   Very fast brain wave activity—that is, over 12 cycles per second—produced by a mentally active organism.

Biofeedback.   The information provided to an individual by some mechanical device concerning the status of one or more of his internal biological events. For example, a flashing light can be set to reflect heart rate or an auditory signal can be triggered when blood pressure goes beyond a certain level.

Cell assembly.   The pattern of neural activity that is caused when an environmental object or event is experienced. When the cell assembly is well developed, the person is able to think of the entire event following the stimulation of the assembly, even if the object itself or the event is physically absent.

Consolidation period.   The period of time when short-term memory of an experience is converted into long-term memory.

Corpus callosum.   A massive bundle of fibers that connects the two hemispheres of the cortex.

Cue function of a stimulus.   That function of a stimulus that provides us with information about the environment.

Delta waves.   A slow brain wave pattern of about 2 to 5 cycles per second, characteristic of deep sleep.

Drug-specific habits.   Habits that appear when a drug is active, but disappear when the drug is inactive.

Electroconvulsive shock.   A severe shock that causes convulsions, thereby preventing the electrical activity that appears to be necessary for consolidation to take place.

Electroencephalogram (EEG).   A recording of the electrical activity in the brain usually taken by placing electrodes on the scalp of the subject. (Also called electroencephalograph.)

Equipotentiality.   The finding that the cortex functions as a whole and that if one part of the cortex is destroyed, any one of a number of cortical areas can take over its function.

Evoked potential.   A burst of electrical activity at some point in the brain caused by the presentation of an external stimulus.

Hippocampus.   A brain structure within the limbic system thought to be involved in the conversion of short-term memory into long-term memory.

Limbic system.   A number of interrelated brain areas believed to be related to emotional experience.

Long-term memory.   Also called secondary memory. The memory of an experience that lasts for a considerable length of time after the experience. Whereas short-term memory is usually measured in terms of seconds, long-term memory can be measured in terms of years.

Mass action.   The finding that disruption of learning and memory is a function of the amount of cortical tissue destroyed.

Microelectrode.   A very small electrode, usually between .5 and 5 microns in diameter, which is used to stimulate and/or record from specific areas in the brain or from individual nerve cells.

Optimal level of arousal.   The level of brain activity that is most conducive to the performance of a certain task (*see the* Yerkes-Dodson law).

Phase sequence.   A sequence of temporarily related cell assemblies. Cell assemblies that consistently follow one another in time form a unit or a phase sequence.

Photic driving. Presenting a visual stimulus at a certain frequency, thereby causing brain waves to occur with the same frequency. (*See Alpha wave driving for an example.*)

Punishment centers in the brain. Areas of the brain that, when stimulated, cause the organism to refrain from whatever behavior preceded their stimulation.

Retrograde amnesia. The inability to remember the events that took place just prior to a traumatic experience, such as an automobile accident.

Reticular activating system. A structure located in the brain stem that appears to be responsible for regulating the electrical activity in the higher centers of the brain.

Reverberating neural activity. A system of self-perpetuating neural activity that lasts for a few seconds after the source of stimulation has been removed. Reverberating neural activity is thought by some to be the basis of short-term memory.

Reward centers in the brain. Areas of the brain which, when stimulated, cause the organism to repeat whatever behavior preceded their stimulation.

Short-term memory. Also called immediate memory and primary memory. The memory of an experience that persists for only a short period of time after the experience.

Split-brain preparation. The arrangement where both the optic chiasm and the corpus callosum are severed, thereby causing the two halves of the cortex to function independently.

Spreading depression. The reduced cortical activity that follows the application of potassium chloride to the cortex.

Visceral conditioning. The conditioning of internal organs under the control of the autonomic nervous system, such as the stomach, intestines, heart, bladder, or arteries.

Yerkes-Dodson law. The observation that if arousal level is either too high or too low, performance is inferior to what it would be if arousal was at an intermediate level. The arousal level resulting in best performance is called the optimal level of arousal.

14

Implications for Education

We begin this chapter with an attempt to relate the major theories of learning covered in the preceding chapters to educational practices. The specification of this relationship is easier for some theories than with others. Theorists such as Thorndike and Skinner, for example, have written extensively about how their views on learning relate to teaching practices. For them, therefore, what follows is mainly a review of the material that was covered earlier in this text. Theorists like Pavlov and Hull, however, never made an effort to extend their theory to the realm of education. With Piaget's theory, the relationship between theory and educational practice, although never stated directly, appears to be fairly obvious. Tolman's theory of learning is especially difficult to relate to education since he postulated six different kinds of learning. In our treatment of his theory below, we emphasize only the kind of learning that he called "cognitive."

After discussing what each of the major theorists says, or seems to say, about education, we will turn to some of the more general differences between cognitive and behavioristic theories as they apply to the classroom.

APPLICATION OF SPECIFIC THEORIES OF
LEARNING TO THE CLASSROOM

Thorndike.

Thorndike would have an orderly classroom with the objectives clearly defined. These educational objectives must be within the learner's response capabilities and they must be divided into manageable units so that the teacher can apply "a satisfying state of affairs" when the learner makes an appropriate response. Learning proceeds from the simple to the complex.

Motivation is relatively unimportant, except in determining what will constitute a "satisfying state of affairs" for the learner. The learner's behavior is determined primarily by external rewards and not by intrinsic motivation. Emphasis is on bringing about correct responses to certain stimuli. Incorrect responses are to be corrected rapidly so that they are not practiced and thereby strengthened. Therefore, examinations are important: they provide the learner and the teacher with feedback concerning the learning process. If the student learns his lesson well, he is to be rewarded quickly. If the student has learned something incorrectly, his mistake must be corrected quickly; thus examinations must be taken regularly.

The learning situation must be made to resemble the "real world" as much as possible. As we have seen, Thorndike believed that learning will transfer from the classroom to the environment outside only insofar as the two situations are similar. Teaching the child to solve difficult problems does not enhance his reasoning capacity. Therefore, teaching Latin, mathematics, or logic is only justified insofar as the student will be solving problems involving Latin, mathematics, or logic when he leaves school. With his identical elements theory of transfer of training, Thorndike opposed the traditional formal discipline or "mental muscle" approach to explaining transfer.

Guthrie.

Like Thorndike, Guthrie would begin the educational process by stating objectives, that is, stating what responses are to be made to what stimuli. Then he would have the learning environment arranged so that the desired responses are elicited in the presence of the stimuli that they are supposed to be attached to.

Motivation is even less important for Guthrie than it was for Thorndike.

All that is necessary for Guthrie is that the student respond appropriately in the presence of certain stimuli.

Practice is important in that it causes more and more stimuli to elicit desired behavior. Since each experience is unique, one must "relearn" things over and over again. Guthrie would say that learning to add two and two at the blackboard is no guarantee that the student will add two and two at his seat. The student must not only learn that two red blocks plus two more equals four red blocks, but he must make new two-plus-two-equals-four associations with apples, or dogs, or books.

Although learning constantly takes place, classroom education is an attempt to purposefully associate certain stimuli and responses. Learning, however, can be easily interfered with outside the classroom if new responses are made in the presence of stimuli similar to the ones the student experienced in school. It is also possible that a student will learn to attach responses to the stimuli in the classroom and another set of responses to similar stimuli outside the classroom. For example, seeing an elderly person in school may tend to elicit "respectful" behavior, whereas an elderly person experienced outside of school may elicit "disrespectful" behavior.

Like Thorndike, Guthrie believed that formal education should resemble real-life situations as much as possible.

Hull.

The major differences among Hull, Thorndike, and Guthrie concerned their emphasis on motivation. You will recall that Hull's was a drive reduction, or a drive-stimulus reduction, theory of learning. As for the issues of specifiability of objectives, orderliness of the classrooms, and proceeding from the simple to the complex, Hull would be in agreement with Thorndike and Guthrie. Learning for him, however, must involve a reducible drive. It is hard to imagine how the reduction of a primary drive can play a part in classroom learning; however, some of Hull's followers have emphasized anxiety as a drive in human learning. From this line of reasoning, it would follow that encouraging some anxiety in students, that would subsequently be reduced by success, would be a necessary conditioning for classroom learning. Too little anxiety would result in no learning (because there is no drive to be reduced) and too much anxiety would be disruptive. Therefore, students who are mildly anxious are in the best position to learn and are therefore easiest to teach. Practice would be carefully distributed so that inhibition would not be built up. The Hullian teacher would intersperse subjects so that the learner would not build up fatigue that would interfere with his learning. Likewise, subjects would be arranged so that those that are maximally dissimilar would follow each other. For example, one reasonable sequence of subjects may be math, physical education, English, art, and history. This, of course, would reduce fatigue and facilitate attention span.

Miller and Dollard (1941) have summarized Hull's theory as it applies to education:

Drive: The learner must want something
Cue: The learner must attend to something
Response: The learner must do something
Reward: The learner's response must get him something he wants.

Skinner.

Skinner, of course, has much in common with the theorists mentioned so far. For example, he would insist that the course objectives be completely specified before teaching commences. Further, he would insist that the objectives be defined *behaviorally*. If a unit is designed to teach creativity, he would ask "What is a student *doing* when he is being creative?" If a unit is designed to teach the understanding of history, he would ask, "What is a student *doing* when he is understanding history?" If educational objectives cannot be specified behaviorally, an instructor has no way of knowing whether or not he has accomplished what he had set out to do. Likewise, if objectives are specified in terms not easily transformed into behavioral terms, it is next to impossible to determine to what extent the course objectives have been met. We will have more to say about behavioral objectives later in this chapter.

The stimuli associated with certain responses are not as important for Skinner as they are for Thorndike, Guthrie, or Hull. Skinner is more interested in starting with the responses as they occur "naturally," or, if they do not occur naturally, *shaping* them into existence. As with most behaviorists, he would start with the simple and proceed to the complex. Complex behavior is thought to consist of simpler forms of behavior. Skinner's approach to presenting material to be learned is best exemplified by programmed learning, to which we will turn in the next section.

As with Thorndike, motivation to Skinner is only important in determining what will act as a reinforcer for a given student. Food deprivation will cause food to become a reinforcer or water deprivation will cause water to become a reinforcer. Secondary reinforcers are very important, too, since these are normally utilized in the classroom. Examples of secondary reinforcers would include verbal praise, positive facial expressions, gold stars, feelings of success, points, grades, and the opportunity to work on what one wants to.

It is also important for Skinner to move from a 100 percent reinforcement schedule to a partial reinforcement schedule. During the early stages of training, a correct response is rewarded each time it occurs. Later, however, it is only rewarded periodically. This, of course, makes the response more resistant to extinction.

All the S–R behaviorists would prescribe a learning environment that allows for individual differences in learning rate. They would either want to deal with students individually, or provide a group of students with material that allows for individual self-pacing, such as teaching machines or specially constructed workbooks. The behaviorists would tend to avoid the lecture technique since there is no way of knowing when learning is taking place or when to administer rewards. We will have more to say about both individualized courses and the lecture technique later in this chapter.

The Skinnerian teacher would avoid the use of punishment. He would reward appropriate behavior and ignore inappropriate behavior, and thereby, hopefully, extinguish it. Since the learning environment is designed so that the student experiences maximal success, he usually attends to the material to be learned. According to the Skinnerians, behavior problems in school are the result of poor educational planning, such as failure to provide self-pacing, failure to use rewards appropriately, offering the material in chunks too large to be easily comprehended, using discipline to control behavior, having rigid plans that all students must follow, or making unreasonable demands on students (such as not moving or not making noise).

Gestalt Theory.

The Gestalt-oriented teacher would stress meaningfulness and understanding. Parts must always be related to a whole so that they have meaning to the student. Historical names or dates will have little meaning unless they are related to current events or to something personally important to the student. An understanding of history is the important thing and it is gained by studying individual events. But the whole understanding of history is always greater than the sum of the individual events.

As we have seen, the Gestaltists view unsolved problems as creating ambiguity or an organizational disbalance in the student's mind, a condition that is unnatural. In fact, ambiguity is looked upon as a negative state that persists until a problem is solved. The student confronted with a problem will either seek new information or will rearrange old information until he gains insight into the solution of the problem. The solution is as satisfying to the problem-solver as a hamburger is to a hungry person. In a sense, the reduction of ambiguity can be seen as the Gestalt equivalent to the behaviorist's notion of reinforcement. However, the reduction of ambiguity can be thought of as an "intrinsic" reward, while the behaviorists usually stress external, or "extrinsic," rewards.

Jerome Bruner, while discussing curiosity as an innate human motive, comes close to what the Gestaltists refer to as a need to reduce ambiguity. Bruner says (1966):

> Curiosity is almost a prototype of the intrinsic motive. Our attention is attracted to something that is unclear, unfinished, or uncertain. We sustain our attention until the matter on hand becomes clear, finished, or certain. The achievement of clarity or merely the search for it is what satisfies. We would think it preposterous if somebody thought to reward us with praise or profit for having satisfied our curiosity [p. 114].

According to Bruner, the teacher's job should not be to find ways of motivating students—they are already motivated. The teacher should take care, however, to encourage these inborn tendencies, especially the will to learn. About the behavioristically oriented teacher who attempts to encourage desired behavior by rewarding it, Bruner says the following (1966):

> You will have noted by now a considerable de-emphasis of "extrinsic" rewards and punishments as factors in school learning. There has been in these pages a rather intentional neglect of the so called law of effect, which holds that a reaction is more likely to be repeated if it has previously been followed by a "satisfying state of affairs." I am not unmindful of the notion of reinforcement. It is doubtful, only, that "satisfying states of affairs" are *reliably* to be found outside learning itself—in kind or harsh words from the teacher, in grades and gold stars, in the absurdly abstract assurance to the high school student that his lifetime earnings will be better by 80 percent if he graduates. External reinforcement may indeed get a particular act going and may even lead to its repetition, but it does not nourish, reliably, the long course of learning by which man slowly builds in his own way a serviceable model of what the world is and what it can be [pp. 127–28].

The Gestalt classroom would be characterized by a give-and-take relationship between student and teacher. The teacher helps the student see relations and to organize his experiences into meaningful patterns. Planning a Gestalt learning experience includes starting with something familiar and basing each step in the educational process on those already taken. All aspects of the course are divided into meaningful units and the units themselves must relate to an overall concept or experience. The Gestalt-oriented teacher would accept the lecture technique as long as it allowed for student-teacher interaction.

Piaget.

Clearly, according to Piaget, educational experiences must be built around the learner's cognitive structure. Children of the same age and from the same culture tend to have similar cognitive structures, but it is entirely possible for them to have different cognitive structures and therefore require different kinds of learning material. Educational material that cannot be assimilated into a child's cognitive structure cannot have any meaning to the child. If, on the other hand, the material can be completely assimilated, no learning will take place. In order for learning to take place, the material needs to be partially known and partially unknown. The part that is known will be assimilated and the part that is unknown will necessitate a slight modification in the child's cognitive structure. Such modification is referred to as accommodation. Accommodation can be roughly equated with learning.

Thus, for Piaget, optimal education involves mildly challenging experiences for the learner so that the dual processes of assimilation and accommodation can provide for intellectual growth. In order to create that kind of experience, the teacher must know the level of functioning of each student's cognitive structure. Since cognitive structure will tend to vary from child to child, so will the material needed to stimulate intellectual growth.

We find, then, that both Piaget (a representative of the cognitive paradigm) and most of the behaviorists reach the same conclusion about education; namely, that it must be *individualized*. Piaget reaches this conclusion by realizing that the ability to assimilate varies from child to child and that educational material must be tailored to each child's cognitive structure. The behaviorists reach the conclusion through their recognition that reward must be contingent upon appropriate behavior and the proper dispensing of rewards requires a one-to-one relationship between the student and the teacher, or between the student and programmed educational material.

Tolman.

In many respects, Tolman and the Gestaltists agree about educational practices: both would emphasize the importance of thinking and understanding. For Tolman, it would be important to have the student test hypotheses in a problem situation. On this matter, Tolman is in close agreement with Harlow's error factor theory, which states that learning is not so much a matter of building up correct responses or strategies as it is a matter of eliminating incorrect responses or strategies. Both Tolman and the Gestalt theorist would encourage small groups for classroom discussions. The important thing is for the student to have the opportunity, individually or as part of a group, to test the adequacy of his ideas. Hypotheses or strategies effective in solving a problem are those that are maintained by the student. The teacher, then, acts as a consultant to assist students in clarifying and then confirming or disconfirming hypotheses.

Like the Gestalt theorist, Tolman would also suggest that the student be exposed to a topic from different viewpoints. This would allow the student to develop a "cognitive map" that could be utilized to answer questions about that particular topic and related topics.

Finally, like the Gestalt theorist, Tolman would say that principles transfer rather than identical stimulus elements or exact procedures. Transfer, according to Tolman, is a matter of transposition, which is the application of a principle or concept learned in one situation to a new but similar situation.

Pavlov.

Pavlovian principles are hard to apply to classroom education, although they are no doubt operating all the time. In general, we can say that every time a neutral event is paired with a meaningful event, classical conditioning occurs; obviously, pairings of that kind take place all the time. When a cologne that was consistently worn by a favorite teacher is experienced later in life, it will tend to elicit favorable memories of school; learning math in a rigid authoritarian atmosphere may create a negative attitude toward math; being made to write something over and over again as a disciplinary action may create a negative attitude toward writing; having difficult subjects in the morning may create at least a mild dislike for mornings; and a likable, knowledgeable male teacher may inspire a young boy student to accept him as a model, or the young girl student to look for someone like him as a mate. The feelings of anxiety associated with failure in school may create an aversion to problem-solving situations outside of school.

Although the influence of classical conditioning in the classroom is strong, it is usually incidental. The principles of classical conditioning, however, can be purposively utilized in an education program, as they were in the case of Albert (see Chapter 7). When Pavlovian techniques are used to modify behavior, the situation appears to resemble brainwashing more than education. To find examples of Pavlovian principles used to modify attitudes, one only needs to carefully observe television commercials. The advertiser's procedure involves pairing a neutral object (the product) with something someone likes (e.g., wealth, health, youth, sex, prestige). Gradually, the product will cause the viewer to have the same feeling that he used to get only from the object or event it was paired with. Next, it is assumed that the viewer will feel successful smoking Brand X cigarettes, be sexier driving a certain kind of car, or be more youthful using a certain hair preparation.

Again, these "incidental" aspects of education are no doubt occurring all the time that a child is in school. The modification of attitudes and emotions involved in learning based on classical conditioning must be taken into consideration in designing any truly effective educational program.

GENERAL DIFFERENCES BETWEEN COGNITIVE AND BEHAVIORISTIC THEORIES

What Is Learned?

In answer to the question the behaviorist would say behavioral habits are learned, whereas the cognitive theorist would answer in terms of a change in cognitive structures. According to the behaviorist, specific responses are learned to specific stimulus situations; according to the cognitivist, an "understanding" is developed which allows for easy response substitution if a commonly used learned response is blocked.

How Are Problems Solved?

Most behaviorists claim a problem is approached in accordance with its similarity to other problems the individual experienced in the past. If the attempted solutions fail, or the learner has never confronted such a problem, he resorts to trial and error behavior until he hits upon a solution. The cognitive theorist maintains that the learner "thinks" about the problem until he gains an insight into its solution. The behaviorist would emphasize *behavioral* trial and error; the cognitivist would emphasize *cognitive,* or vicarious, trial and error.

What Assumptions Are Made About the Learner?

Certainly what a teacher believes to be the nature of the human mind will influence what he believes would be effective teaching practices. We have already seen two examples of this. The behaviorists, who tend to accept Aristotle's and Locke's position that the mind begins as a *tabula rasa* (blank slate), emphasize the importance of sensory experience in formulating the content of the mind. A teacher accepting this position would specify educational objectives in behavioral terms, and then define the kinds of experiences that would bring about the desired behavior. The behavioristically oriented teacher would be more of an arranger than anything else. His most important task is to arrange an environment that is responsive to the behaviors deemed important by the school; that is, he must create an environment that allows the student to be rewarded for behaving in accordance with various course objectives.

The cognitive theorists believe that the mind is not a blank slate at birth and that the mind is active, not passive. The mind is capable of weighing alternatives (thinking) and has the built-in need to reduce ambiguity and to make everything as simple as possible. The teacher accepting this Gestalt point of view is not a mere arranger of the learning environment; rather, he is an active participant in the learner-teacher relationship. The teacher must help the student to see that facts and ideas are part of a larger concept. That the student is able to recite numerous facts without seeing their interrelationship is meaningless to such a teacher. If one took an automobile completely apart and threw all the parts on a pile, it would not be what we ordinarily call an automobile, although all the parts are there. *How* the parts are arranged is at least as important as *what* the parts are. To repeat, the Gestalt point of view always emphasizes that the whole is more than the sum of its parts.

The cognitively oriented teacher's job consists of two things: (1) to induce ambiguity, and (2) help the student clarify the ambiguity. He induces ambiguity by introducing problems and he helps clarify the ambiguity by suggesting strategies for solving the problems. As stated earlier, his classroom practice would involve a give-and-take between himself and his students. Unlike the behavioristically oriented teacher, he would not strongly emphasize working with individual students, and he would be perfectly content to work with small groups. Self-pacing and small-step learning procedures may or may not be important to the Gestalt teacher; their suitability must be determined for each student. He must be able to determine for each student the best strategy for learning; that is, he must know the conceptual basis from where each student is starting before he can help him continue toward understanding the concept being taught. This, of course, is another reason why there must be close contact between the student and the teacher.

How Is the Transfer of Training Explained?

The behaviorist tends to accept Thorndike's identical elements theory of transfer: as the number of common elements in two situations goes up, the tendency to make similar responses in both situations goes up. According to the behaviorist, if you want to enhance transfer of training from classroom education to experiences outside the classroom, you are obliged to increase the similarity between the two situations. For example, if one purpose in teaching mathematics is to provide students with the information necessary for filling out tax forms, the behavioristically oriented teacher would have his students work on tax forms.

The cognitive theorist would tend to emphasize the transfer of principles. Using the tax form example, the cognitively oriented teacher might claim that the learning of mathematical skills will transfer readily to filling out tax forms and grocery shopping, even if tax forms and shopping had not been experienced in the classroom.

The issue of transfer of training, clearly one of the most important problems in education, is still highly controversial. In fact, it appears that the notion of formal discipline, based on faculty psychology, is still alive and well in the American school system. For example, the prominence given the teaching of mathematics in our schools seems to reflect the belief that studying mathematics creates a stronger "reasoning faculty," especially since most Americans require less than a fifth-grade level of proficiency in mathematics for the needs of their daily life. For a discussion of the reappearance of formal discipline in American schools see Kolesnik (1958) or Symonds (1960).

Programmed Learning

Programmed learning incorporates many of the principles of reinforcement theory, although the technique was not invented by a reinforcement theorist. The technique was originally developed by Sidney L. Pressey (1926, 1927). Pressey's "testing machine" was effective, but it did not become popular. Thus, we have another example of *Zeitgeist*—although Pressey's idea was good, it was not appropriate to the spirit of his age at the time he proposed it. It was left to Skinner to rediscover programmed learning and make it popular. Skinner's detailed account of the rationale behind programmed learning can be found in Chapter 5.

1. A mass of data, by itself, would be of little use to a researcher unless he had certain procedures for describing or analyzing it.

2. Procedures used to analyze data are called *statistics*. One important function of statistics is to provide information concerning a distribution of individual datum, or *scores*.

3. Procedures used to "make sense" out of a large number of scores are called

    _____ .   statistics

4. The most common questions researchers ask about scores concern *measures of central tendency* and *measures of variability*.

5. Measures of central tendency provide information about the *typical* or *average* score.

6. Measures of variability provide information about how the scores are spread out—that is, how dispersed they are.

7. Measures of central tendency and measures of variability are both procedures used to

    "make sense" out of a distribution of scores. They are therefore both called

    _____ .   statistics

8. Measures of central tendency are used to find the _____ score.   typical/average/
                                                                              representative

9. In order to find information about the dispersion of scores we use measures of

    _____ .   variability

10. There is no one measure of central tendency; there are many. Which one is used depends on the situation. Three of the most commonly used are the *mode*, the *mean*, and the *median*.

11. The average score in a distribution is found by using a measure of _____   central

    _____ .   tendency

12. The mode is merely the score that occurs most frequently in a distribution of scores.

13. The score occurring most frequently in a distribution is called the _____ .   mode

14. What is the mode of this distribution?

20	
18	
18	
18	_____ 18
17	
17	
13	
12	

15. Is 18 the *average* score of the above distribution? _____   yes

16. Is 18 the *typical* score of the above distribution? _____   yes

17. The *mean*, like the mode, is a measure of _____   central
                                                                              tendency

18. The mean is found by first adding up all the scores in the distribution and then dividing the sum by the number of scores in the distribution. This can be summarized as follows:

    $$\frac{\Sigma X}{N}$$

    Where: Σ = add everything that follows
         X = a score in the distribution
         N = the total number of scores

19. The mean is found by first adding up all the _____ in the   scores

    _____ and then _____ the sum by the _____ of   distribution
                                                                              dividing
    scores in the distribution.   number

Figure 14–1. An example of a linear program where all students cover the same information in the same order (from Hergenhahn, 1974).

Skinner's approach to programming has been called *linear* and involves the following features derived from his theory of learning:

1. **Small steps.** The learner is exposed to small amounts of information and proceeds from one frame, or one item of information, to the next in an orderly fashion. This is what is meant by a linear program.
2. **Overt responding.** The student is required to respond overtly so that his correct responses can be rewarded and his incorrect responses can be corrected.
3. **Immediate feedback.** Immediately after making a response, the student is informed as to whether it is correct or not. This feedback acts as a reward if the answer was correct and as a corrective measure if the answer was wrong.
4. **Self-pacing.** The student proceeds through the program at his own pace.

Figure 14–1 provides an example of a Skinnerian linear program.

There are a number of variations of the linear program. For example, some provide the student with the opportunity to skip information that he is already familiar with. This procedure usually involves giving the student a pretest on a certain section of the program, and if he performs adequately he is instructed to advance to the next section.

Another kind of programming that allows for even more flexibility is the *branching* program. The branching program is much more complicated than the linear program, since it attempts to *diagnose* the student's responses. The branching program usually involves a multiple choice format. After the student has been presented a certain amount of information, he is given a multiple choice question. If he answers correctly, he advances to the next body of information. If he answers incorrectly, he is directed to additional information, depending on the mistake he made. For example, the program may say "If you picked *B* as your answer, go back and review the material on page 24; if you picked *D* as your answer, repeat Section 3; if you chose *A*, you are correct; please proceed to the next section." Diagrams of various programming techniques are shown in Figure 14–2.

Linear Programming

Modified Linear Programs

a. Linear program where information can be skipped if it is too easy or already known:

b. Conversational chaining where the answer to a question asked in a previous frame is answered somewhere in the next frame:

Branching Program

With the Branching program, the student's response is used more as a
diagnostic tool than a learning device. Typically with this kind of program, the student is instructed to move forward in the program if he
answers a question correctly. If he answers incorrectly, however, he is
instructed to different parts of the program *depending on what kind of
mistake the student makes.* He may, for example, be instructed to repeat
an entire section of the program or he may be directed to other information which attempts to clarify his particular type of misunderstanding.
In either case he is again tested and thereafter proceeds through the
program in a manner dictated by his performance on the test.

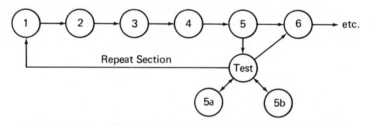

Figure 14–2 .   Diagrams of various programming techniques.

The generalizations from reinforcement theory upon which programmed learning is based can be summarized as follows:

1. An individual must have feedback in order to learn. That is, he must have
   the opportunity to determine whether or not his action or thought was
   correct. Ordinarily, reward acts as feedback in a learning situation.
2. The more quickly a reward follows a desired act, the greater is the likelihood that the act will be repeated. Absence or delay of reward following an act reduces the likelihood that the act will be repeated.
3. The more often an act is rewarded, the more likely the act will be
   repeated.
4. Through the process of differential reinforcement and successive approximation, a student's behavior can be shaped toward a desired goal.
5. A student's behavior can be developed into a complex pattern by first
   shaping the basic elements of the pattern and then combining the elements into a chainlike sequence.

Is Programmed Learning Effective?

Schramm (1964) reviewed 165 studies of programmed learning. Of the 36 studies that compared programmed instruction with the more traditional kinds of instruction, 17 found programmed instruction to be more effective than traditional instruction; 18 found both kinds of instruction to be equally effective, and only 1 found traditional techniques to be more effective than programmed ones. Therefore, the answer seems to be that programmed learning *is* effective, at least in the areas where it has been tried thus far.

The question as to *why* it is effective is not so easily answered. At present, there is widespread disagreement concerning which aspect of programmed learning results in its effectiveness. For example, the Guthrians maintain that programming is effective because it assures that an appropriate response terminates each frame. It is this event, and not the rewarding of overt responses, as the Skinnerians would claim, that makes for effective learning (see, for example, Lumsdaine, 1964). Controversy also exists over the importance of all other aspects of programmed learning, for instance, the nature and importance of knowledge of results, what constitutes a "small step," and the importance of self-pacing. At this time it can be concluded that programmed learning is an effective teaching device, but the essential ingredients that make it effective are still a matter of speculation.

EDUCATIONAL OBJECTIVES STATED IN BEHAVIORAL TERMS

Clearly, the best teaching technique is the one that allows the teacher to most effectively and efficiently meet his course objectives. Any teaching method must be evaluated in terms of course objectives. This means that an instructor must be able to determine whether or not, and to what extent, the objectives of his course have been met. In other words, performance on each course objective must be measurable, and unless the objectives manifest themselves in behavior, they cannot be measured. The course objectives should tell the students what the instructor hopes they will learn in the course, and the evaluative devices, such as examinations, should allow both the instructor and the student to determine to what extent the objectives were met.

In *Preparing Instructional Objectives* (1961) Mager puts the matter as follows:

> Suppose I offered to teach your children to be logical thinkers for $1,000. Now, if I could do it, you would be getting a real bargain.

Robert F. Mager

> But would you agree to such a bargain unless I told you before-
> hand more explicitly what I intended to accomplish and how we
> would measure my success? I hope not. In a sense, a teacher makes
> a contract with his students. The students agree to pay a certain
> sum in return for certain skills and knowledge. But most of the
> time, they are expected to pay for something that is never carefully
> defined or described. They are asked to buy (with effort) a prod-
> uct that they are not allowed to see and that is only vaguely de-
> scribed. The teacher, who does not describe to the best of his
> ability how he intends the learner to be different after his instruc-
> tion, is certainly taking unfair advantage of his students [p. 16a].

Preparing measurable educational objectives is difficult, since educational goals have traditionally been stated in subjective terms. Mager
(1972, p. vi) calls these subjective goals "Fuzzies" because "There is no
way of telling when you have one." In order to "unfuzzify" an abstract
concept or goal, Mager suggests a *goal analysis* involving the following
steps (1972):

1. Write down the goal.
2. Jot down, in words or phrases, the performances that, if achieved, would cause you to agree the goal is achieved.
3. Sort out the jottings. Delete duplications and unwanted items. Repeat steps one and two for any unwanted abstractions (Fuzzies) considered important.
4. Write a complete statement for each performance, describing the nature, quality, or amount you will consider acceptable.
5. Test the statements with the question, If someone achieved or demonstrated each of these performances, would I be willing to say he has achieved the goal? When you can answer yes, the analysis is finished [p. 72].

Elsewhere, Mager (1961, p. 11) offers a comparison between some words used in defining educational objectives that are easily translated into behavior and some that are not (i.e., Fuzzies):

Words open to many interpretations	Words open to fewer interpretations
To know	To write
To understand	To recite
To really understand	To identify
To appreciate	To differentiate
To fully appreciate	To solve
To grasp the significance of	To construct
To enjoy	To list
To believe	To compare
To have faith in	To contrast

It should be noted that what applies to defining course objectives also applies to defining institutional objectives. For example, the extent to which institutional objectives—such as "to realize the interrelatedness of knowledge" or "to fully appreciate the impact of one's values on one's behavior"—have been met would be very difficult to determine.

What often happens is that an instructor will include such course objectives as "to develop an appreciation for" or "to develop a positive attitude toward" or "to note the interrelatedness of" while the grade in the course is based entirely on a midterm and a final examination that test the students' recall of factual material. To be more honest, that instructor should state his course objective simply as "to cause students to memorize the major historical facts surrounding the Revolutionary War." This way, what the student expects is what he gets. Furthermore, the instructor is in a position to evaluate various means of teaching those facts, such as, different textbooks, lectures, programmed learning, or audio tapes. If the instructor insists on believing he is changing attitudes, or appreciations, or understanding, instead of teaching factual material, he will tend to be far less experimental with his teaching techniques. This reluctance to experiment results from the fact that it is far easier to note a change in how well factual material is learned as a function of various teaching techniques, than it is to detect changes in a student's attitude, appreciation, or understanding. That is not to say that understandings and appreciations are not important. Rather, the point is that if understandings and appreciations are to be listed as course objectives, the instructor should state what behaviors he is willing to accept as evidence that students have increased their understanding and appreciation as a function of his course.

Alternative Ways of Meeting Course Objectives.

One advantage in having clearly stated, measurable course objectives is that students can choose among alternative ways of meeting those objectives. A student may wish to take the class as it is arranged by the instructor, or he may meet the course objectives by independent reading, related employment, travel, interviewing certain individuals, or writing a research report. Once course objectives are stated in measurable terms, it is possible to determine the extent to which anyone has met them. It need not matter where or how the necessary information was gathered. If someone can demonstrate that he has met the course objectives, he can be given credit in the course.

If an instructor maintains that a student will miss something important by bypassing the regular course format, he should be able to specify what the student will miss and add it as a course objective. For example, if the instructor maintains that the students gain unique information from his lectures, he should list as one of the course objectives "to gain information from my lectures that cannot be gained elsewhere." Of course, he would be obliged to specify the nature of that information.

How Is a Distribution of Test Scores to Be Interpreted?

Regardless of how course objectives are stated, by far the most commonly used method of evaluating students in a class is the achievement test. The achievement test can take many forms: multiple choice, long essay, short essay, completion items, or true-false. By definition, an achievement test measures to what extent a student has achieved something. More often than not, an achievement test measures to what extent the student has memorized factual information. This is in spite of the fact that objectives for the course may include such terms as "to understand," "to appreciate," "to grasp the significance of," or "to see the interrelatedness of." No doubt, the reason for this discrepancy between course objectives and what is actually tested for is that the extent to which facts have been memorized is relatively easier to measure than such things as "knowing," "understanding," and "appreciating." Very seldom is attitude toward learning measured before and after a course, although one course objective may be to create a positive attitude toward learning.

Since performance on achievement tests is the main factor in determining a student's grade in a course, our remarks here will be directed mainly to that kind of test. Let us take as our example a midterm examination given to a class of 50 students with the following distribution of test scores:

Points Possible = 100
Range = 97–47 = 51 points
N = 50 students
91–100   1111
81–90   ḺḤT 111
71–80   ḺḤT ḺḤT ḺḤT 1
61–70   ḺḤT ḺḤT 1
51–60   ḺḤT 1
41–50   ḺḤT

How is this distribution of scores to be interpreted? Obviously, the students in the class showed different levels of achievement. But why did they? Does the distribution of scores reflect different degrees of motivation in the students? Do the scores vary with the intelligence of the students? Do higher scores reflect a greater degree of interest on the part of the students who obtained them? Is it a combination of the above factors that produce the distribution? Or is it perhaps differences in life circumstances that produce the varying scores? For example, can the variety of scores be generated by the fact that some students have part-time jobs, are married, carry a course overload, or have been ill? In fact, any number of factors could influence test performance when everyone is given the test at the same time.

The instructor may claim that these factors are irrelevant; a student either knows the material or he does not. The instructor may argue that each student in the class had time to prepare for the test and was able to organize his life accordingly. Following this point of view, the midterm becomes a test of organizational ability, and the course content is only a part of what is being tested. In other words, some students will be more ready for the test than others because they were able to deal more adequately with their personal problems. The main problem with this point of view is that "general problem solving ability" was probably not listed as a course objective despite the fact that differing degrees of this ability will play a major role in assigning final grades in the course.

Whenever a distribution of scores on an achievement test is used to assign grades, the implication is that all the information of the course was available for the student, and if he was unable to understand or assimilate the information it is his own fault. In other words, the course is right, and the student is wrong. A growing number of teachers, however, accept the opposite point of view: a distribution of test scores indicates poor teaching. In other words, they believe that when a student performs less than adequately in a course, something is wrong with the course, not with the student.

PERSONALIZED SYSTEMS OF INSTRUCTION

What is now called "a personalized system of instruction" or PSI was originally called the "Keller Plan" after Fred Keller who developed it (Keller, 1968). Keller argues that calling this approach to education the Keller Plan is unfortunate since (1) he was not alone in developing it, (2) someone may try it and fail, in which case he wouldn't want his name

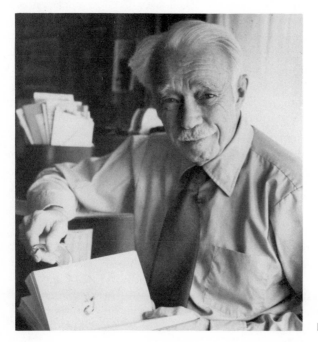

Fred S. Keller

associated with it, and (3) he may come up with an even better plan in the future. So, although Keller can be looked upon as responsible for the development of personalized instruction, we now refer to such instruction as PSI rather than the Keller Plan.

At the present time there is a strong trend in this country toward individualized instruction. Offering an individualized course usually involves four steps which can be summarized as follows:

1. Determine the material to be covered in the course.
2. Divide the material into self-contained segments.
3. Create methods of evaluating the degree to which the student has conquered the material in a given segment.
4. Allow students to move from segment to segment at their own pace.

These are the main ingredients in most individualized courses; but even after one has decided upon individualized instruction, there are a number of arbitrary decisions to be made. For example:

1. What material should be included in the course?
2. How many individual segments should the course contain?
3. What should a segment consist of? (For example, reading assignments, films, audio tapes, field trips, a programmed unit, travel, attending a play or concert or speech, conducting an interview with a politician or an author, conducting an experiment, etc.)
4. How is performance on a given segment to be evaluated? (For example, essay exam, multiple choice exam, oral exam, a research project, a written report, etc.)
5. What degree of proficiency will be required? (For example, an instructor may demand complete mastery in one segment of the course before the student is permitted to commence with the next segment.)
6. Should any time limit be imposed on the students as to when they must finish individual segments or the entire course? (For example, the instructor may say that all students must finish the course no later than the end of the academic term; however, within that period, students can move from segment to segment at whatever pace they feel is best for them.)

What does individualizing a course do to test score distributions? The answer to this question depends on how the instructor deals with item 5 above, degree of proficiency required. For example, if the instructor demands complete mastery of each segment, there will be no distribution of scores. Each student finishing the course will receive the same grade, presumably an A. But the instructor may not demand complete mastery on one segment before the student is allowed to proceed to the next. The instructor may just test over the material in a segment and how well the student does on the test will determine what grade he receives on that segment. Since, in an individualized course, the student decides for himself when he is ready to take a test, the latter procedure also results in a very restricted distribution of test scores.

Even when complete mastery is not required, students in an individualized course will generally obtain *As* or *Bs* as a final grade. This is because, within an individualized course, many personal factors that cause test score distributions are eliminated. If the student is ill, emotionally disturbed, overloaded with other work, in need of additional information, or for whatever reason is not ready to be tested, he simply postpones taking the test. What usually happens in a self-paced course is that there are periods when a particular student will go through two or three segments very rapidly, and he may not take another segment test for a considerable length of time. Presumably personal events in his life are constantly changing, and therefore, one time is better for taking a test than another time.

Complete Mastery and Grades.

It seems that as we learn more about effective teaching, grades will become increasingly meaningless. That is, grades will be replaced by complete mastery of a subject by all students. When a student meets the objectives in a certain course, he will be given credit in that course. When he accumulates the required number of course credits, he will graduate. It will not matter how long that process takes. For example, some students may accumulate the necessary number of credits for graduation in two years, some in three, some in four, some in five, etc. If someone takes a little longer to learn a subject, is it learned less well? Again, it is mainly the time factor that is imposed upon a testing situation that creates varying scores and not differences in intellectual ability. This seems especially true when dealing with college students.

In the future, some students will meet a course's objectives by enrolling in the course and following the standard course format. Hopefully, however, others will meet a course's objectives by following any one of a number of alternative procedures. As more instructors are able to clearly state the objectives for their courses, we undoubtedly will see more students accumulating the information and skills necessary for meeting a course's objectives on their own and demonstrating their degree of competence to the instructor by taking a test or a series of tests. This procedure is generally referred to as "testing out" of a course.

Credit for Proficiency versus Grades.

Which is easier to interpret, grades or credit for proficiency? If a student receives a *C* in statistics, how is this to be interpreted? Does it mean that he learned 70 percent of the course content, and if so, which 70 percent? The same question, of course, would apply to any course in which a student receives a *B*, *C*, or *D*. If, on the other hand, all students can demonstrate complete mastery, a person need only read the course objectives to know what a student knows and what he is capable of doing.

Why should we demand mastery in such areas as driving, swimming, brain surgery, and first aid and not in areas such as history, mathematics, psychology, and philosophy? Is the former group of skills less complex than the latter? Probably not. The difference seems to be in the fact that proficiency in the former skills is defined behaviorally, and proficiency in the latter group is not. Again, as more instructors develop the ability to define proficiency in behavioral terms, we will be able to move toward complete mastery and away from grades.

The Teacher of Tomorrow

PSI has been amazingly successful. Students taking such courses usually want to take more. Instructors and administrators, once skeptical of PSI, are now arguing for its expanded utilization. Entire departments, and in some cases, entire colleges, use PSI exclusively. Although this approach to education started in psychology, it is now being utilized to teach mathematics, language, statistics, English, philosophy, engineering, and political science. (For a review of the effectiveness of PSI in the teaching of college science courses, see Kulik, Kulik, and Carmichael, 1974.)

In his now-famous article "Good-Bye, Teacher" (1968), Fred Keller described his individualized approach to education that we summarized above. Upon noting the superiority of this technique over the more traditional lecture technique of teaching, Keller concludes the following about the teacher of tomorrow (1968):

> He becomes an educational engineer, a contingency manager, with the responsibility of serving the great majority, rather than the small minority, of young men and women who come to him for schooling in the area of his competence. The teacher of tomorrow will not, I think, continue to be satisfied with a 10 per cent efficiency (at best) which makes him an object of contempt by some, commiseration by others, indifference by many, and love by a few. No longer will he need to hold his position by the exercise of functions that neither transmit culture, dignify his status, nor

encourage respect for learning in others. No longer will he need to live, like Ichabod Crane, in a world that increasingly begrudges providing him room and lodging for a doubtful service to its young. A new kind of teacher is in the making. To the old kind, I, for one, will be glad to say, "Good-Bye" [p. 89].

Keller's point, of course, is that instructors will need to become more concerned with how their students learn. The time is near when an instructor no longer will be able to merely dispense information and leave it up to the students to learn it. Tomorrow's instructor, whether cognitively or behavioristically oriented, will need to ponder various classroom formats in order to discover which one is optimally conducive to learning. Such an individual will need to be converted from the traditional college professor to what Carl Rogers calls a "facilitator of learning" or what Keller calls either an "educational engineer" or a "contingency manager."

In summary, the modern teacher will have an attitude of openness, a willingness to try a variety of approaches to teaching, and a receptivity for new information about learning and about the learner. There will be a dedication to task analysis in order to determine what a learning experience consists of. There will be a greater realization that there may be other people or events that can do a far better job of teaching than the teacher can. The teacher will be more willing to delegate responsibility for teaching to individuals or events in a better position to teach than he is. In the final analysis, the modern teacher will be transformed from a knowledge dispenser to an arranger of optimal learning experiences. This will be true at all educational levels. The modern school will be a place where learning experiences are evaluated and strategies for optimal learning for the student are formulated.

The answer to the question, "How best to teach?" is unfolding rapidly these days. The real problem in the future will be to determine what is worth knowing.

DISCUSSION QUESTIONS

1. What would be the basic differences between the behavioristically oriented teacher and the cognitively oriented teacher in their approach to teaching?

2. Why is it important to avoid terms such as "to know," "to understand," "to appreciate," and "to grasp the significance of" while specifying course objectives?

3. Describe the advantages and disadvantages of programmed learning.

4. What is meant by the statement, "Different assumptions about human nature suggest different approaches to education"? Give a few examples of how an assumption about human nature might affect one's approach to teaching.

5. Describe a few trends in educational practices today that are based upon psychological principles.

6. What theory of transfer of training do you feel public school curriculum is based upon? Do you see any remnants of formal discipline in American education? Explain.

7. Summarize the steps involved in individualizing a course.

8. Discuss the pros and cons of lecturing as a teaching technique.

9. Do you feel that it is important that teachers be familiar with various theories of learning? Defend your answer.

10. React to the statement: "Either a student meets the objectives of a course or he doesn't. If he does, he should be given credit for taking the course. If he doesn't, no credit should be given. In other words, the student is either given credit or not, with no shades in between."

11. Describe how, according to Mager, an abstract concept or goal can be "unfuzzified."

GLOSSARY

Behaviorally defined objectives. Course, or institutional, objectives that are defined in terms of the behavior that is exhibited when a student meets a specified objective.

Branching program. A type of programmed learning that directs the learner to different parts of the program, depending upon his performance at any particular point of the program. For example, if he makes a serious mistake, he may be directed to repeat a previous section of the program.

Contingency management. Arranging an environment so that certain responses are rewarded and others are not.

Facilitator of learning. Someone who, according to Carl Rogers, attempts to discover what a student is interested in knowing, and then determines the best way to make that information available to the student.

Formal discipline (also called mental discipline). See Glossary for Chapter 3.

Frame. A term used in programmed learning to describe the small amount of information presented to the learner. In a linear program, the learner proceeds through the program frame by frame until a body of information is mastered.

Goal analysis. A procedure that converts a subjective goal into examples of the kinds of behavior that will be engaged in when the goal is reached.

Immediate feedback (also called immediate knowledge of results). The arrangement whereby a learner is informed about the accuracy of his answers immediately following a learning or testing experience.

Linear program. A type of program that requires each student to go through the same sequence of information in the same order.

Overt responding. A response that can be observed by others, as opposed to a covert response, which is not publicly observable.

Performance-based course. Any course that is arranged so that progress through it, or completion of it, is contingent upon the performance of the student.

Programmed learning. See Glossary for Chapter 5.

Self-paced course. A course arranged so that a student can determine for himself the best pace with which to proceed through the course.

Transfer of training. See Glossary for Chapter 4.

15

A Final Word

In Chapter 1, an effort was made to define learning and to differentiate it from other processes such as habituation, sensitization and instinct. In Chapter 2, the characteristics of science were discussed as they apply to the study of learning. Chapter 3 outlined the historical antecedents of learning theory. Subsequent chapters provided detailed accounts of the major theories that grew out of this rich philosophical heritage. Each of the major theories was listed under one of three paradigms, depending upon which historical theme it followed. The theories that were strongly influenced by Darwin were listed under the functionalistic paradigm. Those theories following in the tradition of Aristotle and Locke were listed under the associationistic paradigm. The theories following in the tradition of Plato, Descartes, Kant, and the faculty psychologists were listed under the cognitive paradigm. In Chapter 13, it was suggested that a fourth paradigm might be emerging—namely, a neurophysiological paradigm—with Hebb's theory being representative of this paradigm.

In this final chapter, we will discuss what the trends seem to be within current learning theory. Our discussion of current trends in no way implies that the information presented in the preceding chapters is obsolete. Almost everything occurring in learning theory today is, in some way, an extension of one of the major theories of learning presented in this book. In order to truly understand such an extension it is necessary to understand the theory from which it is derived.

Thus, we have explored learning theory's past and present. In this chapter, we will attempt to indicate where learning theory seems to be heading and ponder a few questions that it will need to address in the future.

CURRENT TRENDS IN LEARNING THEORY

At least four major trends can be seen in today's approach to the study of learning. First, today's learning theory is more humble in scope. Instead of attempting to explain all aspects of learning, today's theorist is content to investigate some aspect of the learning process. The theories of Estes in Chapter 9 offer examples of the reduced domain of contemporary learning theories.

A second major trend in current research on learning is the increased emphasis on neurophysiological techniques. As we saw in Chapter 13, neurophysiological explanations of learning have come from a position of obscurity during the peak of the behavioristic movement to one of the most popular approaches to the study of learning today.

Third, cognitive processes such as concept formation, risk taking, and problem solving are again a respectable and popular topic of study. Cognitive processes, because of their apparent close relationship to introspection, were largely ignored during the dominance of behaviorism. It should be clear that in turning again to cognitive processes, psychology is broadening its base, but it is not becoming unscientific. Behaviorism was an extreme reaction to the method of introspection and was an attempt to make psychology a science by giving it a reliable, observable subject matter—behavior. There are those who maintain that behaviorism threw out the baby with the bathwater by defining behavior in such a way as to exclude "higher mental processes," such as concept formation and problem solving, or thinking in general. Currently, these areas are of vital interest to psychologists and they are being explored scientifically. As with any other scientific research, the ultimate authority in research on cognitive processes is empirical observation. Theories are devised, hypotheses are generated, experiments are run, and as the result of their outcome, theories are strengthened or weakened. The method is the same as that of the traditional behaviorist; what has changed is the behavior that is being studied. Saltz says (1971):

> After many years of very self-conscious empiricism, the psychology of human learning has begun to show signs of a vigorous interest in new (and often dramatic!) theoretical approaches. We

find the postulations of multiple storage systems for memory; the distinction between learning systems and retrieval systems; the attempt to analyze "what is learned" into a complex system of interacting variables.

Further, there is evidence to suggest that psychologists in the area of human learning may have lost some of their fear of studying complex processes. There has developed a lively new interest in such issues as the nature of concept acquisition; the role of strategies in learning; and the more general question of the nature and function of variables like intention, meaning, and imagery. In short, there is a new interest in the role of the *cognitive,* information-processing variables in human learning [p. vii].

The trend toward cognitive theory by no means indicates that behaviorism is dead. Behaviorism remains a powerful force in psychology and will no doubt remain so for a considerable time. Skinner, in his most recent book (1974) says that true behaviorism has never really been tried. If it had, he maintains, it would be possible to solve many of man's problems. Skinner pleads for the development of a technology of human behavior based on behavioristic notions. He claims older strategies for solving man's major problems based on mentalistic or cognitive theories of behavior have been totally ineffective, and unless a more effective means of dealing with these problems is found, they will persist. Skinner put the matter as follows (1974):

I contend that behavioral science has not made a greater contribution just because it is not very behavioristic. It has recently been pointed out that an International Congress on Peace was composed of statesmen, political scientists, historians, economists, physicists, biologists—and not a single behaviorist in the strict sense. Evidently behaviorism was regarded as useless. But we must ask what the conference achieved. It was composed of specialists from many different fields, who probably spoke the commonsense lingua franca of the layman, with its heavy load of references to inner causation. What might the conference have achieved if it could have abandoned this false scent? The currency of mentalism in discussions of human affairs may explain why conferences on peace are held with such monotonous regularity year after year [p. 250].

Since Skinner is no doubt one of the most influential psychologists in the world today, his plea will certainly not go unnoticed.

A fourth major trend in learning theory today is the increased concern with the application of learning principles to the solution of practical problems. Recently, there have been many attempts to show how learning principles can be used to improve teaching and child rearing. Learning is currently being emphasized in the explanation of personality development. Some of the more effective psychotherapeutic techniques of today are based on learning principles. Learning principles are being used as a basis for redesigning mental and penal institutions. Learning principles are currently being investigated in their relationship to warfare, international relations, legal and judicial procedures, and public health. Learning is being explored as a means of modifying national attitudes towards pollution and population control. And, related to the last point, learning is being studied as a means of instituting cultural change in general. No doubt the next decade will see an ever-growing concern with the application of learning principles to the solution of many human problems.

Some Unanswered Questions About Learning

How Does Learning Vary as a Function of Maturation?

Many investigators have found that the learning that occurs at one maturational stage is not the same as that which occurs at another maturational stage (e.g., Harlow, Piaget, and Hebb). Instead of thinking of learning as a unitary process that either occurs or not, we need to explore further how the learning process may change as a function of maturation. Indeed, such information will be vital in the areas of education and child rearing.

Does Learning Depend Upon Reward?

Most learning theorists would answer this question in the affirmative, but their opinions would vary when it came time to describe the nature of reward. Thorndike's concept of reward would be "a satisfying state of affairs." Pavlov equates reward with an unconditioned stimulus. For Guthrie, it is anything that causes an abrupt change in stimulating conditions. For Skinner, it is anything that increases the rate of responding. For Hull, it is anything that causes drive stimulus reduction. For Tolman, it would be the confirmation of an expectancy. The Gestaltists would liken reward to the reduction of ambiguity. Although these definitions of reward, in some cases, are substantially different, they all point out that some of our innumerable daily experiences "stick" and others do not. The process that causes some experiences to be retained can be loosely referred to as reward. What, if anything, all these versions of reward have in common has not yet been determined.

How Does Learning Vary as a Function of Species?

Animals higher on the phylogenetic scale have more highly developed brains and a more complex central nervous system in general. Can we, therefore, expect to find a difference in learning ability among different species of animals? Bitterman (1960) has found that some species of animals cannot learn at all what another species can learn with ease. To what extent can we generalize what we learn about learning from one animal species to another? What, for example, can studying the learning process in the rat tell us about the learning process in humans? The problem of the generalizability of research findings in learning is currently receiving wide attention.

How Does Learning Vary as a Function of Personality Characteristics?

After operationally defining such traits as introversion or extroversion using existing paper and pencil tests, is it possible that learning ability may be found to differ as a function of such traits? Research has shown, for example, that high-anxious subjects conditioned more rapidly than low-anxious subjects (Taylor, 1951). In Taylor's research, high- and low-anxious subjects were distinguished by using the Taylor Manifest Anxiety Scale. How many other personality traits can be operationally defined and found to interact with learning rate? The answer to this question will be especially important in the realm of education. Since personality is currently thought of as the product of early learning, the question here is really how learning early in life affects later learning, or how the development of a cluster of strong habits influences the development of subsequent habits.

To What Extent Is Learning a Function of the Total Environment?

How does what a child learns in school relate to what he learns from his parents, from television, from books, from toys and games, or from his peers? What happens when the teacher encourages behavior that is not supported by anyone else in the child's life? What happens if the parents are encouraging certain behavior patterns in their child, but his peer group encourages other, and perhaps incompatible, forms of behavior? Of concern here is how the many learning experiences a person has in a short period of time are related to each other.

How Do All of the Above Questions Interact With Type of Learning?

The term *interaction* is one of the most important terms in science. In general, two variables are said to interact when the effect of one variable is different at different levels of the second variable. Aspirin, for example, has different effects on a person, depending on whether or not he consumed alcohol before taking it. If this is true, aspirin and alcohol are said to interact. Lack of sleep may have no effect on weightlifting, but it may have a deleterious effect on typewriting. In this case, the effects of sleep loss on performance are said to interact with task complexity. That is, at one level of task complexity—weightlifting—loss of sleep has little or no effect, whereas at another level—typing—it has a considerable effect.

Assuming that there is more than one kind of learning, it is possible that motivation (drive, for example) may be important for one kind of learning but not for another. Drive may be important for instrumental conditioning, but not for what Tolman called sign-learning. It may be that the laws of classical and instrumental conditioning are the same for all species of animals, but other forms of learning are only found in animals high on the phylogenetic scale. It could be that some learning occurs in an all-or-none fashion, while other kinds of learning may be incremental. It may be that personality type also interacts with type of learning. For example, there may be a difference in learning rate between high- and low-anxious subjects in a classical conditioning situation, but not in a problem-solving situation. A crisscross interaction is even possible in some cases. For example, high- and low- anxious subjects may perform in an opposite manner when the type of learning required of them is changed. This theoretical possibility is shown in Figure 15–1.

Obviously, it is possible that mediational processes are very important for concept formation and problem-solving, but may not be at all important for classical or operant conditioning. Thus, Thorndike's contention that learning is direct and independent of mediational processes would be true of only some kinds of learning. Likewise, the Gestalt contention that learning involves the conscious reduction of ambiguity would also be only partially true. Whether or not "thinking" is important may depend entirely on what kind of learning one is talking about.

Also, it could turn out that everyone's notion of reward is correct. Classical conditioning could, indeed, depend upon the presentation of an unconditioned stimulus. Instrumental conditioning may depend on drive stimulus reduction as described by Hull, or on a "satisfying state of affairs" as described by Thorndike. Other kinds of learning may be more conveniently explained by using the concept of reward suggested by Guthrie, Skinner, Premack, Tolman, or the Gestaltists. The current belief that there are a number of different kinds of learning, rather than one or two, makes all these positions plausible. This, of course, is the approach that Tolman was suggesting in his 1949 article "There Is More Than One Kind of Learning," and more recently by Gagné (1970).

It seems that as more is known about any area, it is easier to make finer distinctions within it. As more is known about the area of learning, it becomes more differentiated. The area of learning has become very heterogeneous, compared to the rather undifferentiated field it was not too many years ago. Like most subjects that we come to know more about, learning has become more complicated instead of less complicated. As it stands today, the field of learning can justify a number of different approaches to its study and a variety of explanations of its facts. As each of the new subdivisions of learning is studied more extensively, we will see more spinoffs from the general field of learning into separate autonomous fields, such as the neurophysiology of learning, cognitive learning,

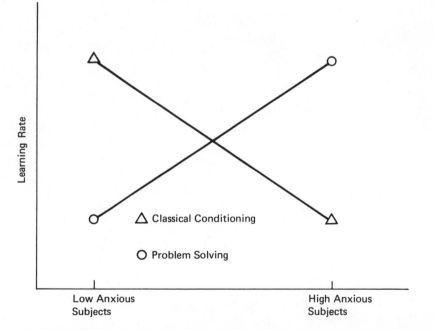

Figure 15–1. A theoretical interaction showing how anxiety level has a different effect on learning rate depending on what kind of learning is involved.

and mathematical models of learning. As these areas themselves become more differentiated, we will begin to see spinoffs from them, for example, "Markov models of learning," "learning and the single cell," and "the effects of early experience on learning." And on it goes. One can see this process of differentiation in the evolution of any science.

DEMONSTRATIONS OF LEARNING

All the learning theorists presented in this book agree that learning produces a change in an organism's behavior, potential behavior, or in his cognitions. Examples of the types of changes in behavior or in cognitions studied by the major learning theorists covered in this text are diagrammed below.

Classical Conditioning (Pavlov)
$$S_1 \longrightarrow R_1 \quad \text{before learning}$$
$$S_1 \longrightarrow R_2 \quad \text{after learning}$$
Where:
S_1 = a tone
R_1 = no salivation
R_2 = salivation

Associative Shifting (Thorndike, Guthrie)
$$S_1 \longrightarrow R_1 \quad \text{before learning}$$
$$S_2 \longrightarrow R_1 \quad \text{after learning}$$
Where:
S_1 = sight of food
R_1 = dog sits up
S_2 = the words "sit up"

Operant Conditioning (Skinner)
$$S_1 \longrightarrow (R_1 \text{ occurs at low rate}) \quad \text{before learning}$$
$$S_1 \longrightarrow (R_1 \text{ occurs at relatively high rate}) \quad \text{after learning}$$
Where:
S_1 = being in a Skinner box
R_1 = pressing the lever

Instrumental Conditioning (Thorndike, Hull)
$$S_1 \longrightarrow (R_1 \text{ has a low probability of occurrence}) \quad \text{before learning}$$
$$S_1 \longrightarrow (R_1 \text{ has a relatively high probability of occurrence}) \quad \text{after learning}$$
Where:
S_1 = being in a T-maze
R_1 = turning right at the choice point

Insightful Learning (Gestalt Theorists)
$$S_1 \longrightarrow r_1 \quad \text{before learning}$$
$$S_1 \longrightarrow r_2 \quad \text{after learning}$$

Where:
    S_1 = a problem solving situation
    r_1 = thinking
    r_2 = arriving at a solution to the problem
Expectancy Learning (Tolman)
    $S_1 \longrightarrow$?   before learning
    $S_1 \longrightarrow s_1$ after learning
Where:
    S_1 = the smell of food
    s_1 = the anticipation of the sight of food
Change in Cognitive Structures (Piaget)
    $S_1 \longrightarrow$ cannot be assimilated into existing cognitive structures
            before learning
    $S_1 \longrightarrow$ can be assimilated into cognitive structures after learning
Where:
    S_1 = an environmental event
Development of Cell Assemblies (Hebb)
    $S_1 \longrightarrow$?   before learning
    $S_1 \longrightarrow r_1$ after learning
Where:
    S_1 = an environmental event such as a chair
    r_1 = the existence of an interrelated group of neurons which, when
         activated, causes the person to think of a chair

No Final Answers About the Learning Process

There are no final answers concerning the nature of the learning process found in this book. But that fact should not bother the student, since in science there are never any final answers. In science, knowledge evolves and evolution depends upon variety. Clearly, most of what is now known about learning came out of the great debates among learning theorists that took place in the 1930s and 1940s. Healthy criticism and defense of one's position seem to provide an atmosphere conducive to the growth of a young science. Fortunately, such an atmosphere still exists in psychology, but the debate among theorists is not as intense as it once was.

Where does this leave the student who is interested in learning about learning? The student has a smorgasbord of approaches to the study of learning before him. He can either choose the one that best satisfies his appetite and concentrate exclusively on it, or he can sample from all of them. While building a house, sometimes a hammer is the most effective tool, sometimes a screwdriver, and at still other times, a saw. The student who decides to sample from the smorgasbord is like the house builder who selects different tools as different problems emerge. A third approach may result if a student cannot develop an appetite for any of the theories developed thus far. Such a student may someday develop his own theory. After all, this is what Thorndike, Pavlov, Skinner, Guthrie, and Tolman did. At this stage of knowledge concerning the nature of learning, all three approaches are necessary.

In the determination of man's behavior, there is no process more important than learning, and if that be so, one of the most worthwhile enterprises a person could engage in is to help unravel the mysteries of that process.

DISCUSSION QUESTIONS

1. Define the term interaction. Give a few examples of interactions not described in this chapter.
2. Discuss four major trends in learning theory today.
3. What is meant by the statement, "The field of learning is becoming increasingly differentiated"?
4. List and briefly discuss several unanswered questions about learning.
5. Why, in your opinion, are there no final answers in science? Relate your answer to the study of learning process.
6. In outline form, respond to the question, "What is the nature of the learning process?"
7. Write what you feel is an acceptable definition of learning.

References

ALLPORT, G. W. *Pattern and growth in personality*. New York: Holt, Rinehart, and Winston, 1961.

AMSEL, A. The role of frustrative nonreward in noncontinuous reward situations. *Psychological Bulletin*, 1958, *55*, 102–19.

AMSEL, A. Frustrative nonreward in partial reinforcement and discrimination learning: Some recent history and a theoretical extension. *Psychological Review*, 1962, *69*, 306–28.

AMSEL, A., & ROUSSEL, J. Motivational properties of frustration: I. Effect on a running response of the addition of frustration to the motivational complex. *Journal of Experimental Psychology*, 1952, *43*, 363–68.

ANDERSON, B. F. *The psychology experiment*. Belmont, Calif.: Brooks/Cole, 1971.

ATHEY, I. J., & RUBADEAU, D. O. (Eds.) *Educational implications of Piaget's theory*. Waltham, Mass.: Ginn-Blaisdell, 1970.

BABKIN, B. P. *Pavlov: A biography*. Chicago: University of Chicago Press, 1949.

BEACH, F. A. Analysis of the stimuli adequate to elicit mating behavior in the sexually inexperienced male rat. *Journal of Comparative Psychology*, 1942, *33*, 163–207.

BEARD, R. M. *An outline of Piaget's developmental psychology for students and teachers*. New York: Mentor, 1969.

BIJOU, S. W., & BAER, D. M. Child development. Vol. 1. *A systematic and empirical theory*. Englewood Cliffs, N. J.: Prentice-Hall, 1961.

BIJOU, S. W., & BAER, D. M. Child development. Vol. 2. *The universal stage of infancy.* Englewood Cliffs, N. J.: Prentice-Hall, 1965.

BITTERMAN, M. E. Toward a comparative psychology of learning. *American Psychologist,* 1960, *15,* 704–12.

BLACK, A. H. The direct control of neural processes by reward and punishment. *American Scientist,* 1971, *59,* 236–45.

BOLLES, R. C. *Theory of Motivation.* New York: Harper and Row, 1967.

BOWER, G. H. The influence of graded reductions in reward and prior frustrating events upon the magnitude of the frustration effect. *Journal of Comparative and Physiological Psychology,* 1962, *55,* 582–87.

BREEN, R. A., & McGAUGH, J. L. Facilitation of maze learning with post-trial injections of picrotoxin. *Journal of Comparative and Physiological Psychology.* 1961, *54,* 498–501.

BROWN, W., & GILHOUSEN, H. C. *College psychology.* Englewood Cliffs, N. J.: Prentice-Hall, 1950.

BRUNER, J. S. *Toward a theory of instruction.* Cambridge, Mass.: Harvard University Press, 1966.

BUREŠ, J., & BUREŠOVÁ, O. The use of Leão's spreading depression in the study of interhemispheric transfer of memory traces. *Journal of Comparative and Physiological Psychology,* 1960, *53,* 558–65.

CHOMSKY, N. A review of *Verbal behavior* by B. F. Skinner. *Language,* 1959, *35,* 26–58.

CRESPI, L. Quantitative variation of incentive and performance in the white rat. *American Journal of Psychology,* 1942, *55,* 467–517.

CRESPI, L. Amount of reinforcement and level of performance. *Psychological Review,* 1944, *51,* 341–57.

DALY, H. B. Learning of a hurdle-jump response to escape cues paired with reduced reward or frustrative nonreward. *Journal of Experimental Psychology,* 1969, *79,* 146–57.

DEWEY, J. The reflex arc concept in psychology. *Psychological Review,* 1896, *3,* 357–70.

DiCARA, L. V. Learning in the autonomic nervous system. *Scientific American,* 1970, *222,* 30–39.

DOLLARD, J. C., & MILLER, N. E. *Personality and psychotherapy.* New York: McGraw-Hill, 1950.

DUNCAN, C. P. The retroactive effect of electroshock on learning. *Journal of Comparative and Physiological Psychology,* 1949, *42,* 34–44.

EBBINGHAUS, H. *Uber Das Gedachtnis* (1885), Trans., H. A. Ruger and Charles Bossinger, *On memory.* New York: Teachers College, Columbia University, 1913.

EGGER, M. D., & MILLER, N. E. Secondary reinforcement in rats as a function of information value and reliability of the stimulus. *Journal of Experimental Psychology*, 1962, *64*, 97–104.

EGGER, M. D., & MILLER, N. E. When is a reward reinforcing?: An experimental study of the information hypothesis. *Journal of Comparative and Physiological Psychology*, 1963, *56*, 132–37.

ESTES, W. K. An experimental study of punishment. *Psychological Monographs*, 1944, *57* (263).

ESTES, W. K. Toward a statistical theory of learning. *Psychological Review*, 1950, *57*, 94–107.

ESTES, W. K. Learning theory and the new "mental chemistry." *Psychological Review*, 1960, *67*, 207–23.

ESTES, W. K. All-or-none processes in learning and retention. *American Psychologist*, 1964, *19*, 16–25. (a)

ESTES, W. K. Probability learning. In A. W. Melton (Ed.), *Categories of human learning*. New York: Academic Press, 1964. (b)

ESTES, W. K., HOPKINS, B. L., & CROTHERS, E. J. All-or-none and conservation effects in the learning and retention of paired associates. *Journal of Experimental Psychology*, 1960, *60*, 329–39.

ESTES, W. K., & STRAUGHAN, J. H. Analysis of a verbal conditioning situation in terms of statistical learning theory. *Journal of Experimental Psychology*, 1954, *47*, 225–34.

FERSTER, C. B., & SKINNER, B. F. *Schedules of reinforcement*. Englewood Cliffs, N. J.: Prentice-Hall, 1957.

FESTINGER, L. *A theory of cognitive dissonance*. Stanford, Calif.: Stanford University Press, 1957.

FLAVELL, J. H. *The developmental psychology of Jean Piaget*. New York: Van Nostrand Reinhold Company, 1963.

FURTH, H. G. *Piaget and knowledge: Theoretical foundations*. Englewood Cliffs, N. J.: Prentice-Hall, 1969.

FURTH, H. G. *Piaget for teachers*. Englewood Cliffs, N. J.: Prentice-Hall, 1970.

FUSTER, J. M. Effects of stimulation of brain stem on tachistoscopic perception. *Science*, 1958, *127*, 150.

GAGNÉ, R. M. *The conditions of learning* (2nd ed.). New York: Holt, Rinehart, and Winston, 1970.

GINSBERG, H., & OPPER, S. *Piaget's theory of intellectual development: An introduction*. Englewood Cliffs, N. J.: Prentice-Hall, 1969.

GOLDSCHMID, M. L., & BENTLER, P. M. *Conservation concept diagnostic kit: Manual and keys*. San Diego, Calif.: Educational and Industrial Testing Service, 1968.

GUTHRIE, E. R. *The psychology of learning*. New York: Harper and Row, 1935.

GUTHRIE, E. R. *The psychology of human conflict.* New York: Harper and Row, 1938.

GUTHRIE, E. R. Association and the law of effect. *Psychological Review,* 1940, *47,* 127–48.

GUTHRIE, E. R. Conditioning: A theory of learning in terms of stimulus, response, and association. In N. B. Henry (Ed.), *The forty-first yearbook of the national society for the study of education. Part II. The psychology of learning.* Chicago: University of Chicago Press, 1942.

GUTHRIE, E. R. *The psychology of learning* (Rev. ed.). New York: Harper and Row, 1952.

GUTHRIE, E. R. Association by contiguity. In S. Koch (Ed.), *Psychology: A study of a science,* Vol. 2. New York: McGraw-Hill, 1959.

GUTHRIE, E. R., & HORTON, G. P. *Cats in a puzzle box.* New York: Rinehart, 1946.

GUTHRIE, E. R., & POWERS, F. F. *Educational psychology.* New York: Ronald Press, 1950.

HARLOW, H. F. The formation of learning sets. *Psychological Review,* 1949, *56,* 51–65.

HARLOW, H. F. Analysis of discrimination learning by monkeys. *Journal of Experimental Psychology,* 1950, *40,* 26–39.

HARLOW, H. F. Learning set and error factor theory. In S. Koch (Ed.), *Psychology: A study of a science,* Vol. 2. New York: McGraw-Hill, 1959.

HEBB, D. O. *The organization of behavior.* New York: Wiley, 1949.

HEBB, D. O. Drives and the C. N. S. (Conceptual nervous system). *Psychological Review,* 1955, *62,* 243–54.

HEBB, D. O. A neuropsychological theory. In S. Koch (Ed.), *Psychology: A study of a science,* Vol. 1. New York: McGraw-Hill, 1959.

HEBB, D. O. *Textbook of psychology* (3rd ed.). Philadelphia: Saunders, 1972.

HEBERT, J. A., & KRANTZ, D. L. Transposition: A reevaluation. *Psychological Bulletin,* 1965, *63,* 244–57.

HELSON, H. *Adaptation-level theory.* New York: Harper and Row, 1964.

HERGENHAHN, B. R. *Shaping your child's personality.* Englewood Cliffs, N. J.: Prentice-Hall, 1972.

HERGENHAHN, B. R. *A self-directing introduction to psychological experimentation* (2nd ed.). Monterey, Calif.: Brooks/Cole, 1974.

HESS, E. H. "Imprinting" in animals. *Scientific American,* 1958, *198,* 81–90.

HILGARD, E. R., & BOWER, G. H. *Theories of learning* (4th ed.). Englewood Cliffs, N. J.: Prentice-Hall, 1975.

HINDE, R. A., & TINBERGEN, N. The comparative study of species-specific behavior. In A. Roe & G. G. Simpson (Eds.), *Behavior and evolution.* New Haven, Conn.: Yale University Press, 1958.

HOLLAND, J. G., & SKINNER, B. F. *The analysis of behavior: A program for self-instruction.* New York: McGraw-Hill, 1961.

HOMME, L., CSANYI, A. P., GONZALES, M. A., & RECHS, J. R. *How to use contingency contracting in the classroom.* Champaign, Ill.: Research Press, 1970.

HOMME, L. E., DE BACA, P., DIVINE, J. V., STEINHORST, R., & RICKERT, E. J. Use of the Premack principle in controlling the behavior of school children. *Journal of the Experimental Analysis of Behavior,* 1963, *6,* 544.

HUBEL, D. H., & WIESEL, T. N. Integrative action in the cat's lateral geniculate body. *Journal of Physiology,* 1961, *155,* 385–98.

HULL, C. L. *Aptitude testing.* Yonkers-on-Hudson, N. Y.: World Book, 1928.

HULL, C. L. Differential habituation to internal stimuli in the albino rat. *Journal of Comparative Psychology,* 1933, *16,* 255–73. (a)

HULL, C. L. *Hypnosis and suggestibility: An experimental approach.* New York: Naiburg, 1933. (b)

HULL, C. L. *Principles of behavior.* Englewood Cliffs, N. J.: Prentice-Hall, 1943.

HULL, C. L. *A behavior system: An introduction to behavior theory concerning the individual organism.* New Haven, Conn.: Yale University Press, 1952.

HUMPHREYS, L. G. Acquisition and extinction of verbal expectations in a situation analogous to conditioning. *Journal of Experimental Psychology,* 1939, *25,* 294–301. (a)

HUMPHREYS, L. G. The effect of random alternation of reinforcement on the acquisition and extinction of conditioned eyelid reactions. *Journal of Experimental Psychology,* 1939, *25,* 141–58. (b)

INHELDER, B., & PIAGET, J. *The growth of logical thinking from childhood to adolescence,* trans. Anne Parsons and Stanley Milgram. New York: Basic Books, 1958.

JAMES, W. *The principles of psychology.* New York: Henry Holt and Co., 1890.

JAMES, W. *Psychology: Briefer course.* New York: Henry Holt and Co., 1892.

JASPER, H. H. Electroencephalography. In *Epilepsy and Cerebral Localization.* Edited by W. Penfield and T. Erikson. Springfield, Illinois.: Charles C Thomas, 1941.

JONAS, G. *Visceral learning: Toward a science of self-control.* New York: Viking Press, 1973.

JONCICH, G. *The sane positivist: A biography of Edward L. Thorndike.* Middletown, Conn.: Wesleyan University Press, 1968.

KATZ, D. *Gestalt psychology: Its nature and significance,* trans. Robert Tyson. New York: Ronald Press, 1950.

KELLER, F. S. Good-bye teacher. *Journal of Applied Behavior Analysis,* 1968, *1,* 69–89.

KELLER, F. S., & SCHOENFELD, W. N. *Principles of psychology.* New York: Appleton-Century-Crofts, 1950.

KIMBLE, G. A. *Hilgard and Marquis' conditioning and learning.* (2nd ed.) Englewood Cliffs, N. J.: Prentice-Hall, 1961.

KIMBLE, G. A., & GARMEZY, N. *Principles of general psychology.* (3rd ed.) New York: Ronald Press, 1963.

KIMBLE, G. A., GARMEZY, N. AND ZIGLER, E. *Principles of General Psychology.* New York: Ronald Press, 1974.

KIMMEL, H. D. Instrumental conditioning of autonomically mediated responses in human beings. *American Psychologist,* 1974, *29,* 325–35.

KOFFKA, K. *Principles of Gestalt psychology.* New York: Harcourt, Brace, and World, 1935.

KÖHLER, W. *The mentality of apes.* New York: Harcourt, Brace, 1925.

KÖHLER, W. *Gestalt psychology.* New York: Liveright, 1929.

KÖHLER, W. *Gestalt psychology: An introduction to new concepts in modern psychology.* (Rev. ed.) New York: Liveright, 1947.

KOLESNIK, W. B. *Mental discipline in modern education.* Madison: University of Wisconsin Press, 1958.

KUHN, T. S. *The structure of scientific revolutions* (3rd ed.). Chicago: University of Chicago Press, 1973.

KULIK, J. A., KULIK, CHEN-LIN, & CARMICHAEL, K. The Keller plan in science teaching. *Science, 183,* 379–83.

LASHLEY, K. S. *Brain mechanisms and intelligence.* Chicago: University of Chicago Press, 1929.

LEÃO, A. A. P. Further observations on the spreading depression of activity in the cerebral cortex. *Journal of Neurophysiology,* 1947, *10,* 409–14.

LEEPER, R. The role of motivation in learning: A study of the phenomenon of differential motivational control of the utilization of habits. *Journal of Genetic Psychology,* 1935(a), *46,* 3–40.

LEEPER, R. W. A Study of a Neglected portion of the Field of Learning: The Development of Sensory Organization. *Pedagogical Seminary and Journal of Genetic Psychology,* 1935, *46,* 41–75 (b).

LeFrançois, G. R. A treatment hierarchy for the acceleration of conservation of substance. *Canadian Journal of Psychology*, 1968, *22*, 277–84.

Lettvin, J. Y., Maturana, H. R., McCullock, W. S., & Pitts, W. H. What the frog's eye tells the frog's brain. *Proceedings of the Institute of Radio Engineers*, 1959, *47*, 1940–51.

Lindsley, D. B. The reticular system and perceptual discrimination. In H. H. Jasper (Ed.), *Reticular formation of the brain*. Boston: Little, Brown, 1958.

Lindsley, D. B., Schreiner, L. H., Knowles, W. B., & Magoun, H. W. Behavioral and EEG changes following chronic brain stem lesions in the cat. *Electroencephalography and Clinical Neurophysiology*, 1950, *2*, 483–98.

Lorenz, K. *King Solomon's ring*. New York: Thomas Y. Crowell, 1952.

Lorenz, K. *Evolution and modification of behavior*. Chicago: University of Chicago Press, 1965.

Lorenz, K. *Studies in animal and human behavior*, Vol. 1. Cambridge, Mass.: Harvard University Press, 1970.

Lumsdaine, A. A. Educational technology, programmed learning, and instructional sciences. In E. R. Hilgard (Ed.), *Theories of learning and instruction*. Chicago: University of Chicago Press, 1964.

Lundin, R. W. *Personality: A behavioral analysis* (2nd ed.) New York: Macmillan, 1974.

McGaugh, J. L., & Petrinovich, L. The effect of strychnine sulfate on maze learning. *American Journal of Psychology*, 1959, *72*, 99–102.

McGaugh, J. L., Westbrook, W., & Brut, G. Strain differences in the facilitative effects of 5-7 Diphenyl-1-3 Diazamantan 6-oL (1757 I. S.) on maze learning. *Journal of Comparative and Physiological Psychology*, 1961, *54*, 502–5.

Mager, R. F. *Preparing instructional objectives*. Palo Alto, Calif.: Fearon Publishers, 1961.

Mager, R. F. *Goal analysis*. Belmont, Calif.: Fearon Publishers, 1972.

Marx, M. H., & Hillix, W. A. *Systems and theories in psychology*. New York: McGraw-Hill, 1963.

Meehl, P. E. On the circulatory of the law of effect. *Psychological Bulletin*, 1950, *47*, 52–75.

Miller, G. A. Some preliminaries to psycholinguistics. *American Psychologist*, 1965, *20*, 15–20.

Miller, N. E. Learning of visceral and glandular responses. *Science*, 1969, *163*, 434–45.

MILLER, N. E., & CARMONA, A. Modification of a visceral response, salivation in thirsty dogs, by instrumental training with water reward. *Journal of Comparative and Physiological Psychology*, 1967, *63*, 1–6.

MILLER, N. E., & DOLLARD, J. C. *Social learning and imitation.* New Haven, Conn.: Yale University Press, 1941.

MILNER, B. Memory disturbance after bilateral hippocampal lesions. In P. Milner and S. Glickman (Eds.) *Cognitive processes and the brain.* Princeton, N. J.: Van Nostrand, 1965.

MORRELL, F. Electrophysiological contributions to the neural basis of learning. *Physiological Review*, 1961, *41*, 443–94.

MORRELL, F. Information storage in nerve cells. In W. S. Fields and W. Abbott (Eds.) *Information storage and neural control.* Springfield, Ill.: Charles C Thomas, 1963.

MORUZZI, G., & MAGOUN, H. W. Brain stem reticular formation and activation of the EEG. *Electroencephalography and Clinical Neurophysiology*, 1949, *1*, 455–73.

MOWRER, O. H. *Learning theory and behavior.* New York: John Wiley, 1960.

MÜLLER, G. E., & PILZECKER, A. *Experimentelle Beiträge Zur Lehre Vom Gedachtniss.* Leipzig, 1900.

MUNN, N. L., FERNALD, D. L., JR., & FERNALD, P. S. *Introduction to psychology.* Boston: Houghton Mifflin, 1972.

MURDOCK, B. B., JR. The retention of individual items. *Journal of Experimental Psychology*, 1961, *62*, 618–25.

MUSSEN, P., & ROSENZWEIG, M. R. *Psychology: An introduction.* Lexington, Mass.: D. C. Heath, 1973.

NOWLIS, D. P., & KAMIYA, J. The control of electroencephalographic alpha rhythms through auditory feedback and the associated mental activity. *Psychophysiology*, 1970, *6*, (4), 476–84.

OLDS, J. Physiological mechanisms of reward. In M. R. Jones (Ed.) *Nebraska Symposium on Motivation.* Lincoln: University of Nebraska Press, 1955.

OLDS, J., & MILNER, P. Positive reinforcement produced by electrical stimulation of septal area and other regions of rat brain. *Journal of Comparative and Physiological Psychology*, 1954, *47*, 419–27.

OVERTON, D. A. State-dependent or "dissociated" learning produced by pentobarbital. *Journal of Comparative and Physiological Psychology*, 1964, *57*, 3–12.

PAVLOV, I. P. *Conditioned reflexes.* London: Oxford University Press, 1927.

PAVLOV, I. P. *Lectures on conditioned reflexes.* New York: Liveright, 1928.

PAVLOV, I. P. *Conditioned reflexes and psychiatry.* New York: International Publishers, 1941.

PAVLOV, I. P. *Selected works.* Moscow: Foreign Languages Publishing House, 1955.

PETERSON, L. R., & PETERSON, M. J. Short term retention of individual verbal items. *Journal of Experimental Psychology,* 1959, *58,* 193–98.

PIAGET, J. *Psychology of intelligence.* Totowa, N. J.: Littlefield, Adams, 1966.

PIAGET, J. *Genetic epistemology,* trans. Eleanor Duckworth. New York: Columbia University Press, 1970. (a)

PIAGET, J. Piaget's theory. In P. H. Mussen (Ed.), *Carmichael's manual of child psychology.* Vol. 1. New York: John Wiley, 1970. (b)

PIAGET, J., & INHELDER, B. *The psychology of the child,* trans. Helen Weaver. New York: Basic Books, 1969.

PLATO, *The republic.* New York: Scribner's, 1928.

PREMACK, D. Toward empirical behavior laws: I. Positive reinforcement. *Psychological Review,* 1959, *66,* 219–33.

PREMACK, D. Reversibility of the reinforcement relation. *Science,* 1962, *136,* 255–57.

PRESSEY, S. L. A simple apparatus which gives tests and scores—and teaches. *School and Society,* 1926, *23,* 373–76.

PRESSEY, S. L. A machine for automatic teaching of drill material. *School and Society,* 1927, *25,* 549–52.

RACHLIN, H. *Introduction to modern behaviorism.* San Francisco: W. H. Freeman, 1970.

Random House dictionary of the English language. New York: Random House, 1968.

RAZRAN, G. The observable unconscious and the inferable conscious in current Soviet psychophysiology. *Psychological Review,* 1961, *68,* 81–147.

RIESS, B. F. Genetic changes in semantic conditioning. *Journal of Experimental Psychology,* 1946, *36,* 143–52.

RUJA, H. Productive psychologists. *American Psychologist,* 1956, *11,* 148–49.

SALTZ, E. *The cognitive bases of human learning.* Homewood, Ill.: Dorsey Press, 1971.

SARTAIN, Q. A., NORTH, J. A., STRANGE, R. J., & CHAPMAN, M. H. *Psychology: Understanding human behavior.* New York: McGraw-Hill, 1973.

SCHRAMM, W. *The research on programmed instruction: An annotated bibliography.* Washington, D.C.: U.S. Office of Education (OE-34034), 1964.

SEARS, R. R. Experimental analysis of psychoanalytic phenomena. In J. McV. Hunt (Ed.) *Personality and the behavior disorders.* New York: Ronald Press, 1944.

SEARS, R. R., MACCOBY, E. E., & LEVIN, H. *Patterns of child rearing.* New York: Harper and Row, 1957.

SEARS, R. R., WHITING, J. W. M., NOWLIS, V., & SEARS, P. S. Some child-rearing antecedents of aggression and dependency in young children. *Genetic Psychology Monographs,* 1953, *47,* 135–236.

SHAPIRO, D., TURSKY, B., GERSON, E., & STERN, M. Effects of feedback and reinforcement on the control of human systolic blood pressure. *Science,* 1969, *163,* 588–89.

SHARPLESS, S., & JASPER, H. Habituation of the arousal reaction. *Brain,* 1956, *79,* 655–80.

SHEFFIELD, F. D., & ROBY, T. B. Reward value of a non-nutritive sweet taste. *Journal of Comparative and Physiological Psychology,* 1950, *43,* 471–81.

SKINNER, B. F. *The behavior of organisms: An experimental analysis.* Englewood Cliffs, N. J.: Prentice-Hall, 1938.

SKINNER, B. F. *Walden Two.* New York: Macmillan, 1948.

SKINNER, B. F. Are theories of learning necessary? *Psychological Review,* 1950, *57,* 193–216.

SKINNER, B. F. How to teach animals. *Scientific American,* 1951, *185,* 26–29.

SKINNER, B. F. *Science and human behavior.* New York: Macmillan, 1953.

SKINNER, B. F. The science of learning and the art of teaching. *Harvard Educational Review,* 1954, *24,* 86–97.

SKINNER, B. F. A case history in scientific method. *American Psychologist,* 1956, *11,* 221–33.

SKINNER, B. F. *Verbal behavior.* Englewood Cliffs, N. J.: Prentice-Hall, 1957.

SKINNER, B. F. Teaching machines. *Science,* 1958, *128,* 969–77.

SKINNER, B. F. Pigeons in a pelican. *American Psychologist,* 1960, *15,* 28–37.

SKINNER, B. F. In E. G. Boring and G. Lindzey (Eds.), *A history of psychology in autobiography.* New York: Naiburg Publ. Corp., 1967.

SKINNER, B. F. *Beyond freedom and dignity.* New York: Knopf, 1971.

SKINNER, B. F. *About behaviorism.* New York: Knopf, 1974.

SMEDSLUND, J. The acquisition of conservation of substance and weight in children: I. Introduction. *Scandinavian Journal of Psychology,* 1961, *2,* 11–20.

SPENCE, K. W. The differential response in animals to stimuli varying within a single dimension. *Psychological Review,* 1937, *44,* 430–44.

SPENCE, K. W. The basis of solution by chimpanzees of the intermediate size problem. *Journal of Experimental Psychology,* 1942, *31,* 257–71.

SPENCE, K. W. Clark Leonard Hull: 1884–1952. *American Journal of Psychology,* 1952, *65,* 639–46.

SPENCE, K. W. *Behavior theory and conditioning.* New Haven, Conn.: Yale University Press, 1956.

SPENCE, K. W. *Behavior theory and learning: Selected papers.* Englewood Cliffs, N. J.: Prentice-Hall, 1960.

SPERRY, R. W. Cerebral organization and behavior. *Science,* 1961, *133,* 1749–57.

SPERRY, R. W. The great cerebral commissure. *Scientific American,* 1964, (1), 42–52.

STEVENS, S. S. Psychology and the science of science. In M. H. Marx, *Psychological theory: Contemporary readings.* New York: Macmillan, 1951.

SYMONDS, P. M. What education has to learn from psychology: VII. Transfer and formal discipline. *Teachers College Record,* 1960, *61,* 30–45.

TAYLOR, J. A. The relationship of anxiety to the conditioned eyelid response. *Journal of Experimental Psychology,* 1951, *41,* 81–92.

TERRACE, H. S. Errorless transfer of a discrimination across two continua. *Journal of the Experimental Analysis of Behavior,* 1963, *6,* 223–32.

THOMSON, C. W., McGAUGH, J. L., SMITH, C. E., HUDSPETH, W. J., & WESTBROOK, W. H. Strain differences in the retroactive effects of electroconvulsive shock on maze learning. *Canadian Journal of Psychology,* 1961, *15,* 69–74.

THORNDIKE, E. L. Animal intelligence: An experimental study of the associative processes in animals. *Psychological Review,* 1898, Monograph Suppl., 2, No. 8.

THORNDIKE, E. L. *The elements of psychology* (2nd ed.). New York: A. G. Seiler, 1905.

THORNDIKE, E. L. *The principles of teaching: Based on psychology.* New York: A. G. Seiler, 1906.

THORNDIKE, E. L. *Animal intelligence.* New York: Macmillan, 1911.

THORNDIKE, E. L. *Education, a first book.* New York: Macmillan, 1912.

THORNDIKE, E. L. *Educational psychology.* Vol. II. *The psychology of learning.* New York: Teachers College, 1913. (a)

THORNDIKE, E. L. *Educational psychology.* Vol. I. *The original nature of man.* New York: Teachers College, 1913. (b)

THORNDIKE, E. L. *The psychology of arithmetic*. New York: Crowell-Collier and Macmillan, 1922.

THORNDIKE, E. L. Mental discipline in high school studies. *Journal of Educational Psychology*, 1924, *15*, 1–22, 83–98.

THORNDIKE, E. L. *The fundamentals of learning*. New York: Teachers College, Columbia University, 1932.

THORNDIKE, E. L. *Human nature and the social order*. New York: Macmillan, 1940.

THORNDIKE, E. L. *Selected writings from a connectionist's psychology*. New York: Appleton-Century-Crofts, 1949.

THORNDIKE, E. L., & WOODWORTH, R. S. The influence of improvement in one mental function upon the efficiency of other functions. *Psychological Review*, 1901, *8*, 247–61, 384–95, 553–64.

THORPE, W. H. *Learning and instinct in animals* (2nd ed.). Cambridge, Mass.: Harvard University Press, 1963.

TOLMAN, E. C. *Purposive behavior in animals and men*. New York: Naiburg, 1932.

TOLMAN, E. C. The determiners of behavior at a choice point. *Psychological Review*, 1938, *45*, 1–41. © 1938 by the American Psychological Assoc. Reprinted by permission.

TOLMAN, E. C. *Drives toward war*. New York: Appleton-Century, 1942.

TOLMAN, E. C. A stimulus-expectancy need-cathexis psychology. *Science*, 1945, *101*, 160–66.

TOLMAN, E. C. There is more than one kind of learning. *Psychological Review*, 1949, *56*, 144–55. © 1949 by the American Psychological Assoc. Reprinted by permission.

TOLMAN, E. C. Principles of purposive behavior. In S. Koch (Ed.), *Psychology: A study of a science*. Vol. 2. New York: McGraw-Hill, 1959.

TOLMAN, E. C., & HONZIK, C. H. Introduction and removal of reward, and maze performance in rats. *University of California Publications in Psychology*, 1930, *4*, 257–75.

TOLMAN, E. C., RITCHIE, B. F., & KALISH, D. Studies in spatial learning. I. Orientation and the short-cut. *Journal of Experimental Psychology*, 1946, *36*, 13–24. (a)

TOLMAN, E. C., RITCHIE, B. F., & KALISH, D. Studies in spatial learning. II. Place learning versus response learning. *Journal of Experimental Psychology*, 1946, 36, 221–29. (b)

UNDERWOOD, B. J., & KEPPEL, G. One-trial learning? *Journal of Verbal Learning and Verbal Behavior*, 1962, *1*, 1–13.

WAGNER, A. R. Conditioned frustration as a learned drive. *Journal of Experimental Psychology*, 1963, *64*, 142–48.

WATSON, J. B. Psychology as the behaviorist views it. *Psychological Review*, 1913, *20*, 158–77. © 1913 by the American Psychological Assoc. Reprinted by permission.

WATSON, J. B. *Behaviorism*. New York: Horton, 1925.

WATSON, J. B. Experimental studies on the growth of the emotions. In C. Murchison (Ed.), *Psychologies of 1925*. Worcester, Mass.: Clark University Press, 1926.

WATSON, J. B. John B. Watson. In C. Murchison (Ed.), *History of psychology in autobiography*. Vol. 3. Worcester, Mass.: Clark University Press, 1936.

WATSON, J. B., & McDOUGALL, W. *The battle of behaviorism*. New York: Norton, 1929.

WATSON, J. B., & RAYNER, R. Conditioned emotional reactions. *Journal of Experimental Psychology*, 1920, *3*, 1–14.

WEIMER, W. B. Psycholinguistics and Plato's paradoxes of the Meno. *American Psychologist*, 1973, *28*, 15–33.

WERTHEIMER, M. Experimentelle studien über das sehen von bewegung. *Zeitschrift Für Psychologie*, 1912, *61*, 161–265.

YERKES, R. M., & DODSON, J. D. The relation of strength of stimulus to rapidity of habit-formation. *Journal of Comparative Neurology and Psychology*, 1908, *18*, 459–82.

ZEAMAN, D. Response latency as a function of the amount of reinforcement. *Journal of Experimental Psychology*, 1949, *39*, 466–83.

Name Index

Allport, G. W., 98, 383
Amsel, A., 149–53, 383
Anderson, B. F., 24, 383
Angell, J. R., 48
Aristotle, 32–33, 35–36, 38, 43, 50, 51, 111, 187, 189
Athey, I. J., 281, 383

Babkin, B. P., 164, 172, 383
Baer, D. M., 83, 383, 384
Beach, F. A., 7, 383
Beard, R. M., 268, 383
Bentham, J., 39, 66
Bentler, P. M., 281, 385
Berger, H., 339
Berkeley, G., 40, 50, 52
Bijou, S.W., 83, 383, 384
Bitterman, M. E., 377, 384
Black, A. H., 340, 384
Bolles, R. C., 139, 384
Bower, G. H., 151, 384, 386
Breen, R. A., 331, 384
Brown, W., 384
Bruner, J. S., 352, 384
Bureš, J., 338, 384
Burešová, O., 338, 384
Burt, G., 331, 389

Carmichael, K., 369, 388
Carmona, A., 341–42, 390
Chapman, M. H., 391
Chomsky, N., 111, 384
Copernicus, 43
Crespi, L., 138, 384
Crothers, E. J., 220, 384
Csanyi, A. P., 113

Daly, H. B., 150, 384
Darwin, C., 43–44, 48, 52, 66, 127, 178, 237–38, 373
deBaca, P., 119, 387
Descartes, R., 38–39, 43, 50, 52, 240, 373
Dewey, J., 48, 384
DiCara, L. V., 343, 384
Divine, J. V., 119, 387
Dodson, J. D., 327, 395
Dollard, J. C., 149, 277, 350, 384, 390
Duncan, C. P., 329–31, 384

Ebbinghaus, H., 44–46, 52, 384
Egger, M. D., 171, 384, 385
Elliott, M. H., 299
Estes, W. K., 26, 83, 103, 212–25, 320, 385

Fernald, D. L., Jr., 390
Fernald, P. S., 390
Ferster, C. B., 110, 111, 385
Festinger, L., 300, 385
Flavell, J. H., 268, 385
Freud, S., 26, 43, 44
Frost, R., 82
Furth, H. G., 268, 281, 385
Fuster, J. M., 326, 385

Gagné, R. M., 11, 379, 385
Gall, F. J., 42, 53
Galton, F., 44
Garmezy, N., 388
Gerson, E., 342, 392
Gilhousen, H. C., 384
Ginsberg, H., 268, 281, 385
Goldschmid, M. L., 281, 385
Gonzales, M. A., 113, 387
Guthrie, E. R., 187–211, 212, 220, 235, 260, 287, 290, 308, 316, 379, 380, 382, 385, 386

Harlow, H., 226–28, 386
Hebb, D. O., 229, 321–32, 333, 343, 373, 381, 386
Hebert, J. A., 258, 386
Helson, H., 119–20, 258, 386
Hergenhahn, B. R., 83, 88, 358, 386
Hess, E. H., 7, 386
Hilgard, E. R., 386
Hillix, W. A., 36, 389
Hinde, R. A., 6, 387
Hobbes, T., 39, 53, 66
Holland, J. G., 83, 387
Homme, L. E., 113, 119, 387
Honzik, C. H., 293, 394
Hopkins, B. L., 220, 385
Horton, G. P., 192, 193, 194, 195, 196, 386
Hubel, D. H., 319, 387
Hudspeth, W. J., 331, 393
Hull, C. L., 113, 125–57, 191, 220, 225, 235, 287, 290, 291, 304, 307, 316, 327, 379, 380, 387
Hume, D., 40, 50, 53
Humphreys, L. G., 107, 387

Inhelder, B., 268, 277, 387, 391

James, W., 48, 53, 58, 315, 387
Jasper, H. H., 6, 339, 387, 392
Jonas, G., 343, 388
Joncich, G., 78, 388

Kalish, D., 294, 295, 296, 297, 298, 394
Kamiya, J., 341, 390
Kant, I., 40–41, 43, 50, 53, 240, 280, 373
Kantz, D., 388
Keller, F. S., 98, 366–67, 369–70, 388
Keppel, G., 225, 394
Kimble, G. A., 3–4, 8, 9, 388
Kimmel, H. D., 343, 388
Knowles, W. B., 325, 389
Koffka, K., 235, 241, 247, 259–61, 388
Köhler, W., 235, 245–246, 247, 248, 249, 255–56, 257, 388
Kolesnik, W. B., 357, 388
Kuhn, T. S., 27–29, 388
Kulik, Chen-Lin, 369, 388
Kulik, J. A., 369, 388
Krantz, D. L., 258, 386

Lashley, K., 319–21, 388
Leão, A. A. P., 338, 388
Leeper, R. W., 307, 388

397

Subject Index

Absolute theory, 257, 263
Accommodation, 270–71, 272
Achievement tests, 364–66
Acts, differentiated from movements, 191–93
Adaptation-level theory, 119–20, 121, 258; reinforcement theory relationship, 120
All-or-none learning, 226 (*see also* Insightful learning)
Alpha wave blocking, 340, 344 (*see also* Brain waves, conditioning of)
Alpha waves, definition, 344
Amplitude of response, 137
Animals, as experimental subjects, 22–23
Annoying state of affairs, 64–65, 79
Aristotle, 36
Arousal; optimal level of, 326–28; relationship to performance (fig.), 328
Arousal function of a stimulus, 325, 344
Arousal theory, 324–28, 344; relationship to reinforcement theory, 327
Assimilation, 270–71, 272
Associationism, 36, 46–47, 52, 163; conditioned responses as bases of, 178
Associationistic paradigm, 50, 187
Associative shifting, 71–72, 79, 141, 201–2; diagram of, 380; figure, 73
Autoclitic behavior, definition, 121
Avoidance conditioning, 11, 13

Backward conditioning, 170, 184
Behavioral objectives, 371
Behavioral potentiality, definition, 13
Behaviorism, 48, 52, 179–80, 184, 262, 374–75; Gestalt theorists opposition to, 238
Behavior modification, 84
Behavior-ratio, 300–301, 302
Belongingness, 74–75, 79
Beta waves, definition, 344
Biofeedback, 343, 344
Brain activity, willful control of, 341
Brain waves; alpha waves, 339, conditioning of, 340; beta waves, 339; delta waves, 339; research on, 339–41; various kinds of (fig.), 340
Branching program, 371 (*see also* Programmed learning)

Cathexes, (*see* Learning, kinds of)
Cell Assemblies, 322–23, 344, 381
Chaining, example on human level (fig.), 145; Guthrie's explanation, 143, 191, 209–10; Hull's explanation, 142–43; involving two people, 100; mental component of, 143; r$_G$-s$_G$ involvement in (fig.), 144; Skinners' explanation, 99–101, 121, 143
Changing contrast detectors, 318
Classical conditioning, 10, 13; comparison to instrumental conditioning, 177–79; diagram of, 380
Clinical method, as used by Piaget, 268
Closure, principle of, 244, 245, 263

Cognitive and behavioristic theories, application to education, 355–57
Cognitive dissonance, 300, 311
Cognitive map, 290, 311
Cognitive paradigm, 50
Cognitive structure, 283; and schemas, 270
Cognitive structures, change in, 381
Common fate, principle of, 243–44, 263
Concentration, 174
Concrete operations, 273, 283 (*see also* Intellectual development)
Conditioned inhibition, 135, 154
Conditioned reflex, 165–66, Pavlov's physiological explanation of, 171–72; procedures involved in producing, 165–66
Conditioned response, definition, 184 (*see also* Conditioned reflex)
Conditioned stimulus, 165, 184
Conditioning, definition of, 13; type R, 85–93 (*see also* Operant conditioning); type S, 85–86 (*see also* Classical conditioning)
Confirmable propositions, 16, 29
Confirmation of an expectancy, 311
Confirmation versus reward, 291
Connection, strength of, 65, 81
Connectionism, 59, 79
Conscious experience and the brain, 246–48
Conservation, 274–75, 283
Consolidation period, definition, 345
Consolidation theory (*see* Memory)
Content, definition, 283; as manifestation of schema, 269
Contiguity, 130
Contingency contracting, 113, 121
Contingency manager, 370, 372
Contingent reinforcement, 94, 121
Continuity, principle of, 243, 244, 263
Continuity-noncontinuity controversy, 226, 230, 248–49
Continuous reinforcement, definition, 121
Convex edge detectors, 318
Copulation, as unlearned behavior, 7
Corpus callosum, 335, 336, 338, 345
Correlational technique, 23, 30
Cortical mosaic, 172, 184
Course objectives, 364
Crespi effect, 139, 154
Critical period, 13; for learning, 7–8
Cue function of a stimulus, 325, 345
Cumulative recording, 90–91, 122

Dark detectors, 318
Darwinism, 50, 163
Darwin's influence on learning theory, 43–44
Delta waves, definition, 345
Demand, as intervening variable, 311
Dependent variable, 22, 30, 147; choice of, 24
Deprivation, 91
Detour problem, 249, 250

Differential reinforcement, 93, 122 (see also Shaping)
Dimming detectors, 318
Discrimination, 184; in classical conditioning, 169–170
Discriminative operant, 95–97, 122; examples, 97; relationship to respondent conditioning, 96–97
Discriminative stimulus, 95–97, 122
Distributed practice, definition, 154
Drive, 154; Guthrie's definition, 210
Drive discriminations (see Learning, kinds of)
Drive, physiological, 205–6
Drive reduction, definition, 155; as necessary condition for learning, 130
Drive stimuli, 140, 155
Drug-specific habits, 338–39, 345
Dynamic stereotype, 173, 184

Echoic behavior, 122
Educational engineer, 370
Educational objectives, 361–64, (see also Behavioral objectives)
Effective reaction potential, 135, 155; relationship to oscillation effect and reaction threshold (fig.), 137
Electroconvulsive shock, definition, 345
Electroencephalogram, 317, 325, 339, 345 (see also Brain waves)
Emphasizer, as role of motivation, 311
Empirical theory, definition, 30
Empiricism, 32, 40–42, 52
Environmental determinism, 180–81
Epistemology, 32, 52, 266, 283
Equilibration, 280, 283; as Piaget's major motivational concept, 271–72
Equipotentiality, 321, 345
Equivalence beliefs (see Learning, kinds of)
Error factors, 228–29, 230
Escape conditioning, 11, 14
Estes' Markov model of learning, 220–25
Estes' stimulus sampling model, 212–19
Evoked potential, 325–26, 345
Excitation, as basic process, 172, 184
Expectancy, definition, 311
Expectancy learning, diagram, 381
Experimental technique, 23, 30
Extinction, Estes' views on, 216; of classically conditioned response, 166, 167, 184; as function of momentary effective reaction potential, 136; of operant response, 93, 94; resistance to, 123

Faculties of the Mind, 40–43
Faculty psychology, 42, 50, 52
Fatigue method of breaking a habit, 210
Field-cognition modes (see Learning, kinds of)
Field expectancies (see Learning, kinds of)
Field theory, 239–40, 263
Figure-ground relationship, 264; as most basic organization in perception, 241–42
First signal system, 176, 184
Fixed interval reinforcement, 122
Fixed ratio reinforcement schedule, 122

Forgetting, Guthrie's theory of, 196–97, 210
Formal aspects of theory, definition, 30
Formal discipline, 43, 52, 68–69
Formal operations, 273, 283 (see also Intellectual development)
Fractional antedating goal response (r_G), 140–46, 151, 155; development of (fig.), 142; involvement in chaining, 142–46, as means of investigating thought processes, 143, 146; stimulation it causes (s_G), 142–43
Fractional anticipatory frustration reaction, 155
Frame, definition, 372 (see also Programmed learning)
Frustration effect, 151, 155
Frustrative nonreward, 149–53
Functional analysis, 114, 122
Functional autonomy, 98–99, 122
Functional invariants, 271, 283
Functionalism, 48–49, 163, 179, 237–38
Functionalistic paradigm, 50
Fuzzy (see Goal analysis)

Generalization, Estes' views on, 216; in classical conditioning, 168–69, 184
Generalized habit strength, definition, 155
Generalized reinforcers, 98, 122
Genetic epistemology, 283; as description of Piaget's theory, 269
Gestalt, definition, 237, 264
Gestalt psychology, 41
Gestalt theory, 220, 235–65, 286, 316, 379, 380; educational implications, 351–53; relationship to Piaget's theory, 279–80
Goal analysis, 363, 372
Guthrie-Horton experiment, 194–96
Guthrie's theory of learning, educational implications, 348–49; summary, 197–98

Habit family hierarchy, 146–47, 155, 291
Habit strength, 130–32, 155
Habits, how to break, 199–201, fatigue method, 200, 201, incompatible response method, 200–201, threshold method, 199–200, 201; sidetracking, 202
Habituation, 5, 14
Heuristic function, definition, 30
Higher order conditioning, 141, 151, 167–68, 184–85
Hippocampus, 332, 345
Hull's approach to theorizing, 127–28
Hull's theory of learning, educational implications of, 349–50; figure summarizing, 148
Hypotheses, as tentative expectations, 291, 311
Hypothetical-deductive theory, 127, 156 (see also Logical-deductive theory)

Identical elements theory of transfer, 68–71, 79
Idiographic technique, 22, 30
Immediate experience, 47, 53
Immediate feedback, definition, 372
Imprinting, 7–8, 14